Listen Again

Listen Again

A MOMENTARY HISTORY OF POP MUSIC

Edited by Eric Weisbard

Experience Music Project

Duke University Press
Durham and London
2007

© 2007 Experience Music Project

All rights reserved

Printed in the United States of America on
acid-free paper ∞

Designed by Heather Hensley

Typeset in Scala by Keystone Typesetting, Inc.

Library of Congress Cataloging-in-Publication
Data appear on the last printed page of this
book.

TABLE OF CONTENTS

Eric Weisbard

Introduction

Pop music turns on moments more than movements:
mysteries, like the proverbial song you hear on the radio
and have to know everything about immediately. The
categories we impose on its bloomings, as would-be
scholars, lovelorn fans, or harried entrepreneurs, are
necessary afterthoughts. But these frameworks are also
profanations: an irritant, usually, to the performers, who
feel stereotyped, and often just as bothersome to hardcore participants who exactly value the singular irreduc-
ibility of their experiences. Does rock and roll belong in
a museum like the one, Experience Music Project, that
has sponsored this book? Many would say no: don't put
grooves behind Plexiglas. Yet the irony is that our reissues, databases, blogs, exhibitry, and bookshelves of
analysis and memoir all ultimately work to corrupt only
the consumerist boundaries of genre and taste, not the
miracles of sound and stance that prompted them.

    So let's try again. If, as now seems increasingly clear,
rallying terms like folk, jazz, blues, rock and roll, soul,
hip-hop, and so on are more confining than illuminating, what should take their place? Perhaps an expanded
view of pop, which has numerous meanings, but, as the
catch-all music fan's term for sticky sounds, inauthentic
identity, and commercial crazes of every sort, remains

the best word for all that is heard, loved, and yet rarely ennobled. Like its predecessor, *This Is Pop*, this book represents work that was presented at the annual EMP Pop Conference—a gathering dedicated to the notion that mixing academics, journalists, musicians, and other culturemongers into one place for one long weekend might produce an intellectual product equal to the clamor of contexts lurking underneath any given *Billboard* week's Hot 100 and Top 200. Each year, the theme of the conference has changed, yet a certain range of concerns remains perennial. Artists who fall between genre lines, songs that sponge up influences from everywhere, strange species of cultural transmission, and studio accidents with unforeseen consequences all register as intellectual hooks: catchy instances of a larger history we are better able to evoke than summarize. Still, it is possible, using the material collected here, to speculate about what may turn out to be landmarks of a revisionist popular music history focused explicitly on pop itself, the neither completely glorious nor completely odious intersection of music and modernity.

Switch blackface minstrelsy and ragtime vaudeville for blues at the start of the story: a masquerade that allowed what W. T. Lhamon, Jr., calls "subaltern song" only within the context of a racialized landscape as polarized and entrenched as our own. Bert Williams, who failed to release an album in the twentieth century, now bridges the nineteenth and twenty-first with his comic speak singing and an identity (New York based, West Indian derived, outlandish and yet showbiz to the core) that many a rapper might recognize. In a linked vein, Marybeth Hamilton resurrects James McKune, the record collector who persuaded jazz obsessives to obsess over bottleneck guitar and scratchy 78s, transforming purist fanship just in time for rock to arrive. Ned Sublette summons up all that was forgotten in a post-Castro heartbeat about hundreds of years of Latin music hybrids, so that "Louie Louie," a cha-cha-chá, sedimented into the cornerstone of all subsequent garage rock: seemingly as monocultural a genre as rock and roll ever produced. And Josh Kun imagines a similar unveiling, a Marx Brothers chant that would restamp Jewishness (and what has been more "pop," pure diaspora, than Judaism?) back onto "passing" music, but his punch line is subtle: that we learn to value the ethnicity of ethnic masquerade.

With Jewish and Latin identities challenging settled popular music oppositions of white and black, with minstrelsy and record collecting recontextualizing the "birth" of the blues, pop history becomes the one thing that pop itself can never afford to be: defamiliarized. Several pieces here, for example, intersect at a complicated angle with hip-hop—a music that has called rock assumptions into constant question with its pop vitality, continued coherence as a genre, and non–baby boomer relationship to the musical and sociocultural past. Michaelangelo Matos looks at the entirely ersatz history of "Apache," which began in the head of a Londoner watching Burt Lancaster playing an Indian and just got stranger from there, yet ultimately became the quintessential b-boy DJ track. Benjamin Melendez, from a surreptitiously Jewish Puerto Rican family (Josh Kun in reverse!), played in a band, the Ghetto Brothers, that Latinized the Beatles (Ned Sublette in reverse!), and led a South Bronx gang, the Ghetto Brothers. His musical and political successor, Afrika Bambaataa, turns up next in Robert Fink's essay, which adds a third element, "post-canonic" classical music, to Bambaataa's well-known incorporation of the German art band Kraftwerk.

Another cluster of essays tries to defamiliarize punk rock, too, by turning it into a story that is less about rock reclamation than pop cultural mediation. David Thomas, a punk legend as the leader of Pere Ubu, invokes as his and the Ohio scene's key influence the unlikely figure of Ernie Anderson, a horror film TV host in the early 1960s and later the voice of *The Love Boat*. Lavinia Greenlaw presents punk in terms of the gendered opportunities it presented an Essex girl who hung out in discos: a new masquerade, no better necessarily, that simply "did what it could." Still, as bildungsroman, it's a happier outcome than the tale of Bill Tate, who for one performance in 1981 billed himself as Buddy Holocaust and was then never heard from again, yet whose less than magic moment still strikes me as a mass cultural product in all that made him and unmade him. Drew Daniel, whose holidays from graduate school backing Björk with his band Matmos have taught him something about crossings, looks at another such instance, as a fictional Germs movie band, fronted by an *ER* regular, plays at a fundraiser with the survivors of the real group.

Throughout this book, we see an attempt to widen the overall scope of the popular music story that rock and roll chroniclers often essentialized, so that a tale of how the songwriters Leiber and Stoller turned a Thomas Mann short story into a Peggy Lee adult pop cabaret song has as much place as the long-repeated narrative of how the duo's earlier hit, "Hound

Dog," passed from Big Mama Thornton to Elvis Presley. So that there is space to ponder Bobbie Gentry, who represents a 1960s country–easy listening–soul synthesis that has subsequently never quite crystallized and never quite faded. Or to rethink the marketing of Grand Funk Railroad, perhaps the most critically disparaged chart-topping rock band of all time, as the embodiment of a populist impulse, however massive in its delivery. Or to notice disco polo, postcommunist Polish disco, whose reception in its heyday by intellectuals in Poland makes Grand Funk look like the Velvet Underground. Battles over taste and categorization are one thing; just below them are thornier issues of cultural valuing and social distinction. This book engages those issues topically, but also stylistically, with writing that ranges from memoir to musicology.

But in the case of American popular music, a more fundamental issue remains basic: the way that a legacy of racism has hopelessly entangled any possibility of asserting an "authentic" popular music or feeling comfortable with inauthentic strands. American popular music, born out of slavery and the African diaspora, out of minstrelsy and racial appropriation, was recoded in the twentieth century, outside of pop itself, as a set of genres with noble lineages and a mostly clean slate. One can decode such moves, as David Brackett does in unpacking the ringing freedom of an E chord and finding a mechanism by which folk-rockers dissociated themselves from R&B. Or itemize work that lives in the shadow of these questions, like Greil Marcus setting contemporary rock versions of tunes by Son House and Dock Boggs against the implacable statement "Somebody has to black hisself up/For somebody else to stay white." Mark Anthony Neal explores two almost magical exceptions, "white chocolate" (rather than "blue-eyed soul") performers, for whom whiteness may actually be a detriment. Jason King, reclaiming a performer, Roberta Flack, often disparaged against a reductive ideal of blackness, creates a powerful interpretive paradigm, "vibe," that both situates her auteurist achievement and unites the hitherto separate continents of quiet storm and ambient.

Magic moments or tragic moments? The tone of this book is far from the hyperbole of press releases or even the "magical resolutions" that cultural studies early on ascribed to subcultural participants. Nor is it a canon of any sort, even an alternate pop one. There is no essentialism to be found here, by which I mean not only the academic disparagement but also the marketing category of the "essential rock albums" and so on. What remains is more than enough: dramatic instances where music was transformed in ways that we are still grappling with. We may have lost our faith in new waves and postmoderns, in music anticipating or effecting broader transformations. But the expanded pop past on display here amounts to what Patti Smith, that rock priestess, once called "a sea of possibility." Is it a better story? At least, it's a bigger one.

W. T. Lhamon, Jr.

Whittling on Dynamite

The Difference Bert Williams Makes

1. The Bottom of the Flow

At the onset of recorded sound, Bert Williams and his partner George Walker billed themselves as "Two Real Coons," thus tossing up for grabs every term in the phrase but the word "two." Right at the beginning they put wink to the promise of recorded documentation. The reality they documented was not individual, not ethnic, but the power of performance protocols on every level of life and culture. Williams wore blackface and white lips, sometimes a ragged chicken suit, and always an enigmatic chortle. His darky business ripened the role's full vocabulary on stage and record. He somehow remained urbane while strutting the cake walk and insisting that "Dancing am de poultry ob motion."[1] He stropped his razor, threw bones, drew cards, and never played by Hoyle. But to what end? Just the way martens prey on porcupines by treeing the spiky creatures, gutting their soft bellies from below, eating their antagonists from the inside out—just so, Williams and Walker held open season on conceptual coons. Isolating the concept on a stage with few props beyond minstrelsy's pancake and cackle, lore grading toward spectacle, Williams and Walker eviscerated whatever "coon" resided in the imagination of their diverse audiences. It was an important and constant gambit for American pop.

Bert Williams sketched strategies for talking back, and for surviving, too, to talk another day. A good example is "Borrow from Me" (1913), a performance from the middle of his career. Walker had died two years before. Their troupe disbanded and Williams's theatrical career had shrunk back again to his solo act in vaudeville. Thus the character he projected was a thoroughly consolidated precipitate of his performance experience. The scene he isolated in "Borrow from Me" used his characteristic confrontation with a manager—who might also be an officer, Pullman car customer, or a mother-in-law—proposing some outrageous scheme. You can hear him on the Archeophone disc as if he were still as alive as his strategy remains necessary.

Williams begins quietly, speaking: "I met a manager here on the streets yesterday. Said, 'I've got a great part for you to play and I am so sure you can get a minute right away—I want you to just listen and see now how sweet this sounds. I'm gonna take out in a day or so *Uncle Tom's Cabin*. You know it's a marvelous show. My cast is most complete, you know, but I thought I'd like to have you to play the bleedhound.' *I said, 'well . . .'*" Here Williams slides slightly out of speech toward melody and rhythm but achieves only recitative for the rest of what starts to sound more like a verse. He goes on: "Bring me the Czar of Russia, just have him come on over here, 'n' blacken up to play Uncle Tom's part. From Mark, the lawyer, I 'spect we better have Mr. Othello—provided, that is, we can find a brother who doesn't come too dark. We have the Statue of Liberty to play Miss Eva and Rip Van Winkle playin' Legree. Now if you can bring me for the cast them folks I've asked you to bring, then *oh* boy, the bleedhound part's for me."[2] It's less the issue of material than emotional reparations that slams into the singer's mind after hearing the manager's offer. During the phrase " 'I said, 'well . . . ,' " emphasized above, one hears him recalling all the demeaning slights managers have offered men like Williams. And then, while he is still grinding out the phrase, inchoate tactics of response start occurring to him. That's the gestation of the song, not in the slights alone but in their cumulation and conversion. The song is about their interest compounding for him and for us. He is in their flow but he is a sluice, too, rechanneling the flow.

One may call Williams "the singer" here because that is his ultimate achievement. Nevertheless, he begins in shock and disarray, unable to sing, and that's where the first passage quoted above leaves him. His answer and confidence build gradually through the rest of the performance. It moves through recitative toward adequate answer, gathering into a tune, as Williams forms and repeats conundrums in the chorus that management can never compensate:

> Bring me the stone that David slew Golia' with,
> And from the apple Adam ate bring me the core.
> Bring me a leaf from the very same tree
> That the dove carried a branch back to brother Noah;
> Bring me that lion that let Daniel live
> And the whale that swallowed Jonah in the sea.
> Bring me everything that I'm asking him to bring,
> 'N, oh boy then he can borrow from me.

Much of what is satisfying in "Borrow from Me" stems from the singer's realizing historical cognates for the manager's initial slight and compressing them into lyric. Giving gravity to the manager's offense and tuning it, "Borrow from Me" demonstrates the power of subaltern song.

Subaltern speech may be halting and self-defeating, as Gayatri Spivak has argued, but subaltern song is different.[3] Although subaltern song does not achieve its aims immediately, it has momentum and cumulative flow. It survives speech and speakers. It gathers slights into memory. Crystallized in song, its echoes persist through repertoires down the eras, staying alive by cycling through all the modes of performance.

There are songs beyond those one breaks into when happy, sad, or in love. Williams's scheme demonstrates how song may ripen until it chants social feeling in a chorus. What's memorable in "Borrow from Me" are its quips. The Statue of Liberty playing Eva, the Czar doing a Tom turn, Rip with a whip: cultural inversions might contribute to fair play. But the statue will not condescend to Eva any more than history will deliver us Daniel's lion or Jonah's whale. So "Borrow from Me" recognizes it will not distribute just deserts. Instead, it rehearses history and our reckoning process from the viewpoint of the bleedhound. In playing with the stories that have slighted Bert Williams's character, "Borrow from Me" does not transcend its conditions. It works through them.

Focusing more on street corner face-offs than political abstraction, his songs and skits seem more insubordinate than resistant. Nevertheless, Williams's performances illustrate the principle argued in different registers by Kenneth Burke and John Lennon: culture is equipment for living, a chair to sit on, alertly. Practiced daily down the years, alertness grows judgmental—which is to say, political. Whether Williams encouraged resistance is a question too simple to answer. His characters explicitly dodged the draft and practiced noncooperation. Rather, the important question to ask about Williams, as about other generative American pop performers, is: How do their antics invert the dominant social signs they project? How might subaltern song organize liberatory values particularly when it wears blackface? Explicit nay-saying is less important here than the way much of the pop public understood that Williams's whole performance said No (steadfastly, if not in thunder), even while his apparent accommodation with the protocols of his time snuck his message past the censors.

What we have to analyze in the pioneering work of Bert Williams are the implications that his gestural style cues. As a realist hatching schemes in a racist and regressive era, Williams mainly seeks and tests strategies for survival. At issue in his work is whether such characters as his Brother Lowdown can reckon and change conditions in the close places where haves meet have-nots. That zone is Bert Williams's beat. That's where his slippery sureness shows that his public has been more likely to mull and complicate social generalizations than have either their governors or the mandarin intellectuals who colluded during Williams's decades to assemble theories of scientific racism. Indeed, can any governor speak more clearly than Williams's beleaguered character in "Nobody"? The mixed success and failure in Bert Williams's case indicate the possibilities of cultural engagement. His publics could see the warping of their lives in Williams's gestures. Through his songs, disparate cohorts of clerks and workers in many metropolitan regions consolidated themselves as one public and clarified their social conditions even unto chants that stuck in the American mind. The structured development of his songs both diagnosed what was happening to this public and suggested their means of coping.

I will circle back to the difference the songs made by reviewing the differences the songs register. Oppression and racism, withering wives, the First World War's draft and the meaning of Africa, managers and bosses: these frequent topics of black farce and song have been rendered sufficiently often that we can now focus on the creativity that fought to redefine them. Later in the century, Miles Davis distilled this point in his autobiography. Gil Evans pointed out to Davis that he ought to layer his own sound on top of compositions he was playing. Davis describes how Evans "would come up and whisper . . . 'Miles, now don't let them play that music by themselves. You play something over them, put your sound in it, too.' Or, when I was playing with some white guys, 'Put *your* sound over theirs,' meaning their *white* sound and feeling. He said this meaning put my shit on top so that the black thing would be on top.[4] Over, under, top, bottom: the history of American culture is the story of push coming to shove, of forces contending on an uneven field. Williams realized early that the consequence of power's play is unforeseen possibility— as when censoring black performance amplified its effect. This paradoxical American censorship involves the taboo against love plots in early black musicals. Aida Overton Walker (who performed with Williams in their musicals and was married to his partner, George Walker) repeatedly told interviewers about this prohibition.[5] Jumbled plots in the Williams and Walker plays, Williams's stuttering movement during their cake walks, and certainly the lyrics of Williams's songs after *In Dahomey* (the first black musical to thrive on Broadway, 1903) all corroborate this gagging and the counter-creativity it spawned.[6]

The taboo inevitably pushed black pop topics toward a politics of double entendre: say one thing, code another. This pressure extended the way censorship of drama in central London (following the Stage Licensing Act of 1737) had opened up burletta and farce as the modes in which working audiences understood themselves and ciphered their complaints. Black-face minstrelsy had come into being precisely as the American elaboration of London's illegitimate theater. And Bert Williams's use of blackface was his way of going explicit with the always-already coded "black" differences of gesture, rhythm, and dance. Blackface constituted Williams's red nose and pig's bladder. Blackface was an excessive signature that levered subtler gestures of low difference into consciousness.

Thus Bert Williams's songs clarified the hypocrisies of power and rallied those who realized nobody had done nothing for them, no time— as in his 1906 recording of "Nobody." This thoroughly cagey song, in which he described himself as whittling on dynamite, ultimately resolves its naive pretenses in its last two syllables, perhaps the most important couple of words he ever recorded:

Naah, ain't never done nothin' to no body.
Naah, ain't never got nothin' from no body, no time.
Ohhh, until I get somethin' from somebody, sometime,
Nn-I'll never do nothin' for nobody, no time.
I won't.[7]

This last line competes to be the calmest, clearest creed in all pop music—much easier to follow than "All you need is love."

Bert Williams licensed himself by seeming not to be a revolutionary performer. There is no threshold instance in which his performances overturned either Western thought or song. Still, his acts sapped Atlantic creeds and affected their soundtrack. His straddle of speech and song pointed toward jazz poetry and hip-hop. His comic sensibility cleared ground for Zora Neale Hurston, Ralph Ellison, and Tom Lehrer. His abbreviated gestures evoked a public fondness that Charlie Chaplin also roused slightly later. Jelly Roll Morton and Duke Ellington both created sonic portraits of Bert Williams. Performers as different as Bob Hope, Johnny Cash, Nina Simone, Ry Cooder, Dave Van Ronk, and Perry Como have covered Bert Williams—all drawing from the core of Williams's repertoire something they could weave into their own disparate styles. Thus Williams contributed to several gradual changes. The ensemble of forces he joined breasted the extant cultural tides then celebrating the top of society. When Williams died in 1922 the tides were already starting to run the other way. Because of the traditions that Williams helped pump and regenerate, American music is still trying to resuscitate what he called the Jonah man tumbled deep at the bottom of the flow. As Jonah, Williams insisted his luck was bad, but he was instituting a pop reading of luck as fortune—meaning more than materiality. To be a *Jonah man* was to rehearse Old Testament suffering, its proverbs and angular humor. It was to join an ancient, ongoing understanding of how injustice works. This reiteration was a secret flow. The lyrics Williams tapped, and their way of coalescing a public, proved a tradition suppressed at the surface but tidal below. Tapping this flow replenished it.

2. No Means No

Note that the backtalk in Williams's recordings incited racially mixed publics. Williams was a class and style man as much as a race man. The constituents covering his songs and touting his humor perceived him in all those ways. The songs Bert Williams committed to cylinder and disc between 1901 and 1922 were among the earliest recorded black songs and performances. They count as landmarks. But their continuing importance depends on the way their revelatory complexity holds up now that we can hear its evidence.[8] What proportions of black separation and interracial affiliation do they articulate? Does Williams's culmination of ragtime sensibility oppose or supplement the strategic authenticities manifest in jazz and blues? If the increasing recuperation of Williams's work attracts commentary corroborating that publics marked his songs both black and interracial, then that will have many implications for our still segregated histories of American pop and its impact on other arts. His case is one that throws those separated histories in doubt.

Williams's songs were way stations in cross-racial tides that began as eddies of performed gestures in American popular culture of the 1830s— before, below, and beside middle-class abolitionism. These anonymous affiliations started flowing from the mutualities of people dislocated in ports, working beside each other in mudsill labor, sharing blankets in flophouses, repudiating together their bosses and pre-ordained fates. A common argot stirred their mutual renunciative gestures. Songs and blackface skits gave them volume and persistent momentum. This seventy-five-year history of mutual nay-saying reached one culmination in Bert Williams but he neither invented nor exhausted it. He is one of those volunteers, appearing above ground but seemingly nurtured from below, growing out of and documenting a musical rhizome that preceded, then mocked, and now augments our currently celebrated strains of blues. In its time, however, the tradition that gave us Bert Williams was hardly underground. Many would have said, did say, it was way too visible and public, too vulgar and transgressive—talking about phrenologist coons, dodging the draft, and giving wives away ("I'll lend you anything I've got on earth but my wife / And I'll make you a present of her"). In brief, it was like a lot of pop that counts: both *in your face,* thus legendary, and *infra dig,* thus suppressed and inadequately documented.

3. Fire Hydrant Theory

[T]he Negro is a very original being. While he lives and moves in the midst of a
white civilization, everything that he touches is reinterpreted for his own use.
ZORA NEALE HURSTON, "CHARACTERISTICS OF NEGRO EXPRESSION"[9]

To tap into the tradition that floated Bert Williams is to confirm that
American and Atlantic pop musics were already suffused with gestures
understood as black well before 1903. That was when W. C. Handy said he
first heard Delta blues on the railroad platform in Tutweiler. Thus Williams was performing race codes also well before 1920, when Perry Brad-
ford and Mamie Smith recorded "Crazy Blues" in New York City. In New
York musicals and then on Broadway; in shows that toured every Atlantic
region except the American Deep South; on wax cylinders then on records; in several silent films and multiple vaudeville follies—that is, in
every extant mode and nearly every place—Williams's popular music,
skits, and plays were singing blackness during three decades before
"Crazy Blues."

In the last years of his career, Williams alluded to and then absorbed
blues into his lyrics and music, gradually ceding ground to its growing
authority. But the performances we now have on disc, taken together,
show that his music was full of the atomic codes that had much earlier
come to identify black music's difference from Euromusic. Black codes so
drenched his songs that codification is clearly their emerging topic—just
the way a fire hydrant is one percent of the time about extinguishing fire
but ninety-nine percent about the messages dogs have left on it. One
object, multiple meanings: man's hydrant is hounds' signpost.

Pop performers often choose among objects, signs of the dominant culture, which have settled into assumed meanings. The performers supplement these signals—be they a way of walking, a mask, a fire hydrant—with
quite different associations. These fetishized figures become compound
palimpsests that pop publics read very differently than do unsuspecting
dominant publics. Just so, Williams's songs garnered, precipitated, and
extracted cultural markers of black difference that his interracial mobility recognized. The mobility enjoyed this sign system perhaps most
when the messages remained illegible to those who followed cues protect-
ing the nobility. His songs consciously flag and activate a blackness that

is not natural but adds up to a fiction that people attracted to this business wanted.

It is exciting to watch the rehearsal of fictive blackness precipitating its increasingly conscious signs of difference. In "Nobody," recorded first in 1906 but staged a year earlier in the musical *Abyssynia*, Williams stutters and slides his delivery. This is somebody's observed private mannerism going social. He is consolidating a socially realized position for blackness. He is joining, exhorting, and parodying his accompanying trombonist. The trombone is itself realizing potential beyond its own marching-band background by imitating human voices and slurring their tones. The way Williams realized these clues made them the more available to others. By 1914, even craven ragtime tunes, like Jean Schwartz's "You Can't Get Away from It," which Williams introduced, insisted that "Syncopation rules the nation." In 1915, Irving Berlin's "International Rag" proclaimed:

> The syncopation's in the air
> You hear the people everywhere [Berlin cites Spain, France, Germany,
>   Italy, England, Russia]
> Wheeeeee
> From every dwelling yelling
> It's the best . . .

These songs were creeds linking supposedly separate cohorts across nation and class, ethnicity and race, gender and style. They flagged, and bragged about joining with, signs of black difference. "Syncopation" is the key term through all these songs, but in this instance "yelling," too, was code for lumpen black expressiveness, and the concept of "blues shouters" would confirm the code in the next decade. Still without analytic frames, these markers solidified and determined what aspects listeners would understand as jazz and blues, today deemed the authentically black forms. Just a few years later, performers and critics would define these forms by refining them from dance music and mass entertainment. Because of his popularity across camps, Bert Williams carted these codes from the plebeian to the public sphere, but it took him a while, just as it did W. C. Handy and others, to know what he was carrying.

Williams's songs were heir to several performance traditions even while other patterns which would be more prestigious were rapidly precipitating both within Williams's own work and external to it. His work projects adaptive processes that are both very personal, a mind deciding its own principles of behavior ("I don't intend to do nothing for nobody"), and wholly social ("the blues is blues, and you can't deny it"). The blues were an undocumented entity when Williams was first acting and recording. As Clarence Williams, W. C. Handy, and others started publishing the lyrics and music of blues, however, and as the form built momentum, Williams began mocking it. He was an equal opportunity mocker. As early as November 24, 1919, with "I'm Sorry I Ain't Got It You Could Have It If I Had It Blues" (by Ted Snyder) and "Lonesome Alimony Blues" (by James F. Hanley) recorded May 6, 1920, in New York City, he was acknowledging the burgeoning form. But by October 25, in "You Can't Trust Nobody" (by Henry Creamer and John Turner Layton), Williams was both mocking and inhabiting what he understood as blues in his regular couplets. Here is part of that song:

> That dark brown lady sang a wicked blues,
> I said a wicked blues, full of mournful[10] news.
> It taint no use to arguefy it,
> For the blues is blues, and you can't deny it.
> It's hard to listen to such sad tales.
> But to everyone that lady would wail:
> Oh its gettin' so you can't trust nobody, none of the time.

In other words, blues illustrates in maudlin fashion what his own songs had been insisting for fifteen years before "blues" was either an accepted category or a distinct form.

. The applause for Williams's humor proves a contrapuntal tendency had survived the dominant racism. This counter-pressure even thrived in the same space at the same time as the prevailing structure. It chose centerpieces of the managers' maintenance system—hydrants—to convey its counter knowledge. Williams's songs gathered and re-expressed attitudes that persisted through the violence and behavior-scourging of mid-century, the lynchings of Reconstruction, the subsequent lawlessness, and the accompanying coarsening of much blackface. Between 1901 and 1922, Williams's songs reorganized the public which had itself taken distinctive shape in the 1830s by mocking the diagnostic American prejudices.[11] The discovery of these songs now reminds us how very many strains were braided into performance traditions in that long moment

Thomas Riis names "just before jazz."[12] During those years, critics devised categories that deemed jazz to be authentic virtuosity, decided blues were the unsullied black song, and sent pop ragtime to the trash heap.

My point is not to denigrate any of the forms we have come to know as jazz or blues. Rather, I want to agree when Marybeth Hamilton tells us we should excavate "entertainment blues—the music of black showbiz—as seriously as those forms which are presently more prestigious."[13] Black showbiz musics surfaced first. They were at least as popular as their successors. They survived the social violence and then the definitional struggles that still beset African American expression on all sides. These musics together have floated Clarence Williams, Cab Calloway, Louis Jordan, Little Richard, Chuck Berry, and James Brown. Hip-hop still rides their tides. Just before critics sifted a putative authentic blackness from the mixed traditions of ragtime and coon songs, we see that Bert Williams integrated black and white cohorts who were attending to vaudeville, popular theater, and sound recordings. In the process, he increased everyone's mutual awareness from a black standpoint. These performances were every bit as authentic as blues and jazz.

Authenticity is relative. The long dawning of that recognition is one more product of the era of technological reproduction. It changes authenticity from the aura of the moment of making, which Walter Benjamin sought, to the wide effectiveness of the reproduction, which Benjamin predicted and lamented. "Bert Williams" was an effectivity which technological reproduction enabled, lore inflected, talent achieved, and a broad public validated. Egbert Austin Williams, Bahamian-born and twice an immigrant to the United States, assembled, wrapped, and recorded "Bert Williams" to show that many sorts of people were kin to his reality.

Heywood Broun reported that Williams "used no gesture which traveled more than six inches."[14] Bert Williams created his effectiveness with small gestures—articulate vowels and restrained consonants, wry smiles askance and stumbling dances. Each curt move fitted Williams's new positioning to a heavily inscribed inheritance. Each move stuck his blackfaced self on top of that legacy. Just as Miles Davis would compose a distinctly black music partly through a deep interaction with the Gershwins and the white Canadian Gil Evans, so too Williams gleaned his offbeat timing, his *pauses* (as he was still calling them), studying pantomime in Europe: syncopation with an Italian paternity! He emphasized his era's massive movement from folk to poplore in the structures of his performances. All these lessons and layerings pile up in Williams's songs.

4. Yes Means No

Williams worked with hailing gestures—other people's and his own. Managers called to him and he had to dodge how they placed him. His own chortles turned greeting into withdrawal. His affirmations declared themselves negations—as in the phrase "YesSuh" in his song "Somebody":

> And the manager looked right straight at me,
> Said, hey now, here's your opportunity.
> Yessuh.
> *Somebody's got to go on'get them cats.*
> Ah, YesSuh,
> Yes Sir! Somebody's got to go
> I'm with you there . . .
> I said, yes sir, I'gree with you,
> Somebody else, yes sir, not me.[15]

"Somebody" is central to a song cycle in which Williams's public eavesdrops on elemental politics taking shape. Let's call these songs the Nobody cycle, after Williams's signature song inaugurating the cluster. Lyrics in this cycle face up to being caught in one's own packaging. It gradually dawns on everyone that the conversation assesses lumpen life. After almost a decade of singing "Nobody" as his encore, Williams wrote and recorded "Everybody" (1915), "Somebody" (with James F. Hanley, 1919), and "You Can't Trust Nobody" (by Henry Creamer and John Turner Layton, 1920).[16] These songs seem to join what they cannot beat. They apparently elaborate abjection. But if that were all they did they would not have been so popular in their day or important still.

The Nobody cycle exactly refutes career moves that jazz and blues purists applaud in separating transcendent art from pop. This decoupling was of course the diagnostic practice during the years the Nobody cycle was churning, at the crossing into the Jazz Age. The argument still goes that art must disavow commodification every way it can, must avoid stereotypes, and must invent or improvise original patterns. But the Nobody cycle does something different. It takes on packaging as an increasing burden in technological eras, another confinement to illustrate and play against. So, too, with stereotypes: in the Nobody cycle they remain realities not to enjoy but to humanize. Williams renders stereotypes as flows falling like Niagara on downcast brothers who discover resources to refigure the signals and divert the flow. Thus the Nobody cycle shows originality as the reassembly of already ongoing practices rather than a bolt from a clear sky. All of which is to say that Bert Williams consolidated minstrel modes as opposed to inventing a new jazz aesthetic, at least as most critics defined it.

Bert Williams's perspective allows reconceiving the jazz/blues threshold as a littoral, a mixing zone that was transported through space and occupied an elastic era. This threshold does not displace New Orleans or Chicago, the Delta or Texas as spawning grounds for jazz and blues, but in augmenting site-specific histories it complicates them. It insists on the roads and the entrepreneurial activities connecting these cities as important. Not only an embarrassing vulgarity populated by coon songs, the pop littoral between 1890 and 1922 was also indispensable for the conception of American vernacular and vanguard art musics. My point is that it deserves study in its own right, rather than as a transitional phase toward now canonical virtuosity. It would help us recall that Clarence Williams, the pianist who wrote, organized, and played on the two earliest recordings of Sidney Bechet's and Louis Armstrong's early masterpiece "Cake Walking Babies from Home" (1925), had done formative time as the MC in the minstrel troupe for which Billy Kersands headlined.[17] Kersands's employee list of those who would later distinguish themselves in jazz is growing longer the more we pay attention. It also included James Bland and Jelly Roll Morton. This littoral was not only a training ground and petri dish but a zone of distinctive achievement, too, not something we should describe only as a hell that jazz fled like bats.

Jazz modernists simplify the option as binary: commerce or art. But listening to Bert Williams, like reading scripts by T. D. Rice or Dan Emmett, like recuperating the careers of William Henry Lane, Ira Aldridge, and Pauline Hopkins, is to find play in the excluded middle. Learning to hear and imagine this interzone as a creative place throws new light on the alternatives that collectors and critics used when they excluded it. Restoring the spectrum makes the binary authenticities relative again. Analysts establishing the jazz threshold have typically redefined virtuosity away from the thorny accommodation Bert Williams achieved. Williams's lyrics, laughs, and gestures hail authority from a lively perspective already in opposition. The modernist aesthetic downplayed these lyrics of the common world in order to elevate the gut-bucket delivery of slide guitarists and such exceptional shouters as Mamie, Clara, and Bessie Smith. The likes of Charley Patton and the several Smiths signified uncommon virtuosities unavailable to the plebes buying the ragtime ideology of alert coexistence that Williams voiced. Jazz and blues critics depreciated modes which admitted that the deck was stacked and unlikely to change soon. That interzone which the emerging black musics avoided was exactly the street where Williams was so productively talking back to managers. In *Invisible Man*, Ralph Ellison would describe this coping strategy of the excluded middle as "running and dodging the forces of history rather than making a dominating stand."[18]

Is running and dodging enough? Surely not. Dignity demands the "dominating stand" that aims for surgical erasure of racist structures and attitudes. But standing up to oppression requires organizational stability that the emerging mobility cannot command. Thus, when direct action fails to clear governing foul play, then Americans of every hue have continually reactivated compromise performances that mock and dodge injustice even while they display it. In the motley lodes of ragtime that Bert Williams mined we have the objective correlative of lumpen consciousness. Its "running and dodging," its capers and chortles, its refusal to be seated and know its place precisely access the public mind that demanded this music. The trick is to see how this relationship codes human trouble, not to scoff at its confusion or vulgarity. We must learn to see blackface modes as a necessary slow alternative to the direct exposition that more secure speakers are privileged to wield. Blackface modes, including ragtime and black pop in general, elaborate a vernacular process that precedes and continues after rites of truth and reconciliation attempt their explicit work.

This indirect engagement discomfits those who seek to achieve racial uplift by nixing objectionable history and scrubbing its residue. But Bert Williams complicates the problem. He was clearly a race man *because* he was doing the chicken-suited clown and inhabiting razor-wielding personae. Clown shoes, blackface masking, and razors were his fire hydrants. They meant one thing to the managers and quite another thing to the bleedhounds Williams organized by layering his commentary on these objects. Doing the darky was his way of turning subaltern speech into subaltern song. It goosed along the backtalk and teased out later incarnations of its particular mode.

Williams was one late link in a train of performative connections that had substantial momentum well before the insatiable appetite of T. D. Rice's Jim Crow character surfaced in the early blackface plays of the 1830s. Rice was then following protocols of English farce that were already operative when Shakespeare assembled Oldcastle and Falstaff. To keep focus, let's board the train when the great black minstrel performer Billy Kersands gave graphic imagery to grotesque appetite late in the nineteenth century. Kersands famously jammed two billiard balls into his mouth. Photographs of this act have taken on a life of their own—corroborating, reenacting, and spinning into a new orbit from the old links. Robert Frank's famous photograph of a tattoo parlor wall in 1950 shows either Kersands or a competitor now with *three* balls incorporated in his smile. The Rolling Stones topped the cover of their 1972 album *Exile on Main Street* with Frank's photo. The uncertainty here is important. No one can specify all the freight riding this line. The difficulty is only partly that Kersands's act is so deforming it renders any performer's face unrecognizable. More importantly, the process is itself anonymous and spontaneous, loric, outside history (even though photography, a modern technology, helps convey it). What is certain is the train's continual fascination. Pa Rainey, Ma Rainey's husband and performance partner—he did stand-up comedy, she sang the blues—later copied Kersands, jamming cups and saucers in *his* mouth. But it is Kersands who always wins the credit. W. C. Handy recalled "Billy Kersands, the man who could 'make a mule laugh' . . . proving on stage that his enormous mouth would accommodate a cup and saucer."[19] Kersands cued Alex Rogers—who wrote the lyrics for "Nobody" and "The Jonah Man"—also to compose Williams's famous skits recorded as "Elder Eatmore's Sermon on Generosity" and "Elder Eatmore's Sermon on Throwing Stones."[20]

Their Eatmore character crucially relocates the gluttonous figure Kersands had personified. The new elder is an offshoot of Williams's favorite target, the manager hectoring common people. "Lot of y'all here this morning think you been washed," Eatmore preaches one Sunday morning, "you ain't even been *sponged*." But this time the manager is sanctified, black, middleclass, and striving. Caught climbing fences with purloined turkey for Thanksgiving dinner, Eatmore is yoked by his hunger to his flock. Williams uses this connection to critique the marginally middle-class public he was reconvening and linking to his lowdown brothers. They were composite parts of the lumpen consciousness that has been the engine of American popular culture since the 1830s. Because of this long heritage, Alex Rogers and Bert Williams could use Eatmore's appetite as a strategic authenticity to puncture dandy pretensions even as its presence folded the striving cohorts into the race. This heritage added another layer of significance to the compound interest in the already complex preacher man. Vaudeville publics would have sniffed him like a hydrant emanating a set of compound signals, all quite legible. This layer would have incited further laughter at his capers.

Ralph Ellison also used the figure of Eatmore to flag authenticity in his posthumous novel, *Juneteenth* (1999). Anyone wondering whether Ellison was inspired by Bert Williams would have to notice how his chief characters—Hickman and Bliss—seem to have been tagged by the same ironic creator who named Eatmore. A crucial scene of that novel has these two old men remembering a tent revival at which they worked as an evangelical team many years earlier, Hickman preaching and Bliss, rising from a coffin, coming back from the dead. Their memories recreate the novel's central scene that names it: the annual celebration of Juneteenth, the day black Texans belatedly discovered their emancipation. Hickman recalls rising to preach to the gathered five thousand celebrants after one legendary Reverend Eatmore had "unlimbered some homiletic there one evening that had the hair standing up," he says, "on *my* head. . . . And it wasn't exactly what he was saying, but how he was saying . . . he was a supermaster! . . . Eatmore had set such a pace that I had to accept his challenge."[21]

One seeks in vain a historical preacher who might have served as a model for Eatmore. The pace-setting "supermaster" is the tidal flow Williams rejuvenated by nabbing, marking, and freeing Eatmore in his skits. In all his essays, stories, and novels, one feels Ellison eager to participate in the cutting contests vernacular black culture stages in all its modes, and here he reenacts transgressive legacies that energized both music and literature. These performed links are what we have in culture instead of genetic hard wiring. Reading, hearing, viewing them sparks the furtive thrill one feels watching chanterelles emerge through rotting leaves after a rain, or watching wet chicks crack their shells. The life process works through these tenderest hatchings.

Such emergence may seem monstrous, though, when hatchings cross modes. Minstrel Kersands's gluttonous grin is reborn in vaudeville as Williams's Elder Eatmore, a turkey-snatching churchman. This newer Eatmore's sabbath pleadings for heavier coins in the collection plate generates Ellison's fictional Eatmore and his much more jubilant considerations of emancipation. Eatmore's American roots in grotesque minstrelsy have turned inside out. This Eatmore inspires a preacher trying to reconnect with people needing freedom. Cultural genesis slides, slippage is prominent, and inversion is the norm. Standing in the flow and trying to get right with cultural imagery—as Kersands, Williams, and Ellison show here—is like trying to wrestle flopping eels into a bucket. Everyone overcompensates. Each grabs partial readings of a slippery message. Nearly always it is less a didactic lesson each recaptures than a gestural style. Not *what* but *"how he was saying"* is generative. The persistence and particularly the surprising twists of performance are what the two elders, Hickman and Bliss, come to realize during their long night of memory.

These grotesque tendrils cross from one mode to another and repeat from one to another era, Elizabethan England to Jacksonian America, Rice to Emmett to Kersands to Williams to Ellison. Their connected codes continually knot us together. Each puts his message on top, not erasing but further compounding the interest that is already passing it on. It's a dangerous world facing down these cumulative slights, being sent out to fight wars, dodging domestic violence, bagging home the festive turkey with nobody coming to help, no time. It's like whittling on dynamite. Managers call us out to fetch the lost Bengal tigers they thought they owned. Subaltern songs demur. They figure out substitute strategies— songs that enter the fray so we can stay home unscratched, cats uncaught. Williams talked back from the deep turbulence where cultural flows tangle. He chocked slights into realizations of lumpen consciousness. His no meant no and so did his yes. He tamped bleedhounds into a mobility and made us conscious how we were already signifying on managers' fire hydrants. He showed how to mock managers' missions safely. It all pumps through Bert Williams: somebody else will have to fetch those cats. Now the circumference of American musical performance is wider and its diameter denser. That's the difference Williams makes.

Notes

1. Bert Williams in *In Abyssinia*, quoted by reviewer in *Boston Transcript*, February 21, 1906.

2. "Borrow from Me" (Jean Havez and Bert Williams, 1910, recorded in New York City, January 13, 1913 [Columbia A1354], available on *Bert Williams: The Middle Years, 1910–1918* (Archeophone, 2002).

3. Gayatri Chakravorty Spivak, "Can the Subaltern Speak?" in *Marxism and the Interpretation of Culture*, ed. Cary Nelson and Larry Grossberg (Urbana: University of Illinois Press, 1988), 271–313.

4. Miles Davis, *Miles: The Autobiography*, with Quincy Troupe (New York: Simon and Schuster, 1989), 184.

5. See undated clippings in the Aida Overton Walker file at the Billy Rose Theatre Collection, New York Public Library.

6. There is a program, with plot sketch, for *In Dahomey* at the Grand Theater on October 20, 1902, in the Billy Rose Theatre Collection, *In Dahomey* file; the *New York Dramatic Mirror* reviewed this production on November 1, 1902. *In Dahomey* opened on Broadway at the New York Theatre on February 18, 1903.

7. The first of the three extant versions of the song that Williams recorded is the only one that includes the final two words, and it is the only version in which he sang the whittling on dynamite verse. This first (1906) version is on Archeophone's 2004 release, *Bert Williams: The Early Years, 1901–1909.*

8. The most important evidence of Williams's performance is on the three new Archeophone discs recuperating all his extant recordings: *Bert Williams: The Early Years, 1901–1909, Bert Williams: The Middle Years, 1910–1918, Bert Williams: His Final Releases, 1919–1922* (Archeophone, 2001). See also the scholarship of James Hatch, Ted Shine, and Thomas Riis: James V. Hatch and Ted Shine, *Black Theatre USA: Plays by African Americans; The Early Period, 1847–1938*, expanded ed. (New York: Free Press, 1996), which includes a reconstruction of *In Dahomey*; Thomas L. Riis, *Just before Jazz: Black Musical Theater in New York, 1890–1915* (Washington, D.C.: Smithsonian Institution Press, 1989); Thomas L. Riis, *More Than Just Minstrel Shows: The Rise of Black Musical Theater at the Turn of the Century* (Brooklyn: Institute for Studies in American Music, 1992); and especially Thomas L. Riis, *The Music and Scripts of* In Dahomey (Madison, Wis.: A-R Editions for the American Musicological Society, 1996). More recently, several new works have appeared on Bert Williams, including a novel by Caryl Phillips, *Dancing in the Dark* (New York: Knopf, 2005), and an analytical study by Louis Chude-Sokei, *The Last Darky* (Durham, N.C.: Duke University Press, 2005).

9. Zora Neale Hurston, *Folklore, Memoirs, and Other Writings,* ed. Cheryl A. Wall (New York: Library of America, 1995), 838.

10. Williams sings "mournful" so that it puns with *moan full.*

11. See my introductory essay, "Constance Rourke's Secret Reserve," xiii–xli, in Constance Rourke, *American Humor: A Study of the American Character,* ed. W. T. Lhamon, Jr. (1931; reprint, Tallahassee: Florida State University Press, 1985). For my fuller account of early blackface as cross-racial resistance, see W. T. Lhamon, Jr., *Raising Cain: Blackface Performance from Jim Crow to Hip Hop* (Cambridge: Harvard University Press, 1998).

12. Riis, *Just before Jazz.*

13. Marybeth Hamilton, "Sexual Politics and African-American Music; or, Placing Little Richard in History," *History Workshop Journal* 46 (Autumn 1998): 168.

14. Ann Charters, *Nobody: The Story of Bert Williams* (New York: Macmillan, 1970), 140.

15. My transcription, and emphasis, from the version on *Bert Williams: His Final Releases, 1919–1922.*

16. Alex Rogers wrote the lyrics and Bert Williams wrote the music for "Nobody" in 1905. A further song in the *Nobody Cycle* would be "I Ain't Got Nobody Much" (1916); its sheet music features Williams on the cover, but he evidently never recorded it.

17. Thomas Morgan, "Clarence Williams," http://www.jass.com/Others/cwm.html (accessed April 16, 2007). Further thanks to Thomas Morgan for sending me this reference: Tom Lord reports that Clarence Williams "ran away with Billy Kersands's minstrel show when just a lad of twelve and toured many season all over the southland" (*Clarence Williams* [Essex: Storyville Publications, 1976], 3).

18. Ralph Ellison, *Invisible Man* (1952; reprint, New York: Random House, 1982), 333.

19. W. C. Handy, *Father of the Blues: An Autobiography,* ed. Arna Bontemps (1941; reprint, New York: Macmillan, 1947), 11.

20. Hear them on *Bert Williams: His Final Releases, 1919–1922.*

21. Ralph Ellison, *Juneteenth,* ed. John F. Callahan (New York: Random House, 1999), 136.

Marybeth Hamilton

Searching for the Blues
James McKune, Collectors, and a Different Crossroads

2 There's a historic landmark that's gone uncommemo-
rated in the borough of Brooklyn, New York. Sixty years
ago, the neighborhood known as Williamsburg was
home to a polyglot population: Italian, Polish, and Irish
immigrant families pushed out of overcrowded Manhattan, and single men of various ethnicities attached to
the nearby Navy Yard. To cater to the latter, the Young
Men's Christian Association set up a lodging house at
179 Marcy Avenue, near a stop on the BMT subway line
and a few blocks in from the Williamsburg Bridge. And it
was there at the Brooklyn YMCA, in a single room sometime in the late 1940s, that the Delta blues was born.

It was born, that is, in the mind of one of the YMCA's
long-term residents, an impassioned record collector
named James McKune. Born sometime around 1910,
McKune was the driving force behind the cohort of music enthusiasts who powered the blues revival of the
1960s, when white Americans and Europeans rediscovered a music that African Americans were leaving
behind. Revivalists set up record labels, issued LP anthologies, and wrote liner notes, articles, and books that
framed the blues as we now know it, a music of pain and
alienation, a cry of African American despair. At the
heart of that tale were a few searing voices that expressed

blues anguish in its purest form: Charley Patton, Son House, Skip James, and Robert Johnson, itinerant loners from the Mississippi Delta, the land where racial oppression hit hardest, the land, so revivalists argued, where the blues began.

This essay explores the tangled roots of the musical form that we know as the Delta blues. As a cultural historian, I am intrigued by why, exactly, this music speaks to us: the lustre it holds for us, the resonance it seems to contain. In particular, I have been struck by its impact on the writing of African American history. In his sweeping study of the turn-of-the-century American South, *Trouble in Mind: Black Southerners in the Age of Jim Crow,* the historian Leon Litwack takes Robert Johnson as his text's guiding spirit: two of the book's eight chapters take their titles from Johnson's songs, and the lyrics of Johnson's "Hellhound on My Trail" provide the closing words of the book. For Litwack, "Hellhound on My Trail" is both prototypical blues and an archetypal tale of the Jim Crow experience, and Johnson himself a black Everyman adrift in the Mississippi Delta, a haunted soul who articulated black Southerners' profound alienation, their experience as "a new generation of interior exiles . . . , exiles in their own land."[1]

Litwack's book is by no means singular. Beginning with Lawrence Levine's monumental *Black Culture, Black Consciousness: Afro-American Folk Thought from Slavery to Freedom,* published in 1977, historians have turned to the Delta blues as a means of accessing the experience of the forgotten and faceless black masses, an experience that historians had too long ignored. As historical evidence, its value lies in its sheer directness. As Litwack puts it, to listen to Robert Johnson "is to feel—more vividly and more intensely than any mere poet, novelist, or historian could convey—the despair, the thoughts, the passions, the aspirations, the anxieties, the deferred dreams, the frightening honesty of a new generation of black Southerners and their efforts to grapple with day-to-day life, to make it somehow more bearable, perhaps even to transcend it."[2] What Johnson's blues provides, in other words, is a kind of audio snapshot of the innermost truths of the past. As Litwack writes, quoting the Delta blues chronicler Robert Palmer: "How much history can be transmitted by pressure on a guitar string? The thought of generations, the history of every human being who's ever felt the blues come down like showers of rain."[3]

In what follows I want to reflect upon this idea of the blues as history transmitted by a guitar string. It is, I think, curious to hear a historian as sophisticated as Leon Litwack frame the blues in this straightforwardly populist way: as the voice of the folk, the pure and unmediated cry of the masses. That reverence for the music's evidentiary powers recalls nothing so much as the claims made, decades ago, for oral history: that it allows us to bypass the dangers of historical interpretation by removing the need for a historian, that it enables us to communicate with the past directly by presenting pure images of past experience.[4]

One effect of that reverence, or maybe its symptom, has been to efface the music's means of transmission, the changing technologies of sound reproduction that brought the blues to its listeners. The awkward fact is that, on first release, the recordings that historians most commonly cite as voicing the fundamental truths of the blues had only negligible sales among African Americans themselves. While exact figures are hard to come by, it is clear that Charley Patton sold only moderately in the 1920s and 1930s; Son House, Skip James, and Robert Johnson sold barely at all.[5] Even in the heart of the Mississippi Delta, the so-called country bluesman had limited appeal. A Fisk University sociologist who surveyed the black bars of Clarksdale late in the Depression found not a single Delta blues-man on the jukeboxes. Top sellers instead were the same as they were in black areas across the United States: Louis Jordan, Lil Green, Count Basie, Fats Waller, all patently urban and unabashedly sexual, their songs laden with double (and sometimes single) entendres, backed by a jazz-inflected sound that pulsed with the rhythms of city life.[6]

I want to reflect upon how the urbane, raucous music that once was the blues became the blues as we know it, a music of the Delta drifter, of existential anguish and pain. Understanding that transformation de-mands that we explore the complex process of cultural recycling that has given listeners in our own era readier access to some blues than to others. It demands that we look at the blues revival, at this transitional moment when white Americans laid claim to an abandoned black music. It de-mands, in other words, that we look at James McKune.

In the reminiscences of those involved in the revival, James McKune looms as a figure of legend: a mysterious loner whose ear for the blues shaped the tastes of a generation, an eccentric iconoclast who wore many faces—a wizard, a prophet, a lunatic. Friends, or rather disciples, clustered around him, but no one knew him very well, and only the barest facts emerge from their stories, many of them hazy and confused.[7] McKune came from Baltimore, or Albany, or North Carolina; he moved to New York City some time in the thirties, or perhaps it was during World War II. His personal life was shadowy, at least to his blues acolytes. "I don't know if this should be mentioned, but he was like a closet homosexual," remembers his fellow record collector Pete Whelan. "I didn't know but [another collector] Bill Givens spotted it right away."[8] What they did spot, all of them, was that he drank, more and more heavily as time went on. By the late 1950s his job as a *New York Times* rewrite man had been long abandoned; for a while he worked as a desk clerk at a men's hostel and sorted letters in a Brooklyn post office, but eventually he lost those jobs too. By 1965 he had moved out of the single room at the Brooklyn YMCA where he had lived for twenty-five years and could be seen wandering the streets of Lower Manhattan, "sockless," one collector remembers, "and apparently brain-damaged from alcohol."[9] In September 1971 his unclothed body was found bound and gagged in a skid row hotel on the Lower East Side. Police detectives surmised that he had been killed by a stranger whom he seems to have picked up for sex.

Out of the fog of half-remembered facts of the unconventional life and the horrific death, one thing remains clear in all his friends' minds: the magnificence of his record collection, the pioneering brilliance of his taste in blues. "There was a guy called Jim McKune who was murdered who was like a grand doyen, if you will, and he was a real mentor," recalls the record collector and blues historian Lawrence Cohn. "I mean, he was listening to Charlie Patton before any of us even knew who Brownie McGhee was."[10] Pete Whelan remembers: "He lived in one room in the YMCA and he had all his records in cardboard boxes under his bed. And he would pull out one and say 'here's the greatest blues singer in the world' [and] I'd say 'Oh yeah?' cause I had just discovered this guy, Sam Collins, who was great. . . . Jim pulls out this Paramount by Charlie Patton. I said 'Oh yeah, sure,' and, of course, he was right!"[11]

What made McKune so influential was not simply that he rediscovered Charley Patton but that he set out a distinctive aesthetic that guided the tastes of a clutch of record collectors who came to call themselves the New York Blues Mafia.[12] Beginning in the late 1940s or 1950s, they gathered each week at each others' homes, displayed their latest finds, played them to a studious silence, and fiercely debated their respective merits. It would be Blues Mafiosi, by and large, who would power the blues revival. Most notably, in 1961, McKune's friend Pete Whelan set up the Origins Jazz Library, a record label that would produce the revival's most influential LPS, *The Mississippi Blues* and *Really! The Country Blues,* both of which put McKune's vision of genuine blues under the spotlight.

What follows is not, in any real sense, a biographical portrait of James McKune. He left only scraps of evidence behind him, far too little for any biographer to draw conclusions about his impulses and motives, and far too elliptical for any historian to put him center stage as a historical actor. Even at the peak of his influence, he can only be glimpsed at the margins: searching for discs at used record stores, holding court with other collectors, indoctrinating his apprentices in his single room at the Y, conjuring up ghostly, gritty voices from the battered 78s that he stored in a cardboard box under his bed.

McKune was a tastemaker, a connoisseur, a cultural arbiter whose authority rested on his ability to distinguish the ersatz from the real, and he was by no means the first white person to exercise those powers of discrimination on the black voice. White connoisseurs of African American song were in evidence in the mid-nineteenth century in the abolitionist cult of the sorrow songs, and their numbers grew later in the century with the international popularity of jubilee troupes, black singers of African American spirituals, songs lauded for their soul-turning beauty and the emotional catharsis they provoked in their listeners.[13] For many turn-of-the-century American intellectuals, the spirituals became the nation's preeminent "folk music," both an expression of national spirit and a rich contrast to the regimented urban industrial order. Yet the celebration of black Americans as a "folk" was increasingly complicated by the changing image of African Americans themselves, wrought by their widespread migration to towns and cities, their movement from quasi-feudal farm tenancy into wage labor, and, after 1920, the emergence of a commercially recorded black music—the blues—reproduced and disseminated by mechanical means.

What follows explores the impact of the recorded blues on that tradition of white connoisseurship. In the process it probes the relation between recording technology and the perceived authenticity of the black voice. As I hope to demonstrate, the idea of a genuine, uncorrupted black voice had—still has—a potency that went far beyond music. I will explore how the connoisseur's search for that voice came to focus on commercially recorded race records—and how it remade the blues itself in the process.

Late in 1927, after spending the better part of the year conducting fieldwork in her hometown of Eatonville, Florida, the African American ethnographer Zora Neale Hurston sent a dispirited report to her Columbia University supervisor, Franz Boas. She had returned to the all-black township after a twenty-year absence to gather material for a dissertation on African American folklore, only to discover that authentic black expressive practices were hardly anywhere to be found. The community she remembered from childhood, vibrant with its love of singing and storytelling, seemed to have lapsed into a passive silence. "Negroness is now being rubbed off by close contact with white culture," she informed Boas, adding in dismay: "The bulk of the population now spends its leisure in the motion picture theatres or with the phonograph and its blues."[14]

It is striking, to say the least, to hear such dismay about "the phonograph and its blues" from Zora Neale Hurston, the self-proclaimed Queen of the Niggerati, the opponent of all things genteel in black art. Hurston would dedicate her life to celebrating the vitality of the black vernacular, the songs of "the man in the gutter" even at their most vulgar and raw. "I was collecting jook songs. Pornographic," she wrote to her friend Langston Hughes in 1929 during an expedition sponsored by their shared patron, Charlotte Mason. "She says the dirty words must be toned down. Of course I knew that, but first I wanted to collect them as they are."[15] In time, Hurston's uninhibited devotion to the raucous and sexy would lead some historians to pose her as a literary sister-in-spirit to blues divas like Ma Rainey and Bessie Smith. Yet no such sense of commonality struck Hurston herself when she encountered Smith and Rainey on record. Instead, she heard the corrupting power of whiteness, mechanised, standardized, factory-made entertainment driving out the indigenous folk songs of old.

If appreciating black music on phonograph was hard for Hurston, it was all the more difficult for white aficionados of African American singing in the years immediately after 1920, when the release of Mamie

Smith's "Crazy Blues," the first blues recording by an African American singer, created the so-called race record industry virtually overnight. One response to the recorded blues was the publication over the next decade of a spate of books and articles, written overwhelmingly by white Southerners, lamenting the decline of authentic black music and drawing on memories to cast themselves back to a kinder, gentler past. "How many memories of my childhood and youth are associated with loved black faces!" wrote Dorothy Scarborough, a native of Texas who by 1920 was teaching at Columbia University in New York. One heard few of those songs any more, and even those were under threat, as the "old-time Negro" gave way to a new one who was not disposed to break into song, who had fully succumbed to what Scarborough described as "the lure of the Victrola and cheap printed music."[16]

Yet if the widespread distaste for race records in some ways simply extended a longstanding lament against mass-produced culture, it also had meanings that were specifically racial. Writers like Dorothy Scarborough tapped into a language and a set of associations that had surrounded the black voice since the Civil War, when the South was flooded with white Northerners, most of them veterans of anti-slavery efforts, who were riveted by the music they found there: by spirituals above all, but also by work songs, the "long, lonely sing-song of the fields," as one listener put it.[17] The music was impossible to describe: beautiful, but also haunting, unearthly—it strained the white listener's capacity to comprehend it, to fix it on paper in musical notes. Writing in the landmark study *Slave Songs of the United States* (1867), William Francis Allen felt the same sense of awe at the sheer *difference* of the black voice. "The best we can do . . . with paper and types, or even with voices, will convey but a faint shadow of the original. The voices of the colored people have a peculiar quality that nothing can imitate; and the intonations and delicate variations of even one singer cannot be reproduced on paper."[18]

In the years that followed the publication of *Slave Songs of the United States*, the elusiveness of the black voice, its resistance to reproduction, became an indispensable axiom, the eye of the needle through which any discussion of African American song had to pass. Deepened by suffering, honed by anguish, the black voice could reach peaks of emotion that white voices could not; through rapt attention, white listeners could absorb it and experience something of the sublime.[19]

All the more unsettling, then, to hear that sublime, untutored, primitive voice captured by this most modern of modern technologies, and to see America's black population shelling out millions to buy up those discs. As many hostile listeners were quick to note, the recorded blues of the 1920s supplied an abundance of glitter and vulgarity (think of publicity photos of Bessie Smith head to toe in feathers and sequins; think of hit releases like "Black Snake Moan," "Meat Cutter Blues," and "I Got the Best Jelly Roll in Town"). But more fundamentally, the very act of fusing the black voice and modern technology made for a kind of mongrel amalgamation that made connoisseurs of the spirituals distinctly uneasy. Few were as blunt as the song collector Robert Gordon, who stated that in preserving black folk song he aimed to help "the whites of the South to keep *one* bunch of negroes from becoming utterly worthless and *modern* in the city coon sense."[20] Yet many shared the feeling underlying Gordon's pronouncement: that the cultural value of African Americans lay in their remaining rural and primitive, children of nature who stood in sharp contrast to the self-controlled, disciplined, rational white self.

The idea of using a recording machine to preserve endangered black voices took hold only in the mid-twentieth century, pioneered in 1933, when the Texas folklorist John Lomax (accompanied by his seventeen-year-old son Alan) obtained recording equipment from the Library of Congress and canvassed Southern penitentiaries for authentic African American music, or, as he put it, "songs that in musical phrasing and poetic content are most unlike those of the white race."[21] On the subject of recording equipment Lomax was evangelical. As he saw it, the phonographic apparatus that he brought with him made possible a truly objective study of black music, "sound-photographs of Negro songs, rendered in their own native element, unrestrained, uninfluenced, and undirected by anyone who had his own notions of how the songs should be rendered."[22] What Lomax was after was the black voice reproduced with machine-like precision, a vision driven less by the ethnographic passion for science than by the zeal of an entrepreneur. "The songs would make a sensation in cultured centers," he noted after a visit to Parchman Prison Farm in Mississippi, "if it were only possible to present them in their native, primitive style."[23] His purpose-built recording machine made that dream a reality. Caught on wax, those evanescent voices could be stored for posterity in a federal repository—as one of Lomax's informants would put it, in a building that would never burn down.

Yet if Lomax's enthusiasm for recording technology was, among song collectors, unprecedented, it was also fraught with contradictions. However much he waxed rhapsodic about his state-of-the-art recording devices, his aim in employing them was to escape from the phonograph, to step outside modernity, to find archaic Negroes who inhabited a world where time had stopped. "Folk songs flourish, grow—are created, propagated, transformed—in the eddies of human society, particularly where there is isolation and homogeneity of thought and experience," he explained.[24] Hence his enthusiasm for recording in prisons, which supplied isolation and homogeneity in abundance. "Negro songs in their primitive purity can be obtained probably as nowhere else from Negro prisoners in state or Federal penitentiaries," Lomax argued. "Here the Negroes are completely segregated and have no familiar contact with whites. Thrown on their own resources for entertainment, they still sing [the "distinctive old-time Negro melodies"], especially the long-term prisoners who have been confined for years and who have not yet been influenced by jazz and the radio."[25] He never doubted that such isolation was possible, even by the mid-1930s, when race records had been circulating for fifteen years. In stressing the shock of his "convict friends" when they heard their own voices replayed on the phonograph, he echoed comic writers like Joel Chandler Harris, who back in 1880 had lampooned Uncle Remus's befuddlement at the workings of "dish 'ere w'at dey calls de fonygraf," his naïve astonishment at the disembodied voice booming out of the horn.[26]

Yet time and again Lomax would be dismayed by the worldliness of the men whose "primitive purity" he was meant to be documenting. He wrote of Lead Belly, the convict-turned-folksinger whom he discovered in Angola State Penitentiary in Louisiana: "His eleven years of confinement had cut him off both from the phonograph and from the radio."[27] But as it happened, Lead Belly enjoyed listening to the radio—he would record a song entitled "Turn Your Radio On"—and he drew inspiration from phonograph records. Such eclecticism dismayed both Lomaxes, father and son, even though Alan Lomax's politics was sufficiently to the left of his father's for him to help sponsor Lead Belly's late 1930s comeback as a proletarian folksinger under the aegis of the Popular Front. Not even Alan

Lomax could find it within himself to tolerate Lead Belly's love for the song creations of Tin Pan Alley, his desire to spice up his sets and recording sessions with songs by the movie cowboy Gene Autry, the yodelling hillbilly Jimmie Rodgers, and the latest Bing Crosby hit.

That the recording machine could provoke black singers to decidedly unfolkish behavior had been apparent to at least one song collector even before the advent of commercial race records. Back in 1907, the young Howard Odum, later the South's premier sociologist, took a graphophone into the Mississippi hills as part of his dissertation research and was continually unsettled by the response the machine generated among the itinerant black guitarists whom he persuaded to sing into the horn in return for small change. As traveling performers at dances and on road-sides, they were accustomed to playing to the crowd, and in their recording sessions they sought to demonstrate their up-to-date repertoires, which was decidedly not what Odum was after. "All manner of 'ragtimes,' 'coon-songs,' and the latest 'hits' replace the simpler negro melodies," he lamented. "Young negroes pride themselves on the number of such songs they can sing, at the same time that they resent a request to sing the older melodies."[28]

It would be too simplistic to argue that James McKune turned to collecting race records because it allowed him to avoid these unsettling encounters. Too simplistic certainly, but at some level true. Clearly, as a means of encountering the uncorrupted black voice, record collecting had a popular potential that field recording did not: it required no significant traveling, no specialized equipment, and it freed the collector from fraught personal encounters, from face-to-face interaction with black Americans themselves.

Such, at least, was true of record collecting when McKune took it up in the early 1940s; a decade or so earlier, when the practice began, things had been rather different. The process of transforming discarded race records into collectible objects had its roots in the late 1920s among a handful of white students at Yale and Princeton with a taste for New Orleans–style, or "hot," jazz. As collectors they were driven partly by love of the music, partly as well by the thrill of the chase. At that time, race records could rarely be purchased at music stores catering to a white clientele, so finding them meant journeying into black neighborhoods, even canvassing door to door.[29] Hunting for hot jazz recordings, at least initially, held out much the same lure as a trip to the Cotton Club in a decade when Harlem was decidedly, if briefly, in vogue.

Over the next few years, those scattered collectors began to cohere into a subculture. In 1934, one of the Princeton contingent, Charles Edward Smith, published an article on hot jazz collecting in the men's magazine *Esquire*, which, as one fellow enthusiast put it, "served notice to widely scattered individuals that there were others who liked the same kind of music, and extended to the public at large the invitation to take up a hobby which was relatively cheap sport."[30] Taking up that hobby was made easier, and cheaper, by the fact that by the 1930s hot jazz was out of favor with African Americans, and recordings by Joe Oliver, Kid Ory, and Jelly Roll Morton could be found in some profusion in junk shops. They could also be found via specialist magazines, like the *Record Changer*, in which collectors could offer items for sale or trade and put out calls for recordings they sought, and in used record stores like the Jazz Record Center near Times Square. Also known as Indian Joe's, it had been founded around 1940 by Big Joe Clauberg, a chain-smoking Native American giant and one-time circus strongman who set it up, initially, as a used book store and a base for publishing *Hobo News*. Every other week Big Joe loaded copies of the paper into his truck and delivered them to points west and south. One of his customers was a juke box operator who offered him used records at a very low price. Big Joe hated driving back to Manhattan with an empty truck, and, besides, his store had lots of free space. Over time, he increased his stock until those bins of used records took over the shop. Business peaked on Saturday nights, when collectors squeezed in to rummage for records while rubbing shoulders with Big Joe's colorful cronies—circus performers, grizzled sea captains, and a permanently inebriated bookie whose habit of sleeping on the shop floor earned him the nickname of Horizontal Abe.[31]

What distinguished hot jazz collecting was the politics that was woven around it by the most active and influential collectors, Charles Edward Smith, William Russell, and Frederic Ramsey. Together they formed part of a transatlantic world of jazz aficionados immersed in the politics of the Popular Front. New Orleans jazz enthralled them as a music "of protest and of pride," inherently progressive in emphasizing collective rather than solo improvisation.[32] Collecting records in the venues they frequented was a sign of progressive social change too. While one could argue that the Jazz Record Center's midtown location made collecting race records more palatable for the faint-hearted by removing the need to go to Harlem to find them, collectors like Ramsey stressed the store's break with habitual marketing practice: it sold Jelly Roll Morton alongside Benny Goodman, black jazz and white jazz in the same shop.[33]

That was record collecting as it was practiced when James McKune arrived in New York. At some point in the mid-1940s, the oddballs and obsessives who haunted Indian Joe's spotted a new face on the scene, a nondescript man of indeterminate age who turned up in the shop every Saturday night. He was extremely thin, of medium height, with sandy hair graying at the temples, dressed in a white button-down shirt, black trousers, white socks, and black shoes, by all appearances his lone set of clothes. Engaging him in conversation was risky. "He had this way of talking," one acquaintance remembers, "he'd make these abrupt gestures, he was very intense, and everybody that he was talking to would be backing up against the wall, because he'd be, not pushing you back, but you'd be afraid of the hands and elbows coming at you."[34] In his pocket he carried a want list that he distributed to used record traders: thirteen hundred 78s recorded in the 1920s and 1930s on the most obscure labels by performers of whom no other collectors had heard.

Late in 1943, James McKune ran his first ad in the Record Changer, and by the end of the decade, the singularity of his wants had drawn him a circle of acolytes. Henry Renard, Ron Lubin, and Pete Kaufman were intrigued enough to write to him (his advertisements gave his address in Brooklyn), and soon they were meeting regularly, along with Stephen Calt, Lawrence Cohn, Ben Kaplan, Nick Perls, Bernie Klatzko, and Pete Whelan, who first encountered McKune in the aisles of Indian Joe's.[35] Most of the men were ten years McKune's junior and unlike the eminences of the "collecting fraternity" were not products of the Ivy League. Pete Kaufman ran a liquor store, Pete Whelan wrote ad copy for a railway magazine, Henry Renard clerked for one of Indian Joe's competitors, Ron Lubin drove a truck for a photographer, and none of them had a lot of money to spend. In McKune they found a mentor. He introduced them to the sites of collector's mythology, the places where the Jazzmen set got their start: the furniture stores under the subway tracks in Queens where Charles Edward Smith unearthed boxes of untouched Okehs and Vocalions; the Polish Music Store, where John Hammond found his Paramounts and Victors; even, incongruously, Bloomingdale's, in whose basement William Russell uncovered a stock of mint condition Paramounts.[36] Saturday afternoons they met at Indian Joe's, where they thumbed through the bins in between swigs from the bottles of muscatel that Pete Kaufman brought along from his store, suspending their searches briefly at three, when a man called Bob turned up with a suitcase of pornographic books. One night each week they convened at each others' apartments and debated the merits of their latest finds. In all of this, McKune took the lead. In July 1950 Kaufman ran an ad in the *Record Changer* offering the substantial sum of three dollars, more than most collectors offered for the most prized 78s, for a copy of "McKune's Comprehensive Want List of 1943." By then, among a small coterie of aficionados he had developed a reputation as a collector's collector, a connoisseur with an unusually discerning ear.

Having traded away more recordings than most people would hear in a lifetime, McKune was the grand old man of the group, and he surrounded himself with an air of inscrutability that emphasized the cutting-edge character of his tastes. "On principle," Whelan recalls, McKune would not pay more than three dollars for any record. To hand over more substantial sums would tarnish what ought to be a radical act of salvage, of rummaging through rubbish and finding treasures ignored by the masses and overlooked by a record-collecting fraternity whose tastes were too often blinkered and staid. McKune had nothing but scorn for collectors like the used record trader Jake Schneider, who became famous among aficionados for amassing nearly half a million recordings.

He had nothing but contempt for fans of white jazz, the bobby-soxers who occasionally ventured into the Jazz Record Center in search of bargain Glenn Miller, but he had no more time for the jumped-up sounds of Louis Jordan, Howlin' Wolf, and Muddy Waters that were dominating the postwar African American soundscape. To hot jazz he was wholly indifferent, and he was frankly bored by the purveyors of "people's music," Lead Belly and other proletarian folksingers promoted by Alan Lomax and Pete Seeger under the umbrella of the Popular Front.

The recordings that James McKune salvaged came from the bottom of the discard pile, the dross that everyone else had rejected, records that, as one collector later put it, were "considered worthless by everyone but [McKune] himself."[37] Alone in his room at the YMCA, playing his 78s at a low volume so as not to penetrate the building's thin walls, McKune listened out for spare, sparse music, oblique, artful lyrics, and intense, passionate, primitive voices, voices supercharged with raw emotion. Politics was absent from those recordings, at least on the surface. As he explained, "After you've listened to the real Negro blues for a long time, you know at once that the protest of the blues is . . . [in the] accompanying piano or guitar," not in anything as unsubtle as lyrics.[38] "Real Negro blues" could be recognized by its inimitable vocal: searing, primitive, yet wholly artless; as McKune put it, it was marked by "an intensity devoid of dramatic effects."[39] As one of McKune's protégés explained: "The voice is dark and heavy, often thick and congested, with a peculiar crying quality. . . . and suffused throughout with an emotional intensity that is all but overpowering (the words seem almost torn from the singer's throat)." These were barely songs at all—more a rhythmic wail of anguish, in which "monosyllabic cries" expressing "strong, uncontrollable feelings" often "carr[ied] far greater meaning than do the song's words."[40] From those voices McKune assembled a pantheon of great "country blues" singers—anguished loners and wanderers like Skip James, Son House, Charley Patton, and Robert Johnson, their very obscurity testament to their ferocious integrity, the rough, ragged intensity of the songs that they sang.

In years to come McKune's protégés would label this music the Delta blues. McKune was far less concerned with geography; his was an imagined landscape, like the "old, weird America" evoked by McKune's friend Harry Smith on his 1952 Folkways anthology.[41] (Smith and McKune had a long-distance trading relationship that extended back to the mid-1940s, when McKune forwarded Smith a list of mint condition Paramounts available at a junk shop on Long Island. Smith bought every one; some turned up on the Folkways Anthology.)[42] Yet unlike Smith's "invisible republic," which mixed the voices of blacks with the voices of hillbillies and refused to specify which was which, the invisible landscape that McKune created was shaped by mythologies of race. At its heart lay that holy grail, the venerable vision of a pure and uncorrupted black voice. McKune's aesthetic restyled that vision in new and more durable form, a form that had sufficient power to survive the triumph of commercial recording. Though the discs McKune celebrated had been recorded and distributed by mass-market channels, they had effectively dropped out of the commercial nexus: everyone had rejected them, African Americans and jazz collectors alike. And while they were mechanically recorded, they had something of the handmade about them. Used 78s were dusty, battered, and scratchy—they had been heavily handled, if not made by hand —and had often been recorded on primitive equipment under poor conditions. Indeed, part of the appeal of McKune's "great country blues singers" may have been the very murkiness of the sound quality. Far from destroying the mystery of black singing, in other words, recording technology conveyed and conferred it, creating discs whose voices sounded peculiar and striking, muffled and contorted by the machine.

It had been in 1944, a year after he took up collecting, that McKune unearthed his greatest discarded treasure, a scratched, worn copy of "Some These Days I'll be Gone," recorded in 1929 by Charley Patton, a singer about whom he knew nothing and whom no other collectors were after. On first hearing Patton's voice sounded almost too primitive, but after that initial shock McKune was transfixed. What overwhelmed him was Patton's artistry, his inventiveness with his materials, the way his rough-edged voice conveyed a breathtaking delicacy of technique. "He tells a story only in part," McKune explained, "singing the same phrases again and again, varying his voice, almost making the guitar part of his voice." On the flip side was the old blues standard "Frankie and Albert," which he sang "as it probably has never been sung before. . . . His is a tale quietly yet passionately told. At the end you are shaken. You play it again and you forget that anyone else ever sang it." What McKune heard in Patton's voice was a transcendent, mystical power: "only the great religious singers have ever effected [sic] me similarly." The only appropriate response to such artistry was to listen "silently. In awe."[43]

The Blues Mafiosi might have rumbled on forever, honing their tastes, refining their want lists, had it not been for an upstart collector who affronted their sensibilities and provoked them to move into the public eye. The offending party was Samuel Barclay Charters IV, a thirty-year-old jazz aficionado and aspiring Beat poet who moved to New Orleans in the early 1950s and began casting around for new sounds when the Dixieland revival dried up. Equipped with magnetic tape and a contract from Moses Asch, he spent the next few years scouring Alabama for skiffle bands, the streets of New Orleans for Mardi Gras Indians, and the Bahamas for calypso musicians, including the brilliant guitarist Joseph Spence. In New Orleans he got to know the jazz historian Frederic Ramsey, who was then undertaking the Southern treks that would result in a much-praised book of photojournalism entitled *Been Here and Gone*. One glance at Ramsey's photographs fired Charters's imagination and led to a book and an LP issue in 1959 on Folkways Records, both entitled *The Country Blues*.

At heart, *The Country Blues* was a work of advocacy. What struck Charters as important in black music was its sheer emotional intensity. His experiences in New Orleans in the 1950s, as the civil rights movement intensified, had alienated him from what he saw as a racist, conformist mainstream, and that sense of disaffection would mount in the following decade, when he aligned himself with the New Left, wrote poetry protesting the Vietnam War, and ultimately left the United States altogether. In setting out to uncover the "country blues," Charters envisioned it as an intensely personal music that "became the emotional outlet for Negro singers in every part of the South."[44] The term itself he appears to have lit upon in consultation with Ramsey, who used it in liner notes in the mid-1950s, but Charters gave it a new kind of prominence, raising it to the level of a brand name. At a fairly late stage in preparing his manuscript, he seems to have met up with Pete Whelan and other Blues Mafiosi to listen to some of their rare recordings. But he was not really interested in rarities; his aim was to "keep the focus where the black audience put it," and so he put most of his effort into recovering sales figures from the files of record companies and the industry trade press.[45] The book that resulted barely mentioned Charley Patton, gave a bit more attention to Robert Johnson, but put the spotlight on Lonnie Johnson, Leroy Carr, and Big Bill Broonzy, the musicians whose recordings black Americans of the 1930s had bought.

When the book was published to glowing reviews, with Charters lionized for recovering a forgotten art form, McKune was incensed. He contacted Trevor Benwell, publisher of the British-based collectors' magazine *Vintage Jazz Mart* and offered to write a riposte. The result was a column pointedly entitled "The Great Country Blues Singers," which would run intermittently until 1965. Its first installment is as close as McKune ever got to issuing a manifesto. "This essay makes up for what Sam Charters did not say, or did not say fully enough, in his book *The Country Blues*," he began. "I know twenty men who collect the Negro country blues. All of us have been interested in knowing who the *great* country blues singers are, not in who sold best."[46]

Beneath the aggrieved territoriality in McKune's words lay a distaste for the whole premise of Charters's project: his decision to use the tastes of African American record buyers as a kind of aesthetic guide. McKune took it as given that the masses could not discriminate, and in his eyes it did not matter whether those masses were white or black. To think otherwise was to resurrect the most philistine brand of left-wing populism, to confuse solidarity with connoisseurship, to pose the appreciation of black music as in itself a political act. While Charters insisted on mining every moan or wail for its social significance ("hours in the hot sun, scraping at the earth, singing to make the hours pass"), the whole point of McKune's *VJM* columns was to evaluate the singers as artists. That, he insisted, was what would-be collectors of country blues needed: advice from experts who had been "listening to blues records since 1943" and who possessed the training, the cultivation to understand "greatness," to distinguish the pedestrian from the artful, the ersatz from the real.

To display that training and cultivation (and to expose Charters's mistakes), the Blues Mafia set out to make the truly great voices public. Sometime around 1960, Pete Whelan canvassed his fellow enthusiasts for the least-battered copies of their most treasured 78s, hired a tape engineer, a partner with money, and set about making taped reproductions. The long-playing albums that resulted began appearing in 1961 on an independent label that Whelan dubbed the Origins Jazz Library. As the name suggested, Whelan envisioned the LPs as a kind of reference collection of primordial sounds, the soil from which jazz sprang, primitive music as an art form in its own right. Just how inadequately Charters had performed his task the label made clear in its first two releases: OJL-1, devoted to Charley Patton, whom Charters had wholly neglected; and OJL-2, an anthology of blues greats pointedly titled *Really! The Country Blues*. Wasn't Charters's country blues real, an interviewer asked Whelan twenty years later. "It was real," he responded. "Just not real enough."[47]

Stephen Calt later estimated that about half of OJL's customers were Europeans, the other half a mix of seasoned collectors and young guitarists keen to broaden their repertoires. For OJL-2, *Really! The Country Blues*, Whelan ordered only five hundred pressings, and it would take over two years for sales to exhaust that first batch.[48] Still, it was enough. Almost immediately, the OJL recordings became the bible of new, younger blues enthusiasts like John Fahey, often musicians themselves and entranced by the rough-hewn voices, the scratched, grainy sound, and the sense of acquiring secret knowledge, of eschewing Charters's easy answers and participating in a vanguard. For the future *Deep Blues* author Robert Palmer, who encountered the albums as a musician in Memphis, they were "the definitive country blues anthologies," a view held as well by Jeff Todd Titon, whose exposure to the albums would lead him to study ethnomusicology and write the influential book *Early Downhome Blues*.[49] Other fans included a young historian named Lawrence Levine, just completing his graduate work at Columbia and beginning the investigations into African American folk songs that would result in *Black Culture, Black Consciousness*; Greil Marcus, who discovered the albums in his local record store in Berkeley; and the veteran jazz collector Marshall Stearns, an English professor turned musicologist and the director of the Institute for Jazz Studies, which he helped to establish in 1953.[50]

So intense was the country blues mania that even the Library of Congress took notice. In 1962 it released *Negro Blues and Hollers,* an LP compilation of field recordings made in 1941–42 by Alan Lomax, John Work, and Lewis Jones in the Mississippi Delta, which had lain untouched and forgotten in the Library's vaults for twenty years. To write the liner notes, they turned to Stearns. "Literature on the country blues is hard to come by," he noted—Samuel Charters, though raising the form's public profile, had made only "a beginning." "To get to the heart of the matter, one has to dig deeper": to the Origins Jazz Library reissues of country blues rarities and to the "unique articles" in *Vintage Jazz Mart* by "James McCune [*sic*], the dean of country-blues fanciers." The value of McKune's articles lay in dispensing with sociology to focus on the form's "artistic merits." Country blues recordings as he defined them were "archaic in the best sense . . . gnarled, rough-hewn, and eminently uncommercial." In them one heard a music "fixed in time and space," unaffected by technology or the market, "tied down to—and unerringly reflect[ing]—the geographic area, the local manners, and the exact vernacular of a specific place."[51] That specific place was the Mississippi Delta, which thanks to McKune we could now identify as the locus of blues authenticity, the land where the blues was born.

Stearns's liner notes brought McKune momentarily into the limelight, the closest he would ever come to public recognition as a country blues expert. Yet they also contained the seeds of what would become a re-branding. By the mid-1960s, the phrase "country blues" being, it seems, too tainted by Charters's misapprehensions, aficionados relabeled the music "Delta blues." McKune himself never employed the term. Yet it was his taste that codified the sound, one that proved uncannily market-able, owing in part to its resonance with broader cultural trends. "Pure blues," for McKune, took the form of voices that were searing, personal, and to his ears apolitical. This would become one of the keynotes of the revival: real, authentic blues was not protest music. On this score, in time, even Samuel Charters came to agree. "If the blues simply mirrored the protest of the moment they would finally have little more than an histori-cal interest, like the songs of the suffragettes or the Grange movement," he wrote in the wake of the OJL reissues. Instead, the Negro turned to the blues "as the expression of his personal and immediate experience." The result was "a poetic language" that spoke of "a larger human reality," timeless truths of alienation and loss.[52]

Despite their apparent distaste for politics, the revivalists' own lan-guage was profoundly political. It echoed the values and aesthetics of the postwar American intelligentsia, which conspicuously recoiled against the cultural radicalism of the Red Decade.[53] In their criticism of literature, painting, and theater, Cold War intellectuals celebrated art that was uni-versal, poetic, and nonideological. In the process they staked out a new role as "guardians of the self," champions of the personal, the individual, against the forces of political conformity.[54] The Delta blues, I would ar-gue, formed part of that cultural moment. To call it a regional music is misleading, for the Delta it spoke of was a state of mind. A music of anguish and alienation, of existential loneliness, it had its roots in the imaginations of a coterie of record collectors, their sensibility shaped by an obstinate nonconformist, an eccentric self-made outcast.

James McKune, in the end, is the enigma at the heart of the Delta blues, and not least because he so abruptly falls out of its story. Though his protégés succeeded brilliantly at pushing his aesthetic into the spot-light, he himself played no direct part in the process. As his vision of blues infiltrated the mainstream, McKune wrote no liner notes, managed no artists, set up no record labels, opened no blues clubs. His *vjm* columns, always sporadic, ceased altogether in 1965, and sometime that year he moved out of the Williamsburg ymca for a room in a Manhattan hostel near 34th Street. Eventually he drifted to the Lower East Side and found a room at the Broadway Central Hotel, a once-elegant watering hole gone to seed. Though the lower floors retained a kind of lowlife glamour—home to the Mercer Arts Center, a gathering place for New York's nascent punk underground, where by 1973 the New York Dolls would be in residence— McKune settled on the floors above, given over to single rooms inhabited by junkies, hookers, and derelicts, into whose ranks he quietly slid. When police found his body in September 1971, the only clue to his earlier life lay in a letter in the room from Bernie Klatzko, one of the stalwarts of the Blues Mafia. There was no trace of a record collection: McKune had either sold it or given it away.

Perhaps McKune's movement away from the blues was inevitable. The pleasures of collecting lie in creating a personal system, an alternative universe of aesthetics and taste. Lose control of that universe and the collector's pride and bravado become envy and frustration; his excitement and euphoria become depression and despair. Perhaps McKune's story illuminates the dark side of collecting, the devastation of the connoisseur who finds that his private passion is private no longer, that his role as a tastemaker has been usurped.

The biographer Hermione Lee has spoken of the writer's temptation, when coming to the end of a work of biography, to try to bring that life to a poetic conclusion, to try to make the death in some way sum it up.[55] I don't know—I may never know—what propelled McKune into his fascination with blues, but it is hard not to speculate about how his aesthetic resonated with his inner needs. McKune dedicated his life to finding a blues voice that was intense, raw, defiantly marginal, and he ended his days as a homeless, friendless wanderer, dying in circumstances as violent, mysterious, and sexually charged as Robert Johnson himself. It's too pat, but perhaps not wholly unjustified, for me to end on that note, to place McKune down and out on skid row clinging fiercely to his blues vision—living the life of the alienated drifter, scorning the pull of the marketplace, uncorrupted to the very end.

Notes

1. Leon Litwack, *Trouble in Mind: Black Southerners in the Age of Jim Crow* (New York: Knopf, 1998), 478.
2. Ibid., 457.
3. Ibid., xvii.
4. Michael Frisch, "Oral History and *Hard Times:* A Review Essay," in *The Oral History Reader*, ed. Robert Perks and Alistair Thomson (London: Routledge, 1998), 29–37.
5. Robert Palmer, *Deep Blues: A Musical and Cultural History of the Mississippi Delta* (New York: Viking, 1981), 123–24. For a detailed discussion of musical taste in the Mississippi Delta, see also Elijah Wald, *Escaping the Delta: Robert Johnson and the Invention of the Delta Blues* (New York: Amistad, 2004), 83–102.
6. "List of records on machines in Clarksdale amusement places," folder 7 (Lists), Fisk University Mississippi Delta Collection, Archive of Folk Culture, Library of Congress, Washington, D.C. The list, compiled by the sociologist Lewis Jones, dates from 1941 or 1942.
7. Henry Renard, "Letters from McKune," *78 Quarterly* 1, no. 3 (1988): 54–62; Bernard Klatzko, "Postscript to the McKune Story," *78 Quarterly* 1, no. 4 (1988); 93; Stephen Calt, *I'd Rather Be the Devil: Skip James and the Blues* (New York: Da Capo, 1994), 216–17; Joel Slotnikoff, "Pete Whelan Interview," http://www.bluesworld.com/PeteWhelanInterview.html (accessed April 16, 2007).
8. Slotnikoff, "Pete Whelan Interview," 3.
9. Calt, *I'd Rather Be the Devil*, 217.
10. Quoted in Jim O'Neal, "I Once Was Lost, But Now I'm Found: The Blues Revival of the 1960s," in *Nothing But the Blues: The Music and the Musicians*, ed. Lawrence Cohn (New York: Abbeville Press, 1993), 376.
11. Slotnikoff, "Pete Whelan Interview," 3.
12. O'Neal, "I Once Was Lost, But Now I'm Found," 376.
13. Jon Cruz, *Culture on the Margins: The Black Spiritual and the Rise of American Cultural Interpretation* (Princeton, N.J.: Princeton University Press, 1999); Ronald Radano, "Denoting Difference: The Writing of Slave Spirituals," *Critical Inquiry* 22 (1996): 506–54.
14. Quoted in Robert Hemenway, *Zora Neale Hurston: A Literary Biography* (Urbana: University of Illinois Press, 1977), 92.
15. Zora Neale Hurston to Langston Hughes, undated (spring/summer 1929) and October 15, 1929, in Langston Hughes Papers, James Weldon Johnson

Memorial Collection of African American Arts and Letters, Beinecke Rare Book and Manuscript Library, Yale University.

16. Hemenway, *Zora Neale Hurston*, 280–81.

17. Charles Peabody, "Notes on Negro Music," *Journal of American Folklore* 16 (1903): 152.

18. *Slave Songs of the United States,* ed. William Francis Allen, Charles Pickard Ware, and Lucy McKim Garrison (New York: A. Simpson and Co., 1867), iv–v.

19. Radano, "Denoting Difference," 518–19.

20. Quoted in Deborah Kodish, *Good Friends and Bad Enemies: Robert Winslow Gordon and the Study of American Folksong* (Urbana: University of Illinois Press, 1986), 140.

21. John A. Lomax, " 'Sinful Songs' of the Southern Negro," *Musical Quarterly* 20 (1934): 181. On Lomax, see Nolan Porterfield, *Last Cavalier: The Life and Times of John Lomax, 1867–1948* (Urbana: University of Illinois Press, 1996); and Jerrold Hirsch, "Modernity, Nostalgia, and Southern Folklore Studies: The Case of John Lomax," *Journal of American Folklore* 105 (Spring 1992): 183–207.

22. Lomax, " 'Sinful Songs' of the Southern Negro," 181.

23. Undated letter written in Parchman, Mississippi, in file marked "General Correspondence, 1933–1939," John Lomax Papers, Archive of Folk Culture, Library of Congress.

24. John A. Lomax, "Report of the Honorary Consultant and Curator," from *Report of the Librarian of Congress for the Fiscal Year Ending June 30, 1934,* reprinted in *Archive of American Folk Song: A History, 1928–1939, Compiled from the Annual Reports of the Librarian of Congress* (Washington, D.C., 1940), 27.

25. Lomax, "Report of the Honorary Consultant and Curator," from *Report of the Librarian of Congress for the Fiscal Year Ending June 30, 1933,* reprinted in *Archive of American Folk Song,* 24.

26. Joel Chandler Harris, *Uncle Remus: His Songs and His Sayings* (New York: D. Appleton and Co., 1881), chapter 6: "The Phonograph."

27. John A. and Alan Lomax, *Negro Folk Songs as Sung by Lead Belly* (New York: Macmillan Company, 1936), xiii.

28. Howard W. Odum, "Folk-Song and Folk-Poetry as Found in the Secular Songs of the Southern Negroes," *Journal of American Folklore* 25 (July-September 1911): 259.

29. Stephen W. Smith, "Hot Collecting," in *Jazzmen,* ed. Frederic Ramsey, Jr., and Charles Edward Smith (New York: Harcourt, Brace and Company, 1939), 287–99.

30. Ibid., 289.

31. Henry Renard, "The Life and Times of Big Joe Clauberg and his Jazz Record Center," *78 Quarterly* 1 (1989): 62–66.

32. Alan Lomax, *Mister Jelly Roll* (New York: Duell, Sloan and Pearce, 1950), vii.

33. The Popular Front jazz subculture is discussed in Michael Denning, *The Cultural Front: The Laboring of American Culture in the Twentieth Century* (London: Verso, 1997), 328–38; David W. Stowe, *Swing Changes: Big-Band Jazz in New Deal America* (Cambridge, Mass.: Harvard University Press, 1994); and Bernard Gendron, " 'Moldy Figs' and Modernists: Jazz at War (1942–46)," in *Jazz among the Discourses,* ed. Krin Gabbard (Durham, N.C.: Duke University Press, 1995), 31–56.

34. Interview with Pete Whelan, July 6, 2003.

35. Pete Kaufman, "A Recollection of Big Joe's . . . ," *78 Quarterly* 1, no. 2 (1968): n.p.

36. Slotnikoff, "Pete Whelan Interview," 11–12.

37. Calt, *I'd Rather Be the Devil,* 216.

38. James McKune, "The Great Country Blues Singers (3)," *VJM Palaver,* September 1961, 7.

39. Ibid.

40. Pete Welding, "Stringin' the Blues," *Down Beat,* July 1, 1965, 22.

41. Greil Marcus, *Invisible Republic: Bob Dylan's Basement Tapes* (London: Picador, 1997), 87–126.

42. Rani Singh, ed., *Think of the Self Speaking: Harry Smith—Selected Interviews* (Seattle: Elbow/Cityful Press, 1999), 23, 25, 71.

43. James McKune, "The Great Country Blues Singers (2)," *VJM Palaver,* June 1961, 3.

44. Samuel Charters, *The Country Blues* (New York: Rinehart, 1959, reprinted 1975), 19.

45. Charters, *Country Blues,* xviii.

46. James McKune, "The Great Country Blues Singers (1)," *VJM Palaver,* April 1961, 3–4.

47. Slotnikoff, "Pete Whelan Interview," 2.

48. Calt, *I'd Rather Be the Devil,* 249.

49. Palmer, *Deep Blues,* 281; Jeff Todd Titon, "Reconstructing the Blues: Reflections on the 1960s Blues Revival," in Neil V. Rosenberg, *Transforming Tradition: Folk Musical Revivals Examined* (Urbana: University of Illinois Press, 1993), 224.

50. See Lawrence Levine, *Black Culture, Black Consciousness: Black Folk Thought from Slavery to Freedom* (New York: Oxford University Press, 1977), 478, n. 16, and 483, nn. 85, 87, where Levine draws on the OJL reissues.

51. Marshall Stearns, liner notes to *Negro Blues and Hollers*, originally published 1962, reissued in 1997 on Rounder Records (CD 1501).

52. Samuel Charters, *The Poetry of the Blues* (New York: Oak Publications, 1963), 17, 173.

53. For a more extensive discussion of this point, see Marybeth Hamilton, "Sexuality, Authenticity, and the Making of the Blues Tradition," *Past and Present* 169 (November 2000): 132–60.

54. Daryl Michael Scott, *Contempt and Pity: Social Policy and the Image of the Damaged Black Psyche, 1880–1996* (Chapel Hill: University of North Carolina Press, 1997), 73.

55. Hermione Lee, "How To End It All: Biography and Death," paper delivered at the *History Workshop Journal* conference on Biography and History held at Birkbeck College, London, on October 28, 2000.

Josh Kun

Abie the Fishman
On Masks, Birthmarks, and Hunchbacks

3

Do not imagine that you, of all the Jews, will escape with your
life by being in the King's palace.
ESTHER 4:13–14

Everybody knows there is no fineness or accuracy of suppres-
sion; if you hold down one thing you hold down the adjoining.
SAUL BELLOW, *THE ADVENTURES OF AUGIE MARCH*

Home? I have none. Family? No.
PHILIP ROTH, *PORTNOY'S COMPLAINT*

1. My Inner Abie

My last name is pronounced the way nobody wants it to
be, with a "u" that might as well be an "oo." It is not a
Korean name, though that hasn't prevented me from
being mistaken for a Korean by junk mail distributors, or
from being made an honorary Korean, as I was on my
first junior high field trip when the order of the alphabet
on the school roster put me in the same wilderness re-
treat cabin as the Kims and the Lees and the Kwons. It is,
in actuality, a Hungarian name, passed down to me from
my American-born father—whose first name matches
that of Thomas Kuhn, which, despite the letter of difference in the last names, has not prevented people from
thinking my father should be footnoted anytime any-

body uses the phrase "paradigm shift" to explain a major change. My father got the name from his Hungarian-born father, who was never able to tell me much about where it came from beyond that. The name also belonged to a famous Hungarian dictator but nobody in our family has ever been able to tell me much about that either.

By the time I was old enough to know that Jewish last names were often shortened by the time they hit American shores, I asked my grandfather if we were once Kunstein or Kunowitz, the way my mother's father's last name, Kamins, was once Kaminsky. My grandfather—who was modern Orthodox, who took my father to Talmud and Torah classes when he was just old enough to read, who had somehow convinced my father that he would grow up to be a rabbi and not a gastroenterologist—insisted that in fact our last name "used to be shorter." Apparently, not only were we such non-assimilationist Jews that we made our name longer and even more Jewish than it was but we were also related to Josef K.

For Jews, names are the outer shells of inner struggles. Their length, their cadence, their absence or presence of–bergs or–steins, their sheer multisyllabic Jewy-ness, their ability to make someone ask "Is that a Jewish name?" have long been signs of deeper, more complicated stories of Jewish self-performance and visibility, stories that often house the residue of painful memories, shame, and loathing. The names we change and the names we keep are merely the props of our performances, the most common traces of the vexing question of what it means to perform oneself as Jewish.

For me that performance has meant the following. I am the grandson of poor Orthodox Hungarians and Reform country club–belonging, Cobb salad–eating Russians who married Swedish nurses who converted. I am the nephew of Auschwitz survivors who became upholsterers and horse-track regulars. As for my parents, my mother insists on celebrating Easter and Christmas because they have nice decorations and my father keeps a few pictures of his grandparents and great-uncles buried in a cluttered desk drawer, but otherwise I was raised to think that it's better to not remember so much.

I grew up in the shadows of the 20th Century-Fox studios, breakdancing at bar mitzvahs, moussing my hair, wanting it blonde like the Protestant kids at my private school who got to fox trot and waltz at cotillions and beach clubs, the ones where rich black kids were asked if they were there to do the windows and rich Korean kids (not me) were only allowed a day pass. I was convinced that the Jewishness of my grandparents would just get in the way of my being who I thought I wanted to be. The Russian Swedes weren't the problem—they had Trans-Ams and aqua Benzes. The Hungarians were the problem. Warm milk and cold cabbage. Money hidden in couch cushions. Schizophrenia, madness, shock therapy. Thick accents that smelled like herring.

I am now a walking mix of Jewish self-hatred and annoying philo-Semitism. For my thirty-first birthday, a friend gave me a t-shirt with the Star of David on the front and the words "self-hater" on the back. At the time I was still living in an Orthodox neighborhood, in my paternal grand-parents' old house with a garage full of boxed memories. I'm a critic who often writes about Jewish pop culture and there has never been a perfor-mance of Jewishness in popular culture that I have been able to fully celebrate. I get angry when Spielberg makes films about Jews and angry when he doesn't. I get angry when Jews sing of being Jewish, and angry when they don't. I am a staunch opponent of assimilation and a staunch opponent of anyone who opposes assimilation. I want Jews to maintain their difference, yet I also want to preserve the option for sameness.

I say things like, "If you are a Jew, act like one." I also say things like, "If you are a Jew, act like whatever you want." I also say "Just be Jewish" and then complain in disgust, "Please, stop being so Jewish."

Jean Amery once called it, "The necessity and impossibility of being a Jew," and I couldn't agree more.[1]

2. Abie and Roscoe

The story I want to tell concerns a certain Abie—let's call him Abie Cohen—who changes his name to Roscoe Chandler and pretends that he is no longer Abie. Then somebody recognizes him, sings a song that outs him, and he must choose, now that he has been outed as himself and not himself, outed as being not one but two, the impostor and the real, which masquerade he will continue to wear, which secret he will keep. Will he choose his adopted name and culture? Or will he wear his birthmark on his surname?

To get to the story, I first need to tell an old Groucho Marx joke that goes like this: A Jew and a hunchback are walking down the street and when they walk past a temple, the Jew turns to the hunchback, nudges him in the ribs, and says, you know I used to be a Jew. The hunchback looks back at him and says, Oh really? I used to be a hunchback.

The joke wasn't very popular after Hitler turned its punch line into the basis for genocide. Mickey Katz used to tell it in the fifties, but nobody much appreciated it when he did. Like Groucho, Katz was an aggressively out Jew—let's follow Ronald Smith and call them antic-Semites—who made performing his Jewishness part of his musical shtick. The joke was made for Jews like Katz and Groucho because it was a revenge joke—the Jew who stayed a Jew reminding the passer, the assimilator, the masked, who they once were. To use Hannah Arendt's terms, it was the kind of joke pariahs, Jews in Eastern and Central Europe who willingly opted out of dominant elite society, told about parvenus, the Jews who made their Jewishness a secret and opted in.

The punch line's thin ice—where antic-Semitism begets anti-Semitism—is its echo of anti-Semitic groupthink in which the Jew was eternally the Jew, an immutable creature that had no hope of true assimilation. For Judaism there was conversion, the logic went, for Jewishness there was nothing, no cure. Arendt has argued that one of the results of Jewish assimilation into the political and social ranks of twentieth-century Western Europe was that the special markers of Judaism as a religion and "the Jews" as a political or social entity began to lose their meaning and value and be replaced by a quality of identity, "a structure of feeling"—to borrow Raymond Williams's phrase—called Jewishness. "Jewish origin, without religious and political connotation," Arendt wrote, "became everywhere a psychological quality, was changed into 'Jewishness,' and from then on could be considered only in the categories of virture or vice."[2]

Assimilation also led to the very obsession that drives this inquiry; with the birth of Jewishness came the birth of the worry over visibility. The more Jewishness became about the private and assimilation became about the public, the more Jews, and everyone else, obsessed over just what this (innate?) Jewishness was. Or as Arendt puts it, "Jews were obsessed by it as one may be by a physical defect or advantage, and addicted to it as one may be to a vice."[3] I wonder if Arendt ever told Groucho's joke. Jewishness is like a hunched back, immutably there for the obsessing.

A Jew is a Jew is a Jew.

Now, imagine Groucho saying that very phrase, cigar in hand, eyebrows grabbing his hair line, and you get just how thin the ice can be. "For it is an axiom of that identity that a Jew is a Jew is a Jew," writes Leon Wieseltier. "But the study of Jewish history showed that axiom was a necessary fiction."⁴ Turns out that Groucho knew that too; he knew all about the necessary fictions of identity.

The hunchback joke appeared in slightly altered form in the Marx Brothers 1930 film *Animal Crackers,* where it became a song, or rather a taunt that became a song. In the same film where Groucho masquerades as the vaunted Captain Spaulding just back from Africa, Chico and Harpo realize that they recognize Roscoe W. Chandler, the elite art dealer who is about to reveal a prized new painting. They know he is not Chandler but Abie from Czechoslovakia, Abie the fish peddler. And they know because he has an enormous birthmark on his right forearm. He begs them to not reveal him, but they insist—chanting "Abie the Fishman! Abie the Fishman!" in a taunt of a song—while circling him. As the scene unfolds, they pickpocket him, taking both his wallet from his pocket and, in the scene's great twist, his birthmark from his arm.

Here we have the first Jewish outing anthem, the song that, over and over, threatens to return Roscoe to Abie. But Roscoe/Abie is no Queen Esther, the woman responsible for what is perhaps the greatest outing moment in biblical history. After concealing her Jewishness from her new husband, King Ahasuerus, Esther outs herself to save the Jews from his genocidal plot. She was in hiding until she made a political decision to reveal her identity—in Eve Sedgwick's words, "a firm Jewish choice of a minority politics based on a conservative reinscription of gender roles."⁵ Roscoe does not make any choice at all. He is outed by the nosy, singing intruders, revealed to be a stranger and an outsider just like them.

What fuels their song is the discovery of the hunched back—the birthmark, the biological truth, the mark of the Jew—but then, as if anticipating the slippage from antic-Semitism to anti-Semitism, it too comes off. The mark is also a mask. Roscoe is indeed Abie, but not because of biology, not because a Jew is a Jew is a Jew, but because of culture and profession, because he is a Czechoslovakian fish peddler. Looks like Arendt was right again: "Each society," she wrote, "demands of its members a certain amount of acting. The ability to present, represent, and act what one actually is."⁶ The actually of Roscoe is what Chico and Harpo—themselves masquerading as Italians—are after, not because he's a Jew

Fig. 1. Chico and Harpo discover Abïe the Fishman: Still of Harpo Marx, Louis Sorin, and Chico Marx in *Animal Crackers* (Paramount, 1930). COLLECTION OF JOSH KUN.

but because he's pretending not to be. They put into song what "Mottke the vest maker" put into body blows in Michael Gold's novel *Jews without Money,* published the same year that Abie hit the big screen. Mottke didn't sing songs about Jews who passed, he beat them up: "If his name is Garlic in the old country he thinks it refined to call himself Mr. Onions." Who did these Jews thinks they were? Who did they think they were fooling?

Catching the pretenders was a favorite Marx Brothers game. They reveled in the compulsory theatricality and roleplaying of society but didn't like it when others acted but didn't admit they were acting. In comparison to their counterparts of the time—George Burns or Jack Benny, for example—the Marx Brothers didn't want to crack wise from beneath the mask, they wanted to make the mask the joke itself. As Barry Rubin reminds us, the Marx Brothers chose stage names that broke the rules of Hollywood assimilation, names "far more ridiculous than anything brought from Eastern Europe: Leonard to Chico, Julius to Groucho, Adolph to Harpo, Milton to Gummo, and Herbert to Zeppo."[7]

By being Groucho and Chico instead of Julius and Leonard, they could use a song like "Abie the Fishman" as a weapon against those who chose Roscoe over Abie. Their song, then, is their blackmail—the sound of knowing a secret, knowing what he's hiding—his old past handed back to him through the threat of exposure. The song's performance is full of anarchic release, a fantasy of ethnic revelation and reversal, of discovery of a secret identity then turning that discovery into power.

The song is like a magic spell—sing it and the mask comes off.

And imagine if it really worked. Imagine if Abie the Fishman became a magic, conjuring mantra that could reverse invisibility and turn Jews back into Jews; just by singing, names would be reversed. Could you imagine the fallout in the music world?

Abie the Fishman, Abie the Fishman, and then POOF!:

Al Jolson is Asa Yoelson, George Gershwin is Jacob Gershovitz, Irving Berlin is Israel Baline, Barry Manilow is Allan Pincus, Marc Bolan is Marc Feld, Doc Pomus is Jerome Felder, Herbie Mann is Herbert Solomon, Bob Dylan is Robert Zimmerman, Gene Simmons is Chaim Weitzman, Paul Stanley is Paul Eisen, Geddy Lee is Gary Weinrib, Mama Cass is Ellen Cohen, Lou Reed is Lou Rabinowitz, Richard Hell is Richard Myers, Joey Ramone is Jeffrey Hyman, Perry Farrell is Peretz Bernstein, Carole King is Carole Klein, Taylor Dane is Taylor Wonderman, and Janis Ian is Janis Fink (even though she already copped to her Abie/Roscoe masquerade on her 1968 album *The Secret Life of J. Eddy Fink*).

What a powerful weapon it could be! The extortion! The bribes! The plummeting of Kiss album sales!

Indeed, when the "Abie the Fishman" song is unleashed on Roscoe, it has a threatening quality to it, as if all name-changers live with the fear that one day they will be found out. The song rattles Roscoe like a "Boo!" shouted out from the dark shadows over and over again. It was as much about *unmasking* Roscoe, then, as it was *frightening* him with the past he thought he had left behind. Jewishness as a self-reflective horror movie— *Abie's aliiiive! He's back from the grave!* Donald Weber has already laid out this territory, though for him it's more that the experience of being Jewish in America is like a never-ending walk through a haunted house. For Weber, to be Jewish in America is to always be haunted by an "Old World" past—old names, old identities, strange accents, strange manners—and to always be grappling with the ragged and unkempt ghosts who won't leave the present alone. Drawing on the work of the German sociologist Norbert Elias, Weber points to "the potential dangers latent in the 'outsider's' identification with an idealized cultural authority: the desire to imitate, to pass, to be accepted as a member of the society one esteems, and seeks acceptance by—a version, we might say, of the drama of Americaniza-tion."[8] The desire comes with its own built-in risk, the great fear of the assimilated Jew: to be found out, for the game of hide and seek to end, for the ghosts to be seen in the real light of day. "The Jew in me," the poet David Meltzer once wrote, "is the ghost of me, hiding under a stairway."[9]

The concealing of the ethnic ghost hidden beneath the stairway or beneath an art dealer's tuxedo was an issue on everyone's minds in the "melting-pot" pop world of the day. Paul Whiteman's 1930 featurette *The King of Jazz* ended with the vignette "The Melting Pot of Music," a dra-matic musical celebration of assimilation and passing in which musicians of all different backgrounds and accents enter the same melting pot and come out as cowgirls singing "Stars and Stripes Forever." Along with Jews, there were Spaniards and Italians, Russians and Mexicans, Poles and Irish. Though there were no African Americans. Their music was the medium of the melting, the sound of the American masquerade, but the people behind the music were never part of the final American stew.[10]

This musicalization of the melting pot, with black music as the me-dium of choice, had already been famously at work just three years earlier when Hollywood Jews debuted the first talking feature, *The Jazz Singer*, the night before Kol Nidre. Here was another Abie transformation: Jakie Rabinowitz puts on blackface to become Jack Robin, chooses the great white way over the not so great Jewish way of the cantorate, kills off his father, and chooses a Southern mammy over his bereft Yiddishe momme. The brothers Warner who made the film were leading the way of studio Jews who, as Neil Gabler and Otto Friedrich have so deftly shown, were Jewish in private but didn't put Jews on the screen. If jazz was a medium of melting into assimilative whiteness, then cinema was its technology, an industry run by Abies and Jakies reborn as Roscoes and Jacks and based on Jewish passing and Jewish fantasy. Inventing worlds they couldn't actually live in.

Indeed, it was this early period in the growth of the entertainment industry that the masquerades of American Jews began to rely on various engagements with African American music and popular culture, thereby setting up another "axiom" of "that" identity: Jews engage black music and black culture through appropriation and masquerade in order to perform themselves as white. This is Michael Rogin's take on *The Jazz Singer*, whereby the Jew whose whiteness is in question (Al Jolson/Jakie

Fig. 2. Abie dons the black mask: Cover image from Al Jolson and Eddie Cantor, *The Immortals—Jolson and Cantor* (Epic, n.d. [circa 1950s]). COLLECTION OF JOSH KUN.

Rabinowitz), dons blackface as a way of distancing himself from the very blackness he mimics. "Jack Robin plays a person of color instead of being confused by one," Rogin argues. "By painting himself black, he washes himself white."[11]

Abie blacks up to become Roscoe.

This axiom led to another: Jews engage black music and black culture to be hip, to abandon the squareness of their own culture for the alleged coolness of blackness—Norman Mailer's "white negro" recast as the "Jewish negro" who wants to be down. This oft-told tale has been newly revived by John Leland, who counts the relationship between blacks and Jews as central to America's understanding of hipness.[12] Linked to this Jewish interest in black coolness (after all, part of the very notion of American Jewishness is that Jews have always needed "others" to be cool) is the third axiomatic route of black-Jewish interplay, the Jew who engages black music and black culture to actually identify as black. Mezz Mezzrow is the classic example here, the Jewish jazz musician who distanced himself from his Russian Jewish roots and allied himself with African Americans, going so far as to think himself black, "a colored guy . . . Race, Negro."[13]

Abie becomes not Roscoe the art dealer, but Roscoe the pot dealer and jazzman.

The history of Jewish musical masquerade, though, goes far beyond the well-traveled terrain of black-Jewish exchange and appropriation. For Abie's other racial and ethnic conduits into Roscoedom, we need only to consider this 1958 remark from the Jewish humorist Harry Golden about the Jewish love for Latin music: "The history of Jews in America, from *sha sha* to *cha cha*." Golden's awareness of both Jewish shape-shifting in general and Jewish shape-shifting through Latin American rhythms came at the tail end of various Latin crazes that had been changing the American pop soundscape since the 1930s. As with African American music, Jewish engagement with Latin music took many forms. For every Jew who did not vanish behind disguise and masquerade—Jews like Irving Fields who may have once worn the Latin mask of Campos El Pianista (literally, "fields the pianist") but ended up famous for interpreting Yiddish songs in Latin tempos—there was Alfred Levy, who spent his entire career in Latin music recording under the name Alfredito.[14] In 1966, he went boogaloo for a Cotique release that showed him dabbling in Latin soul and R&B, and among the songs on the list was "Sweets for My Sweet," the result of its own set of black-Jewish-Latin masquerades. Written by two Jews (Doc Pomus and Mort Shuman) for an African American vocal group (the Drifters), the song was built around a Latin shuffle with chord changes on loan from "Guantanamera."[15]

Abie picks up a conga, bangs out a mambo, and becomes Roscito.

The power of the Marx Brothers' Abie theme was rooted not only in its aggressive unmasking but in its reference to the Abie character so prominent in the era of the "Hebe comic." Abie was often the name given to the stock "Hebrew" character performed by comics and writers in the first decades of the century. No name said "Jew" in the mainstream pop cultural imagination like "Abie." So when the Marx Brothers reminded Roscoe he was Abie, they were reviving an image: the baggy pants, oversized derby, mispronunciations, wild gesticulations of performers like David Warfield, Joe Welch, and Julian Rose.

In his study of these Jews masquerading as Jews, Harley Erdman has

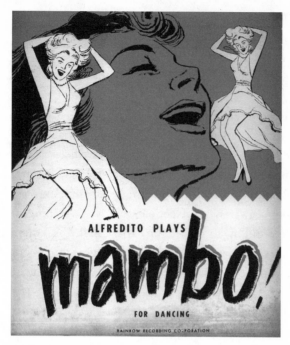

Fig. 3. Abie becomes Roscito: Cover image from Alfredito, *Alfredito Plays Mambo!* (Rainbow Records, n.d. [circa 1950s]). COLLECTION OF JOSH KUN.

suggested that even these performances of Jewish visibility were rooted in the anti-Semitism that had helped force so many Jews to don a non-Jewish mask in the first place. "The polarities of aggressive and world-weary Jew evident throughout these sketches," he argues, "reflected the older Gentile staging traditions of the aggressive/unscrupulous and effeminate/incompetent Jew."[16] Gentile echo or not, for the Hollywood screenwriter Ben Hecht the end of the Abie era was still a tragedy of assimilation and conformity: the Abies of the world had been kidnapped by Hollywood's "Simple Simon Jews" who were "frightened at the crude reminder of their immigrant beginnings, hoping to blot out all consciousness of Jews in their country by breaking all the mirrors they could."[17] The Marx Brothers' Abie theme, then, was the mirror put back together.

And as such, its impact has extended beyond the 1930s. In recent years, the Abie song has made a comeback. On his 1998 album *Busy Being Born* recorded for John Zorn's Radical Jewish Culture imprint, the guitarist Gary Lucas expanded the Abie theme into a two-minute guitar-plucked tease that eventually releases whatever anger, mania, and madness is coiled up inside the assimilation process. In 2005, Abie got yet another tribute, only this time not by a Jew but by Don Byron, the African American clarinetist, who included his own "Abie the Fishman" on his latest album, *Ivey-Divey*. It's one of the few original compositions Byron tackles on *Ivey-Divey*, which is mostly a series of sideways meditations on the techniques of Lester Young and Miles Davis. His "Abie" has no dialogue from the film, none of the nagging mischief of the Marx Brothers' "Abie," nor any of Lucas's vitriolic dissonance. But Byron's clarinet does plenty of nervous bobbing and weaving, dodging Jack DeJohnette's drum fills and Jason Moran's piano chases like a clever, kinetic chameleon. Byron makes the Abie story into a playful cat-and-mouse game, a nail-biter that ends as abruptly as it begins.

Byron and Abie are perfect for each other. Whether it was on his *Tuskegee Experiments* debut (where he tackled medical racism against Southern blacks) or 1998's *Nu Blaxploitation* (where he linked Hendrix, Mandrill, and hip-hop to riff on race in post–civil rights America), Byron has always been interested in how marginalized music performs identity and how identity performs music. But the last time he dealt specifically with Jewishness was on 1993's *Don Byron Plays the Music of Mickey Katz*. There his subject was Katz, the clarinetist and comedian, who ambushed the quivering 1950s Jewish American mainstream with unapologetic Jewish madness. Katz relished his role as the carnivalesque, "too Jewish" outsider, the Borscht Jester pariah who kept speaking Yiddish even after self-hating club owners and radio DJs urged him to stop. Katz was Roscoe's opposite, an Abie who was out to make Abies of everyone else. He took Tennessee Ernie Ford's coal-mining rendition of "Sixteen Tons" and made it into a kosher deli work song. Johnny Mercer's smooth "Old Black Magic" became a rough "Old Black Smidgick." Sheb Wooley's "Purple People Eater"—the one who once had bobbysoxers running for their lives —was now "poiple," ate "kishkes," and saw the world through "eyes like latkes." Katz would have gone after Roscoe too.[18]

3. Zelig, Can You Hear Me?

That the history of Jews in American popular music would be rife with Abies performing themselves as Roscoes is symptomatic of the central role that masquerade, passing, shape-shifting, and vanishing have all played in Jewish history itself. As a people linked to no single national homeland, a people of diasporic movement and flow, a people of exile and scattered seeds, the dominant feature of Jewish life has never been the fixity of identity.

A Jew has never been a Jew has never been a Jew.

The dominant feature has been the opposite—transformation, change, adaptation. As a professor of mine put it years ago, Jews are like tofu: they take on the tastes and smells of what surrounds them. Which in the typically circuitous logic of Jewish identity debate was also the very trait which anti-Semitism makes part of its central attack: the Jews are tricky, they could be lurking anywhere, don't trust appearances. Anti-Semitism likes it both ways: the Jew is immutable, and eternally mutable at once; always the same and always mercurial. They could be fair in Britain and Germany, in the words of Samuel Stanhope Smith, "brown in France and Turkey, swarthy in Portugal and Spain, olive in Syria and Chaldea, tawny or copper-coloured in Arabia and Egypt." That Jews are, as Sander Gilman has put it, "the adaptive people par excellence," can be seen as being both emancipatory and entrapping, a strategy of survival through camouflage or proof of the incurable Jewish disease of camouflage, proof that Jews can infect anything. "The Jew," Gilman writes, discussing Lyotard, toward the end of his study of "the Jew's body" as an anti-Semitic nexus, "caught up in such a system of representation, has but little choice: his essence, which incorporates the horrors projected onto him and which is embodied (quite literally) in his physical being must try, on one level or another, to become invisible."[19]

Let us, then, agree on this simple command for now: The definition of "Jewish" must always be followed by a series of questions: When? Where? And most importantly, Who wants to know? For the reasons for masquerade have always varied—for Sephardic Jews expelled from Spain in the fifteenth century, masquerading and soon becoming Christian in the centuries-long tradition of the conversos was a survival tactic. But so was keeping your heritage hidden as a crypto-Jew, an obedient Christian on the street, a secret Jew at home. Concealment as a Jewish way of life that guaranteed life itself. As Janet Liebman Jacobs has shown, it was the crypto-Jews, not the conversos, who were the most threatening and the most at risk; concealing their Jewish identity—what she calls "using secrecy and subterfuge as weapons against cultural annihilation"—was an act of seditious heresy worthy of fatal punishment.[20]

Of course, the performance stages of twentieth-century U.S. pop culture and pop music are not fifteenth-century Spain, and signing recording contracts with Warner Brothers or Universal is not the same as being subject to the Edicts of Grace that made "Judaizing" into an unpardonable sin. In music, Jewish masquerade was not a means of survival as much as it was a way of entering the American mainstream on its terms, not your own.

Woody Allen captured the dilemma best in his 1983 film *Zelig* where he introduced us to a shape-shifting Jew who, due to a psychological disorder, is anyone but himself: a black trumpeter, a white gangster, Pagliacci. To truly be a Jew, Zelig suggested, was to never be a Jew. "It's safe to be like the others," Zelig told his shrink under hypnosis, "I want to be liked." There is a Zelig, but he is defined by his changes, defined by the masks he wears.

The history of American popular music is full of musical Zeligs, so much so that I've started thinking about "audio-Zeligism" as the dominant performance mode of American Jewishness. We are used to this line of inquiry in cinema and television, where outing Jewish actors is a favorite pastime of Jewish audiences. "Both the screen's first and latest heartthrobs—Theda Bara and Winona Ryder—are Jews," David Mamet wrote, as one example of this, in 1994. "But how would one know if one did not know?"[21] But what about music and musical masquerade? Whether it be Berlin and Gershwin dreaming up plantation fantasies of a mythical South or black romance on Catfish Row, Eli Basse and the Barry Sisters dreaming up fantasy versions of Cuba and Puerto Rico, the Urick Brothers becoming the Ames Brothers and swirling up some of the best fifties audio vanilla, Leiber and Stoller writing songs as if they were black men and black women, Herb Alpert putting on a sombrero and inventing what Tijuana sounds like, Phil Spector speaking through black girl groups and releasing Christmas albums, Peretz Bernstein (son of a Queens diamond dealer) inventing LA narco-decadence as Perry Farrell, and David Lee Roth (grandson of Ukranian immigrants in Indiana) keeping his name and his nose, while using Borsht Belt tummeling to re-invent rock and roll theatrics: *Jump . . . go ahead . . . why not? . . . you might as well . . . so jump . . . jump already.* "It's funny," Roth has said, "Here I am the son of a Jewish doctor, and the Van Halens are sons of a musician, a world traveler. They wound up married with children, and I'm by myself, never happy staying in any one place for too long."[22]

So with all of this, we might ask a similar question that Gabler and Hecht and many others asked of Hollywood: for all of the Jews in American pop—on the mic and in the studio and behind the desk—how many songs actually are about Jewish life? These are not, by and large, Jews in hiding like Roscoe, but they are Jews who perform themselves as something other than Jews. Because they make music *in* disguise, their music is *about* disguise.

And yet as I write these lines, I bristle at them. What does that mean, "other than Jews"? Maybe this is American Jewishness—not Judaism, not religious practice and observation bound by Halahkic law and matrilineal birthright—but Jewishness, secular, cultural practice in its most raw, most contradictory, most natural state. Maybe stories of Jews writing stories about non-Jews *is* the story of Jewish life. "The subject of the Jews is really inescapable," Barry Rubin winks, "though much of it concerns those escaping being Jews."[23] Chico and Harpo did not out Roscoe then, they outed what he did—became a Zelig, changed shape, hid one identity inside another.

Maybe the "Abie the Fishman" song has led us somewhere else, to the dominant aesthetic of secular Jewishness itself: the music of masquerade.[24]

4. Abie's Son

What would the Marx Brothers do with Bob Dylan, popular music's greatest living masquerader, the ultimate audio-Zelig of them all? An actual son of an Abie (Abraham Zimmerman), Dylan began his career with a decision to shape-shift and trade his birth identity for another. The young Robert Zimmerman wanted out of being Zimmerman, out of small-town Minnesota, out of his dad's electrical store, and wanted into what he heard coming from the radio and the Victrola machine: Hank Williams, Johnnie Ray, Web Pierce, Howlin' Wolf. It was the Monroe Brothers' 1936 recording of "Drifting Too Far from the Shore" that made Zimmerman feel like he was not who he was raised to be, his first sign that his past was the thing he would soon leave behind. As he told Martin Scorsese in *No Direction Home*, "The sound of the record made me feel like I was somebody else, that I maybe was not even born to the right parents or something."

Dylan's new self was finessed in Greenwich Village. The apartments where he crashed (Dave Van Ronk's among them) were identity laboratories, perfect sites for concocting new selves out of bits of Clausewitz and Robert Graves, Zoot Sims and Judy Garland, Jimmie Rodgers and Harold Arlen, Don Juan and Kublai Khan. It was, as Dylan writes about leaving Minnesota in the first volume of his autobiography, *Chronicles,* an experience akin to fifteenth-century discovery—an East Village Columbus learning the ways of a strange new world that will allow the real him to finally be born.

From then on, his career was a string of re-invention, both for the sake of creative rebirth and for the sake of public evasion. The more the public and the critics pigeonholed him, the more he was apt to change his shape—a Guthrie-esque drifter, a Van Ronkian raconteur, a born again Christian, a Zionist, an orphan. His one buried Abie had become multiple Roscoes. In that way, *Chronicles* reads like a Zelig manual. He charts the birth of Bob Dylan out of the alias ashes of Elston Gunn and the Scottish kingliness of Robert Allyn. He writes of wittingly leaving his past, leaving his Russian immigrant grandparents, his Midwestern parents, all traces of the world he inherited. *Chronicles* is the story of rejecting inheritance and embracing newness—a rebirth with a new name, a chance for a new start. When Dylan sings about Jews killed in the camps on "With God on Our Side," he doesn't identify with them—he's one of the Americans outraged that "they" were put in mass graves.

Abie wasn't hiding. He was dead. "One of the early presidents of the San Bernardino angels was Bobby Zimmerman," Dylan writes. "And he was killed in 1964 on the Bass Lake run. The muffler fell off his bike, he made a U-turn to retrieve it in front of the pack and was instantly killed. That person is gone. That was the end of him."[25]

In an act of good old-fashioned parricide, Dylan also killed his parents the same way he killed his old self. In his first interview with the publicist for Columbia Records, Dylan said he knew nothing of his family, that "they were long gone." It was a point he reiterated in his 2005 interview with Ed Bradley on *60 Minutes,* where he said of his early years in Minnesota: "Some people get born, you know, to the wrong names, the wrong parents. . . . You call yourself what you wanna call yourself. This is the land of the free."

In Genesis 22, the story is supposed to work the other way around. Abraham is supposed to sacrifice Isaac, the father willing to bind his son for death to secure a covenant with a domineering God. Dylan sang about this in 1965's "Highway 61 Revisited": "God said to Abraham, kill me a son . . . Abe says where do you want this killin done?" But on the page and on *60 Minutes,* Dylan switches the Torah up—he gives us the binding of Abraham and he's the Isaac who's put to the test. When Abie dies, it's Dylan who does the symbolic killing.

Dylan's greatest performance of his Zeligean Jewishness came in 1961 —just one year before he recorded Woody Guthrie's "Jesus Christ"—with "Talkin' Hava Negeilah Blues," in which "Hava Nagila" (the Jewish theme song of all Jewish theme songs) is intentionally spelled wrong. "Talkin' Hava Negeilah Blues" is a knowing folk blues goof on Dylan's "hidden" identity. We hear him struggle—painfully, comically—to sing the words of this "foreign song" that he "learned in Utah": "ha, va, na, gee, ha-va-na-gee, geeee, laaa, ha-va-na-gee-lahhh, yodelayhehoo."

Maybe even more than Lucas's or Byron's Abie odes, "Talkin' Hava Negeilah Blues" is the best Abie song of all. In this performance, Dylan is both Roscoe and Abie, the hidden identity and the new identity, the father and the son. On the one hand, the song is foreign, he can't pronounce it, it's not his. Yet Dylan winks at us. It is his, he just chooses to not perform it as it should be performed. The chorus is strained, tortuous, and stuttered, because Dylan knew who he was and he knew who he was pretending to be. Which leaves "Talkin' Hava Negeilah Blues" as a song about not singing "Hava Nagila," a performance about the refusal to perform.

Instead of the Marx Brothers singing at Roscoe, this is Roscoe singing to himself. Roscoe shows us Abie by not showing us Abie, a musical reminder that even his birthmark is a mask.

Notes

1. Jean Amery, *At the Mind's Limits: Contemplations by a Survivor on Auschwitz and Its Realities* (Bloomington: Indiana University Press, 1980), 82.
2. Hannah Arendt, *The Origins of Totalitarianism* (New York: Harcourt Brace, 1973), 83.
3. Ibid., 84.
4. Leon Wieseltier, *Against Identity* (New York: William Drenttel, 1996), axiom 28.
5. Eve Kosofsky Sedgwick, *Epistemology of the Closet,* as excerpted in *Queer Theory*

and the Jewish Question, ed. Daniel Boyarin, Daniel Itzkovitz, and Ann Pellegrini (New York: Columbia University Press, 2003), 54. I thank Larry Gross of the University of Southern California for reminding me of Sedgwick's treatment of the Esther story in the context of queer theory and outing discourse.

6. Arendt, *Origins of Totalitarianism*, 84.

7. Barry Rubin, *Assimilation and Its Discontents* (New York: Random House, 1995), 80.

8. Donald Weber, *Haunted in the New World: Jewish American Culture from Cahan to the Goldbergs* (Bloomington: Indiana University Press, 2005), 7.

9. David Meltzer, *David's Copy: The Selected Poems of David Meltzer* (New York: Penguin, 2005), 41.

10. Michael Rogin, *Blackface, White Noise: Jewish Immigrants in the Hollywood Melting Pot* (Berkeley: University of California Press, 1996), 140. Also see my own discussion of this in *Audiotopia: Music, Race, and America* (Berkeley: University of California Press, 2005).

11. Rogin, *Blackface, White Noise*, 102.

12. John Leland, *Hip: The History* (New York: HarperCollins, 2004), 204. See also Jonathan Schorsch, "Making Judaism Cool," *Best Contemporary Jewish Writing*, ed. Michael Lerner (San Francisco: Jossey-Bass, 2001).

13. Maria Damon, "Jazz-Jews, Jive, and Gender," *Jews and Other Differences: The New Jewish Cultural Studies*, ed. Jonathan Boyarin and Daniel Boyarin (Minneapolis: University of Minnesota Press, 1997), 172. The reasons given for Mezzrow's identification often lead to a fourth route: blacks and Jews are partners in disenfranchisement who can bond over histories of oppression. Irving Howe, Michael Alexander, and Leland have all offered versions of this argument, with Howe famously explaining away Jewish blackface as "one woe speaking through the voice of another." For this idea, see Irving Howe, *World of Our Fathers: The Journey of the Eastern European Jews to America and the Life They Found and Made* (New York: Bantam, 1976), 553. Leland describes it as "a story of outsiders . . . an alliance of the pariah" in *Hip*, 204. For the most perplexing extension of this argument, see Michael Alexander, *Jazz Age Jews* (Princeton, N.J.: Princeton University Press, 2003).

14. For more on Jewish-Latin musical exchange in general, see my "Bagels, Bongos, and Yiddishe Mambos, or The Other History of Jews in America," in *Shofar: An Interdisciplinary Journal of Jewish Studies* 23, no. 4 (Summer 2005): 50–68. For more on Fields's career, see my liner notes for the 2005 re-issue of the Irving Fields Trio's *Bagels and Bongos* (Reboot Stereophonic).

15. For the complete story of the Brill Building period that Pomus sums up as

"just Jewish Latin," see Ken Emerson, *Always Magic in the Air: The Bomp and Brilliance of the Brill Building Era* (New York: Viking, 2005).

16. Harley Erdman, *Staging the Jew: The Performance of an American Ethnicity, 1860–1920* (New Brunswick, N.J.: Rutgers University Press, 1997), 105.

17. Ben Hecht, *A Guide for the Bedevilled* (New York: Charles Scribner's Sons, 1944).

18. For more on Katz's take on Jewish concealment, see his autobiography, *Papa, Play for Me* (Middletown, Conn.: Wesleyan University Press, 1999), and my *Audiotopia*.

19. Sander Gilman, *The Jew's Body* (New York: Routledge, 1991), 177, 236.

20. Janet Liebman Jacobs, *Hidden Heritage: The Legacy of the Crypto-Jews* (Berkeley: University of California Press, 2002), 10.

21. David Mamet, *Make-Believe Town* (Boston: Little, Brown, 1996), 135.

22. This citation culled from a Roth fansite, www.rotharmy.com. See also Roth's autobiography, *Crazy from the Heat* (New York: Hyperion, 1997). I thank Daphne Brooks for reminding me that Roth belongs to this great tradition.

23. Rubin, *Assimilation and Its Discontents*, xi.

24. Echoes of this idea can be found in Yuri Slezkine's claim that Jews have long worn "Mercury's Sandals" in that they, like so many other itinerant ethnic strangers, have been the offspring of the god Mercury—the go-betweeners, the border crossers, the brokers, the interpreters, the tricksters who are insiders and outsiders at once, "unarmed internal strangers." See his *The Jewish Century* (Princeton, N.J.: Princeton University Press, 2004).

25. Bob Dylan, *Chronicles, Volume One* (New York: Simon and Schuster, 2004).

Ned Sublette

The Kingsmen and the Cha-Cha-Chá

4

DOT-DOT-DOT. DOT-DOT. DOT-DOT-DOT. DOT-DOT.

When the Kingsmen recorded "Louie, Louie" in April 1963, it had been four years since the Cuban Revolution, and as far as the United States was concerned, Cuba had disappeared.

In the 1950s, Cuba had been omnipresent in United States media and culture. Every week, fifty million people watched *I Love Lucy,* in which the band-leading Cuban comedian Desi Arnaz played a comical Cuban bandleader named Ricky Ricardo. Everyone could da-dum *Lucy*'s theme song, composed by Arnaz's Santiago de Cuba homeboy Marco Rizo. Americans' idea of dancing was largely Cuban. American nightclubs had Latin themes and booked Latin dance bands, and working musicians were expected to be able to play Latin numbers. But by the 1960s, with Cuba the object of a United States embargo that still remains in effect today, the island nation had been forgotten as a source of music.

By the time people began to talk about rock and roll as having a history, Cuban music had vanished from North American consciousness.

The Kingsmen had no idea that the "Louie" lick came from a cha-cha-chá, but it did. Richard Berry, the Louisiana-born twenty-one-year-old African American singer-songwriter from South Central Los Angeles who composed "Louie" at the height of the cha-cha-chá boom in 1956, later recalled: "It was an R & B dance song. And it was still a cha-cha. At that time, everyone was doing the cha-cha-chá."[1]

In those days, knowing how to dance with a partner, communicating coordinated movements by touch, was one of the basic social graces. People took lessons to be able to dance well. And when they danced, they danced to something called live music, pardon my sarcasm. If you look at, say, *The New Yorker*'s listings from 1952, you'll see that hotel ballrooms routinely booked two dance bands—an American band and a Latin band. The Latin bands alternated on the bandstand with white dance bands for white audiences, and they also split the bill with black bands playing for black dancers. They were thus a point of contact for both sides of a still-segregated musical world. At the Palladium, on 53rd Street and Broadway, Latin bands played for the most integrated crowd in New York—Puerto Ricans, African Americans, Jews, Italians, everybody, offering a musical, dancing, and social experience that older New Yorkers still reminisce about.

The mambo had exploded in 1949, made famous by the Cuban bandleader Pérez Prado from his base in Mexico City. Its hyperkinetic calisthenics weren't so easy for amateur dancers, but the cha-cha-chá—which followed on its heels, so to speak—replaced mambo's polyrhythm with something more like a beat and offered an easy, catchy step: *1-2-cha-cha-chá*. The cha-cha-chá erupted in Havana in 1953, with a single by Ninón Mondéjar's Orquesta América on Panart, the first and largest independent Cuban label. Both sides of the 7-inch 45 rpm record were hits: "Silver Star" and "La Engañadora," compositions by the group's violinist, Enrique Jorrín.[2] According to the label on the disc, "Silver Star" was a danzón, but its chorus went: *Cha-cha-chá, cha-cha-chá, es un baile sin igual* (cha-cha-chá, cha-cha-chá, is a dance without equal). The other side, "La Engañadora" (The Deceiver), with lyrics that made fun of a Havana girl's prosthetic voluptuousness, was labeled "mambo-rumba," but it too was a cha-cha-chá.

By the following year, when Elvis Presley recorded his first hit, "That's All Right (Mama)," the cha-cha-chá had caught on everywhere. In 1955, as the early classics of rock and roll were appearing, Orquesta América had an enormous hit, with practically untranslatable percussive lyrics that went: *Vacilón, qué rico vacilón / Cha-cha-chá, qué rico cha-cha-chá.* The composer of "Rico Vacilón" was Rosendo Ruiz, Jr., a well-known Havana composer and the son of a legendary Cuban *trovador* (guitar-playing singer-songwriter). In late 1955, or maybe early 1956, another of his cha-cha-chás, "Amarren el Loco" (Restrain the Madman), was recorded for the GNP label by the Cuban pianist René Touzet, who led the number one Latin band in Los Angeles. The tune was rechristened with a title Americans could remember: "El Loco Cha Cha." (Cubans *never* say "cha-cha," because they know the name of the dance mimics the sound of the dancers' feet on the floor: there's always a third "chá.")

Touzet's recording of Ruiz's tune was the source for the "Louie, Louie" lick. It's the *tumbao,* or what Americans call the groove, that kicks it off and locks it down all the way through. You can jam on it as long as you can keep the dancers excited, using a variety of musical devices that Latin musicians deploy as a matter of course.[3] The "Loco"/"Louie" lick was apparently created by Touzet, or perhaps an uncredited arranger in his employ; Ruiz told the Cuban music journalist Rafael Lam that it was not part of the tune as he composed it.[4]

Richard Berry encountered "El Loco" while singing with Ricky Rillera and the Rhythm Rockers, a Los Angeles dance band led by two Filipino brothers, for a largely Mexican audience that wanted to dance cha-cha-chá. Inspired by the "El Loco" tumbao, Berry wrote words and a tune to go with it, creating "Louie, Louie." By 1963, his song had traveled to Seattle, and after following a complicated path of transmission from band to band, it was recorded in Portland, Oregon, by the Kingsmen.[5]

Touzet's lick emerged more or less intact into the Kingsmen's version of "Louie, Louie." (I say more or less, because Touzet—and Berry—phrased it DOT-DOT-DOT / DOT DAHH, but the Kingsmen played all the notes as short DOTS, without that elongated last note of the phrase, thus missing a crucial bit of uplift.) The Kingsmen's lead vocal retained the Latin-like rhythmic flow of Richard Berry's melody, compatible with the two-bar rhythmic template Cubans call the clave. The lyrics were only partly intelligible in the Kingsmen's version, and there arose what we would now call an urban legend that the song had dirty words, giving it a risqué reputation that caught people's attention. But what made it stick to become a classic of the garage-band repertoire was that fabulous lick, with that tense silence, so characteristic of Cuban music, between the DOT-DOT-DOT and the DOT-DOT. You could hang out on it as long as you needed to, and it was easily playable by anyone, even by people with little musical training. Like the Kingsmen. Or all the garage bands that played "Louie" in every city, suburb, town, village, and even in farmhouses (I can attest) all across the United States of America.

In other words, to the familiar white-kids-copying-African-Americans rock and roll genesis story we add a twist: the African American that the white kids were copying was playing a cha-cha-chá. Rock writers have long known about the cha-cha-chá origin of what Marsh rightly calls "the world's most famous rock 'n' roll song," but I think they've mostly missed the point: it wasn't an exotic detail. It wasn't something that was left behind when the song became rock and roll. It was central to what "Louie, Louie" was. And "Louie," while a textbook example, is far from an isolated case. Without Cuban music, American music would be unrecognizable. Nor was the Cuban influence merely one of many equally significant flavors. Cuba exercised an important formative influence on music in the United States, or, as we imperially call it, American music. But then, I've come to think of Cuban music as the fundamental music of the New World.

Why Cuba?

I wrote a book to try to answer that question.[6] I won't reprise all my arguments here, but suffice it to say that the slave trade from Africa to Cuba began earlier, and lasted longer, and carried more Africans, than the slave trade to mainland North America. Havana was a major center of music from the early days of Spanish colonization of the New World, and the influence of music from Cuba—an island bigger than the rest of the Antilles put together—was felt in the United States not once, but repeatedly, from early on.

You can find similarities between African American and Afro-Cuban music—call and response, importance of rhythm, and spirit possession, to name three—but the differences are at least as striking. Certainly, the two distinct musics reflect the differences between the way slavery was conducted in the two locations. One territory spoke English, the other

Spanish; one was Protestant, the other Catholic. The African drums (as well as the languages and religions, intimately tied to the drum) were prohibited throughout British North America, thus favoring the use of fiddle and banjo, traditions which do not appear in Cuba;[7] meanwhile, the drums were tolerated, albeit with restrictions, in the Spanish colonies. But not only that.

Beyond the differences imposed by the slaveholders' culture, the two musics also reflect differences between two great musical regions of sub-Saharan Africa: the semi-arid region of the western Sudan (not to be confused with the present-day nation of Sudan, it's the region directly below the Sahara), versus the musical tradition from further south. You could think of it as savannah Africa versus forest Africa. This judgment is supported by both musicology and the demographics of the slave trade.

Two-thirds of the Africans brought to Louisiana during its French period, and many of the first enslaved Africans in South Carolina, were shipped from the Senegambia, the northernmost territory to be exploited in the transatlantic slave trade, where Islam had been a presence since the eleventh century. In the case of Louisiana, it appears that many were Bambara, from hundreds of miles inland, thrown onto the slave market as a consequence of the Segu rebellion and carried downriver.

But while people shipped from Senegambian ports were central to the founding of Afro-Louisiana, they had not been part of the founding of Afro-Cuba almost two centuries earlier. In 1526, Spain specifically excluded by royal decree the importation of slaves from Islamized areas to its colonies in the New World. Instead, the base layer of Afro-Cuban culture is Kongo. Notwithstanding the diversity of African cultures that were brought to both Cuba and the United States, and while recognizing the presence of the Kongo diaspora throughout the New World, it appears that these distinct beginnings were important in determining key aspects of the two places' easily distinguishable musical styles.

The music of Sudanic Africa is, and was for centuries, influenced by Koranic chanting. Its melismatic vocal style stretches out vowels, ornamenting them and bending the pitches; that's one of the defining characteristics of African American song, noticeably absent in the Afro-Cuban way of singing. It's a griotic tradition, with verbose narrative texts (cf. the blues). In the savannah, where drums were harder to make than in the forest, African cognates of the banjo and the fiddle—the two classic African American instruments in slavery days—dominated. Even today, in that part of Africa, you can hear that loping time flow, similar to what Europeans called 6/8, emphasizing the upbeats, with a similarity to the African American shuffle rhythm that is still apparent.[8]

By contrast, the music of the Kongo—a forest region, where drums were everywhere, in the form of fallen trees—is more polyrhythmic, with multiple percussion instruments playing at once. It's not Arabized: Islam did not penetrate there. There were no griots in the Kongo. The most typical melodic instrument, the *sanza* (or *mbira*), plays rhythmic loops of fixed pitches, not bent-pitch notes. Everyone participates, playing their own part, and what they play is organized according to a rhythmic key that everyone respects.

A letter written in New Orleans in 1819 reads: "On Sabbath evening the African slaves meet on the green by the swamp and rock the city with their Congo dances."[9]

Rock the city. New Orleans was the first American town to rock, perhaps because it was the one with the closest tie to Havana. When General Alejandro O'Reilly took charge of French-speaking New Orleans on behalf of Spain in 1769, he arrived from Havana with a force of two thousand men that outnumbered the white citizenry of the town. It was the Spanish who gave New Orleans the formal structure of a city, with a Spanish governor who reported to the captain-general of Cuba. And it was during the Spanish period in Louisiana—which lasted until 1803, and which, to be provocative, we could call the "Cuban period," or even the "Kongo period"—that significant numbers of Kongo people were brought to the colony, part of a jumble of Africans that arrived from ports up and down the west coast of Africa during that time. In Louisiana, they joined an older, already well-established, Afro-Louisianan culture, largely Senegambian in origin, that had emerged during Louisiana's time as a French colony. Their music thus went on top of a basic track that had already been laid down decades before. By then, Louisiana culture was already becoming a gumbo—to use a clichéd but inescapable metaphor, from a Kikongo word meaning "okra." (Okra in Cuba is called *quimbombó*—same word; in Louisiana, okra was called *kin gumbo*.)

From the Spanish period on, and continuing well into the twentieth century, the great port city of Havana—larger than any city in British North America at the time of the American Revolution—was in frequent communication with the smaller city of New Orleans. It's no accident that they were also two of the greatest black music centers. This was not, by the way, a "Caribbean connection": New Orleans and Havana, along with Veracruz, are not on the Caribbean but the Gulf of Mexico, making for a circum-Gulf musical region worthy of acknowledgment on its own.

The cultural link between New Orleans and Havana was not only Spanish but also African. Even after Louisiana became a state in 1812, New Orleans boasted the one place in the United States where blacks could play African-style drums and dance African-style dances in public. That was Congo Square, sacred ground of American music, where on May 1, 1808, a traveler observed "twenty different dancing groups of the wretched Africans, collected together to perform their *worship* after the manner of their country."[10]

By the 1830s, as the original drum-makers from Africa were beginning to die out in New Orleans, the *habanera* had become an international hit. The rhythm had been kicking around the Antilles for much longer: BOOM . . . BA-BOP-BOP, or, for the musically literate, dotted eighth, sixteenth, eighth, eighth. ONE (two) AND THREE FOUR.[11] Robert Farris Thompson identifies this rhythm as the Kongo *mbilu a makinu,* the call to the dance.[12] We know it as *tango,* a word that became pretty much interchangeable with *habanera,* a name that tells you where it was disseminated from. Not where it originated, but where it was branded, if you will: in the great city of Havana, where at the end of the eighteenth century a journalist complained that the idle youth danced till morning and that there were fifty dances every night.

The power of the habanera is that upbeat in the middle of the bar, on the AND of 2. If it's in the bass, you're already rocking. You can find the habanera rhythm in the work of Louis Moreau Gottschalk, the first great piano virtuoso of the United States and the most famous American musician of the nineteenth century. Gottschalk, whose music is too little known today, was a French-speaking white New Orleans Creole. His grandmother was a refugee from Saint-Domingue (better known by its subsequent name of Haiti, it played a key role in the histories of both Cuba and Louisiana); an important figure of Gottschalk's childhood was his black nanny, also from Saint-Domingue. Gottschalk spent most of his life traveling; he died in Rio de Janeiro of a ruptured appendix at the age of forty. During extended stays in Cuba, he learned to play the *contradanza* in Cuban style from the composer Manuel Saumell and traveled to the eastern part of the island, where he was impressed by the drums of the Saint-Domingan–descended *tumba francesa* group.[13] The habanera rhythm propelled Gottschalk's composition "Bamboula," a celebrated piano piece composed in 1848, when he was eighteen, but it appears in the right-hand part only. In 1860, after having been to Cuba, Gottschalk had a big hit—in those days the medium was printed sheet music—with a contradanza published in New Orleans titled "Ojos Criollos," subtitled "Danse cubaine." By then the habanera / tango rhythm had migrated to the bass. Listening to "Ojos Criollos" today, it sounds very much like ragtime, but it was a *danse cubaine* that preceded ragtime by thirty-five years.

The habanera provided the show-stopper of Bizet's *Carmen,* and it was the rhythm of Jelly Roll Morton's famous "Spanish tinge," without which, he said, "you will never be able to get the right seasoning, I call it, for jazz."[14] It's been played in New Orleans since before the invention of sound recording. For that matter, the habanera—immensely versatile, depending on the tempo and what drums you assign to what note—is still all over the Antilles. With a new set of timbres and played faster, it's the rhythm underlying reggaetón, a music that, in traveling from Jamaica to Panama to Puerto Rico, provides a contemporary demonstration of the process at work throughout the region over the centuries.

The word "tango," referring generically to dances of black people, appears in a 1786 document in New Orleans. The dance that became known worldwide in the mid-1910s as *tango* was Argentine in its style and its drama, but the underlying rhythm was imported in the nineteenth century from Havana to Argentina, a country without a large black population. It was, after all, the *habanera.*

The first American tangos, composed by African Americans, were on the Cuban not the Argentine model, beginning with "Trocha: A Cuban Dance," by Will Tyers, published in 1896, during the Cuban War of Independence that with North American intervention in 1898 became the Spanish-American War. In 1900, during the four-year American military occupation of the island, W. C. Handy traveled to Cuba as part of Mahara's Minstrels. Later, with the Argentine tango in vogue internationally, Handy used the habanera rhythm in "Memphis Blues" (1912), but he had already heard that rhythm in Cuba. The habanera was even more prominent in Handy's biggest hit, "St. Louis Blues," which came out in 1914, at the height of the tango's popularity in the United States.

The tango informed early jazz. Most early jazz musicians spent a lot of time hearing or playing some form of tango, and the dance was popular with black Americans, becoming a craze in New Orleans in 1913.[15] Decades later, a similar process saw the "rhumba," the mambo, and the cha-cha-chá melt into rock and roll.

Two hits stand out as landmarks of the Cuban musical penetration into the American consciousness: "The Peanut Vendor" (1931), sung by Antonio Machín with Don Azpiazu's Havana Casino Orchestra, and Dizzy Gillespie's "Manteca" (1948).

"The Peanut Vendor" ("El manisero" in Spanish) became one of the most recorded tunes in the world. Dance bands from New York to Paris to Tokyo added it to their repertoire, which meant absorbing some of the rudiments of how to play Cuban music. Louis Armstrong recorded it immediately, though he played it in swing time (and in his vocal, *maní*— peanuts—became "Marie.") The song kicked off a "rhumba" craze that remained to become a permanent part of the musical landscape. (A confusion here: the tune was a *son* instead of a rumba, but *rumba* is a more memorable word to English-speaking ears, so it was used, with an extra "h" providing orthographic mystery.)

The rhumba boom came along just in time for talking—and singing— pictures. From the 1930s into the 1960s, it was almost mandatory to have at least one Latin rhythm number in stage and screen musicals. That would be a study all its own, but suffice it to say that even *My Fair Lady* had a Latin-inspired tune, "I Could Have Danced All Night," though it's played and sung in a very British way. It's the song in the show that's about dancing.

"The Peanut Vendor" polyrhythmicized the way Americans thought about music. Part of its novelty was that it used Cuban percussion (though not congas, still held in bad odor in polite Cuba because of their associations with the lowlife). It wasn't just what those instruments sounded like. It was the roles they had when they locked together in a percussion section. These instruments had developed in order to be able to play in a polyrhythmic texture, and their influence stimulated the development of the American trap set in a more polyrhythmic direction.

Among its other distinctions, "The Peanut Vendor" was the first big hit to feature maracas, which are prominent on the record. Some people—though not Latinos—may think of maracas as a joke. They're not. You know how, in the rock and roll rhythmic formulas that became more and more stultifyingly codified with each passing decade, the hi-hat plays a stream of eighth notes? That's what the maracas did in "The Peanut Vendor." American music wasn't doing that; drum kits didn't have hi-hats yet. When the hi-hat did appear, it allowed a drummer to do what the maracas did.

No jazz bandleader played maracas, but Machito (Frank Grillo) was a first-class *maraquero,* snapping out an articulate rhythm on maracas and singing in clave against them while he fronted Machito and His Afro-Cubans. Founded in 1940, it was the first black-identified Latin band in the United States and, though it has been largely ignored by jazz historians, it was one of the greatest bands this country ever produced.

Machito's brother-in-law and music director, Mario Bauzá, was a mentor to Dizzy Gillespie and hooked him up with the Cuban rumbero Chano Pozo. Dizzy's recording of Chano's "Manteca" featured Chano playing what Cubans call a *tumbadora,* and what English speakers call a conga drum, a Cuban invention based on a typical Kongo construction. Dizzy and Chano's collaboration marked the integration of that instrument into jazz, and subsequently into other types of American music. Chano taught Dizzy's musicians how to play a polyrhythmic texture, which in turn made possible something American bands didn't previously play: a one-chord groove tune, with no chord changes, just layers of rhythm. Chano was not only a percussionist; he was a great popular composer whose tunes, sung by Machito and others, had preceded his arrival in the United States. His tunes drove Dizzy's musicians crazy, because they didn't change up—they just hung out there, grooving, years ahead of their time. The bass lines had to jump with a "bump" on the *and* of 2, not swing along 4 to the bar.

Two other instruments that came from Cuba were treated like novelties in the United States, part of the demeaning of Latin culture and music as kitsch: the bongó and the *campana.* Though relegated to beatnik clichés in American pop culture, the bongó is a subtle, intellectual instrument, penetratingly loud in spite of its small size, with the function of "speaking," a tracing of the way drums still serve to communicate speech across distances in forest Africa today. The campana, which in Spanish means "bell"—in English we condescendingly call it a "cowbell"—is the unsubtle power of iron. In a Latin band, the bongó player sets his bongó down and switches over to the campana when things get hot, kicking the tune into high gear. Think of the rock and roll records where the bell is essential: "Time Has Come Today," "Honky Tonk Women" and its knock-off "All Right Now," "Mississippi Queen," "We're an American Band," "Old Time Rock and Roll." And untold numbers of R&B, funk, and disco records.

Imagine pop music without maracas, conga, bongó, campana. Drum machine makers couldn't: our post-drum-machine music has routinely included simulations of Afro-Latin instruments as a basic part of the palette along with virtual kick-snare-hat-crash sounds. They're not only useful but necessary, in the expanded polyrhythmic space afforded by having independently programmable instruments. But even without the Latin instruments' specific sounds, the rhythmic ideas they articulated have become commonplace.

From the beginning, rock and roll was a negotiation between shuffle time and straight eighths. Given the enormous popularity of Latin music at the time, and the degree to which African American music was swinging, this largely meant a negotiation between the feels of African American swing and Afro-Cuban clave.

In swing (or shuffle) time, quarter notes are divided into pairs of un-equal eighth notes, with the first note somewhere around twice as long as the second. A feeling of lift, essential to the dancer, comes from giving that shorter upbeat note an accent, or push. Meanwhile, Cuban music, with its straight, even eighths, gets its rhythmic power from the eternal undulation of polyrhythms around its two-bar clave, with an emphasis on the fourth beat of the measure and a relative de-emphasis of the first. These two feels are consistently distinct in the discographies of the two musics in the decades preceding "Manteca": the vast preponderance of African American records from that era are in swing time. Cuban popular music, meanwhile, *never* shuffles, unless it's copying the American style, and it rarely sounds natural doing so. A shuffle feel isn't well suited to the kind of polyrhythm that Cuban music needs. Add to that the difference between African Americans' melismatic singing style and Cubans' syllabic singing style, and these two feels imply different styles of singing, and ultimately even a different poetics.

The clave is a rhythmic concept that takes various forms, but the most basic expression of it is a two-bar rhythm that you've heard all your life: ONE (two) AND (three) FOUR / (one) TWO THREE (four). When you hear that rhythm in North American music, it tends to be used as a beat—as in "Bo Diddley," "Hambone," "Hand Jive," and so forth. In Cuba, that rhythm is played by the two hardwood sticks known as claves, but they don't have to be playing for the clave to be in effect, because in Cuban music, clave is not a beat. It's a rhythmic *key,* the rhythmic equivalent of being in the key of C. Just as you don't have to be holding down a C-major triad all the time to play in the key of C, you don't have to be clicking out the basic clave rhythm on a pair of sticks to be playing in clave.

A rhythmic key is a powerful idea, not treated in European music theory. The Ghanaian musicologist J. H. Kwabena Nketia, speaking of African music, called this key a *timeline,* but in Cuba it came to be called a clave. While a lot of Antillean music has that two-bar feel, in Cuba the clave was consciously elevated to an organizing principle—a way of lining up a stack of rhythmically independent rhythmic parts so that they'll work together. It's what you have to have to coordinate a polyrhythm. Anybody can play any of a number of complementary rhythms, and everyone will know from any one of them where the clave is. It's all meant for dancing, and the dancer, who gets different parts of his or her body moving more or less independently, is part of the polyrhythm.

As African American music evolved, it didn't need a clave to hold it together, because as intensely rhythmic as it could be, the rhythm was composed of fewer elements. Dizzy Gillespie believed that "with [a] few exceptions when they took our drums away, our music developed along a monorhythmic line. It wasn't polyrhythmic like African music."[16] To which I would add that repression in America wasn't the only reason for the less polyrhythmic texture, and some polyrhythm was certainly present in African American music. And the textures of African American music have continued evolving, becoming more polyrhythmic in recent decades. But Gillespie was hitting at a basic truth: historically speaking, there's nothing in the American discography approaching the texture of the rumba of Matanzas, Cuba.

Both at the time of "The Peanut Vendor" and again with "Manteca," the influence of Cuba made African American music more polyrhythmic. Meanwhile, jazz, which had a level of harmonic complexity way beyond that of Cuban dance music, was traveling down to Havana from New Orleans and driving the Cubans wild.

In the post-"Manteca" world, when African American music with straight eighths started to emerge as a hip new trend, it audibly channeled Latin style. Meanwhile, the idea of rock and roll was gaining traction, and the mambo and the cha-cha-chá were part of the air that first-generation rock and roll breathed.

When "Rock around the Clock" hit Number One in the July 9, 1955, *Billboard,* the record it displaced had held the spot for nine weeks: "Cerezo Rosa," or, in English, "Cherry Pink and Apple Blossom White," a sloweddown cha-cha-chá by Pérez Prado. In "Rock around the Clock" the debt to Latin music is apparent despite the swing-boogie rhythm—listen to the strong clave feel of the lead vocal. Bill Haley's less successful follow-up was "Mambo Rock," which, though it wasn't anything close to a mambo, quoted "The Peanut Vendor" in three different spots. The quickie movie called *Rock around the Clock* featured, besides Haley, a Latin band doing four numbers.

The cha-cha-chá was still pervasive in the United States the first week of 1959, when the Cuban *revolución con pachanga* triumphed.[17] On January 7, 1959, one day after a victorious Fidel Castro was interviewed in Matanzas by Ed Sullivan, Sam Cooke recorded "Everybody Loves to Cha Cha Cha." That week, tunes on the *Billboard* Hot Hundred included Tommy Dorsey's "Tea for Two Cha Cha Cha," Edmundo Ros's "I Talk to the Trees Cha Cha," the De Castro Sisters' "Teach Me Tonight Cha Cha," and, at Number 80, a rocked-out, cha-cha-chá-ized version of an old Mexican *son jarocho,* "La Bamba," by Ritchie Valens, which peaked at Number 22 after Valens's (and Buddy Holly's) death a month later. The name "La Bamba," with that intervocalic "mb," betrayed its distant Kongo predecessors. To a Mexican, the tune was emblematic of the region of Veracruz, right across the water from Havana and New Orleans, and in musical communication with Havana for centuries.

The story of "La Bamba" is very much like that of "Louie": the tune entered Valens's live repertoire because the crowd his band played for in Los Angeles wanted to dance cha-cha-chá.[18] The band found they could stretch out on that two-bar loop as long as they needed to. For the recording session, perhaps to compensate for Valens's amateurism, producer Bob Keane hired the best studio drummer in Los Angeles, who tapped out the *1-2-cha-cha-chá* on a woodblock (something Cuban musicians would never do, since Cuban dancers don't need their step marked out that literally). That drummer, who also played on Valens's other three-chord anthem, "Come On, Let's Go," was Earl Palmer, who had relocated to LA from New Orleans in 1957. At the age of sixteen, Palmer had stowed away on a United Fruit Company steamer for a three-day vacation to Havana, a not uncommon getaway for black New Orleanians. "The captain wasn't very pissed," he recalled. "I think this was something he used to do. Do you realize Havana, Cuba, in 1941 was one of the wildest places on earth?—gambling and prostitution and dope all over, and *music hipper than anything I'd heard to that day.*"[19]

Possibly the most recorded drummer in history, Earl Palmer slammed out a number of hits in his hometown of New Orleans with Dave Bartholomew's band—the first R&B studio band, which quickly became the first rock and roll studio band. Palmer recalled the tradeoff between shuffled versus straight eighths in a founding classic of rock and roll, recorded September 14, 1955: "Little Richard moved from a shuffle to that straight eighth-note feeling. I don't know who played that way first, Richard or Chuck Berry. Even if Chuck Berry played straight eighths on guitar, his band still played a shuffle behind him. But with Richard pounding the piano with all ten fingers, you couldn't so very well go against that. I did at first—on 'Tutti Frutti' you can hear me playing a shuffle. Listening to it now, it's easy to hear I should have been playing that rock beat."[20]

At that time in New Orleans—still in active maritime communication with the port of Havana—the Cuban feel was well established, to say the least, and not only in the music of Professor Longhair. The Hawketts' 1954 "Mardi Gras Mambo," with Art Neville on vocals, had nothing to do with the form or timbre of mambo as Cubans knew it, but it had one note to a syllable—no melisma—and was in straight-eighths time with what Americans called a "rhumba" beat. "We gave it a little mambo snap to cash in on the craze of the day," recalled Neville, who was in high school at the time.[21]

"Mardi Gras Mambo," which became a Carnival perennial in New Orleans, had previously flopped in a country version. But I say, when you talk about a black artist in the 1950s doing a country number, or vice versa, look for a Latin element. Conventional rock history frames Chuck Berry's first hit, "Maybellene," recorded May 21, 1955, as a black guy doing a country song, which it was. But what do you hear on "Maybellene"? Maracas, in your face. "Maybellene" 's maracas were probably (though there seems to be some question) shaken by Jerome Green, who had none of Machito's elegance but could certainly get a beat going.

Green is better known for working with Ellis McDaniel, aka Bo Diddley, whose first hit, the eponymous "Bo Diddley," recorded on March 2, 1955, was perhaps the most rhythmically influential record of early rock and roll. Like much of Diddley's repertoire, it was driven by open-tuned guitar, barring with one finger up and down the neck in the manner of an African musical bow, together with a backbeat snare and that very un-Delta-blues instrument, the maracas. Though its famous beat is pretty much the same as the basic two-bar clave, it was played with swung instead of straight eighths. Bo Diddley described its origin differently over the years to different interviewers, no doubt being thoroughly tired of the question. George R. White quotes him: "I'd say it was a 'mixed-up' rhythm: blues, an' Latin-American, an' some hillbilly, a little spiritual, a little African, an' a little West Indian calypso . . . an' if I wanna start yodelin' in the middle of it, I can do that too."[22] But in the context of the time, and especially with those maracas, "Bo Diddley" has to be understood as a Latin-tinge record. A rejected cut recorded at the same session was titled only "Rhumba" on the track sheets.[23]

Like everything on Chess Records, "Bo Diddley" was recorded in Chicago, where T-Bone Walker first attracted attention in the 1940s at a club called the Rhumboogie. The electric blues cats were very well aware of Latin music, and there was definitely such a thing as rhumba blues; you can hear Muddy Waters and Howlin' Wolf playing it. Otis Rush's "All Your Love," recorded with Ike Turner's band in 1958, was probably the classic of the genre. This was not only happening in Chicago, of course. Ray Charles came with "What'd I Say," a Latin-blues fusion, in 1959, and the very Latin-sounding "Unchain My Heart" in 1961.

There were a lot of tunes in the fifties with a hybridized swing and Latin feel, in as wide a variety of ways as musicians could imagine. Tennessee Ernie Ford's version of Merle Travis's "Sixteen Tons," recorded September 21, 1955 (the first single I ever bought, at the age of five), had a particularly magical combination of the two feels. It swings hard, but the bass implies Latin and the vocal moves in clave. Little Willie John's 1956 "Fever" became a big hit two years later for Peggy Lee, who copied John's arrangement closely, though giving it more of a jazz sound and less of an R&B sound, stripping away the horns but keeping the strong clave feel in the vocal over a Latin-style bass, against swinging drums and backbeat fingersnaps (like those in "Sixteen Tons"). In 1950s Bakersfield, California, recalled Buck Owens, "We played rhumbas and tangos and sambas, and Bob Wills music."[24] Out there in my natal town of Lubbock, Texas, Buddy Holly's style had a lot of Afro-Cuban feel.[25] Even as seemingly non-Latin a number as "Peggy Sue" began (when it was still called "Cindy Lou") with what the Crickets drummer Jerry Allison called "like a Latin—I think it was maybe a rhumba beat" before he came up with the driving paradiddle that characterized the finished tune.[26]

Another rock and roll rhumba was Elvis Presley's "Hound Dog," written by Jerry Leiber and Mike Stoller and previously recorded by Big Mama Thornton.[27] There was a pronounced Latin feel to many of Presley's hits. One of my faves, "Stuck on You," his 1960 comeback single when he got out of the Army, has lyrics that move like a Latin tune, strongly in clave, but over a shuffling band. The tune, by Aaron Schroeder and J. Leslie McFarland, was part of a professionalized pop style that dominated the interregnum between Buddy Holly's Crickets and the Beatles. Generally if somewhat inaccurately remembered as the Brill Building sound, it was largely the creation of Jewish songwriters who were crazy about Latin music. After work, the good times of the Palladium beckoned, just three and a half blocks up Broadway from the piano-furnished offices of the Brill Building.

Ken Emerson's *Always Magic in the Air*, about the songwriting partnerships of the Brill Building scene, rightly puts the Latin influence front and center, noting, for example, that "[Doc] Pomus had grown up within earshot of Puerto Ricans who lived down the block in Williamsburg . . . [his songwriting partner Mort] Shuman described himself as 'a mambonik' who 'wrote rock 'n' roll but lived, ate, drank and breathed Latino.' "[28]

Emerson's book is rich reading, but in the case of one of his finds, a clarification is perhaps called for. If the Brill Building had a rhythmic cornerstone, it would be DOMM, DA DOM rest—dotted quarter, eighth, quarter, quarter rest. Or maybe with a CHICK from a snare or hi-hat on the fourth beat instead of a rest. That's the beat that underlines tunes like "There Goes My Baby," "Be My Baby," and "Stand by Me." According to Emerson, it was a Brazilian beat called the *baion*, borrowed from *Anna*, an Italian movie released in the United States in 1953, yielding in Leiber's and Stoller's hands "the Italian bastardization of a Brazilian samba to an ersatz Russian string-orchestration on a rhythm-and-blues record by an African-American quartet."[29] Also known as "El Negro Zumbón," the lyrics were in Spanish, not Portuguese, and the song was frequently recorded by Latin artists; Pérez Prado cut it in 1953, long before "There Goes My Baby."

Following Leiber and Stoller's lead, Emerson refers to the rhythm as the baion throughout his book. But, as he indicates, the pedigree was already confused. *Baión* is the Spanish version of the word; in the northeast of Brazil, where it comes from, it's called the *baião*, and while it does have that rhythm, played by the bass-register drum called the *zabumba*, it's a quick, double-time dance, with a feel very unlike that of the mid-tempo Brill Building records.[30] Italian movie and all, that DOMM, DA DOM CHICK, especially at mid-tempo, especially in midtown Manhattan in the Palladium era, is just another way of playing our old friend the habanera, or, to take it back to the Kongo, the *mbilu a makinu*. It's the tango.

I make this point because that Brill Building rhythm, played at a comfortable mid-tempo, survived to become the default template of white people's music, especially in the 1970s and 1980s, after the dangerous prospect of rhythmic variety had been squelched by the virtual segregation of tightly targeted radio formats. Whether in Fleetwood Mac's "Dreams," or any of thousands of others, that now mechanically regulated tango beat was heard daily in what was left of rock and roll. Meanwhile, the new kids got rid of rhythm pretty much entirely, replacing it with thrash, which is why I never gave a fuck about punk rock.

During the seven-year interval between Richard Berry's composition of "Louie, Louie" and the Kingsmen's recording, Fidel Castro came from Mexico on the *Granma* to Cuba's Oriente province, rolled triumphantly into Havana, declared Cuba's revolution to be socialist on the eve of defeating the Bay of Pigs invasion, and stared down both Kennedy and Khrushchev in the missile crisis. There would be no more dances coming in from Havana to the United States. Meanwhile, the image of the band of longhaired, bearded revolutionaries had become the international ne plus ultra of young male virility. It would take several years for rock groups to appropriate the look, but once they did, there were hirsute quartets everywhere, styling themselves as sexy revolutionaries.[31]

In the sixties, rock and roll was consciously reinvented and paraphrased, especially by British musicians, who put a frame of historicity around it, revering and in some cases remaking records by a previous wave of African American musicians who were not well known by the mass audience that came to see the new groups. In many cases they were copying Latin-tinge records by African Americans (case in point: John Mayall and the Bluesbreakers with Eric Clapton covering Otis Rush's "All Your Love"). As this new rock and roll came up—this time, mostly played by white guys—the Cuban-derived feel actually got stronger, even as the memory of Cuba as a source got fainter now that Lucy and Desi were divorced, communist Cuba had been embargoed by the United States, and Cuba had disappeared from the world's music industry. The new generation got to it indirectly, often without quite realizing what it was.

They needed a bag of tricks to play straight eighths with. By the mid-sixties, the new rockers had left the shuffle behind, perhaps because that easy-sounding feel is tricky to play—that is to say, the white kids couldn't swing. Instead, they redefined rock and roll as straight eighth notes. They rocked, but they didn't roll. Shuffles remained big in country; the highly centralized Nashville major-label system didn't permit self-contained groups to record, relying instead on crack studio professionals who could play the hell out of a shuffle. There were some mid-sixties rock and roll shuffles: the Beach Boys' "Help Me, Rhonda" was one. But then, the drummer on that date was a real drummer—Earl Palmer's Los Angeles competitor, Hal Blaine.

Comparing the music of that period with what came after, one of the remarkable things about it was its diversity. Radio stations played a heterogeneity of styles: Johnny Cash and the Supremes, back to back, on the same station. Ever since the disco era and the fragmentation of media into generic streams, the idea has been to fit into the mix, that is, to sound very much like everything else. Radio programmers have become stylistic enforcers, and with everything sounding so similar, the choice of what record to play rests ever more on how much promotional money is paid. But in the sixties, music tried *not* to fit in. You needed to make your record sound *different* from everyone else's, so it would stand out in the clutter. The best way to do that in three minutes was to build your record around a distinctive rhythmic hook, and—whether the people who did it were conscious that's where they were looking or not—the biggest source of rhythmic ideas was Latin music.

In the 1950s, the incorporation of Latin elements into first-generation rock and roll had been more or less deliberate. In the sixties, with Cuba forgotten, in most cases the rock and roll guys weren't listening to Latin records and copying them directly; they were copying sort-of Latin beats and riffs, which they may not have recognized for what they were. Latin rhythm was a vaguely comprehended legacy. Exhibit "A" is the forgotten cha-cha-chá genesis of "Louie, Louie."

There has been much mythologizing about "three-chord rock." But there were two kinds of three-chord rock. One was based on the blues, which distributed three chords over twelve bars: four bars of E7, then two bars of A7, and so on. But the other three-chord rock, at least as important if not more so, was derived from Afro-Cuban music. It looped the three chords in a two-bar cycle—the "Louie"/"La Bamba" template. That three-chord loop was introduced to American audiences in "The Peanut Vendor," though its deployment in rock and roll perhaps even more closely resembled Machito's first hit from 1941, "Sopa de Pichón," which happily cycled its two-bar loop while American jazz bands were busy playing song forms and blues changes. Rock and roll bands of the sixties were often hobbled by limited musicianship, but they could handle straight eighths and repeating three-chord loops, with a bass bump on the *and* of 2, and then they nailed it in place with a sturdy backbeat. There were scads of these tunes, especially between 1964 and 1967. There was even a soft-pop top ten version of "Guantanamera," a three-chord Cuban tune composed in 1928.

Probably the most important single producer of Cuban-rhythm rock and roll—to me, the most underrated figure of sixties pop—was Bert Berns, a Palladium mambo dancer who, before beginning his career as a professional songwriter/producer in the Brill Building scene, spent much of the winter of 1957–58 hanging out in Havana.[32] Berns's untimely death in December 1967 is an appropriate marker for the passing of the rock and roll era; it was around that time that live performances in the studio started to become productions instead, giving way post–"Pet Sounds" and post–"Sgt. Pepper" to carefully layered overdubs, with a price paid in rhythmic energy and musical drama. It became more possible to fix mistakes, lowering the bar for players.

Berns, who fused Latin and gospel feels—something African American musicians were already doing—co-wrote and produced the Isley Brothers' epochal and thoroughly Cubanized "Twist and Shout" (1962, with "Spanish Twist" on the B side), which the Beatles' version couldn't touch. Much of the material on Berns's Bang records label was Cubanoid: several of Neil Diamond's early hits, like "Cherry, Cherry," or the McCoys' "Hang on Sloopy." Van Morrison's "Brown-Eyed Girl"—Morrison's biggest radio hit, still in high oldies rotation forty years later—was a Bang record, produced by Berns, with the New York studio pro Bob Bushnell on bass. Directly or indirectly, the "Brown-Eyed Girl" bass line derives from the playing of Israel López "Cachao," who more or less created the modern style of Latin bass in the late thirties while playing with Arcaño y sus Maravillas, but who was also highly visible playing with Eddie Palmieri in New York clubs during the Bang days. Arsenio Rodríguez, the greatest Cuban bandleader of all, released his penultimate album on Bang; in a music-biz example of what Fernando Ortiz would have called reverse transculturation, *Viva Arsenio!* (1966) included a cover of "Hang on Sloopy" sung by Arsenio, presumably because Berns owned the publishing.

Another Palladium mambo fanatic was promoter Bill Graham, creator of the archetypal sixties rock venues. The Palladium was Graham's first image of what a musical experience should be and provided him with his greatest—perhaps his only—moments of happiness. He recalled the euphoria: "In the middle of a song, the whole orchestra would suddenly stop playing except for the bass line. But nobody would stop dancing. We'd all clap our hands and keep the clave beat and everybody simply surrendered to the passion of the music—thousands of us. We'd keep perfect time till the solo was over and the entire band would come back in and take it on home. *Thousands* of us. And everybody felt good. Everybody felt *so* good."[33] A generation of American kids would experience a less rhythmic, more hallucinatory version of this at Graham's dance concerts in the era of the love-in. It was Graham who pointed the Mexican American Carlos

Santana away from leading a blues band by turning him on to what was going on in the tropical Latin world, and who played him Tito Puente's "Oye Como Va" (a rewrite of Cachao's "Chanchullo").

Motown picked up the manufacture of pop music where the Brill Building left off—right down to the girl-group sound—creating in the process an original black-on-black melting pot of styles that rarely relied on twelve-bar blues changes and definitely had its Latin tinge. Not only the opening piano-and-percussion of "Ain't Too Proud to Beg" (1966) recall Latin music; the break is built on Eddie "Bongo" Brown's congas. When the Motown house band moonlighted, they cut "Cool Jerk," a flat-out R&B *guaracha* with a very Cuban-sounding *coro*.

Speaking of guarachas, compare the Rascals' "Good Lovin'" (1966) to Sonora Matancera's "Caramelos" (1960) featuring Celia Cruz—it's the same lick, that same endless three-chord loop, and even the structure of a Latin jam. When you listen to the Olympics' 1965 original of "Good Lovin,'" the mambo style is even more apparent.

I have a Cuban friend that I like to listen to oldies radio with. We pick out the Cubanisms pretty much at random as they float by. Like, say, "Smoke on the Water," whose four-bar crunch riff is something any Latin band could have played, though a little less, uh, heavily. "Break on through to the Other Side"? A mambo, complete with an organ solo imitating typical horn-section figures. On and on this goes. Even something as twee as Petula Clark's "Downtown" was a Britpop Latin-tinge tune.

To say nothing of the Beatles. "And I Love Her" is a bolero, complete with bongó and claves. Or my favorite example: John Lennon's guitar riff that begins and defines "Day Tripper." It's a mambo, turned into rock and roll. Listen to Machito's "Freezelandia" (1952), and you can hear a very similar riff to the "Day Tripper" lick, developed in a very similar way through doubling of instruments. Whether or not the Beatles ever actually heard "Freezelandia" before they came up with "Day Tripper" is irrelevant, as far as I'm concerned; the style had long been there for them to pick up on. When they get to the "she was a dayyyy tripper" part, they handle it like a Latin band. Sort of. *1-2-cha-cha-chá*.

The group that most defined rock and roll in the sixties was arguably the Rolling Stones. Their image is that of British whiteboys imitating old Southern blues guys, right? But early footage of the band shows them playing Buddy Holly's "Not Fade Away," with Mick Jagger playing maracas. Well, they *are* imitating black American musicians: Jerome Green, not Machito, was Jagger's inspiration to pick up the maracas (a gesture subsequently copied by Davy Jones of the Monkees, who was then seen waving them around by millions of American kids every week on TV). Almost all the Stones' sixties hits, the Jagger-Richard compositions, are in Latin time. There's no better example than that "hey-hey-hey" drum break of "Satisfaction," when everything else falls away but the unvarying *1-2-cha-cha-chá* that's been going on from the first bar; it's exactly the same part that Earl Palmer played on woodblock throughout "La Bamba." The difference is that the Stones weren't playing for dancers who were actually doing the cha-cha-chá. But that insistent rhythm still had its effect, making listeners want to move, even if they no longer knew how. The Stones followed up "Satisfaction" with another cha-cha-chá–derived rock tune, "Get Off My Cloud." Jagger plays maracas on "Let's Spend the Night Together" and even says "cha-cha-cha."

"Sympathy for the Devil" begins with an extended percussion-only introduction. If you look at the Jean-Luc Godard film that shows the Stones working up that song,[34] you can hear that it was a dirge, and a dull one at that, before someone got the idea to call in Rocky Dijon to play congas, making it come alive, supported by maracas played in the Jerome Green tradition. And please ignore Keith Richards's once having said it was a "samba," duly repeated by scribes in article after article; it's not. It's an Afro-Cuban groove. Sort of.

Most American cities don't have a visible concentration of Puerto Ricans, but they became New York City's largest Latin population sometime around 1930 and have been vital to musical life in that broadcast and recording capital. Puerto Ricans played the Cuban styles all along and made them their own.[35] After 1959, with the musical powerhouse of Cuba entering a state of revolutionary isolation, a new generation of Puerto Ricans was thrust onto center stage in New York Latin music. This generation, who lived side by side with African Americans, at first came up with the R&B-Latin fusion of *bugalú*—a homegrown New York Latin music—producing such delights as Pete Rodriguez's "I Like It Like That" and the Joe Cuba Sextet's "Bang Bang." Some of the Puerto Ricans who came up in New York at this time became true giants of American music: I'm thinking particularly of Ray Barretto and Eddie Palmieri, who both started their bands in 1961. By the 1970s, the salsa boom was well underway, creating one of the most brilliant (and underappreciated) recorded legacies in American music.

Meanwhile, conga drums had become one of the signature sounds of African American musical nationalism, ultimately even acquiring a faux-African pronunciation unknown in Cuba: *kungaz*. Along with the one-chord groove tune that the conga helped define, the instrument was an important part of the sound of another of America's great cultural achievements: funk.

When I asked Bobby Byrd (James Brown's music director in the glory days) about funk, I had expected that, being a pianist, he might say something about the harmony—the insistent use of sevenths, or something like that. Instead, he told me: "It was the syncopation of the instruments—everybody playing a different part. Okay, now we winded up with a seven-piece band, but everybody had a different part to play. That's where the funk part of it became. Everybody playing a different part and it's all fitting together like a glove."

That's exactly what Latin bands did, and exactly what American bands up until that time did not do. Funk polyrhythmicized the R&B combo the way the mambo had earlier polyrhythmicized the jazz band. But then, Bobby Byrd and James Brown, like Chuck and Bo, like Elvis, came of age in the mambo era. The example of Cuban music was everywhere in those days.

The amnesia that kept Cuban music out of the narrative of rock and roll history was enforced by the trade embargo against Cuba by the United States.

For a moment during the Carter presidency, and more extensively in the 1990s and early twenty-first century, important steps were taken toward normalization of musical relations between the two countries, though the trade embargo has not been lifted since President Kennedy imposed it. A 1988 law made it explicitly legal to import and license Cuban recordings into the United States. It did not, however, become legal for United States record companies to employ Cuban musicians directly or commission new recordings from them. Companies from any other country could do those things, because only the United States embargoes Cuba. Thus it was legal for the American label Nonesuch to license *Buena Vista Social Club* for sale in the United States, once it had been produced by the British label World Circuit, but it would have been illegal for Nonesuch to finance the album's creation.

By the late nineties, it had become common to see Cuban musicians playing in United States cities, though they had to jump through a lot of hoops to get here. And it was increasingly possible for United States citizens to travel to Cuba legally under certain conditions; still, Ry Cooder had to pay a $25,000 fine for having traveled to Havana illegally to make *Buena Vista*.

Visiting Cuba (always legally, I hasten to add), I have heard the music of five different African groups (Congo, Carabalí, Arará, Gangá, Yoruba), sung in ancestral languages and played on ancestral drums by practitioners of the traditional religions. It's a treasure house of African culture, alive in Cuba for the benefit of the whole world. In the eastern part of the island, I have seen three different groups dedicated to playing the tumba francesa that so fascinated Gottschalk. To say nothing of Cuba's hyperactive contemporary music scene. It's still a thoroughly musical island, with a discerning public that demands professionalism as well as flavor.

But communication between the two countries was badly damaged after the change in government occasioned by *Bush v. Gore*. United States policy in the age of *bushismo* has been unremittingly hostile to any kind of contact, cultural or otherwise, between us and them. As I write this in 2006, the United States has allowed no Cuban musicians to enter the country since 2003,[36] and refuses to let all but a handful of its own citizens go to Cuba. It's not just a trade embargo against Cuba; it's a cultural embargo against ourselves.

No wonder we don't recognize "Louie, Louie" as a cha-cha-chá.

Notes

1. Quoted in Dave Marsh, *Louie Louie: The History and Mythology of the World's Most Famous Rock 'n' Roll Song* (New York: Hyperion, 1993), 45.
2. Cristóbal Díaz Ayala, "Orquesta América," in *Encyclopedic Discography of Cuban Music, 1925–1960*, http://gislab.fiu.edu/SMC/discographynew.html (accessed April 16, 2007).

3. Marsh tells us that before recording "Louie," the Kingsmen played it for a solid hour and a half one night at a dance. Marsh, *Louie Louie*, 88.

4. Personal communication, Rafael Lam.

5. Dave Marsh's previously cited (and highly recommended) book describes the song's evolution in detail.

6. *Cuba and Its Music: From the First Drums to the Mambo* (Chicago: Chicago Review Press, 2004).

7. Black people played violin in Cuba—especially free blacks, who staffed the orchestras—but Cuba has no fiddling tradition like that of the United States. The banjo does not appear in Cuba except as a North American import.

8. For an extended discussion, see Gerhard Kubik, *Africa and the Blues* (Jackson: University Press of Mississippi, 1999).

9. Quoted in Dena Epstein, *Sinful Tunes and Spirituals: Black Folk Music to the Civil War* (Urbana: University of Illinois Press, 1977), 96.

10. Quoted in ibid., 93; emphasis in original.

11. I use the lower-case on "two" to indicate that the second downbeat of the measure is silent.

12. Robert Farris Thompson, *Tango: The Art History of Love* (New York: Pantheon, 2005), 115.

13. See S. Frederick Starr's *Louis Moreau Gottschalk* (Urbana: University of Illinois Press, 2000; reprint of 1995 Oxford University Press edition under the title *Bamboula!: The Life and Times of Louis Moreau Gottschalk*), an excellent biography that gives a detailed portrait of the place and time.

14. Alan Lomax, Mister Jelly Roll: The Fortunes of Jelly Roll Morton, New Orleans Creole and "Inventor of Jazz" (New York: Duell, Sloan and Pearce, 1950), 62.

15. I learned about Crescent City tango mania from a lecture by Jack Stewart, at Satchmo Summerfest, August 6, 2005, in New Orleans.

16. Dizzy Gillespie with Al Fraser, *To Be, or Not . . . To Bop: Memoirs* (Garden City, N.Y.: Doubleday, 1979), 290.

17. Ché Guevara's phrase; the pachanga, popular at the time, was the last Latin dance craze to migrate from Havana to New York.

18. Beverly Mendheim, *Ritchie Valens, The First Latino Rocker* (Tempe, Ariz.: Bilingual Press / Editorial Bilingüe, 1987), 34.

19. Tony Scherman, *Backbeat: Earl Palmer's Story* (Washington, D.C.: Smithsonian Institution Press, 1999), 44; emphasis added.

20. Ibid., 91. A disclaimer is perhaps in order: the idea of "swung" versus "straight" eighths is understood to be a general concept, broadly recognized as true by musicians, as per Palmer's comment here, but not implying rigidity. Drummers are not metronomes, and a spectral analysis of the playing of

rumberos in Matanzas won't show perfectly even duple time, just as programming a shuffle on a drum machine in exact triplets will sound dead. There is an intricate play of tension going on at the micro-level.

21. David Ritz, *The Brothers Neville* (New York: Da Capo, 2001), 63–64.

22. George R. White, *Living Legend: Bo Diddley* (London: Castle Communications, 1995), 59.

23. Ibid., 223.

24. AP obituary for Buck Owens, March 25, 2006.

25. On my album *Cowboy Rumba* I had the privilege of singing "Not Fade Away," Buddy's rewrite of Bo Diddley's very rumba-like "Mona," together with the Cuban rumba heroes Los Muñequitos de Matanzas. I can die happy now.

26. In the video documentary *The Real Buddy Holly Story,* Allison demonstrates at the drum set how the tune originally sounded as a "rhumba."

27. See Ken Emerson, *Always Magic in the Air: The Bomp and Brilliance of the Brill Building Era* (New York: Viking, 2005), 8.

28. Ibid., 123.

29. Ibid., 60.

30. Most of Brazil heard the *baião* for the first time in 1946, when the accordionist Luiz Gonzaga, the Baião King, gave his tune "Baião" to the Rio de Janeiro pop vocal group Quatro Ases e Um Coringa. See Dominique Dreyfus, *Vida do Viajante: A Saga de Luiz Gonzaga* (São Paulo: Editora 34, 1996), 112–13.

31. The late-period bearded Jim Morrison image? Neo-Ché. Four decades after his death on October 9, 1967, Ché turns up on more T-shirts around the world than all the rockers of the sixties put together.

32. I am indebted to Joel Selvin for sharing with me some of his work on Berns.

33. Bill Graham and Robert Greenfield, *Bill Graham Presents* (New York: Doubleday, 1992), 49.

34. Called *Sympathy for the Devil*; Godard's original cut, titled *One Plus One*, reportedly included more footage of the song's development. Cf. also the Stones' strong live performance of the tune, complete with congas and maracas, in the film *Rock and Roll Circus*.

35. The three biggest bandleaders of the Palladium era were Machito and two Puerto Ricans, Tito Puente and Tito Rodríguez.

36. There was one bizarre exception: musicians attached to a Cuban nightclub revue were allowed into the United States in 2004 to play at the Stardust Hotel and Casino in Las Vegas, a curious story which is beyond the scope of this essay.

David Thomas

Ghoulardi
Lessons in Mayhem from the First Age of Punk

5

The first and possibly only *native* punk movement in America ended in the mid-1960s and was to be found, not within rock music, but within the fluid boundaries of local radio and TV media communities. The garage punk bands of the sixties should be seen as an evolutionary growth of rock music as a folk phenomenon; the American punk activity of the late seventies as a pop artifice promulgated by foreign cultural imperialists and promoted by corporate interests, Madison Avenue arrivistes, and chicken-hawking sexual deviants. It was designed, by intent or circumstance, to subvert and short-circuit what was already an emerging wave of third generation rock youth represented by such literate bands as Television, Talking Heads, Pere Ubu, the Residents, MX80 Sound, and others. Simultaneously, a media-induced state of datapanik served to bury meaning within a flood of anodyne and charming data-chaff.

Driven by local circumstances, inspired by local characters, and fueled by the sort of unrefined exuberance to be expected in the last wild days of a technological frontier, isolated pockets of punk activity were capable of throwing up sometimes astonishing phenomena that blossomed and then withered unnoticed outside a limited geography. Where, in former times, mountains, deserts, and rivers might have served to isolate communities, in the fifties and sixties broadcast throw and reception range would act in a similar way. These were the days of regional radio hits—localized charts were the norm rather than the exception. These were the days of the wild child personality radio jocks, and their story has been told often and in great detail. Less known, less appreciated and far rarer were the wild child TV punks. There were, of course, influential national figures such as Ernie Kovacs, Soupy Sales, and Steve Allen, and radio antecedents such as Arthur Godfrey, but spotted here and there across the country were equally innovative and often far more idiosyncratic local characters. The one I know about is Ernie Anderson. He is the father of director Paul Thomas Anderson (*Boogie Nights*), and between 1963 and 1966 he was the biggest thing in Cleveland, unrivaled even by the mighty Jim Brown. His presence dominated the city's landscape at a time when Cleveland was the second largest Hungarian-language city in the world. His catch-phrases entered and still remain in the local vernacular. His antics and jokes were recounted in every school and bar and factory and office. He outraged the great and the good. But even so, at the peak of his popularity, the family restaurant chain Manners Big Boy would produce blue milk shakes in plastic cups emblazoned with his image and his slogan, "Stay sick and turn blue!"

Ernie Anderson left Cleveland after 1966 and moved to Los Angeles where he eventually became the voice of ABC, *Monday Night Football,* Ford Motors, and most memorably *The Love Boat*. Over the decades imitators who traded in his persona rose and fell and rose again in markets bounded by Cleveland and Detroit. He died in February 1997. On TV, in Cleveland, he was known as Ghoulardi.[1]

While radio jocks trade heavily in the persona marketplace, ultimately they prosper or fail depending to a significant degree on the popularity of the playlist. Success on TV, however, is more thoroughly reliant on the immediacy of the mask and the masquerade—certainly in the case of Ghoulardi, a Friday night/Saturday afternoon monster movie host constrained by a local TV budget to packages of the cheapest Hollywood B-movies. *The Disembodied, World without End, Ghost Diver, Sh! The Octopus, The Haunted Sea, From Hell It Came*—the list makes *Attack of the Fifty-Foot Woman* look like quality. Most people were not tuning in to see the movie.

The Cleveland/Akron underground of the mid-seventies has been subject to speculation and keen interest because of the "otherness" of the bands it spawned. But why was it such a specific and limited generational window? What was the source of such rage, such disaffection from not only the mainstream culture but also from the so-called counterculture—in fact from any subculture you'd care to mention? What could produce such a contradiction as this set of radical innovators who embraced consumerist media with such enthusiasm?

The answer for many of us is simple. We were the Ghoulardi kids.

I was nine in 1963 when Ghoulardi went on air. He was forty. I was thirteen when he quit in 1966. After him I believe that I could only have perceived the nature of media and the possibilities of the narrative voice in particular ways. Describing how he devastated the authority of the media, and of the Great and the Good, how he turned the world upside down and inside out, it seems, is nearly impossible for an outsider to appreciate. Some prankster sloganeering, lots of whacked hipster dialect, some primitive blue screen technique, and lots of firecrackers exploding inside plastic Rat Fink dragster models, all sandwiched between movie segments over the course of ninety minutes on the TV every Friday night—how unsafe could that be? You have no idea. Ghoulardi was the Flibberty Jib Man—Ken Nordine's drifter who can enchant the populace of a town with nothing more than the sound of his voice.

This may sound improbably portentous for a mere monster movie host but you really had to experience it—experience the mayhem—to appreciate how powerful this masquerade was. Everyone who saw Ghoulardi will tell a favorite story—like the night he set off an egregiously large home-made explosive device sent in by a fan—he was always setting off fireworks and blowing up things in the studio—and quite clearly the off-camera crew were telling Ghoulardi not to light it up and you could see people running across the studio, the camera abandoned to skew off balance, pointing at the floor, and then the entire room was stunned senseless for some minutes . . . live . . . smoke, curtains on fire, people stumbling around.

Or the night he repeated the "What, me worry" phrase for ten minutes, progressing through the range of all possible inflections and dramatizations . . . or certainly enough of them. (Ghoulardi would sometimes set out, perversely, to induce tedium as its own form of mayhem. In a *Gun-*

smoke parody he and supporting characters sat around a table not saying anything, not moving—stone cold nothing—for a minute. "Let me think," he said, and then he sat there.)

But the most memorable and distinctive feature of the Ghoulardi show involved the lexicon of audio, film, and blue screen drop-ins that he and his crew developed to artfully disrupt any linear experience the audience might hope for, and to generally punk out the proceedings. Some of the staple film drop-ins included clips of an English gurning competitor, two trains colliding, an improbable winged aircraft collapsing inward, and a fat lady dancing like a ballerina. Audio drop-ins were likely to be bits of polkas, Rivingtons and Trashmen riffs, or Scream Jay Hawkins eruptions.

The best of the drop-ins were the live blue screen improvisations, each timed out to the second and cued by an engineer looking at a stopwatch. The technique, traceable to John Zacherle in New York City, was probably developed independently by Chuck Schodowski, Ghoulardi's "producer/ engineer." (Certainly, in Schodowski's hands, it was used to far more artful effect.) In a haunted house Ghoulardi appears in a hallway warning, "Don't open that door!" Dropped in next to a caveman gnawing on a bone, he offers to take him out for a pizza. And there is a particularly memorable scene from *Dr. Cyclops,* repeated to great effect in *Attack of the Crab Monster,* where Ghoulardi drops into a cave scene among a bunch of nervous characters and he's running from side to side waving his arms and jumping ludicrously up and down.

The B-movie was for Ghoulardi a canvas, an open invitation to spread mayhem, and generally engage in ransacking any sense of good taste, worthiness, or respectability that local TV might aspire to. The amateurish enthusiasm and naive intention of the B-movie encourages a kind of communal abstraction that approaches folk culture, and the frequent lack of a coherent agenda leaves lots of wiggle room for whatever personalized context or agenda an audience—or TV host—chooses to overlay.

But Ghoulardi was in a different league from other monster movie hosts. He eschewed the gothic makeup, and Bela Lugosi affectations. Even his name subverted the genre—the first syllable is the setup, the last two the sucker punch. Chef Boyardee, maker of canned spaghetti . . . *Et voilà!* Ghoul-ar-dee!

Made up in a fright wig, fake mustache, and goatee in constant peril of peeling away, wearing a lab coat covered in badges and campaign buttons, and sporting sunglasses with one lens missing, he subverted all possible expectations. On prominent display were a Nixon-Lodge button, an "LBJ for the USA" button, and an "I've Had Enough, I'm Voting Republican" button.

Think of Ghoulardi as a last hurrah of that pop culture masquerade, the rebel without a cause. Just a guy with a bad attitude. Apolitical, nonaligned, drifting across the landscape content to leave behind nothing more than mayhem. "What are you protesting against?" "Whatta ya got?" Except in Ghoulardi's case the exchange between him and a weary station manager on yet another Monday morning went like this—Station Manager: "Why don't you just behave?" Ghoulardi: "I don't HAVE to behave!"

The politicization of sixties pop music—and the effective end of the rebel without a cause mask—was certainly well under way when Ghoulardi bowed out in 1966. Ghoulardi hated pop. He was a jazz fan. He and Schodowski orchestrated the musical side of their mayhem with mainly instrumental rock, jazz, and blues clips—the Ventures, Booker T, Tom King and the Starfires, Oscar Peterson, Jimmy McGriff (who wrote "Turn Blue" for Ghoulardi)—along with . . . polkas. Duane Eddy's "The Desert Rat" was his theme tune. Frankie Yankovic's "Who Stole the Kishka?" figured prominently. The instrumental tracks featured lots of raw guitar. The fewer vocal tracks were pointedly aggressive nonsense like the Rivingtons' "PAPA-OOM-Mow-Mow" and "The Bird's the Word," or barely articulate rages like Screamin' Jay Hawkins's "Constipation Blues" and "I Put a Spell on You."

Ghoulardi didn't do safe. In the days when Huntley and Brinkley and Walter Cronkite and any number of local luminaries were demigod arbiters of truth and reality, Ghoulardi launched an assault on their credibility, ravaging the third-rail untouchable righteousness of the media priests. The most devastating effect was achieved with a single word, three syllables, one question mark: "Dor-o-thy?"

Dorothy Fuldheim was a frumpish intellectual drawn from academia to serve as a nightly commentator on Channel 5 news. She was the grande dame of the media elite, the great and the good were tucked up snug and warm inside her huge handbag. The master of mayhem, the rebel with no cause, Mr. Bad Attitude, locked her in his sights and homed in. Ghoulardi understood the medium better, far better, than did his targets in the media.

"Dor-o-thy!?" It was only a question—usually followed by a drop-in of the exultant intro to "Who Stole the Kishka?"—but the incredulity of the delivery was withering in its impact. "The Emperor has no clothes," it shouted out in the irrefutable language of the inarticulate front-end that is television. What response is possible? Logic? Reason? Counter-argument? Impotent, the great and the good could only bemoan the corruption of youth.

Years later in the early seventies in Cleveland there was an art terrorist crew, on the fringes of the Coventry Road / *American Splendor* crowd, called Fred & Ethel Mertz. They "adjusted" billboards—always smiley-faced, perfectly coifed local TV news portraits—with the slogans "Question Authority" or, more often, "Nuke the Whales." They painted on sun-glasses and goatees. They were Ghoulardi kids.

One more chapter of the Ghoulardi story needs to be described and relates most significantly to his downfall. It concerns "Parma Place," a minisoap opera incorporated into his program slots. Parma is a western suburb of predominantly Polish extraction. The vocal performance that is "Dor-o-thy?!" had been previously honed and perfected with the exclama-tion "Par-Maa?!" to such effect that Parma City Council would spend much effort countering the mischaracterization of their town. Parma Place featured three "certain ethnic characters," as they were described, played by Anderson, Schodowski, and the wife of a well-known local DJ. They were usually seen sitting on a couch watching TV and talking about what they had been doing or might do—if they only could stop watching the TV. It was parochial, unabashedly working-class ethnic, and full of local inside jokes.

So one night at Severance Hall, home of the imperious George Szell and the Cleveland Orchestra, then at the very peak of its powers, Maestro Szell introduced a violinist, noting that he had grown up in Parma. From all accounts a shockingly large proportion of the audience, considering the classiness of the joint, erupted with the "Par-Maa?!" question.

The hammer had to come down. This had gone too far. And Ernie Anderson himself had grown tired of the part and of the escalating has-sles. He quit. He moved on. He left behind a generational window of kids with a different sort of POV.

So, without Ghoulardi would there have been the Cramps—a band so thoroughly co-optive of the Ghoulardi persona that when they first appeared Clevelanders of the generation were fairly dismissive? Would there have been an Electric Eels dressed in tin foil running a lawnmower over the stage? Or Tin Huey, a truly strange band full of odd people telling odd stories, playing oddly mutated instruments? Or a Rocket from the Tombs with a name that so obviously synthesizes sci-fi and horror B-movie-isms? The Mirrors sang about the people who live on the inside of the earth. Pere Ubu drew on a Ghoulardi-esque persona for its identity.

Consider the characteristics of these bands. Foremost is a distinctive narrative voice which is an idiosyncratic mixture of the observational, the self-participatory, and the intrusive other—by which I mean the notion that the telling of a story should involve the incorporation of additional, intrusive povs that might run in parallel, or at some angle to the central narrative, crossing it, intruding, overlaying, contradicting, deprecating, or even ignoring it. Certainly we, the Ghoulardi kids, could have encountered, and eventually did, this form of surreality in various literary and art traditions, but we were introduced to the basics from some guy on the TV, at a young age, unencumbered by the baggage of pretension, elitism, or dogma. To tell a story this way was simply how you did things—it wasn't sophisticated, or clever, or important. But it made a neat mess. And that was cool. Consider the startling musical inserts and abrupt image jumps beloved by these bands, the enthusiasm for noise and abstract sound, the appreciation of absurdity and extremism, the sense of the theatrical but an abhorrence of artifice. Running a lawnmower across the stage— the equivalent of shooting off fireworks in a TV studio—sounds about as artifice-laden as you can imagine but you had to be there, you had to see it—the diminutive cripple Dave E partnered with the hulking Aryan bleach blonde John Morton—and it all looked pretty normal—well, natural, or right or, uh, clear—dare I say organic? (You had to be there.)

These bands were fronted by guys with extreme persona, odd hosts archly mediating a musical experience, each serving as a funhouse lens through which the musicians look outward at the audience and through whom, in turn, the audience receives context, perspective, and scale. The observer is himself watched. The narrator is generated by the story he tells.

In Charlotte Pressler's seminal piece about the Cleveland scene of the mid-seventies, "Those Were Different Times," she asks a question she is not able to answer:

Why, for example, are so many of the people in this story from the same background? Most of them were from middle or upper-middle class families. Most were very intelligent. Many of them could have been anything they chose to be. The Sixties drop-outs dropped in to a whole world of people just like themselves but these people were on their own. You can ask, also, why they all turned to rock n roll. Most of these people were not natural musicians. [They] would probably have done something else, if there had been anything else for them to do. One can ask why there wasn't; why rock n roll seemed to be the only choice.

Maybe the answer to her question is that rock music provided the best medium, the most readily available masquerade through which to pursue artful mayhem, to practice the narrative extremism of the host mediator, and to leave a mark worthy of Mr. Anderson's approval.

Note

1. Reference material throughout comes from Tom Feran and R. D. Heldenfels, *Ghoulardi: Inside Cleveland TV's Wildest Ride* (Cleveland, Ohio: Gray and Company Publishers, 1997).

David Brackett

Magic Moments, the Ghost of Folk-Rock, and the Ring of E Major

6

To think of magic moments in music is to emphasize the temporal, albeit in at least two different ways. The arrival of a magic moment focuses our attention on the present, creating one of the few instances in life when we are not reflecting on the past or future. Yet, reflecting on magic moments creates the opposite effect, plunging one into the world of memory. Writing about magic moments thus raises a paradox, in that one scrutinizes a past experience that eclipsed a sense of past and future when it initially occurred. The heightened narrativity of such a retelling initially limits the possibility of external verification of the magic moment in question, forcing the reader to accept on faith the implied distinction between magical and non-magical moments. In other words, the act of recounting one's memories makes no claims to approach "the real," instead adopting a rhetorical posture closer to that of storytelling, and thus, of fiction.[1] These distinctions—between an experience of present-ness and of dwelling on the past, between magical and mundane moments—collapse as experiences of the present come to be understood as already inflected by condensations of memory.[2]

The choice of a magic moment for this essay was sparked by the proximity of one such moment to the

Example 1. Elvis Costello, "It's Time" (0:32–0:42).

This ma- gic   mo - ment_____   con-cludes when this   ci - ga-rette ends___

Example 2. The Drifters, "This Magic Moment" (0:13–0:20).

This   ma - gic   mo - ment___   so   dif' - rent and   so   new

words "this magic moment," as they occur in a passage of Elvis Costello's "It's Time" (shown in example 1).

This passage transports me from the present to 1996 when I first heard Elvis Costello sing it, initiating a paradigmatic swirl of associations that leads to the Drifters' 1960 recording of "This Magic Moment" (see example 2).[3]

The lyrics of both of these songs reflect on the complex sense of multiple temporalities implied by the notion of a "magic moment." The phrase "this magic moment" occurs twice in the lyrics of the Drifters' recording: the first of these moments, the singer tells us, is "so different and so new" because "I kissed you"; the second occurs "while your lips are close to mine"—suggesting that repeating the kiss is enough to make that magic feel like the first time. Both of these lines are set to a classic doo-wop I-vi-IV-V harmonic progression but are updated with the "uptown" sound of swirling strings inaugurated by the Drifters' release from the previous year, "There Goes My Baby," and modified by "the Latin tinge" permeating popular music during the period.

The magic moments in the lyrics of "It's Time," on the other hand, feel more like they may be the last time such moments occur. In the latter song, "this magic moment" first "concludes when that cigarette ends"; then in successive verses it "concludes when they turn out the light"; and finally it "conclud[es] our mutual fate." Thus, the Drifters' magic moments evoke beginnings, kisses, and eternity, while Costello's conjure up "conclusions" marked by burning cigarettes and extinguished lights. The magic moments in both songs become metonyms, evoking the past in the present, but they differ in their relationship to a notion of originary pleasure: the Drifters, by perpetuating the belief that it can be recovered and last forever; Costello, by doubting that it ever existed in the first place.

Costello's fatalistic narrative, so reminiscent of what he termed the "revenge and guilt" that saturated his early approach to lyrics, refers us to the earlier, sweeter magical moment of the Drifters through the use of a borrowed verbal phrase. But one other aspect of "It's Time" evokes the pop music world of the 1950s and early 1960s, another possibly, yet possibly not, accidental instance of quotation or near-quotation, this time occurring in the succession of sonic events. I already mentioned the so-called doo-wop harmonic progression employed in "This Magic Moment," a series of chords almost as common in early rock and roll as the twelve-bar blues progression. In the passage following the words "this magic moment" in "It's Time," it's possible to hear shards of this doo-wop progression, broken up and extended, with other chords occasionally interpolated; a progression never played straight through, but nonetheless clear enough to form patterns to which the song keeps returning. In fact, from the words "this magic moment" on, the doo-wop progression forms a reference point for the harmonic progression of "It's Time," even though it is never stated in its pure form.

Example 3 illustrates how "This Magic Moment" uses the I-vi-IV-V progression in unadulterated form twice (three times if one includes the introduction) before introducing a contrasting harmonic progression (see example 2 for a more detailed view of the first half of the first of these repetitions). The situation with "It's Time" is more complex: the progression represented in Example 3 begins on the words "this magic moment" (shown in more detail in example 1) in the *middle* of the progression, on the "IV" chord. The song then cycles through variants of the I-vi-IV-V progression four times, altering it each time, while avoiding one of the most defining features of the progression (certainly in terms of Western music theory)—the movement from V to I that clearly marks the beginning of a new repetition. The only "authentic," V-I cadence occurs after the words "well I suppose that depends," with the arrival on the tonic chord (I), which coincides with the words "if you go" (the movement from the end of statement 1 to the beginning of statement 2 in example 3). This section of "It's Time," beginning with the words "if you go," is further emphasized by a dramatic change of texture with the entry of bass guitar and "real" drums.

Example 3. Use of "doo-wop" progression in "This Magic Moment" and "It's Time."

I	VI	IV	V
"This Magic Moment"			
1. C	Am	F	G7
2. C	Am	F	G7
"It's Time"			
.5.		A (A#°7)	
1. E	C#m	A (A#°7)	B (G#m) B >>
2. E (G#7)	C#m	A	
3. E	C#m		B (D#m/A#)
4. (G#7)	C#m	A (A#°7)	
5. (A) E			

Yet my interest in "It's Time" does not stem entirely, or even mostly, from its reference to a song released some thirty-six years earlier: to my ears, the magic moment of the song occurs neither with the mention of ever-deferred and displaced magic moments in the lyrics nor in the evocation of chord progressions from days gone by, but rather in the musical gesture that concludes each verse of the song—a ringing open A chord that resolves to an open E (see example 4), what in music-theoretical terminology would be called a plagal cadence (also termed an "amen" cadence because it is sung at the conclusion of Protestant hymns). The arrival at these chords is carefully set up by several factors: the harmonic progression discussed earlier, the arch of the long vocal line, and a gradual build-up of texture.[4] This particular way of using the open E chord recalls other similar usages, usually involving a movement from A to G-sharp on the third string of the guitar. This usage of the E-major chord, a kind of "sonic emblem" involving the specific timbre of the highly amplified (though not particularly distorted) electric guitar, references another line of pop music history, one that stretches back to the "classic rock" of the mid-sixties.[5]

For guitarists, the E-major chord in open position provides a particular kind of satisfaction (in fact, Henry Rollins linked the pleasures of playing this chord to male-oriented auto-eroticism); and traces of this visceral pleasure undoubtedly resonate with listeners, whether or not they are guitarists.[6] It has a uniquely full, bright sound, resulting from several factors: the root of the chord is played on the lowest open string of the

Example 4. Movement from A to E at 1:42 of "It's Time."

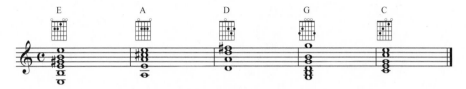

Example 5. Spacing of open chords on the guitar.

instrument in its conventional tuning; it uses all six strings of the guitar; the highest note is also the root and is also played on an open string; and the spacing of the pitches of the chord almost perfectly conform to the music-theoretical ideal (see example 5). This correspondence by itself may not help explain its effect, except that this ideal bears a strong relationship to the arrangement of pitches in the overtone series (a series of faint pitches sounding above every pitch—termed the fundamental—that we actually hear): low pitches further apart, high pitches closer together. Thus the upper five pitches of the open E chord are in a relationship to the lower pitch that reinforces the overtones of that lower pitch—music theorists may yet debate whether the open E is the real chord of nature.[7]

By way of comparison (see example 5), other commonly used open, major chords available on the guitar have their root on an open string, but not on E (A major, D major), or the root is on the E string, but the string isn't open (G), or the root is neither on low E, nor open (C major). G major is probably the closest competitor to E in terms of its sonorous quality, but both its highest and lowest pitches are stopped (i.e., not open), and the spacing of pitches does not correspond to the overtone series in the manner of the E chord. The G chord, therefore, while much beloved by folk guitarists, and very versatile, lacks the brilliant ring of E, and, because of where the open and stopped strings are situated, is not as easy to control on the electric guitar. However, as I will discuss later, songs using these other chords as their tonic chord also derive a distinctive overall sonority.

The particular usage of the E chord that I have been discussing, the one

Example 6. Neil Young, "Barstool Blues" (0:43–0:46).

Example 7. The Beatles, "Nowhere Man" (0:14–0:17).

Example 8. Bob Dylan, "I Don't Believe You" (0:02–0:15).

featuring the movement from A to G-sharp on the G string, did not arise out of the ether. Rather, Costello, in employing this usage, links "It's Time" with other recordings dating back to the mid-1960s, creating a fairly consistent line of intra-generic reference. Examples 6 through 8 all rely on a similar usage of the E chord.

In all three of these recordings (all four if we include "It's Time"), the sound of the open E chord is an essential ingredient, equal, I would argue, to the impact of melody, chord progression, rhythm, timbral nuances of the voice, and so on. Because of the centrality of this sound to the effect of the recordings, if one were to attempt to capture the flavor of these arrangements in a cover version, it would not really be possible to transpose the song to another key. Dylan, in fact, originally recorded the last example, "I Don't Believe You," in a solo version two years earlier in the key of D. Transposing the song to E was among the many extensive and significant changes made between the two versions, yet one of the most audible benefits of this change was to make available the particular sound of that key on the guitar.[8]

Similarly, the demo version of "It's Time" reveals that Costello also originally conceived the song in a different key. The change of key from F in the demo down to E, in addition to giving Costello a bit more room at the top of his voice, makes the brilliance of the E chord available on the guitar, which then becomes a major ingredient in the sonic reconception of the song. A further interesting point about the demo is that it highlights the genre connections between "It's Time" and gospel/rhythm and blues (and, hence, the genre world of the Drifters) more than the official version, largely through the use in the demo of 6/8 meter, and a slower, more lilting tempo (the quarter-note triplets in the official version—see example 1—survive as vestiges of the meter used in the demo).

Arraying these examples together raises several questions. First, what is the expressive use to which the "sonic emblem" of the open E is put? In other words, what, if anything, do the verbal/semantic worlds implied by the words of these songs have in common that makes the use of the open E with 4–3 suspension (or "E sus4" in guitar nomenclature) particularly well-suited to projecting their meaning? The lyrics of "It's Time," "Barstool Blues," and "I Don't Believe You" all deal with relationships that are in the process of ending or have already ended, while "Nowhere Man" describes someone lost in uncertainty. If we were to assume that musical gestures were completely neutral, then we could quickly move to the idea that our E chord straightforwardly reflects or translates the quality of "ending, loss, romantic despair, depression" heard in the lyrics. Yet while words may give us a key to the "human universe" inhabited by the music, the music (and especially the singing voice) inflects the words, as the different versions of "I Don't Believe You" and "It's Time" well illustrate.[9] The qualities that *I* hear in these recordings—"defiance, strength, resolution in the face of adversity, yearning, sneering"—illustrate the ambiguous, yet not completely open-ended quality of musical meaning. The brilliant ring of the open E chord with a 4–3 suspension stresses certain potential interpretations of the lyrics, calls our attention to latent aspects of voices and personae, while softening or downplaying others.[10]

Yet this chain of specific word-music linkages, while compelling, addresses only one aspect of connotative meaning. Another telling aspect may be found along the translucent and shifting borders that mark genres and the socio-cultural associations attached to them.[11] The use of a musical device such as this gesture involving the open E chord evokes historical associations with (what I am calling here for lack of a better name) "folk-rock," a genre which became meaningful in relation to other genres during the mid-1960s (or the summer of 1965, to be more precise), and which became the prototype for later constructions of classic rock. In all three periods under consideration here, 1966, 1975, and 1996, the E-chord gesture evokes (something like) folk-rock through its contrast with other genres that would be unlikely to include such a gesture. This particular E chord references folk-rock partly through its difference from other usages of the open E that may refer to other genres, most notably, to those derived from the blues. In order to accept this distinction, one would have to examine the very different way in which the E chord is used in blues and blues-derived genres; one of the most striking differences, for example, is how, in blues-related genres (but not in folk-rock), the third (G-sharp on the first fret of the G string) alternates ambiguously with the open G, creating a "blues third" effect (see example 9). This bluesy usage of the open E characterizes recordings such as Link Wray's 1958 "Rumble" (where the resounding E chord that dominates the sound-scape of the song is clearly situated in a blues tonal context), which otherwise might seem to be prime examples of antecedents for the open E as heard in "It's Time."[12]

The move toward excision of blues tonality in folk-rock creates a momentary boundary and distinguishes it from two historical genres usually considered to be important influences on rock and roll: blues and country. Rather than the "lowdown" funkiness of blues tonality, the "purity" of the major thirds in folk-rock evokes musics outside the American vernacular, the most obvious examples being either British Isles traditional music or European classical music. One effect of this move is to create a form of rock and roll–derived popular music—in the process of being christened "rock" circa 1965—with distinctive connotations of middle-class whiteness, opposed to the African American connotations of blues and rhythm and blues, or the rural, working-class whiteness of country.[13]

Folk-rock thus fulfilled the need for a genre that was distinctively white. It also simultaneously created a genre that was distinctively hip, achieving this hipness through an insistence on artistic autonomy and an invocation of bohemian discourses around alternative practices of accreditation—or, in other words, around the idea that value emanates from the approval of other artists rather than from economic success or established academic/critical criteria. These factors helped differentiate folk-rock from less hip,

Example 9. Stereotypical blues guitar lick in E.

white-associated genres such as teen pop and pre–rock and roll-styled pop.[14] While other hip styles performed by white musicians co-existed at this time with folk-rock, these genres, such as blues-rock and hard rock, all maintained obvious ties to historical and contemporaneous genres that were strongly associated with African Americans. These white musicians therefore always ran the risk of being seen as derivative, at a remove of one step from the "real thing," or as somewhat devalued copies of an original that remained beyond reach. Folk-rock seemed to satisfy the desire for the newly expanded mass of white, middle-class, post–secondary school producers and consumers for a music that did not reek of an earnest duplicate, however skillfully delivered.[15] Costello's transformation of "It's Time" from gospel/doo-wop to a song with closer ties to folk- (or classic) rock thereby obscures, through a process of generic "whitening," the connection of its magic moments with those in the Drifters' recording of that name.

This is not to say that the work of all artists associated with folk-rock avoids blues tonality, although the recordings of archetypal folk-rockers, the Byrds, come fairly close. Blues inflections are rarely far away in Dylan's work—even in "I Don't Believe You" the opening guitar riff resembles that of Chuck Berry's "Memphis," and Robbie Robertson's guitar fills make frequent use of blues-based phrases—and the Beatles recorded several blues- and country-derived songs on *Rubber Soul*, the album on which "Nowhere Man" appeared. The point here is that one of the clearest defining differences between folk-rock and earlier rock and roll, contemporaneous rhythm and blues, and country is the use of these ringing, non-bluesy, folk-based, open guitar chords, of which the E with a suspension is a prime example.[16]

Similar to how the folk-rock of "Nowhere Man" and "I Don't Believe You" distinguished itself from other genres coexisting in the mid-1960s, so did the allusions to folk-rock in "Barstool Blues" and "It's Time" mark their identity within the popular music field of their eras. "Barstool

Example 10. Typical folk-rock melodic embellishment of open A and D chords.

Blues," appearing on Neil Young's *Zuma* in 1975, contrasted with other "hard rock" songs on the same album, such as "Drive Back," or the out-and-out "folk" of "Through My Sails." A glance at the top-ranked albums in *Billboard*'s charts of that year reveals contrasts between Young's album and the funk of Earth, Wind & Fire's *That's the Way of the World*, the pop-rock of Elton John's *Captain Fantastic and the Brown Dirt Cowboy*, and the hard rock cum heavy-metal of Led Zeppelin's *Physical Graffiti* (though the eclecticism of *Physical Graffiti* probably resembles that of *Zuma* more closely than the others). Costello's "It's Time" finds companionship on his album *All This Useless Beauty* with his folk-rock Byrds' tribute song, "You Bowed Down," but contrasts elsewhere with numerous ballads, the neo-soul "Why Can't a Man Stand Alone," or the country-ish "Starting to Come to Me." Looking across the pop music spectrum of 1996, Costello's work has less in common with the best-sellers of the day than the examples from 1966 or 1975, differing mightily from hip-hop albums such as the Fugees' *Score,* or from Céline Dion's retro-pop *Falling into You,* though sharing certain models in "classic rock" (if little else) with *Fairweather Johnson* by Hootie and the Blowfish.

One could say, in a guitar-o-centric world, that "It's Time," "Nowhere Man," "I Don't Believe You," and others are "about" the E chord in the same way that songs by the Byrds, like "Mr. Tambourine Man" and "Turn, Turn, Turn," are about the D chord, and like their "I'll Feel a Whole Lot Better" is about the A chord. The Byrds don't (to my knowledge) have an E-chord song of the type I have been describing. D and A, while not possessing the resounding ring of E, have other properties that, we might speculate, are better suited to the Byrds' purposes. These chords enable a 4–3–2–3 melodic motion, a type of movement that is not possible with E, because the third of the E chord is only a half-step above the open string (see example 10 and compare with example 5). Costello's aforementioned tribute to the Byrds' mid-1960s oeuvre, "You Bowed Down," written originally for the Byrds' leader Roger McGuinn (and recorded by him in 1991) is, not surprisingly, in D and uses ringing open D and A chords whenever possible.

The interface between performance practice, the technology of musical instruments, and the social history of genres contributes to the paradigmatic depth of the magic moment I have been describing. But I would argue that the particularity of this moment is not unique. My choice of what may seem to many to be an obscure track on an obscure album is thus not driven by the desire to bestow artistic legitimacy on "It's Time" but rather by the almost random coincidence of a conference theme with a line in that song. The arbitrary nature of song selection suggests that such performances of personal and socio-historical excavation should be possible with a wide range of cultural artifacts.

Magic moments trigger memories that strive to connect chains of otherwise disconnected associations and events. What is ephemeral, an instance that disappears in a blink of an eye, may in later instances be organized, framed in a narrative. Such is frequently the fate of not only magic moments but, one might argue, of unmagic moments as well, of communication in general, of the experience of symbolic forms in time, and thus, of music in particular. These chains of memories lead listeners to different positions in social spaces located at different points in history: on the one hand, to an African American rhythm and blues group going "uptown" and crossing over to new audiences, new sounds, rhythms, and instruments, as new possibilities for combining pop, rhythm and blues, and rock and roll were being explored; or, on the other hand, to white bohemians betokening countercultural movements and the institution of cultural capital within the popular music field.

Postscript: Black or White?

A camera swoops down from outer space to a suburban tract home where Macaulay Culkin listens to headbanger music. Annoying his baseball-watching father and tabloid-reading mother, Culkin responds by strapping on an electric guitar and blowing his father back into the outer space from which the camera descended. Dad lands in "Africa" where a riff based on an E sus chord accompanies a dancing Michael Jackson, who is surrounded by "African" warriors. The riff initiates a blues-based chord progression, and Jackson's "Black or White" (1991) begins. This E sus chord most strongly recalls a song like the Rolling Stones' "Soul Survivor" from *Exile on Main St.* (1972), yet even this adaptation of the riff in a hard-rock guise, I would argue, retains the style-identity connotations of its emergence within the genre of folk-rock. The combination of this riff with Jackson's soul-derived singing and the techno-based rhythm track thus attempts to enact the song's refrain, "It doesn't matter if you're black or white," in musical terms. This musical-semiotic fusion finds echoes both in the famous video-morphing sequence toward the end of the song and in Jackson's own notorious physical transformation. Multiple acts of cross-racial ventriloquism also play off the cultural referents of these musical components: Jackson plays air guitar to the track recorded by Slash, while in the middle section (where the riff temporarily ceases) Culkin mimes to a rap performed by Bill Bottrell (this section ends with the line "I'm not going to spend my life being a color"). Does this paean to multiculturalism that revels in diversity as an assemblage of totalized essences, and resembles nothing so much as a United Colors of Benetton ad, reveal Michael Jackson to be a musical archaeologist? Never underestimate the King of Pop.

Notes

1. Michel de Certeau, *The Practice of Everyday Life* (Berkeley: University of California Press, 1984), 79.

2. Simon Frith concludes his discussion of music and the experience of time by arguing for the ability of music to focus our attention on the present moment. *Performing Rites: On the Value of Popular Music* (Cambridge, Mass.: Harvard University Press, 1996), 157. See Jonathan Kramer, *The Time of Music* (New York: Schirmer Books, 1988), for an extended study of the relationship between music and the experience of time.

3. This train of associations illustrates what can be understood as the intensely connotative quality of listening/hearing music, especially "song" with its multiple semiotic axes. Even this brief excerpt of "It's Time" contains another verbal phrase, "concludes when this cigarette ends," that sparks off another chain of associations, in this case leading to songs such as "A Good Year for the Roses" and "These Foolish Things" in which discarded cigarettes evoke dying relationships or absent loved ones. For more on connotative processes in popular music, see Philip Tagg, *Kojak: 50 Seconds of Television Music; To-*

wards the Analysis of Affect in Popular Music (Göteborg: Musickvetenskapliga institutionen vid Göteborgs universitet, 1979); Philip Tagg, *Fernando the Flute* (Liverpool: Institute of Popular Music, University of Liverpool, 1991); Philip Tagg and Bob Clarida, *Ten Little Title Tunes: Towards a Musicology of the Mass Media* (New York: Mass Media Music Scholar's Press, 2003); and for an overview of semiotic processes in popular music in general, see Richard Middleton, *Studying Popular Music* (Milton Keynes: Open University Press, 1990), 172–246.

4. In fact, I would argue that the deviations from the doo-wop progression in "It's Time" do contribute, in good functional-harmonic fashion, to the impact of the "big E chord" by delaying resolution of the harmonic-melodic motion of the song in order to heighten tension.

5. Due to the capacity of this musical gesture to elicit corresponding physical movements (especially among guitarists—see Frith, *Performing Rites*, 141–42), its meaning could arguably lie in the realm of "primary signification" as well as in the field of connotations explored here (see Middleton, *Studying Popular Music*, 224–27, 264–67; and Charles Keil, "Motion and Feeling through Music," in *Music Grooves*, ed. Charles Keil and Steven Feld (Chicago: University of Chicago Press, [1966] 1994), 53–76.

6. The pleasures of the E chord are also illustrated by a scene in the middle of *School of Rock* (2003), in which Jack Black teaches one of his students, a solemn classical guitarist, how to play an E chord, "rock" style.

7. The term "chord of nature" has been used by theorists of Western art music such as Jean-Philippe Rameau and Heinrich Schenker in reference to the major triad; both theorists used the overtone series to support this claim. The overtone series has also been pressed into the service of other systems to support claims of naturalness, as in, for example, the creation of a forty-three-note scale by the twentieth-century composer Harry Partch. See also Robert Palmer's discussion of the impact of guitar overtones, amplifier distortion and reverb, and recording studio effects on the history of rock and roll, "The Church of the Sonic Guitar," *South Atlantic Quarterly* 90, no. 4 (fall 1991): 649–73.

8. Another motivating factor was undoubtedly that it places Dylan's voice in a slightly higher register, making it easier for his voice to "cut through" the amplified accompaniment.

9. The idea that lyrics refer to the "human universe" evoked by the music comes from Dave Laing, *The Sound of Our Time* (London: Quadrange, 1969), 99 (quoted in Middleton, *Studying Popular Music*, 228). I am aware that, strictly speaking in music-theoretical terms, the use of A resolving to G-sharp in an

E-major chord may not always be a "suspension." I am here merging music-theoretical terminology with the guitarists' vernacular use of the term as would be typically learned through reading chord symbols, although I will note that in all of these examples, strong-weak rhythmic placement of the A and G-sharp mimics the pattern of the suspension/appoggiatura in functional tonal music.

10. The suspension/appoggiatura also has connotative properties in Western art music in the period ca. 1600–1900, where it is frequently used to evoke longing/yearning or, to use a contextually appropriate term, *sehnsucht*.

11. An unproblematic evocation of the concept of genre certainly risks presenting the popular musical field as a static, spatialized arrangement, with different kinds of music clearly demarcated from one another. The most thorough-going problematization of the concept of genre may be found in Jacques Derrida, "The Law of Genre," in *On Narrative*, ed. W. J. T. Mitchell (Chicago: University of Chicago Press, 1980), 51–77. For work that argues for a carefully qualified use of genre in relation to popular music, see Franco Fabbri, "A Theory of Musical Genres: Two Applications," in *Popular Music Perspectives*, ed. David Horn and Philip Tagg (Göteborg: IASPM, 1982), 52–81; Frith, *Performing Rites*; Keith Negus, *Music Genres and Corporate Cultures* (London: Routledge, 1999); Jason Toynbee, *Making Popular Music: Musicians, Creativity and Institutions* (London: Arnold, 2000); David Brackett, "(In Search of) Musical Meaning: Genres, Categories, and Crossover," in *Popular Music Studies: International Perspectives*, ed. David Hesmondhalgh and Keith Negus (London: Arnold, and New York: Oxford University Press, 2002), 65–83; and David Brackett, "Questions of Genre in Black Popular Music," *Black Music Research Journal* 25, no. 1 (2005): 65–84.

12. See Palmer, "Church of the Sonic Guitar," for a discussion of many other blues-based examples from the 1950s and 1960s.

13. I want to stress here the difference between "folk-rock" and "folk," which, even in its late-1950s, early-1960s guise as the "urban folk revival" was remarkably more inclusive in terms of race and gender; this held true for the performers associated with it as well as its more widespread social connotations. Folk-rock, and hence rock, succeeded in presenting itself as an anti-mass mass form that followed in the footsteps of the urban folk revival, but with the important addition of a modernist "art for art's sake" mode of "authenticity." See Keir Keightley, "Reconsidering Rock," in *The Cambridge Companion to Pop and Rock*, ed. Simon Frith, Will Straw, and John Street (Cambridge: Cambridge University Press, 2002), 109–42.

14. By invoking "whiteness" in this context, I am not referring to a racial essence but rather the way in which a genre would have been likely to be associated

with a social group identified as "white" at a particular historical conjuncture; i.e., "whiteness" becomes meaningful as a tendency within a field of social relationships that is reconstituted from moment to moment. I have tackled this issue at greater length elsewhere; see Brackett, "(In Search of) Musical Meaning," "What a Difference a Name Makes: Two Instances of African-American Music," in *The Cultural Study of Music: A Critical Introduction*, ed. Martin Clayton, Richard Middleton, and Trevor Herbert (New York: Routledge, 2003), 238–50, and "Questions of Genre in Black Popular Music." Bernard Gendron succinctly sums up the importance of the issue of racial distinctiveness and its role in cultural accreditation in a certain strain of early rock criticism in *Between Montmartre and the Mudd Club: Popular Music and the Avant-Garde* (Chicago: University of Chicago Press, 2002), 186–87, 219–21. For more on alternative discourses of cultural accreditation, see Pierre Bourdieu, *The Field of Cultural Production: Essays on Art and Literature*, ed. Randall Johnson (New York: Columbia University Press, 1993), and, again, Gendron, *Between Montmartre and the Mudd Club*.

15. See Mikhail Bakhtin, *Speech Genres and Other Late Essays*, trans. Vern W. McGee, ed. Caryl Emerson and Michael Holquist (Austin: University of Texas Press, 1986), 60–102 (esp. 95–100), on how distinctions between genres (in this case, what Bakhtin terms "speech genres") depend on different implied audiences, what he calls "addressivity"; and see Bourdieu, *The Field of Cultural Production*, 29–73, for a discussion of how positions in the cultural field may correspond to positions in social space through variable logics of artistic prestige and economic success. By "producers," I am referring to both "producers" in the music industry sense, as well as to musicians who produce the sounds heard on recordings. To understand the expanded sense of artistic positions available to baby boomers, which was a major factor in the development of an autonomous mode of legitimation within the sphere of commercial music, it is interesting to read Tom Wolfe's account of the conflict between Phil Spector circa 1964 and the representatives of the old-guard music industry ("The First Tycoon of Teen," *The Kandy-Kolored Tangerine-Flake Streamline Baby* [New York: Farrar, Straus and Giroux, 1965], 47–61. Reprinted in David Brackett, *The Pop, Rock and Soul Reader: Histories and Debates* [New York: Oxford University Press, 2005], 111–17). A *Billboard* article from the summer of 1965 when the folk-rock boom was at its peak supports the idea of shared values between producers, consumers, and industry gatekeepers, as the producer Lou Adler notes that "many of radio's young disk jockeys have beliefs which coincide with" those of the folk-rock songwriters ("Record of Absurd Gets Serious Play," *Billboard* [August 14, 1965], 1, 57).

16. The mode of playing the electric guitar, of which the open E is an example par

excellence, suggests not only a presentation of a new type of white subjectivity but also a new form of white masculinity. By repeating gestures, assuming postures, coordinating arms, hands, and fingers—as well as head, neck, torso, and pelvis—just so, playing the guitar works to form the body. That is, by holding the guitar a certain way, making particular physical gestures in order to play certain chords and produce certain sounds, a norm is established that molds subjectivity in the course of subjecting the guitarist to an ideal physical attitude. Successive generations of guitarists will come to inhabit the corresponding way of presenting their bodies and psychic identities in the course of performance. Thus, this E-chord gesture (and the playing of other open, ringing chords on the electric guitar) can also be understood as forming not only a type of masculinized body but a mode of male subjectivity as well. Indeed, let the studious yet triumphant stance of the folk-rock guitarist be contrasted with others who would play the open E, with Pete Townshend's windmill strums of open chords standing as the limit case. See Steve Waksman, *Instruments of Desire: The Electric Guitar and the Shaping of Musical Experience* (Cambridge, Mass.: Harvard University Press, 1999) for a discussion of the interrelationship between gender and race in the self-presentation of electric guitarists such as Chuck Berry, Jimi Hendrix, and Jimmy Page. This line of thought was suggested by Mitchell Morris following the presentation of an earlier version of this essay.

Discography

Beatles. "Nowhere Man." *Rubber Soul*. Parlophone, 1965.

Byrds. "I'll Feel a Whole Lot Better." *Mr. Tambourine Man*. Columbia, 1965.

———. "Mr. Tambourine Man." *Mr. Tambourine Man*. Columbia, 1965.

———. "Turn! Turn! Turn! (To Everything There Is a Season)." *Turn! Turn! Turn!* Columbia, 1965.

Costello, Elvis. "It's Time" and "You Bowed Down." *All This Useless Beauty*. Warner, 1996.

———. "It's Time" (demo). *All This Useless Beauty*, expanded edition, re-release. Rhino, 2001.

Dion, Céline. *Falling into You*. 550 Music, 1996.

Drifters. "This Magic Moment." Atlantic, 1960. Re-released on *The Very Best of the Drifters*. Rhino, 1993.

Dylan, Bob. "I Don't Believe You." *Another Side of Bob Dylan*. Columbia, 1964.

———. "I Don't Believe You." *The Bootleg Series, Vol. 4: Bob Dylan Live 1966: The "Royal Albert Hall" Concert*. Columbia/Legacy, 1998.

Earth, Wind & Fire. *That's the Way of the World*. Columbia, 1975.

Fugees. *The Score*. Ruffhouse, 1996.

Hootie and the Blowfish. *Fairweather Johnson*. Atlantic, 1996.

Jackson, Michael. "Black or White." Epic, 1991.

John, Elton. *Captain Fantastic and the Brown Dirt Cowboy*. MCA, 1975.

Led Zeppelin. *Physical Graffiti*. Swan Song, 1975.

McGuinn, Roger. "You Bowed Down." *Back from Rio*. Arista, 1991.

Rolling Stones, The. *Exile on Main St*. Rolling Stones, 1972.

Wray, Link. "Rumble." Cadence, 1958.

Young, Neil. "Barstool Blues." *Zuma*. Reprise, 1975.

Videography

Jackson, Michael. *Video Greatest Hits: History*. Sony Music Entertainment Inc.,
1995.

Holly George-Warren

Mystery Girl
The Forgotten Artistry of Bobbie Gentry

7
She has been called the J. D. Salinger of rock and roll. The Mississippi-born singer/songwriter/guitarist/producer Bobbie Gentry is every bit as mysterious as the steamy, Delta-flavored story-song she recorded in 1967 that made her a star. Gentry never revealed what Billie Joe MacAllister threw off the Tallahatchie Bridge in her original "Ode to Billie Joe"; she has remained silent and completely out of the public eye for a quarter-century, with requests for performances, recording sessions, and interviews going unheeded. Though artists as diverse as Lucinda Williams, Rosanne Cash, Jenny Lewis, Tom Jones, Beth Orton, and Shelby Lynne sing her praises, a publicist at her former label, Capitol, doesn't even know Bobbie Gentry's gender ("nothing exists on him in our files," he responded in 2002 when asked for info on Gentry).

Gentry's self-imposed exile is all the more enigmatic in this age of second acts, revived careers, and the scramble to regain celebrity. The richly drawn characters populating Gentry songs like "Fancy" often desperately seek fame and fortune, doing whatever it takes to get it. Yet Gentry herself stepped aside from the recording business after a mere five-year run. Her very contradictions, as well as her rags-to-riches life story, make her the perfect subject for, well, a Bobbie Gentry song. Her pioneering artistry—bringing the American South to life via her masterful songwriting, particularly on her first innovative concept albums—should have made her a legend. Instead, anonymity and a handful of compilation CDs are all that exist. Her back catalog is out of print.

Roberta Lee Streeter was born in rural Chickasaw County on July 27, 1944, to Robert and Ruby Streeter, who also had a son, Robert Streeter, Jr. Bobbie Lee, as she was called, had Portuguese ancestry and was raven-haired with dark, luminous eyes. The Streeters lived a hardscrabble existence, which Gentry has only briefly touched on in interviews, letting her lyrics do her talking for her: "We didn't have electricity," she has said tersely, "and I didn't have many playthings." Her mother wanted a better life and set out for southern California, where she remarried several times. Bobbie Lee moved in with her grandparents, who also had no electricity or indoor plumbing.

Bobbie Lee was drawn to music as a child. Living in the Delta, she must have heard some blues and honky-tonk, but it was church music she credited with making the impact. "Life in the South is a very different life than in other parts of the country," she pointed out in 1971. "The church was terribly important to us. It was in the church that I learned my music. I'd teach myself to play the piano by watchin' Ginnie Sue, the pianist at the Pleasant Grove Baptist Church. Funny thing is she only played the black keys, and I'd sit up in the loft thinkin' that was the only way to play the piano." Bobbie Lee's supportive grandmother traded a milk cow for an upright piano for her granddaughter. At six, she could already play a bit by ear, picking out a tune, "Skater's Waltz," that she had heard on the radio. Soon, she wrote her first song, "My Dog Sergeant Is a Good Dog."

To go to school, she moved in with her father in Greenwood (one of the towns where the Delta blues first emerged). Then, in 1957 at thirteen, she joined her mother in Palm Springs, California. With the family fortunes somewhat improved, she continued her musical education, teaching herself guitar, banjo, bass, and vibes, while writing songs and playing occasionally at local country music clubs. Deciding she needed a stage name, she chose Bobbie Gentry, after seeing the steamy 1952 potboiler *Ruby Gentry*, directed by Texan King Vidor and starring brunette beauty Jennifer Jones as the poor white-trash seductress Ruby, Charlton Heston as her brutish paramour, and Karl Malden as her rich husband Old Man Gentry. After graduating from Palm Valley High School, Bobbie Gentry set off for nearby Las Vegas, where she found work at a casino dancing in a Folies Bergère–style revue.

Gentry's songwriting continued unabated, and she performed at clubs on her nights off. In the mid-sixties, she moved to Los Angeles to attend college, studying philosophy and eventually transferring to the Los Angeles Conservatory of Music. There she took classes in composition, music theory, and arranging. Playing acoustic guitar and singing, with a bass player and drummer to back her up, she booked gigs at a Pasadena nightspot. At some point, she hooked up with a musician named Bobby Perris, who, in exchange for her playing rhythm guitar on his recordings, engineered a twelve-song demo of her singing her own compositions and playing acoustic guitar. The future radio/TV announcer Jim McKrell happened upon a Gentry gig one night and, impressed, took her tape to his then-boss, the music publisher Larry Shayne. Shayne signed her to a publishing deal and shopped the demo to Capitol Records A&R man Kelly Gordon, a transplanted Southerner who primarily worked with R&B artists. Intrigued by Gentry's rhythmic finger-picking and sultry alto, Gordon caught one of her club performances and flipped.

Getting her signed to Capitol was no easy matter, however. Apparently, the conservative head of A&R at the label heard "Ode to Billie Joe" and thought it was about disposing an aborted fetus from the side of the bridge. Though he didn't want to give Gentry a recording contract, he finally authorized Gordon to cut a single with the singer.

Thanks to Golden Oldies radio, almost everyone in the Western world has heard Bobbie Gentry's breakthrough, signature single. Its four min-. utes and fifteen seconds tell the compelling story of a pair of Delta teenagers who share a deep dark secret that ultimately leads to the boy's suicide and the girl's lifelong bereavement. Rich details of rural farm life render "Ode" more a short story than a pop song; in fact, its literary merits were praised in a 1997 feature in the *Oxford American* and its lyrics have been quoted by such novelists as Ian Frazier and Larry McMurtry. In a 2002 essay for salon.com on Italians' stoicism toward death, the humanities professor and author Camille Paglia used "Ode" to make her point: "Country people are notoriously blunt and unsentimental about accidents and disasters," she wrote, "which traumatize today's squeamish, overprotected middle-class professionals. Bobbie Gentry's 1967 hit song, 'Ode to Billie Joe,' preserves something of that premodern flavor when a crusty farmer, indifferent to his daughter's feelings, reacts to the news of a young man's fatal plunge off a bridge by remarking, 'Well, Billie Joe never had a lick of sense. Pass the biscuits, please.' "

Just as striking as the song's unresolved denouement were its spare guitar lines juxtaposed against atmospheric cellos and violin arrangements, as well as the vocalist's sensual, Southern-flavored singing and conversational tone. Originally, "Ode" had been considered something of a throwaway. Gordon's first choice for a single was the bluesy swamp-rocker "Mississippi Delta," with its driving, percussive guitar and Gentry's sing-songy spellout—M I double S I double S I double P I—inspired, she later explained, by an old Delta voodoo hex. (The Alabama-born country-soul singer Shelby Lynne covered the song in the 1990s.) According to studio records, "Mississippi Delta" was the A-side of a 45 issued in July 1967, with "Ode" the flip.

The composer/arranger/conductor/producer Jimmie Haskell had already been in the business for seven years, playing accordion on the Elvis Presley soundtrack *GI Blues,* applying his classical training to string arrangements for Capitol Records, including Rosemary Clooney, and working with the legendary producer Nik Venet on projects ranging from Greek bouzouki music to the Lettermen. Gordon, he remembered in a recent interview,

> introduced me to Bobbie Gentry and played me something called "Mississippi Delta." Had that become the A-side, she would have been known as a gravel-voiced rock & roller. He went through a bunch of tunes for the B-side, where she just sat on a stool and played her guitar, and we came to this one called "Ode to Billie Joe." I said, "What do you want me to do with it?" He said, "Anything. Just put some strings on it so we won't be embarrassed." I said OK. Up to that point I'd been used to being given demonstration recordings in which the entire ideas were present on the records, and they said to just expand the demo. In this case, there was no demo of strings, nothing. He said, "No one will ever hear it anyway."
>
> The song sounded to me like a movie—those wonderful lyrics. I had a very small group of strings—it was serendipity that we had two cellos and four violins. I decided to make one of the cellos a bass. Of course,

since a cello bass would've become monotonous playing a standard bass line, I thought, What can I write that would fit her guitar playing? She played a five-string Martin, fingerpicking. I made the bassline do the least amount of notes that I could write for a cello bass and still have it sound interesting—five notes every four bars. I had the cello player play pizzicato all the way through. The other cello I made a normal cello play with a bow. Then I thought, This is a long song, so I better not have the strings play all the way through. So they play on the intro, then they don't play for an entire minute, except the bass cello. Then I began playing figures that related to the lyrics. I was branching out in my own head for the first time, creating something that I liked because no one was ever gonna hear it and I wouldn't have to worry about what I wrote. Bobbie was rather quiet, observing everything. I seem to recall her making only one comment during the entire recording.

Though Haskell received only $250 for his contribution to "Ode," he says his work on the song has continued to pay off, bringing him such clients as k.d. lang and Sheryl Crow, who specifically requested his "Ode" sound for tracks on their albums *Drag* (1997) and *The Globe Sessions* (1998), respectively. An "Ode" legend that has persisted over the years is that the original song ran over seven minutes and gave all clues necessary to draw conclusions about what got flung from the bridge and why Billie Joe jumped. Haskell says he has only ever heard the version he arranged, however, and neither Gordon nor Gentry ever referred to a longer one.

Released in August 1967, "Ode" sold 750,000 copies its first week, a phenomenal achievement in 1967 for an unknown with no advance hype or MTV to push it (though a promotional "Ode" video was later produced by Capitol, which starred the radiant, barefoot, and blue-jean clad Gentry lip-synching on a bridge). The single knocked "All You Need Is Love" out of *Billboard*'s Number One spot, where it lodged for a solid month, before being overthrown by another Southern newcomer, Alex Chilton's Box Tops and their first hit, "The Letter." The singer-songwriter Rosanne Cash, who was twelve that summer, remembers "long, serious conversations with people about what exactly was thrown from the bridge. We were all very opinionated about that." Cash is still a fan. "[Gentry's] images are as stark as Paul Strand photos—her voice as a writer is so real. And her voice reminds me of Sophia Loren's body—all woman, dark, curvy, seductive, vulnerable."

Gentry's own exotic looks didn't hurt her popular appeal. "Her path was stunningly swift: from records to television to films to worldwide fame," Capitol Records reported. She performed the number on such programs as *The Smothers Brothers Comedy Hour,* and virtually every major news magazine did a feature on her. *Mademoiselle* gave her the M'lle. Award as one of the "outstanding women of the year." The Welsh singer Tom Jones recalls the first time he caught Gentry on the telly. "I thought 'Ode to Billie Joe' was a fantastic song to start with, and then I saw her do it on *Top of the Pops* in England, and she looked like a model! I thought, Christ! Looka this! She's looking as good as she's singing!"

Across the pond in Australia, the future founder of the punk pioneers the Saints was also captivated: "I grew up in a semi-rural working-class area and there was a fair bit of country music on the radio at the time, but 'Ode' really stood out," the singer/songwriter/guitarist Ed Kueppers recalls. "Though it wasn't a local song, it felt like the whole thing could have taken place down the road from me. But by making the mundane magical, it transcended the more standard, descriptive country songs. It reeked of all the unknown and mysterious things that surround you in childhood, with its references to hot weather, preachers, muddy river banks, and adult conversations that you're not supposed to be listening to and only get half the meaning of." Even Bob Dylan, sequestered with the Band at Big Pink, in West Saugerties, New York, got caught up in "Ode." The basement tapes were rolling when Dylan ad-libbed his hysterical parody of the song's conversational tone and attention to the mundane details of life: "After a while we took in the clothes / nobody said very much / just some old wild shirts and a couple pair of pants / which nobody really wanted to touch / Mama come in and picked up a book / An' Papa asked her what it was / Someone else asked, "what do you care?" / Papa said, 'Well, just because.'" Originally entitled "The Answer to Ode," "The Clothesline Saga" was released on *The Basement Tapes* in 1975, around the same time that a film version of the song went into production.

When probed, during countless interviews, about the song's mysteries, Gentry was never forthcoming. Years later, she wrote that "these questions are of secondary importance in my mind. The story of Billie Joe has two more interesting underlying themes. First, the illustration of a group of people's reactions to the life and death of Billie Joe, and its subsequent effect on their lives is made. Second, the obvious gap between the girl and her mother is shown when both women experience a common loss (first Billie Joe and later Papa), and yet Mama and the girl are unable to recognize their mutual loss or share their grief."

In the midst of all the hoopla, Gentry, Gordon, and Haskell raced back into the studio to capitalize on the success of "Ode to Billie Joe." Since Gentry had plenty of original material, seven of her compositions joined "Ode" and "Mississippi," along with a sultry cover of the P. J. Proby hit "Niki Hoeky," to make her debut album, *Ode to Billie Joe*. Recorded in a heartbeat and released in September, *Ode to Billie Joe* furthered Gentry's vivid recollections of her verdant homeland. With their intimate, autobiographical details, rich descriptions, and Southern colloquialisms, "Chickasaw County Child," "Lazy Willie," "Sunday Best," and "Papa, Won't You Let Me Go to Town with You" are sonically and lyrically of a piece with "Ode" and "Mississippi Delta," making the album feel more like a carefully planned concept work, in the vein of *Sgt. Pepper's*, than a thrown-together batch of numbers to capitalize on a hit. "Bugs" is a laundry list of every kind of pesky varmint swarming the Delta, with lifelike skeeter sounds courtesy of Haskell's strings. Gentry's haunting ballad "I Saw an Angel Die," with its bluesy harmonica, conjures the torrid drama and longing of an illicit, doomed love affair.

A Number One album on the pop charts and multiple Grammy winner, *Ode* also topped the country market, and Gentry was asked to co-host the first ever Country Music Awards. Her merging of a soulful pop and country sound, which attracted a large contingent of both C&W and pop listeners, reflected a specific moment: other Grammys that year went to Glen Campbell, Aretha Franklin, Johnny Cash and June Carter, Tammy Wynette, Sam and Dave, *Sgt. Pepper's*, and the 5th Dimension's "Up Up and Away," which won record and song of the year for the band and Jimmy Webb. But Gentry's impact also foretold the success of a blended pop-blues-country style that would explode in popularity three-plus decades later in artists ranging from Wynonna to Shania Twain to Gretchen Wilson. But because Gentry did not fit strictly into any one of these formats—pop, country, or blues—and zigzagged sonically between them, her place in music history has been largely ignored and/or forgotten. The fact that her work and influence still reverberate within the music of other singular artists who, too, cannot be categorized, such as Rilo Kiley's Jenny Lewis and the singer-songwriter Lucinda Williams, is further validation of Gentry's pioneering oeuvre.

With all this success behind them, the *Ode* team returned to the studio in early 1968, enlisting the horn arranger Shorty Rogers. One of the unsung masterpieces of the 1960s, *The Delta Sweete* took *Ode to Billie Joe* one step further. This time, no doubt about it, it was a full-blown concept album—the tracks seguing with no space between the grooves. Interspersed with Gentry originals are classics drawn from among the Deep South's best: a slinky version of Jimmy Reed's "Big Boss Man," punctuated by bluesy harmonica and funky bass; a sly twist on Mose Allison's "Parchman Farm"; a humid take on John D. Loudermilk's "Tobacco Road"; and a raucous tomboy approach to Doug Kershaw's "Louisiana Man." Gentry's own songs veer from the proto-rap numbers "Reunion" (a kind of sequel to "Papa Let Me Go to Town with You") and "Sermon" to the lushly baroque "Penduli Pendulum," "Jessye Lisabeth," "Refractions," and "Courtyard." The latter four chamber-pop masterpieces all exude a foreboding sense of tragedy and loss, with hints of mysticism amid the poetry of the lyrics. Gentry is at her most sensual on "Mornin' Glory," sounding as if she recorded the song while sprawled across rumpled satin sheets.

Her own personal life had merged with the professional: Kelly Gordon —about six years Gentry's senior—had fallen madly in love with his discovery, leaving his wife and children for her. The two lived together for a while, but with Gentry constantly traveling, the relationship gradually disintegrated. (Tragically, Gordon died of cancer some six years later at age thirty-five; near the end of his life, according to Haskell, he moved into Gentry's guest house, where she cared for him until his death.)

Delta Sweete is nearly always cited as an influence by Gentry acolytes, one of whom, the Australian singer-songwriter Clare Moore, singles out the album's murder ballad "Parchman Farm," which she herself has recorded:

> The arrangements on *Delta Sweete* are really fantastic—I love the string part that comes in at the end of "Parchman Farm." It creates an eerie soundscape by which you can digest the last [surprising] line of the song. And the fact that the singer is a woman changes the song's meaning completely. When I listen to guys singing it, it reminds me of Johnny Cash's "Cocaine Blues" on *Live at San Quentin.* All the inmates whoop and holler when he sings the line, "I shot that fat bitch down!"—possibly explaining why some of them are incarcerated in the first place! The male version of "Parchman Farm" seems like an hom-

age to the hard-done-by gunman. In *her* version, I imagine that Bobbie is the dead wife, stopping to systematically catalogue the bastard's present and potential suffering, before heading on up to heaven for a bit of bloody peace!

Though *Delta Sweete* has since gained a cult following among such musicians as Moore and Lucinda Williams, the album flopped in 1968. Its swamp-rocking single, "Okolona River Bottom Band" (featuring an uncredited male voice with a Delta drawl similar to the one on "Bugs"), only chugged up to Number 54.

Unbowed, Gentry gave the Delta another shot on her follow-up, *Local Gentry*. Recorded later that year, the album was again produced by Gordon with horn arrangements by Rogers, minus Haskell. Continuing in the Mississippi vein are the hothouse flower "Sweet Peony," good-timey "Papa's Medicine Show," and down-home "Ace Insurance Man" (with spoken vocals by her uncredited Delta man again). Gentry's baroque side came through with the mordant "Casket Vignette," whose protagonist is a coffin salesman callously fast-talking a bereaved fiancé, and the brutally tragic waltz "Recollection." Gentry's co-write with Gordon, "Sittin' Pretty," slides back and forth between cheesy pop and jazzy R&B; the rest of the album is filled with Beatles covers. Again, no chart action.

Around this time, someone got the idea to put Gentry in the studio with Capitol's hot new male star, Glen Campbell, another big Grammy winner in 1968 via "Gentle on My Mind" and "By the Time I Get to Phoenix." Previously, Campbell had co-headlined a ten-date tour with Gentry, and she'd guested on his hit TV show, *The Glen Campbell Goodtime Hour*. Campbell says that during the recording sessions (co-produced by Gordon and Campbell's producer Al DeLory), Gentry was "loose as a goose. She wasn't uptight. She was very easy to work with. I came up with some [songs], she came up with some. We sang things we wanted to sing." Their album together, *Bobbie Gentry and Glen Campbell*, leaned toward a country-flavored easy-listening sound, with "Mornin' Glory" turned into a cheery his 'n her duet, which snuck into the lower rungs of the pop singles chart. It was the Gentry-Campbell take on the Everly Brothers, however, that ignited the public's imagination: "Let It Be Me" and "All I Have to Do Is Dream" went Top 15 on the country charts, and Top 40 on pop, with the album cruising to Number One on the country chart.

Campbell recalls that Gentry and Gordon had recently split up when the duo got together but has denied that he and Gentry were an item—a rumor at the time. Their album liner notes didn't dissuade speculation about their offstage chemistry, raving, "Some of the world's treasures have resulted from the bringing together of things that belong together—like Bobbie Gentry and Glen Campbell, as it turns out. Looking back, it's hard for anyone to say, but maybe they should have begun as a team. They have the affinity, one for the other, that's unusually rare." In his 1994 autobiography, *Rhinestone Cowboy*, Campbell flatly states, "I was never in love with her, nor she with me," in response to press reports of an affair. His then-wife, Billie, was reportedly insanely jealous of Gentry. And who could blame her? According to Jimmie Haskell, "The first thing men noticed about her were her legs—the most amazing legs in the world! When you got to talking to her, there was this magnetism, this warmth. She exuded female attraction."

Surely, Gentry's sex appeal became both a blessing and a curse in her attempts to establish herself as a serious artist in control of her career. Increasingly, her television appearances relegated her to dancing around in tight-fitting pantsuits and minis, emphasizing her below-the-belt attributes. Like her U.K. soul-singing peer, Dusty Springfield, Gentry's over-the-top image (including luscious false eyelashes and pancake makeup) was embraced by a large gay audience, including drag queens. The effect on her musical legacy has been to marginalize her work—except for *that* song—rather than to include her in the echelons of such rock-identified singer-songwriters as Joni Mitchell.

Gentry's work with Campbell particularly pushed her into the realm of "entertainment," rekindling her stardom, primarily in the country music field and overseas. She scored another U.K. hit from her next release, 1969's *Touch 'Em with Love,* which sank without a trace in the States. Bacharach-David's "I'll Never Fall in Love Again," which reached Number One in the United Kingdom, exemplified the kind of 5th Dimension/Dionne Warwick–style material that predominated on the album. She cut *Touch 'Em* in Nashville, with a new producer, Kelso Hurston. The album's highlight, the rousing title track, was written by John Hurley, the author of the Springfield "Son of a Preacher Man," which Gentry also covers here. Only two Gentry compositions appear, the gospel-tinged "Glory Hallelujah, How They'll Sing" and the forlorn "Seasons Come, Seasons

Go." Her U.K. smash netted her a BBC television show, which could be seen internationally, boosting both her and Campbell's overseas profile, he recalls. "Television really kicked things off for both of us," he says. "I did her [TV show] in England . . . and that was shown all over the world—Australia, New Zealand, Hong-Kong, everywhere . . . I started selling records like crazy in Europe and Asia, and she did too—off the strength of that TV show." According to the program's producer, Stanley Dorfman, the show's MOR pop flavor was primarily Gentry's doing: "She wrote the show," he told the BBC in 2005. "She knew what she wanted."

Back in the States, Gentry headlined the Vegas/Reno casino circuit. Performing at glitzy Harrah's, in Reno, she met its owner, the multi-millionaire car collector Bill Harrah. In 1969, after a brief courtship, the two shocked their friends by marrying; Gentry was twenty-five, Harrah was fifty-eight (it was his fourth nuptials, and Gentry's first). The marriage lasted only about ten weeks, falling apart after Gentry returned to London to perform, according to Harrah's former wife Scherry Harrah (who remained close to her ex, after marrying and divorcing him twice before he wed Bobbie): "[Bobbie] was supposed to be appearing at the Queen's Theater in London and Tom Jones was on the same bill. She got up about five or six o'clock in the morning for rehearsal, and she thought Bill would stay in bed, but he went down and sat in the back of the the-ater and found out that what they were doing on the stage was *not* in the script."

Apparently, Gentry made out quite well financially from the divorce. And for someone whose early life was fraught with deprivation, financial security must have been a longtime goal. Haskell recalls:

> She told me one time that her mother had been married several times and that one of those times was to a wealthy man and that the other times they were not wealthy, and she said, "Rich is better than poor." She said, "*I'm* gonna be rich." I'm quite sure she handled her money very carefully. One time, she had me conduct the Memphis Symphony when she was doing a Pops concert. . . . After the concert, which went very well, I met her mother and her grandmother, which was de-lightful. They were lovely people. The grandmother said, "Bobbie, Mr. Haskell is such a gentleman. I thought he was excellent." And Bobbie said, "He should be for what I'm paying him!" She was always con-cerned about money.

Gentry's next musical move was to go to Muscle Shoals, Alabama, to work at Fame Studios, with the producer Rick Hall, where Aretha Franklin had cut the initial recordings for her Atlantic Records breakthrough, 1967's *I Never Loved a Man the Way I Loved You*. Hall called on Haskell to do the string arrangements. When he arrived at the rural studio, Bobbie "was wearing a little fur jacket," Haskell remembers, "and I said, 'Well, Bobbie, I see being married to Bill Harrah has done you very well. That's a nice jacket.' And she said, 'I paid for this with my own money!'"

The album, *Fancy,* yielded a title track story song nearly as powerful as "Ode." Born poor white trash, beautiful Fancy is groomed as a hooker by her sickly, impoverished mom. She lands a slew of wealthy catches, ending up in a mansion, with no shame, no regrets. Gentry's sharply drawn lyrics are backed by Muscle Shoals' most soulful players. The fabulous cover portrait (rumored to have been painted by Gentry, it's uncredited on the record sleeve) depicts the singer in full Fancy regalia. The rest of the album consists of easy-listenin' covers plus a pair of blue-eyed soul numbers: a humid take on Leon Russell's "Delta Man" and a saucy version of Hall's "Find 'Em, Fool 'Em, and Forget 'Em" (which was remade in the early 1980s by the LA punk band the Mentors into "Find 'Em, Feel 'Em, Fuck 'Em, Forget 'Em"). An enchanting folk-rock track, James Taylor's "Something in the Way He Moves," features Gentry's softest singing. Hall also produced a superb, non-LP single, "Apartment 21," a kind of confessional, singer-songwriter–style number that barely slipped into the Top 100. "Fancy" fared nicely, though, hitting Number 31 pop. (After the song went Top Ten country for Reba McEntire in 1990, and was later used in a high-profile, Reba-endorsed chips commercial, it has become associated primarily with her, resulting in its being frequently performed by wobbly-voiced amateurs at country shindigs and karaoke bars who usually introduce it with, "Here's my favorite Reba song . . .").

The early 1970s found Gentry traveling constantly between England, doing BBC specials along with hosting a U.S. Armed Forces radio show, and Vegas, where she headlined the glamorous Crystal Room at the Desert Inn. Eventually moving to an exclusive gated community in the desert, she signed on to a high-class nightclub revue for a million-dollar paycheck. She proudly described her latest "baby" to a journalist at the time: "I write and arrange all the music, design the costumes, do the choreography, the whole thing. I'm completely responsible for it. It's totally my own

Fig. 1. Sheet music for Bobbie Gentry's "Fancy," published by Larry Shayne Music, Inc., 1970. COLLECTION OF HOLLY GEORGE-WARREN.

from inception to the performance. Besides that, I produce my own records. I originally produced 'Ode to Billie Joe,' and most of the others, but a woman doesn't stand much chance in a recording studio. A staff producer's name was nearly always put on the record."

Gentry finally did get the producer credit on 1972's *Patchwork*, her final recording for Capitol. An eclectic return, all twelve tracks are Gentry originals, including the country and western–style "Billy the Kid" (complete with whistling and tongue clucking), the folky buddy song "Benjamin," the Latin-tinged weeper "Beverly," and the movie-soundtrack-like "Marigolds & Tangerines." For the first time, Gentry's lyrics—all handwritten—were included in the album's packaging (again, uncredited and by the same artist who painted *Fancy*'s cover), with the singer wearing a long, gypsy-style patchwork skirt. Though a rather upbeat album, its two most striking songs exude a jaded ennui: the breezy "Number One Fan" and the introspective "Looking In." On the former, about an ardent admirer, Gentry glibly sings the somewhat ambiguous line "God bless you and keep you, from your Number One Fan." "Looking In," conversely, projects the exhausted artist's point of view, with Gentry, in her most velvety voice, purring, "So I spend my days thinkin' up new ways / To do the same old thing / The seasons come and go without a name / And I spend my nights at the bright spotlights / Wishin' I could let the people know / There's no chance to win or lose without the game."

Though "Number One Fan" and "Looking In" sounded as if Gentry were fed up with the Vegas lifestyle, she had found camaraderie there. Tom Jones remembers Vegas as where he really got to know her, when he, Gentry, and Elvis Presley would congregate following their nightclub appearances. "Elvis would be at the Hilton, I would be at Caesar's Palace, and she would be performing somewhere, and we would get together at night at Elvis' suite at the Hilton," Jones vividly recalls. "He'd always get his backing singers into his suite with an electric piano and we would sing. Bobbie was one of the few other people who were invited into that thing. We'd mostly sing gospel stuff. She was great looking, fantastic, outspoken—but she was more like one of the guys, a star in her own right. She and Elvis seemed to get on well together. She would be up all night with us."

Vegas, though, seems to be where the creative energy and life got sapped out of Gentry (a fate, of course, which also befell the King). Only a minimum of songs have surfaced since the release of *Patchwork* (sadly and unjustly another flop). In 1974, she composed and sang a blue-eyed soul shuffle for the soundtrack of *Macon County Line* (starring Leif Garrett and Max Baer, Jr.). That same year, she hosted a pilot for a variety show, *Bobbie Gentry's Happiness,* which wasn't picked up. Then, she traveled home to the set of *Ode to Billy* [sic] *Joe,* directed by Baer, Jr., and starring Robby Benson as Billy Joe and Glynnis O'Connor as his girlfriend (named Bobbie Lee). The movie's ad slogan promised "What the song didn't tell you the movie will!" The melodramatic plot revealed that a drunken Billy Joe had been raped by an older man and, suffering from shame and guilt, was unable to consummate his love for his longtime girlfriend Bobbie Lee. (Bobbie Lee threw her favorite rag doll off the Tallahatchie Bridge to demonstrate to Billy Joe that she was ready to lose her virginity.) Eventually, the stricken Billy Joe leaps from the bridge. Gentry's hit song reentered the charts upon the film's release, as did a new version recorded for the movie.

Gentry's life changed again when, on October 15, 1975, she married the singer/songwriter/guitarist (and former Gram Parsons bandmate) Jim "Spiders and Snakes" Stafford. The couple's stormy union produced a son, Tyler. Stafford, who has since remarried and had a family, refuses to discuss his ex-wife (even acquaintances like Glen Campbell and Wanda Jackson are surprised to hear the two were once married). Stafford's Web site, which promotes his shows at his own theater in Branson, Missouri, briefly mentions Gentry in his official biography: "By now a minor celebrity, Jim hosted a network summer variety show replacement series [in 1975], *The Jim Stafford Show,* . . . which . . . also gave him a chance to showcase his exceptional ability as a guitar player. This was also where he met and married Bobbie Gentry. . . . In 1980, following a divorce from singer Bobbie Gentry, Jim appeared in Clint Eastwood's *Any Which Way You Can.*"

Since then, Gentry has completely dropped out of sight, apparently moving to different parts of the country depending on her son's educational needs. She spent much of the 1990s in Georgia, living on the exclusive resort Skidaway Island, remarried to a wealthy golfer, while Tyler went to school nearby. In recent years, she has returned to the Los Angeles area, where Tyler attended college. All requests for interviews, recordings, and performances have been rebuffed, though Haskell says she asked him in the late nineties to write arrangements for a song she was recording. (Unfortunately, Haskell was unable to connect with her at the time and hasn't heard from her since.) Another record executive visited Gentry and even convinced her to play her Martin guitar for him, but nothing came of his offer to record her.

There are frequent postings on the Bobbie Gentry website chat board from various relatives in Mississippi and California reminiscing and/or pleading with her to get in touch:

I grew up going to Mississippi family reunions at the farm that Bobbie (Roberta Streeter) grew up [on]. Always a cool cousin that'll sing to the family! Jim Stafford was there at the last one I went to.—Brad Streeter

She is my aunt. She does not want her whereabouts known. She does not sing anymore and is in seclusion.—Cindy Lu Streeter Thomas

Bobbie is my second cousin, her mother is first cousins with my father. Her mother's maiden name was Ruby Bullington. Heard all the great stories about her when I was growing up as well. Never got a chance to actually meet her.—Laura

Bobbie is living in West Hollywood, Ca. She is a very private person. She will never perform again.—Vegas

Bobbie is my cousin that I grew up adoring and hoping that I would grow up to be just like her. Her mother, Ruby, was my favorite aunt. We last saw Bobbie right after her mother died years ago. She disappeared and we never heard another word from her. That really hurts. I feel as though none of her family here in Palm Springs ever meant anything to her. I wish we knew the reason. We all love and care about her.—Laurie Shipman

My mother is Carol Ann Grantham from Greenwood, Mississippi. If Bobbie ever reads this site, my mother hopes you are doing well. She still talks about that plaid hand-me-down coat that she got from you.—Tracy

It is obvious that many of you have honest and genuine concerns regarding Bobbie's well being and her whereabouts. Here is what I believe I can safely post without giving too much away: Bobbie lives on the upscale side of a relatively small community in Los Angeles County. She seems to live an average lifestyle . . . and appears to be perfectly content with her existence. She is neither in seclusion, nor in hiding, or anything like that. Occasionally I see her (usually driving her car), and from what I can determine, she is still very attractive. She is still slim, and she still has that infectious grin of hers. Her movements are quick and easy, which leads me to believe that she is in excellent health. I haven't talked to her. In fact, I will never approach her in person unless it is in a setting where politeness would dictate to exchange a few friendly words of mutual recognition. Bobbie clearly wants to distance herself from her past—her days in Palm Springs as well as her time in show business, and I think that I understand her reasons for doing so. In closing, there is no need to worry about Bobbie. Keep your postings coming—I'm sort of sure that she reads this site and believe me, she is doing very well.—Roger

In the meantime, Gentry's work has been resurrected by such acolytes as Shelby Lynne, Beth Orton, whose homage, "Bobby [sic] Gentry," appeared on *The Other Side of Daybreak* (2003), and Lucinda Williams, who has been outspoken about Gentry's influence. On CMT television, during her *Crossroads* concert with Elvis Costello in 2001, Williams told him why she's such a fan: "It was really original stuff, the stuff she was doing. She was writing her own songs. She was one of the first female singers . . . who sang in a lower register. I felt real comfortable with that, because before that I was listening to singers like Judy Collins, Joni Mitchell, and Joan Baez. They all had these beautiful high voices. Then here comes Bobbie Gentry, and she had this lower, kind of smoky voice. It was kind of country, but it wasn't typical country. It was a blend. I just really identified with it." For *Rolling Stone*'s 2003 issue devoted to women musicians, Williams wrote, " 'Ode to Billie Joe' fit right into this Southern Gothic tradition. It had that mystery, that darkness. It was a different voice, a blend of blues and country and folk that was totally unique. It was swampy, smoky, whiskey-stained and low."

Perhaps, one day, Gentry will be coaxed out of retirement. If she is, will she pursue the deep, soulful artistry of her early albums, or choose the glitzy Vegas entertainment route? Regardless, with such artists as Williams, Orton, and Lynne singing her praises, Gentry's pioneering body of work may become known to more than just a small following of fans. For now, every time "Ode to Billie Joe" comes on the radio, the mystery lingers.

Franklin Bruno

"Is That All There Is?" and the
Uses of Disenchantment

8 In 1896, the twenty-one-year-old Thomas Mann completed his first significant piece of fiction, having abandoned his ambitions toward lyric poetry not long before.
"Enttäuschung," later translated into English as "Disillusionment," is more a sketch than a story, not far removed
in manner and length from the works of E. T. A. Hoff-
man or Robert Walser. At a Venice café, the young narrator notices a stranger, whom he initially mistakes for an
Englishman, aimlessly pacing the Piazza San Marco. After a few evenings of eyeing one another, this "extraordinary man" pours out his life story, without prompting, to
the narrator. He is a clergyman's son whose first inkling
of the chasm between reality and the "pulpit rhetoric" of
his upbringing comes when his family's house catches
fire. " 'So this,' I thought, 'is a fire. This is what it is like to
have the house on fire. Is this all there is to it?' "

Other disappointments follow, among them the adolescent realization that "the dry agonies of baffled lust"
are nothing compared to the torturous thought: "So this
is the greatest pain we can suffer. Well, and what then—is
this all?" He concludes: "So I dream and wait for death.
Ah, how well I know it already, death, that last disappointment! At my last moment I shall be saying to myself: 'So this is the great experience—well, and what of it?
What is it after all?' "

In 1996, Polly Jean Harvey told substantially the same tale, minus Mann's framing device, on *Dance Hall at Louse Point,* her duo album with the producer John Parish, over Parish's guitar and Mick Harvey's funereal organ pads. Details have changed: the singer is now carried from the burning house by her father, and a circus, absent from Mann's version, is now among the things from which "there was something missing." But the story's recurring question, which now leads to a sung refrain, remains:

> Is that all there is?
> Is that all there is?
> If that's all there is, my friends
> Let's keep dancing
> Let's break out the booze
> And have a ball
> If that's all . . . there is.

Of course, a great deal happened in between. In particular, Peggy Lee recorded Jerry Leiber and Mike Stoller's "Is That All There Is?" in an arrangement by the young Randy Newman. Released in September 1969, several months after the recording, the single became a left-field hit, topping *Billboard*'s recently introduced Adult Contemporary chart—then called "Easy Listening"—for October 18 and 25, and peaking at Number 11 on the Hot 100 for November 5, some evidence of its cross-generational appeal. It's not as though this was a bad week for pop: though the 5th Dimension's "Wedding Bell Blues," at Number One, is little-remembered, numbers 2, 3, and 4 were "Come Together," "Suspicious Minds," and The Temptations' "I Can't Get Next to You." The record earned Lee a Grammy for Best Contemporary Vocal, Female, though it lost out as Record of the Year to the 5th Dimension's "Aquarius" / "Let The Sunshine In," a medley of songs from *Hair,* Broadway's answer to the Living Theater.

The resonance of "Is That All There Is?" with a mass audience argues against the now-commonplace reduction of pop history—especially that of the 1960s—to rock history. In one respect, the record's success at the time of release has an obvious, even facile, explanation, given the mixed fortunes of the left. To speak only of America: by 1969, protest movements had seemingly achieved meliorist successes in both civil rights and the effort to end direct U.S. involvement in Vietnam, with troop withdrawals beginning in July. At the same time, it must be remembered that the "Vietnamization" of the conflict was presided over by the recently inaugurated Richard Nixon, an ur-establishment figure overtly hostile to The Movement; and that the assassinations of Martin Luther King and Robert Kennedy the previous year had served as symbolic reminders that change would come at no small cost. The cultural landscape was just as shaky: August alone saw both Woodstock and the Manson Family murders. Under these circumstances, a song answering radical existential doubt with resigned hedonism might well strike a nerve.

But in provenance and genre, Lee's record had little to do with its cultural moment, at least as it is retrospectively understood. Consider the principals: a singer closely associated with big-band swing and 1950s "quality music," a pair of songwriters whose role in the transition from rhythm and blues to early rock and roll can hardly be overstated, and an orchestrator (Newman, the scion of an extended family of film composers) soon to emerge as one of the 1970s most anachronistic and unclassifiable artists. This group of people had no business coming up with an actual hit record—not at the very moment when, we're told, rock solidified its place as popular music's alpha dog, a position it occupied until the rise of hip-hop as a global music; the moment at which the counterculture, for better or worse, became *the culture*. The success of "Is That All There Is?" suggests that, as late as 1969, matters were more fluid, and that pre-rock and non-rock voices could still, on occasion, make themselves heard.

This is not to underestimate the ways that the conversation had changed. In 1957, Lee had left Decca Records for a second stint with Capitol, where she had been a flagship artist earlier in the decade. By the mid-sixties, her singles consistently made respectable Adult Contemporary showings, but she had not scored an across-the-board pop hit since 1963: Leiber and Stoller's "I'm a Woman," a distaff respelling of "I'm a Man" full of the team's customary vernacular wit. At the time of "Is That All There Is?" her previous single had been a misguided stab at Blood, Sweat, and Tears' "Spinning Wheel." Presented with "Is That All There Is?" Stoller recalls that "the label thought it was some kind of weird, uncommercial shit. This was when Capitol was selling lots of Grand Funk records. It was the last thing Peggy had in the can." It languished there until Lee bartered an appearance on *The Joey Bishop Show* for the single's release.

The late 1960s was a transitional period for the songwriters as well.

After selling their Red Bird label in 1966 and returning to freelance work, the team who had said, "We don't write songs, we write records," would from then on produce many more that they *didn't* write. They were also moving in new artistic circles, making contact with vanguard modernists in their respective fields; like the Beatles, but unlike many others who have attempted to negotiate the bridge between high and low, the team did so from a position of entrenched success on "their" side of the divide. Leiber's name pops up repeatedly in *Digressions on Some Poems by Frank O'Hara,* Joe LeSeuer's recent memoir of the New York poetry and painting scene; Stoller, meanwhile, studied with the post-serialist composer Stefan Wolpe. Completed by 1966, "Is That All There Is?" was a product of this period. Clearly ill-suited to other artists they were working with at the time, notably the Coasters (who recorded their "D.W. Washburn" for a 1968 comeback) and Brook Benton, the song was initially considered "weird, uncommercial shit" by its authors as well. Leiber says, "It was really geared to be band five, side one on an album—you know, the place you put something you don't expect to go anywhere. When it became a hit, I was surprised and wildly gratified."

Even so, it would be misleading to call "Is That All There Is?" an art song. Despite its source in Mann's high modernist text and the modest dissonance of its underlying harmonies, it uses language that anyone can understand, and the chorus has a melody nearly anyone can sing. The team's ambitions beyond the pop charts leaned more toward the musical stage than the concert hall; in this respect, it may be more accurately considered a repurposed theater song, though one that barely made it across the footlights. In 1965 or early 1966, Leiber encountered and adapted sections of "Disillusionment," the earliest piece in Mann's American collection *Stories of Three Decades.* (The spoken sections' source was no secret—it was later mentioned in several journalistic profiles of Lee.) The piece remained a recitation until the team presented it to the English musical theater star Georgia Brown, who was slated to do a BBC special after leaving the Broadway cast of *Oliver.*

According to Stoller, "Jerry had given me the vignettes and I had set them to music. Around that time Georgia came to Jerry's house in New York, and she wanted to do this show. She liked the song, but said, 'You have to connect this with a refrain of some kind.' So we grabbed a refrain from something else we were working on—something like, 'They all wear clothes with the very same lining/Cash bank notes on the 7th day,' and Georgia said, 'That's perfect.' But after she left we looked at each other and said, "That doesn't make any sense at all." The addition of the now-familiar chorus, shaped the material into recognizably song-like form and introduced the lyrics' sole rhyme, the half-buried *ball/all*. The chorus also alters the point of the original story: where Mann's character's response to his discoveries is merely to "dream and wait for death," Leiber's draws an active consequence of sorts: "Let's break out the booze and have a ball."

With the song completed, the team flew to London for the telecast of *Georgia's Back* in June or July of 1966. To the songwriters' knowledge, no recording of this debut performance survives. But a demo recording made around the same time, with Stoller playing tack-piano and Leiber supplying the vocal, does. The fragment released on the 2001 compilation *The Songmakers Collection: Music from the Brill Building* cuts off before the first sung chorus, but its melody can be heard as a piano intro. In this version, the music is a pastiche of Kurt Weill's and Bertolt Brecht's Berlin theater songs, as Stoller freely admits. The verses' distinctive alternation between F minor and A-flat minor appears, in the context of a longer progression, in bars six and seven of "Surabaya Johnny," while the rhythmic accompaniment figure recalls "Pirate Jenny." The important resemblance, though, is simply at the level of form: as with many of the freestanding songs from *The Threepenny Opera* and *Happy End*, the alternation between spoken verses (though Weill's are typically notated as pitched *Sprechstimme*, rather than speech proper) and a melodically expansive, even sentimental chorus is key to the piece's overall "cabaret" feel.

These Weimar trappings determined the team's next attempts to place the song. Leiber's ideal singer—Clara Waldorf, of Brecht's own Berliner Ensemble—was clearly impractical. The closest New York equivalent was Marlene Dietrich, then concentrating on nightclub appearances. "I asked Burt Bacharach, who had conducted for her, to learn the song so someone she already knew could play it, instead of these two strangers. We went up to her apartment in the East Sixties, she brought out tea and cookies, and talked about the Kennedy compound for two hours, until I was cross-eyed." Finally, Dietrich listened, and demurred, claiming that her current repertoire focused on glamour, not depth.

The first recording of the song, a year before Lee's, was by Leslie

Uggams. Uggams had been an opening act at the Apollo at age six; by the early 1960s, she was a featured performer with TV's sing-along king, Mitch Miller. After her Tony in 1967 for Comden and Green's civil rights–themed musical *Hallelujah, Baby!,* she was being recast as half-soul-singer, half-all-around-entertainer, somewhere between Dianne Carroll and Dionne Warwick. On her Atlantic debut, unfortunately entitled *What's an Uggams?,* the song appears alongside two other recent Leiber/Stoller songs ("Flying," previously cut by Carmen McCrea, and "Some Cats Know") and four by Bacharach and David, including "What the World Needs Now."

Unfair as it is to judge Uggams's version against Lee's, one can hardly help feeling that the song is ill-served by her openly stagy approach. She attacks the ends of verses with more disgust than disaffection ("Is *that* . . . all there *is* . . . to *love?*) before cold-shifting to a brittle, oddly thin delivery for the choruses. Pat Williams's arrangement is overfurnished; the opening verse retains the demo's tack-piano, with a banjo doubling the percussive effect, but the rest devolves into a slurry of string parts and confusingly articulated polyrhythms. For the final chorus, *Tonight Show* horns kick in as the tempo slows and Uggams belts one to the back row. The emotional state of the character in the song could be described any number of ways, but "eager to please" isn't one of them.

Uggams's record left no lasting mark. Leiber and Stoller next attempted to place the song in a restaging of *International Wrestling Match,* originally a non-musical play by Jeff Weiss, which had won an Obie for its January 1969 run at La Mama Theater Club. Leiber recalls this as a typical off-Broadway production for the time, less a play than a string of theatrical episodes, including one involving Jacqueline Kennedy and a number of sailors. (No one seems to remember if this was the point at which "Is That All There Is?" was to have been inserted.) Producer Ted Mann eventually pulled out of the project after disputes with the director, but the plan lasted long enough for the play's title to appear as a teaser line ("From the forthcoming production . . .") on the label of early editions of the Lee single and commercial sheet music.

The play was still in the works when Lee enthusiastically accepted the song. Apparently unaware of its previous history, she became convinced that it had been conceived with her in mind; the authors did not tell her otherwise. Though Leiber and Stoller produced the session themselves,

Newman was given an unusually free hand with the arrangement, perhaps owing to the writers' dissatisfaction with previous attempts to capture the song. The demo and Uggams's recording are particularly valuable in clarifying the extent of Newman's contribution. This arrangement becomes *less* elaborate as it goes on; though the tack-piano and Williams's banjo have been dropped, the third and fourth verses are quite similar in feel to the original piano demo. But in the second ("circus") verse, Newman introduces a horn countermelody that has come to seem part of the song and recurs in many later cover versions. Even more radically, Newman entirely rewrote the music under the opening verse—no previous recording begins as a waltz, and the supporting harmonies have no obvious connection to those supplied by Stoller.

In this setting, the song finally finds itself—or lets Lee find it. Taken on its own, one can complain that the chorus borders on undergraduate existentialism: *The Myth of Sisyphus* via *Play It as It Lays*. The lyric strains to be profound, but in Lee's handling, it simply is. Part of this is technique, part of it is taste, and part of it is persona. With her whip-smart timing and arm's-length approach to a song's text, Lee was the most clinical of the great pop singers; because of this, she could also be the most deeply, unreachably wounded. To every smoldering "Fever" or calculating "Hey Big Spender" in her catalog, there is a numbed, traumatized flipside, from "Sing a Rainbow," the cracked-prism nursery rhyme she sang as a moll-turned-mental patient in the film *Pete Kelly's Blues,* to "When the World Was Young," a *chanson* on lost innocence with English lyrics by Johnny Mercer, which she recorded at various junctures in her career, always with a glassine, impermeable depth indistinguishable from sheer surface.

Lee treats Mann/Leiber's questions not as challenges but as opportunities for revelation, as if the discovery that life hasn't earned its advance press could be, in its own way, something wondrous. Her performance isn't overtly theatrical but genuinely dramatic. Something *happens.* In the first two choruses, when she doesn't quite sing the title, instead using it as a half-spoken transition, and then begins to phrase against the archaic swing of Newman's backing, her transformation from a schoolgirl to a lifer in the demimondaine is audible, in the very moment it occurs. After the "love" section, she begins the chorus, only to cut it off cold ("so let's keep–") and sail into the final verse, breaking the fourth wall: "I know what you must be saying to yourselves / If that's the way she feels about it, why doesn't she just end it all?"

It's not clear who added this touch; the same half-chorus of music occurs at the same spot in Williams's arrangement, but Uggams simply hums wordlessly through the section. One final change, though, is entirely Lee's. Leiber notes, "She either couldn't or wouldn't do one line as written. In the last verse, when she's talking about death, she says, 'Oh no, not me, I'm not ready for that final disappointment.' But what I wrote was, 'Oh no, not me, I'm in *no hurry* for that final disappointment.' What's implicit there is a kind of cynical, but amusing, German one-liner, but Peggy didn't get it." You can find Leiber's original line in any printed version; the lyricist still checks before approving sheet music reprints. In suggesting that the "final disappointment" is still something to be dreaded—that it might still *hurt*—Lee's version takes a bit of the edge off the original text. But either variation is less detached than the sentiment in Mann's original: "I dream and wait for death."

One place where Leiber's original line can be heard is on *Live at the Tropicana*, a 1970 album by Guy Lombardo and His Royal Canadians. Lombardo had led his organization through sweetened, dance-orchestra renditions of the hits of the day since 1924, and no change in musical fashion was about to alter his mode of operation. On this outing, the material includes the New Vaudeville Band's "Winchester Cathedral" and the themes from *Dr. Zhivago* and *The Prime of Miss Jean Brodie*. In this context, the presence of "Is That All There Is?" is disconcerting, for all the wrong reasons. Guitarist Ty Lemley—as pictured on the back cover, a square-jawed Steve Lawrence type—delivers the spoken sections uncomprehendingly, with all the emotional connection of the shipping news, sounding as though he had lived through no experience, good or bad, whatever. Lee's reserved reading is positively operatic by comparison. This is the only recording of the song that might convince listeners to answer "Yes" to its central question.

In *Always Magic in the Air*, Ken Emerson's 2005 history of the Brill Building, "Is That All There Is?" figures as the last hurrah of an entire mode of pop production. More modestly, it was the final significant chart appearance, at least with a new song, for both Lee and Leiber and Stoller. Lee returned to a heavy touring schedule, and an eponymous album was hastily assembled, with songs and arrangements by various hands, including Leiber and Stoller's "Whistle for Happiness" and two—"Love Story" and "Linda" (re-gendered as "Johnny")—from Randy Newman's debut LP. The songwriters' plan to write and produce their own full-length follow-up for Lee was placed on hold until long after the record's momentum had ebbed. *Mirrors*, released in 1975 on A&M, was clearly meant to pick up where the single left off, in both mood and musical style, while also recognizing that the principals had aged. "Ready to Begin Again" opens the album with some of the bravest lines a once-glamorous female vocalist could sing: "My teeth are at rest in the glass by my bed/and my hair lies somewhere in a drawer." Other songs range over political allegory ("Professor Hauptmann's Performing Dogs"), parental abandonment ("The Case of M.J."), and the recent murder of the former matinee-idol Roman Novarro ("Tango"), with musical echoes not only of Brecht and Weill but of Jacques Brel and even Randy Newman. The closing "Longings for a Simpler Time" is as poker-faced a pastiche of Americana as anything in Newman's catalog, especially when one considers that the song's embroidered-sampler view of the past ("When girls were girls and boys were boys . . . when life was grand in this sweet land") hardly reflects the songwriters' youth as Los Angeles hipsters with black girlfriends. The album was originally intended to begin with a reprise of the 1969 hit; later CD reissues restore it to the running order. "If we had done *Mirrors* at that time, it might have been more successful," Leiber says now, "but I consider it very successful."

The song crossed the high-low divide again in 1978, on *Other Songs by Leiber & Stoller*, a little-remembered (and not-yet reissued) Nonesuch album by the soprano Joan Morris and the pianist-composer William Bolcom, one of a long series of similar recordings presenting the work of various American songwriters, from Eubie Blake to Vincent Youmans, in piano–vocal recital format. Bolcom's piano reduction of the Newman arrangement is perfectly serviceable; Morris's delivery has all the faults typical of legitimate singers' attempts to meet vernacular style halfway. Still, the song suffers less damage at her hands than "I've Got Them Feeling Too Good Today Blues" (one of several borrowed from *Mirrors*) or the selection's only nod to rock and roll, the Cheers' 1955 hit "Black Denim Trousers and Motorcycle Boots."

Maligning Leiber and Stoller as high-cultural strivers for being involved in this project is easy, and ultimately too facile. They were no longer writing the sorts of songs that could be successfully placed with pop artists, and they knew it. The liner notes mention, optimistically, that the newer songs included are "intended for forthcoming Broadway productions." What wasn't obvious at the time was that the primacy of the very style they helped build in the fifties and early sixties had already begun to erode the viability of musical theater as a possible outlet for their new work. When Leiber and Stoller finally reached Broadway, it was with 1995's *Smokey Joe's Café,* which threaded a plot through thirty-three songs, all but one ("Pearl's a Singer") from their peak years as R&B and rock and roll writers—songs which by then could be heard as nostalgia by a baby-boomer audience longing for, and likely misremembering, "a simpler time." It's no accident that "Is That All There Is?" doesn't appear in that show.

The song's afterlife began in 1980, when disillusion had become less a discovery than a way of life, with a single on the prescient no-wave/disco label ZE Records by Cristina—the performing name of the former Harvard student and *Village Voice* theater reviewer Cristina Monet. Her one previous release had been "Disco Clone," on which her inflatable-sex-toy lead vocal was less central than a swirling, salsa-laced arrangement and a spoken turn by the then-unknown Kevin Kline. Her "Is That All There Is?" was recorded in a tiny studio in Avenue A, with backing by labelmates Kid Creole and the Coconuts, whose August Darnell wrote the bulk of her first full-length album soon after. Led in by a few bars of sourly detuned piano, the music is a rough, expedient adaptation of the original, with Stoller's chord progression strung along a thin, single-note guitar riff, overlaid with party noises and sax squeals by James White, another member of the ZE repertory company.

But like Lee's, this record is the singer's show. Her former husband and label cofounder Michael Zilkha recalls that Cristina improvised the verses in (at most) three takes, freely altering the incidents in Leiber's lyric to suit a more decadent milieu. In retrospect, the loose, spoken structure of the song's verses makes it surprising that no one had thought to "update" them before. The first verse merely adds the detail that her mother burned the family's house down ("she was like that") but the second trades the circus for a nightclub: "There were bored-looking bankers dancing with beautiful models, and there were boys with dyed hair and Spandex t-shirts dancing with each other. . . . And when I went home, I said to myself, 'Is that there all there is to a disco?' " Next, she falls in love: "He'd beat me black and blue, and I loved it—I'd have killed for that guy." Finally, she asks the listener, "Why doesn't she slit her throat and shut up?" The final choruses, inevitably for their moment, replace "booze" with " 'ludes," and the last changes Leiber's constant "if" to " 'cos that's all there is"—the question that survived from Mann's story stated as a seemingly incontrovertible conclusion.

As Zilkha says, "Cristina couldn't sing, but her records were very good conceptually." Between one thousand and two thousand copies were released on ZE via Island in England, where members of Blondie gave it a strong push on a BBC record-rating program. Within two weeks, what one article at the time called "legal frighteners" from Leiber and Stoller's publishing company had served the label with cease and desist orders and threatened further action. The record never saw official release in America, and its appearance on early pressings of the compilation *Rodney on the Roq, Vol. 1* was later replaced with a track by the California punk Rik L. Rik.

"I'm not sure they had a case," says Zilkha now, "but I just didn't have the money to fight it. We always had enough money to make records, but I was keeping Kid Creole and Was (Not Was) on the road, and we were operating at a half-million dollar loss every year until the third Kid Creole record—I just couldn't spend fifty thousand on legal bills." Though he estimates the single might have sold 150,000 copies unchecked, his main disappointment at the time of our interview was that the song couldn't be included on *No Thanks!,* Rhino Records 2003 box set of canonical punk recordings, or on the reactivated ZE's own reissues.

Leiber and Stoller make no apologies for their action against the record, and one wouldn't expect them to—they may be great American artists, but they're also great American businessmen. Leiber calls the version "an atrocity," though he recognizes "that it was meant to be partly funny and partly angry," while Stoller says, "It was breaking for a hit, and I thought it was a horrible burlesque that entirely missed the point. There are the lyrical changes, but there are musical ones as well—we went after it on the basis that it had been substantively changed, and could hurt the value of the copyright." Even without making general pronouncements about intellectual property, it is hard not to point out that the changes

Elvis Presley made in the version of "Hound Dog" that Leiber and Stoller wrote for Big Mama Thornton have not hurt that copyright much—or that the songwriters might count themselves lucky that no one had ever intervened to protect Thomas Mann's interest in the material.

There have been other covers since, of varying degrees of faithfulness, by Tony Bennett, Bette Midler, Chaka Khan, Giant Sand, and Firewater, among others. But it seems fitting to conclude with PJ Harvey's, released a century after Mann's story first appeared. The track, one of the few covers Harvey has ever recorded, was first heard on the soundtrack album to *Basquiat,* Julian Schnabel's biopic of the painter Jean-Michel Basquiat, who serves as the focal point of the director's knowing portrait of the New York art world in the cash-flushed 1980s. As Schnabel obviously knows, Basquiat walked his own tightrope between high and low modernisms for much of his too-brief career, with a foot in both downtown music and visual art scenes, and would have been well acquainted with the ZE extended family.

Further cinematic evidence of these connections can be found in Edo Bertoglio and Glenn O'Brien's *Downtown 81,* also known as *New York Beat Movie,* in which Basquiat doesn't precisely act but nonetheless stars. This film, which intersperses a thin noir storyline with club and studio performance clips, was shot when its title indicates, but much of the footage was thought lost until 1999, when the filmmakers had many of the participants redub their dialogue, with the poet Saul Williams becoming the voice of the late Basquiat. The cast is a who's who of East Village high-low foment: a pre–*Stranger Than Paradise* Ester Bazint and John Lurie, Warhol survivor Cookie Mueller, Fab Five Freddy, and (in non-musical cameos) every member of Blondie. Of the ZE stable, Kid Creole, James White, and DNA all appear, while none other than Michael Zilkha is credited as executive director on the film's belated commercial release.

In fact, Cristina may be one of the few significant participants in the scene who *doesn't* appear for at least a fleeting moment. Despite this conspicuous absence, it seems likely that Harvey's version, which is entirely faithful to Leiber's text, owes its existence—or, at least, its appearance in *Basquiat*'s recreation of the world *Downtown 81* documents—in large part to Cristina's "atrocity," which was almost certainly unavailable for use by Schnabel (or his music supervisor). Even Harvey's version appears only on the soundtrack album. In the film's DVD release, only

Lee's recording is heard, obscured by the noise of a gallery opening depicted as the peak of Basquiat's rise from street poet and graffiti artist to exoticized darling of the collector class; the point, that is, from which he can only decline.

Postscript

I conducted the phone interviews with Jerry Leiber, Mike Stoller, and Michael Zilkha that form the spine of this essay in March 2004, a month before presenting a shorter version at that year's Pop Conference. In December 2004, ZE issued the first-ever CD versions of Cristina's 1980 debut album (originally eponymous, now *Doll in the Box*), as well as 1984's Don Was–produced *Sleep It Off*. The former includes her version of "Is That All There Is?" as a bonus track, with a confusing writing credit that reeks of legal compromise: "Leiber Stoller 1980—Additional lyrics Cristina." This marks the track's first official release since the original single was withdrawn. None of my interviewees suggested that this release might be in the works—and Zilkha's comments about other reissue projects strongly implied that the songwriters had resisted overtures made up to that time. I can't confirm that our interview had anything to do with Leiber and Stoller's agreeing to the release, but I admit I wouldn't be displeased if being asked about the record in a less business-oriented context—which I did with some trepidation—helped soften them up. It's also possible that they came to recognize that Cristina's version had done —could do—no harm to their work, or to Peggy Lee's. Or, perhaps, they realized the folly of controlling the meaning of a song about the loss of meaning.

Benjamin Melendez, as told to
Henry Chalfant and Jeff Chang

Ghetto Brother Power
The Bronx Gangs, the Beatles, the *Aguinaldo*,
and a Pre-History of Hip-Hop

9

Benjamin Melendez's is an extraordinary life. While hip-hop history is often told in broad, macro strokes, the micro-history of Melendez's story offers insight into the social conditions, the racial consciousness, and the collective street creativity that led to the emergence of hip-hop in Bronx neighborhoods in the early 1970s. Perhaps the most important event that swung the Bronx from the borough's political, economic, and social abandonment of the 1960s to the street-level youth uprising of the 1970s was the 1971 gang peace treaty. The treaty came at a time when gangs had proliferated across the borough, and gang violence was peaking. In December the Ghetto Brother peacemaker Cornell Benjamin was killed while trying to stop a fight between a number of other gangs. Melendez and the Ghetto Brothers president, Carlos Suarez, aka Charlie Melendez, played a central role with key leaders from the Black Spades, the Savage Skulls, the Turbans, and dozens of other street organizations, in organizing the treaty.

Melendez also led the Ghetto Brothers' band, and after the peace treaty, they began to play on Friday nights in front of their clubhouse on 163rd and Prospect. It was safe for youths to gather on the streets again. The band's sound—a hybrid of Latin, rock, and soul—and their public appearance seemed to point toward the imminent cultural change. By the summer of 1974, music filled the Bronx from DJ Kool Herc's West Bronx spot in Cedar Park to Afrika Bambaataa's dances in former Black Spades territory in the Bronx River Projects.

Born to Puerto Rican immigrants and raised in New York City, Benjamin moved from Greenwich Village to the Bronx in 1963. His family was part of the mass exodus of poor, Black, and Brown families displaced by Robert Moses's effort to build a Lower Manhattan Expressway. In the Bronx, the building of the Cross-Bronx Expressway accelerated the borough's downward spiral. Half of the whites left the borough during the sixties, and government disinvestment and deindustrialization followed. Slumlords bought up decrepit buildings, milked them for rents for a time, and in the end, burnt them down. By 1970, many blocks were abandoned, with hundreds of ghost-shell buildings.

Against this backdrop, youth gangs returned to the Bronx.

My brother came back from Vietnam in 1973 and said, "Benjy, you have no idea what life was like in Vietnam." I said, "What are you talking about? I live in Berlin. Look at the South Bronx, it's like Berlin after 1945."

Ten years before, I had moved from the Village—14th street—up to Stebbins Avenue in the Bronx. I befriended a guy named Huey at Junior High School 133. So Huey asked me one time, "Hey Benjy, why don't you join my club?" I liked the idea of being with all these guys. My greatest hero was John Wayne.

I said, "What's the name of your club?"

He said, "The Cofon Cats."

You know to this day I don't even know what the hell that means. I looked it up in the dictionary, even looked in the encyclopedia. Couldn't find it! So Huey must have come up with that name.

But after a while, I thought, this ain't doing it. The way they were running the club, there wasn't too much organization. I told Huey, "I don't like this. I'm gonna leave." So I went to the block, I went back home, I started to thinking, I said, "I really don't want to start a gang. I just want to start something with my brothers."

The club was me, Robert, Victor, then later on Huey because we adopted him as a brother, and another friend we adopted named Raymond. I came up with a lot of names but the one I liked the most was the Ghetto Brothers. On 158th Street and Trinity Avenue, I befriended

Charlie Suarez and then he joined. I wanted us to fashion ourselves after the Hell's Angels.

My family was *Marano*. We were secret Jews. My father would call us every Friday night, pull down the shades, we would do the prayers. After everything was done, he said, "Go outside. Be quiet." We were never allowed to talk about it. So even though the Hell's Angels and a lot of the gangs had swastikas, I never allowed that.

Once, I was preaching to the Ghetto Brothers in the clubhouse. Here I am, one of the leaders of one of the largest gangs in the South Bronx, all dirty and mean, and someone said, "Benjy, somebody's at the door for you." I looked and it was my father. He said, "Come over here." He grabbed my ear, and walked me like this from our headquarters all the way to where we lived on Tiffany—in the street, in front of everybody! We went upstairs. He said, "Turn on the water." I said, "Pa?" And then he gave me a bath. Can you imagine the hell I took from the guys the next day?

My father was my world. But a lot of the guys I knew were brought up by single parents. That's why the Ghetto Brothers were important, because we provided that family structure. There were rules and regulations. One of them was you still had to go to school, you couldn't come to the clubhouse until after three. We also had the Ghetto Sisters. They were not sex objects. I did not permit that. Another rule was that when you had parties, don't be messing around with the sisters. You would pay for it. There were two incidents when two Ghetto Brothers paid for it.

The GBs grew to have divisions all over, from New Jersey to Connecticut. In fact, though I never met him, I heard that Eddie Perez, the mayor of Hartford, is an ex-Ghetto Brother. You had people who disagreed with Ghetto Brother policies leave the group and start another group. Out of the Ghetto Brothers, you had the Savage Skulls, Savage Nomads, Roman Kings, Taino Brothers, the Renegades. The Ghetto Brothers were so big at one time, we used to call the Bronx Ghetto Brother City.

From there it just started festering. The little gangs that were there, they started to spread as a result. And remember, we're talking about power. People had the attitude of: I want to be the leader. I want to show the people that I'm bad. The newspapers and the media—anything they wrote, these guys actually lived it. If they wrote, "They are the meanest gang in the Bronx," these guys lived it. So all these gangs popped up because guys wanted to be the leader.

Each gang had a president, a vice president, and a warlord. The warlord was the guy who would arrange for the war with the other gang. The president had tried negotiation, it didn't work out, the vice president tried, it didn't work out. Now we're going to have to go to war over this turf or over this girl.

The warlord's responsibility was to get with the other warlord and say, "OK this is what we're gonna do. What are you gonna bring? Wanna go with the hands? Wanna bring guns?" The GBS—no, everything was always with the hands. Some gangs did something called "throwing steps," where the warlords got down and danced. It didn't happen with us, but it did with other groups. I thought it was weird! But I started seeing the evolution of that much later, in the mid-seventies, when the GBS were waning down.

One day Charlie brought this guy in named Cornell Benjamin. We called him "Black Benjy." At that time in the GBS, I dropped the "warlord." I didn't want any more warlords. I said, "Ben where do you work at?" He said, "I work on 161st Street, I work as a drug counselor." "How long have you worked there?" "Oh at least four-five years." "Oh OK that's good." I'm listening to this guy—well-spoken, very charming, very articulate. So I said to Charlie, "I'm gonna make this guy the third staff leader, I'm gonna make this guy our spokesman, this guy's gonna be our peacemaker." This guy had a way of bringing in kids, and I saw that and I liked that.

We became the police around the area. We'd say, "Listen guys, they aren't going to do it for us. We have to be looking out for our brothers and sisters. Yo, my brothers you can't sell drugs around here. Go down the block. Sisters, I'm sorry but you can't be prostituting here. You're gonna have to go somewhere else where there aren't little children." People complied, because we didn't threaten them with violence. Some clubs did. But you know the codes in that area, you don't tell on your boys. Instead, I confronted the brothers, told them that's not how we do things down here, that's not how we work. We're going to have to set an example.

After Cornell Benjamin was killed, all the newspapers all came up to me on 158th Street—the *Daily News,* the *New York Times,* you name it. All the gangs were there, looking, waiting for one word: War. I said, No we're not gonna have any war. I said, "Brothers look at all these newspaper guys. They ain't writing anything, we're not giving them what they want. They look at us like we're a bunch of savages. But nah, we're not going to give them that."

I told the Ghetto Brothers, we sent Black Benjy out there for peace. To declare war, his peace will be in vain. We're not gonna do it. I cannot risk any of these guys again—I'm thinking these guys have mothers, fathers, wives. Charlie, I understand where he was coming from, he was pissed off. And a lot of Ghetto Brothers wanted the natural thing—go out there and take revenge. But this is what the media wants.

I used to tell the Ghetto Brothers, "What makes the world go round? Not love. Risk." One cold night in December, we were sitting there in the clubhouse, at least about fifteen or twenty Ghetto Brothers. One of the GBs, Louie the Santero, asked me, "Benjy who do you consider here your best warrior?" I said, "Brothers, a warrior is not one who carries the blade, he's not one who carries the .45, he's not one who carries those chain, a true warrior is a man of peace. To go out there to take a risk, to go to the Black Spades, to go to the Turbans, to go to the Savage Nomads alone, that takes a lot of courage."

Was I scared? Damn right, I was scared. Somebody had to do it. So I gave them a definition of what a new warrior is. I said, "Brothers we got to get together, this is getting out of hand." The public peace treaty meeting was very short. It was convened by the Madison Square Boy's Club. It was being filmed. There were cops in attendance. Charlie led the meeting, and before they got started, he asked them to leave. Since we already knew the presidents, the vice presidents, the warlords of these clubs, we used certain signs to each other—don't say nothing.

That's why the meeting was short. The following day or the day after is when we got the presidents, some of the vice presidents and some of the warlords together and then we convened the real peace treaty meeting. We all agreed this was the time when we would have to drop everything and do something positive in the community.

After that, the Ghetto Brothers band started playing in front of the clubhouse. We just plugged our amplifiers into the light pole. We saw the GBS every morning, give 'em a big hug. We'd tell them, "You ready to rock and roll? Get all the guys together for Friday night. We're gonna have a big party at 163rd and Prospect." Music brings a message. You play guitar, you play conga, people are gonna listen. They don't listen to you when you're preaching. So we thought, let's do it through music. And when we did songs, "Viva Puerto Rico Libre" or "Independista," people started to listen. When we started playing songs about the brothers coming together, people started to listen.

We did not go to school to learn how to play music. We watched, we saw people. My youngest brother Robert learned how to play rhythm by listening to Beatles tunes, Santana, and my brother Victor learned from him. I learned also by watching. We're all self-taught. When we were at parties we used to have the record player, we used to play the Beatles, then we'd play Blood, Sweat and Tears, then we'd play Chicago. Then later my brother brought down Sly and the Family Stone and James Brown. We were fusing all this music together—rock, Latin, soul. And we fused all these people together—people that like rock, with people that like Latin, with people that like soul. We added everything together and there was a message behind it. My brother Victor, who drummed and did a lot of the arranging, was really into James Brown. He would say, "Listen, follow my lead." That's when the dancing came in. Nobody really dances to rock and roll, the way people dance to salsa or soul. But when we added that element, that's when everyone started to get down.

I came from a family where in the household all you heard was old Argentine and Spanish music. That was the music we heard, not Joe Bataan, not Celia Cruz, not Tito Puente. It really started with the Chipmunks. This is how me and my brothers learned harmony, by listening to these guys! Then came the Beach Boys, then came the Four Seasons. Then came the Beatles and everything changed. But the Beatles crossed all barriers of races. When we started playing guitars, we brought in Beatles music. We introduced the Beatles to the Savage Skulls and the Savage Nomads they loved it. When we were doing "Help" or "I Want to Hold Your Hand," they would say, "Who wrote that?" We'd say, "Oh, we did!"

Jimi Hendrix comes into the scene, Santana too. When Santana comes in, we said "Nah that can't be. I think he took that from us." We were doing rock and roll, heavy rock and roll with timbales and congas. Then Grand Funk Railroad comes into the scene—"I'm Your Captain." That song, I would tell the Ghetto Brothers, referred to Charlie or to me. Then someone would come to me and say, "Hey I bought that Grand Funk Railroad album the other day, and they don't have that beat on there!" I'd say, "Nooo we've got that! That's us."

Whoever heard of doing Beatles with timbales and congas? We mixed the two. But then we also mixed the *aguinaldo* from my father's time. So there was the melody of those three tunes. But we were educating the community, telling the young brothers, "Listen this is part of your music too." The *aguinaldo* is like the *bomba*. In Puerto Rico, if you wanted to tell a story of someone you love or something that happened into the community, they'll put it into words. The song would be like the newspaper. What happened that day, they would sing about.

Before he went to sleep at night, my father made up a lot of songs, usually about the prophet Moses. He'd say, "Listen to this!" He'd start banging and making up words and when he finished, you clapped and said, "Pa . . . that was great!"

The *aguinaldo* was very influential in our family. In our time, *aguinaldo* was played without congas, that came later. In Puerto Rico geographically, they put the Africans in the outskirts of the island, and the people on the mountain, *jíbaros,* looked *blanco,* white. Those are the people that play *aguinaldo.* When you go to the edge of the island, it's more about drums, it's more about *bomba.* So my brother Victor said we should mix them both. That's what we did with "Viva Puerto Rico Libre."

There was a guy who owned a record label called Mary Lou who heard us playing out on the street one Friday night. He came up to us and said, "I have this record studio, I'll pay for it and you guys will have your own album." You can imagine how we must have felt. So he paid us five hundred dollars, one shot, went into the studio, recorded everything, one-shot. The sad thing about the record is that we didn't have the market and nobody promoted it.

The next street club that really got involved in a lot of music was the Black Spades. They would play their stuff out there with the big speakers. When they were around the projects in Morris or Castle Hill, there would be a guy walking around with a dolly bringing out the speakers. Then they would just start playing the music out in the street. I really liked that. When I saw what they were doing and heard this new sound, I said to the Ghetto Brothers, "Guys, check this out! This is the *new* ghetto expression." Some of them—especially the black brothers—took a liking to that and went in that direction. And the rest was history.

Steve Waksman

Grand Funk Live!
Staging Rock in the Age of the Arena

10 Grand Funk Railroad advertised the release of its first
album, *On Time,* in the December 1969 issue of *Circus*
by drawing attention to a series of successful appearances at large rock festivals and concerts around the
United States. The group was "born" at a rock and roll
revival in Detroit (near their home location of Flint,
Michigan); they showed 125,000 in Atlanta that "it's not
how big it is, it's how you use it"; they helped the people
in Cincinnati to "get off"; managed to "thunder through"
a crowd of 30,000 in Nashville; in Texas they got all of
what 180,000 had to give; and in LA the band and the
audience "came."

Leaving aside the crude sexual innuendo, two things
fascinate me about this ad. First is the geography of it:
the band creates a symbolic touring circuit for itself,
starting in the Midwest and heading south, before wind-
ing up in the Golden State. Notably absent is New York or
any other location in the Northeast; Grand Funk is a
band for the Sun Belt and the Rust Belt, at least to start.
More importantly, Grand Funk uses its success at playing to large crowds to legitimate their commercial appeal. One can take this as the first measure of the band's
effort to sell itself as a "people's band," in opposition to
critics and "hip" tastemakers. I think it can also be seen

as a measure of the shift that was underway in the staging of live rock as the 1960s came to a close. I cannot say definitively, but I believe this to be the first time a band was sold on the basis of the size of the audiences to which it performed (as opposed to the number of people who bought its records, lest we forget that fifty million Elvis fans couldn't have been wrong in the 1950s). The crowd was becoming a commodity in popular music to an unprecedented degree, and the large-scale concert was in the process of becoming a standardized element of the rock industry, a process that would come to fruition in the emergence of arena rock over the next few years. Accompanying this change in mode of production was a change in the meaning of live rock performance, which no American band symbolized at the dawn of the 1970s more than Grand Funk Railroad.

"Live music" remains a relatively underexamined phenomenon in popular music studies. As a field, we seem to be afraid that positing the unique significance of the live event opens the way toward the sort of romanticization of unmediated experience that so many of us have questioned in our various research efforts. Sarah Thornton's "Authenticities" chapter in *Club Cultures* is a notable exception and includes some important insights concerning the relative value of "live" and "recorded" music. By her account, the term "live" did not become a common point of musical vocabulary until the 1950s, when recordings had assumed the dominant role of representing "music" to the majority of listeners.[1] Since that time, Thornton argues, live musical performance has played an increasingly diminishing role in public spaces of musical consumption, as the discotheque and then the modern dance club have moved the action "from the stage to the dancefloor."[2] The one counterexample she raises to this trend is that of the arena or stadium concert, about which she notes that the Beatles were the first band to hold such concerts and "were possibly the last band to get away without dramatically changing their style of performance to accommodate this new environment."[3] After the Beatles, Thornton claims, arena and stadium concerts were more predicated upon the intensification of spectacle and the use of technologies designed to ensure a performance of maximum impact, and the live event as a whole no longer existed as an autonomous phenomenon but as a supplement to the business of selling records.

Thornton's genealogy of the category of "live music" is compelling, but her explanation of the changes wrought by the shift to arena rock is less so; her narrative of changing authenticities does not do justice to the specificity of the late 1960s/early 1970s moment when arena rock emerged. More attentive to the particular weight of this moment is Ellen Willis, in a short piece titled "Crowds and Freedom." Willis begins by noting that "the power of rock 'n' roll as a musical and social force has always been intimately connected with the paradoxical possibilities of mass freedom or collective individuality."[4] For Willis, this paradox begins to take shape not in live performance but through the collectivity created out of mass-mediated cultural forms such as radio, records, and television, through which a shared repertoire of sounds and images became the common currency of a heterogeneous and dispersed population, each of whom "integrated the music into our lives or our lives into the music in our own way."[5] Live crowds, in her analysis, "functioned largely as a confirmation of the existence of the community," a function that Willis suggests was particularly strong for arena or festival crowds.[6] Rock concerts, in other words, brought together a community that was already conscious of its interconnectedness through the effects of mass media. Yet some concerts had more weight than others as events where community was confirmed and consolidated. Woodstock, by Willis's estimation, dramatized the possibilities of mass freedom as well as the fragility dwelling within that term; and Altamont was "the countermyth that could no longer be denied," after which the idea that the crowd could be a source of freedom largely receded from the ideological edifice of rock and roll.[7]

The post-Altamont moment in U.S. rock history is the moment at which arena rock starts to become the prevailing form of live rock performance; and if that moment was experienced by some as an ending, for others it was just as strongly a beginning. Steven Tyler was one such figure. In 1969, the future singer of Aerosmith had played in a number of New England–based rock ensembles and achieved a good measure of regional notoriety but had not yet made the break for larger-scale success. He received a taste of what that success would be like, though, when Led Zeppelin came through the Northeast on their 1969 tour. Tyler had an "in" with the British rockers—his friend Henry Smith had joined Zeppelin's road crew. In Boston, he caught the band at the Tea Party, Boston's version of a rock and roll ballroom, where he claims he was moved to tears by the middle section of "Dazed and Confused."

When Zeppelin played New York City some weeks later, though, it was not at the comparably sized Fillmore East but at Madison Square Garden. Through his friendship with Smith, Tyler was afforded admittance to the Garden during sound check; and the sight of the empty arena provoked a vision: "When I got there, the road crew and the union people were all eating and the band hadn't arrived. The stage was empty and so were the 19,000 seats. The silence was deafening. I walked out to the stage and lay down, with my head hanging backward off the edge. I was overwhelmed by instant delusions of rock and roll grandeur, imagining that I was roaming the land, raping and pillaging, disguised as an ambassador of rock. And I said to myself, *Someday a band of mine is gonna fill this fuckin' place.*"[8] One can read into Tyler's reverie the worst excesses of 1970s rock: the unabashed narcissism of the rock and roll star, and the accompanying, unremitting masculinism, with its attendant sexual caste system structured around the relationship between male stars and female groupies. For my purposes, though, the passage reveals one matter above all, that the space of the arena was invested with profound meaning in itself, and figured prominently in the broader set of cultural fantasies promoted by rock—perhaps especially hard rock and heavy metal—during that decade. In the eyes of Steven Tyler, and no doubt of many other musicians and fans, the arena was an icon of success in its own right; and the possibility of drawing an arena-sized crowd stood for an intensely coveted form of rock and roll grandeur.

Grand Funk Railroad began their own ascent to stardom in this moment as well. Between 1969 and 1974, the band scored ten gold records, at a time when a gold record was awarded for sales of over one million units. They also played a steady stream of concerts to arena- and festival-sized crowds. Throughout their rise to success, critics watched with a skeptical and at times hostile eye. Most critics deemed the music of Grand Funk an unsatisfying simplification of the power trio format that had been popularized by late 1960s ensembles like Cream and the Jimi Hendrix Experience. Typical was Dave Marsh's review of their 1970 album, *Live:* "Are they as slow and doped out of their wits as their audiences? Are they THAT naive and unsophisticated? . . . I really tried to listen to the music but, halfway through, I had to shut it off."[9] When the band's success continued to escalate despite critical hostility, Grand Funk Railroad became a problem for critics to resolve: how could a group with such obvious lack of musical merit gain such a strong hold over the rock audience? This concern came to a head in 1971, when the band became the first since the Beatles to play at New York's Shea Stadium, with a capacity of over 50,000.

The Shea Stadium concert was the culmination of a determined move to mass success engineered by the members of Grand Funk Railroad— Mark Farner, Don Brewer, and Mel Schacher—and their manager, Terry Knight. During the early years of their success, Knight was the band's public mouthpiece and publicity mastermind. Among his grander gestures was a billboard advertising the Grand Funk album *Closer to Home;* located in the heart of Times Square in New York, where it took up a whole city block, it remained for three months in early 1971 at a cost of $100,000. Knight would defend the necessity of such measures by noting that radio play was all but closed to Grand Funk, and critics were almost uniformly opposed to the group. Brash and self-important, Knight showed considerable skill at maintaining one of the most characteristic and yet most delicate balances in rock: presenting Grand Funk Railroad as a group of underdogs while celebrating and justifying their enormous popularity.

According to Terry Knight, Grand Funk Railroad were the ultimate anti-establishment band, standing for "the people" against the power of government and media. When members of the press largely snubbed a press conference arranged to address the Shea concert, Knight went on the offensive, declaring that the media were scared of Grand Funk in a way that they had no reason to be with the Beatles. As he proclaimed in an interview following the aborted press conference: "The media is worried about our power. Anybody that can draw 55,000 people together at one time has got some kind of power. . . . Back when the Beatles were famous 55,000 people just meant a lot of screaming girls. Now, 55,000 people to *them* maybe means the possibility of a Mark Farner standing on stage and saying, 'now brothers and sisters take that city down!' "[10] Feminizing the rock audience of the preceding decade by way of disparaging it, Knight drew a distinction between the Beatles and Grand Funk Railroad that was politically groundless—the Beatles were far more political than Knight here suggests, and GFR were not so radical—but rhetorically powerful. It was not just that Grand Funk Railroad symbolized the shift from the 1960s to the 1970s in rock but that Knight used them as such symbols to build their appeal. He further offered a definition of the audience to complement his portrayal of the band, as a group of people who were young but not *too* young, who were not "just" girls but a collection of "brothers and sisters" whose attraction to rock and roll made them automatic rebels ready for action.

Interviewing Knight, the journalist Kenny Kerner eventually became exasperated by such rhetoric. "Why do you keep using those words? *Our* people? *Your* people? Brothers. Sisters. That's such garbage. . . . How can you bring everybody together if you first separate them?" Knight defended himself on political grounds, declaring that when "they" are promoting Vietnam, lines of separation are necessary. But Kerner pushed his point, and in so doing laid bare some of the stakes involved in Grand Funk's success: "The reason for the Beatles great popularity was that they had universal appeal . . . Grand Funk is coming on to the music scene and saying that *these* people are the ones we're playing for. . . . The Beatles didn't separate . . . Grand Funk is taking their people out of the entire population and catering exclusively to them."[11] This unusual exchange, in which an interviewer genuinely challenges his subject, reveals the tensions emerging in the early 1970s around the mass appeal of rock. Grand Funk had the capacity to draw larger crowds than just about any other band of the moment, but their appeal nonetheless seemed exclusive. By their very popularity, they had driven a wedge in the perceived ability of rock to represent its audience in a unified and unifying way.

Greil Marcus elaborated upon this conception of the meaning of Grand Funk's success in the midst of an extensive rumination on the conversion of rock into a part of mainstream culture that he wrote for the June 1971 issue of *Creem*. Discussing the changes that overcame rock during the late 1960s, Marcus asserted that a once "secret" medium had become assimilated, and that "mainstream assimilation has brought not power but dissipation."[12] In this moment of fragmentation, Marcus observed, "It's certainly possible that the only place in rock and roll . . . that still moves with the excitement and that still has the power to maintain the values of exclusive possession that have made this music matter for fifteen years is the place now occupied by Grand Funk Railroad."[13] Further noting that Grand Funk had achieved such prominence despite a number of limiting factors (lack of radio play, hostile critical response, indifference to the band among many diehard rock fans), Marcus went so far as to suggest that

"Grand Funk is not merely fragmenting the audience, like most everyone else; they may be *dividing* it." Yet the group's ultimate importance for Marcus rested not in the divisiveness of their impact but in the apparent connection they had with a newly constituted wing of the rock audience, a younger wing that rejected some of the standards and assumptions of the critic and his peers. Others might be unattuned to their message, but Grand Funk seemingly had a direct line of communication with these younger fans. In Marcus's description, Grand Funk concerts dramatized and consolidated this bond in the strongest terms: "A Grand Funk concert sets up, defines, invites and entertains a community which forms itself around that event. The 'goal' is to get off—and in the mystery of the rock, you get off on what's yours. A Grand Funk concert is exclusive. Only certain people want to get in. They know who they are, too. Fuck that critic shit, man, siddown. This is the best thing going, and not only that, this is the biggest group in the world, and I . . . *am in the same room*."[14]

A month after Marcus's commentary appeared, Grand Funk Railroad played their Shea Stadium concert. The show was part of the tour for their fifth album, *Survival*, which took place through the summer of 1971. In keeping with Knight's promotional approach, the *Survival* tour as a whole was designed to demonstrate the range of the group's influence and popularity. Of the fourteen dates on the *Survival* tour, the Shea Stadium concert was one of only two held in the continental United States. The remaining appearances took the band to Germany, Holland, France, Italy, and England in the weeks prior to Shea Stadium, and then to Hawaii and Japan in the days following that concert. Grand Funk Railroad returned to the United States to conclude the tour with a show at the Yale Bowl in New Haven, Connecticut.[15] By the time they played at Shea the band had become a well-oiled arena rock machine, as was evident in the gesture with which they opened their concerts during the year. Rising from the massive sound system carried by the band to introduce each show were the opening strains of Richard Strauss's *Thus Spake Zarathustra*, which by 1971 had assumed a secondary designation as the musical theme from Stanley Kubrick's mind-expanding 1968 science fiction film, *2001: A Space Odyssey*.[16] The pounding tympani and famous crescendo of the composition's opening measures powerfully set the stage for the concert experience to come and heightened the sense of expectation that accompanied the beginning of a Grand Funk show.

Three reviews, appearing in the weeks and months after the Shea Stadium concert, captured the contradictory grandeur of the event. That the concert was reviewed at such length in three nationally circulating magazines—*Rolling Stone, Harper's,* and *Creem*—was itself a sign of the weight that it was seen to carry. While concert reviews were common in two of these publications, rarely did they occupy more than a page of commentary. Grand Funk Railroad's concert at Shea, on the other hand, was treated as feature article material and became an occasion for three of the country's most respected critics—Timothy Ferris, Richard Goldstein, and Lenny Kaye—to offer their impressions not just of the concert but of the Grand Funk phenomenon.

Ferris's *Rolling Stone* review was the first to see print and was the most ambivalent of the three in its judgment of the band's significance. Although *Rolling Stone* had recently run a favorable Lester Bangs review of Grand Funk's latest album, the magazine had typically looked upon the band and the associated heavy metal genre with a dubious eye. Ferris's take on the Shea Stadium concert was in keeping with that stance. He was by no means entirely unsympathetic with the band, but he emerged from the concert far from fully convinced of Grand Funk's power in either musical or cultural terms. That said, *Rolling Stone* ran Ferris's review as a front page item, granting it status as the most newsworthy story of the issue, and the story most likely to grab attention on the newsstand.

Setting up the review of the concert, Ferris provided a concise version of the band's origins in the "workingman's town" of Flint and their subsequent rise to prominence. Grand Funk Railroad's success, for Ferris as for so many other observers, had at its center Terry Knight and his remarkable ambition. Claiming that the group's music was a secondary consideration, Knight explained the band's appeal to Ferris: "What the audience is hearing and seeing is Mark holding his guitar over his head and saying, 'You see this, Brothers and Sisters, you see me? I'm free. I own this stage. It's mine and it's yours, and we're free and you can be free.'"[17] The key point for Knight was that Grand Funk Railroad made this freedom seem possible for the band's audience as well. In effect, Knight was showing his Michigan roots here. The rhetoric was clearly borrowed from that of another regional band, the incendiary MC5; and Knight was styling himself as a refashioned version of that band's original manager and political visionary, John Sinclair. However, whereas for Sinclair and the Five, the politics existed inside the music, taking shape as a politics of noise, for Knight it was the symbolism of the musicians more than the music itself that transmitted the most powerful message.[18]

Ferris retained a certain detachment from these assertions, but he did turn to a Flint journalist, Steve Wayley, for support of Knight's position. Wayley acknowledged Knight's efforts to "choreograph" the career of Grand Funk, but he held firm to his belief that the band represented an important type of freedom, the sort "that you feel when you completely lose yourself at a rock concert."[19] Watching Grand Funk Railroad at Shea, Ferris did not partake in such freedom. Although there were certain musical moments that impressed him, such as a passage in one of the band's best-known songs, "I'm Your Captain," on the whole he was struck by the relative sameness of Grand Funk's repertoire. This quality was exaggerated by a sound system that, to his ears, was "pushed to such distortion that everything sounded as if it were being played full blast on the world's biggest car radio."[20] However, he was also struck by their ability to motivate a crowd in such a capacious setting, and by the end of the show he was at least willing to grant that Grand Funk Railroad came across far better in concert than on record. Drawing his conclusions about the concert and the band, Ferris was left with the impression that "there really isn't much mystery to Grand Funk." They represented a moment at which the audience for rock was expanding, and their success was the result of Terry Knight's skill at selling them as a "lowest common denominator" attraction. But Ferris was drawn to make a further observation, distinguishing Grand Funk from "the great groups of the Sixties." The latter "managed to combine the raw force of rock 'n' roll with the complexity of their own backgrounds." Grand Funk, by contrast, was all raw force and was thus indicative of a polarization between the "cerebral and the shake-ass" that had beset rock music in the new decade.[21]

Writing in the non-rock-oriented venue of *Harper's*, Richard Goldstein was far more impressed than Ferris with the import of Grand Funk Railroad, if not with the particulars of their music. Like Ferris and so many other commentators on the band, Goldstein gave requisite attention to Terry Knight and his promotional savvy. His main concern, though, was closer to that of Greil Marcus: who was Grand Funk's audience, and why did they so attach themselves to this band? The answer, for Goldstein as for Marcus, was that Grand Funk Railroad appealed to the younger set of rock fans, to "people between the ages of fourteen and eighteen," whom he described as a "hidden source of energy, precisely because they have no vested interest in popular culture, except as it reflects their immediate needs." From his vantage point in the midst of Shea Stadium, Goldstein further elaborated that "the people who come out to see Grand Funk perform are the lumpen young . . . who have no sense of the Sixties, and therefore no equipment for experiencing rock."[22] This was an audience who was not prepared to gauge rock according to the norms of an earlier era; and Grand Funk Railroad was, for Goldstein, in a position to provide new coordinates.

The most important way the band did so was through their accessibility, a quality that came through in the relative amateurishness of their performance. That amateurishness carried a promise of connection between band and audience, even in the inflated dimensions of Shea Stadium; it connoted the ways in which the members of Grand Funk were new sorts of rock stars, less "shaman" than "pal," less elevated than approachable. How Grand Funk Railroad carried themselves as stars, in turn, was connected to the undifferentiated quality of the sound they generated at Shea, and the ways in which that sound required a new style of listening to be fully appreciated. Goldstein's comments on this point constitute one of the most illuminating statements on the unique aesthetics of arena and stadium rock: "If you listen close and tight, the way you've trained yourself to hear Jerry Garcia of The Grateful Dead, there is virtually nothing to grab onto . . . Grand Funk's music is flat and bright. . . . You have to pull away before its force begins to show. Only when you have established your own willingness to be casual, when you have opened your ears to include the whole stadium, does the power of Grand Funk Railroad become manifest. It is the power of an engine: impersonal, mechanical, and with sharp edges of Lucite and gears of polished steel. . . . The stadium shakes with every beat; my seat vibrates under me; a jet plane flying low is silenced by the chords."[23] Timothy Ferris was not able to hear these dimensions of Grand Funk. He was listening for fidelity and clarity of a sort that could not exist in an acoustic environment like Shea Stadium; and when he did not find it, he complained of the distracting amount of distortion, characterizing the band's sound as that of a big car radio. Goldstein, by contrast, realized that the music in such a setting was bound to communicate as much by feel as by sound. What mattered was not whether one could hear all the finer points of the band's music—this was not music in which the finer points were meant to draw attention. It was instead music designed to generate a total effect, which was further amplified by the dimensions of Shea.

Lenny Kaye was also attuned to this new sound and its accompanying environment. His review in *Creem*, the last of the three to appear, was the longest and most detailed account of Grand Funk's performance. Unlike the other writers, Kaye gave clear indication that this was not his first experience with the band. Thus, his impressions of Shea were based not only on the novelty of the event but on his existing impressions of the group in concert. He observes, as the band break into their first song: "They're loud, much louder than the other times I've seen them, but also richer, not as ear-splitting and trebly. A volume you can live with, can thrive on, just over the threshold of distortion."[24] Kaye is also more attentive to the band's stage presence, for as he notes, "Grand Funk are a show band, first and foremost." When burly frontman Mark Farner sheds himself of his shirt, the writer recognizes it as part of the band's ritual, a sign that Grand Funk is truly ready to get down. Almost as if on cue, the audience acknowledges the sign, and their already forceful enthusiasm becomes that much more audible. As a seasoned Grand Funk observer, Kaye is not especially struck by the responsiveness of the crowd, which was a running feature of the group's concerts. What does strike him is the power of the band's music, which sounds to him far improved from his earlier encounters. Don Brewer and Mel Schacher laid a "solid foundation" for Farner, whose guitar playing stressed "back-up chords" rather than full-scale solos. Combined, the trio proved a "peculiarly powerful mixture" for Kaye and created "a totality of drive, and as they move from song to song, you can feel them easing into the experience of playing at Shea . . . building from it in a natural rise that never loses their rapt command over the audience."[25]

Grand Funk appeared very much in command of the concert. But throughout the bulk of the show, according to Kaye, the response of the audience was no more intense than at any other performance by the band. As the concert proceeds, Kaye is compelled to admit that "there's a definite lack of hysteria in the air, a feeling that the whole night has still not passed beyond the bounds of control."[26] That was about to change. Farner paused for effect, quieting the audience so he could dedicate the next song to the recently departed Jim Morrison. The song was "Inside Looking Out," characterized by Kaye as "the universally acclaimed all-time fav-o-rite of Grand Funk live performances." "Inside Looking Out" was one of the songs on which the band stretched out considerably in concert. Featuring a lyric that elliptically referred to being high on marijuana, it also contained one of Farner's most extroverted and extended guitar solos and included one of the central bits of audience participation within the group's set.

It was this latter element of the song that assumed a new dimension at Shea. Farner addressed the crowd directly, complimenting their good vibe, asking if they felt alright, then urging them to clap their hands. "The kids are in their glory," wrote Kaye, who seemed to be partaking in the action even as he was reflecting on it, "up on the chairs, leaning over the fences, joining in for all their worth." And just at that instant the stadium lights went on to illuminate the night-time assembly, "a million little suns erupting into glory, all focused on fifty five thousand who are rippling along like so many seas, a huge mirror reflecting the suddenly-small three people on stage, a true notion of where the party has been all along."[27] The crowd was displayed to itself, made conscious of itself as a crowd at the climax of the evening in a gesture that demonstrated both Grand Funk's power over the audience and the extent to which the band was beholden to the assembled mass. Kaye here describes a moment analogous to what Elias Canetti called the "discharge," when "distinctions are thrown off and all feel equal . . . It is for the sake of this blessed moment, when no-one is greater or better than another, that people become a crowd."[28]

Kaye considered the remainder of the show to have been an afterthought. Yet Grand Funk's choice of closing song was certainly of consequence under the circumstances: a cover of the Rolling Stones' "Gimme Shelter." The song had appeared on the band's most recent album, *Survival,* but here took on a new dimension, signalled by Mark Farner's introduction of it as "our generation's national anthem." For all the talk about the Beatles surrounding Grand Funk's appearance at Shea, it is striking that they ended their set paying tribute to the Stones—all the more so given how fresh Altamont was in the minds of many rock fans. Indeed the film, *Gimme Shelter,* that documented the Stones' performance at Altamont was even more recently released; and as Robert Duncan has argued, it was that film by Albert and David Maysles that truly memorialized the event as standing for the mythic end of the sixties, culminating in footage of a young African American getting stabbed to death by one of the Hells Angels members hired to provide "security."[29] It was no coincidence that the same filmmakers, the Maysles Brothers, were hired by Grand Funk to film the Shea Stadium concert, shooting footage that remains unreleased.

However much Grand Funk might have evoked Altamont in bringing their own concert to a close, Lenny Kaye was left with a very different vision of rock and roll as he reflected on the band and their performance. He classified the group as "moralistic," preaching a simple set of values that revolves around the dictum "do anything you want, as long as you don't do anyone else harm in the process." Moreover, Kaye suggested that the members of Grand Funk seemed to genuinely believe the articles of faith they put forth, "not because Terry Knight told them to, but because they're the living embodiment." As such, the group stood for a key strain of rock and roll mythology, which Kaye summarized:

> Rock 'n' roll is built on a myth. That being a guitar flash or a wizard drummer or a laid-back bass player is better than being anything on this earth. That the American Dream didn't fade away when we ran out of West to conquer. That it doesn't take brains, or money, or position, or anything, really, to have that golden chance to go all the way. . . .
>
> Grand Funk knows all this, and if they're not totally aware of their position in the myth, they certainly sense it subconsciously. Their strength doesn't lie on the stage, in their instruments, in their 8,000 watts of power. Their strength lies with their audience, who'll stay with them . . . as long as the group reflects a part of where they want to be, and then will split at the first sign of betrayal. . . .
>
> Grand Funk isn't a rock 'n' roll band.
>
> They're a big fan club. The best fuckin' fan club in the world.[30]

Grand Funk Railroad, for Kaye, personified the hopes of the rock audience as it had been reconstituted in the 1970s. Against the suggestion of Ellen Willis, who linked the end of the 1960s with the end of the myth of mass freedom in rock, Kaye finds a certain idealism intact. He also posits, in a move that foreshadows the thesis of Greil Marcus's *Mystery Train*, that the prevailing mythos of rock is congruent with the mythos of "America" at large. As with Marcus's later analysis, what seems at stake for Kaye is a set of values related to "the American meaning of the word democracy," in which the individual pursuit of opportunity is set against the promise and the pitfalls of mass belonging, of joining the crowd.[31]

In rock and roll, "opportunity" represented a potent mix of creative freedom and financial reward, and the most successful rock stars of the late 1960s and early 1970s fused these elements into a lifestyle of bohemian luxury that was as much a part of the allure of rock as the music itself. Grand Funk Railroad achieved a version of this lifestyle but joined it to an image that was Terry Knight's finest creation. As much as the band were clearly striving for the higher echelons of rock stardom, they still seemed within reach. Sure, they were stars, but they were not necessarily star material; by some accounts they could hardly even play their instruments properly. In the moral world that Knight constructed around the group, their very ordinariness made them powerful representatives of the people for whom they performed. If that notion was a hype, it was a hype that resonated within the terms of rock as they existed in the first years of the 1970s, when the rock and roll industry was learning how to dramatically expand its reach, and when the larger-than-life aura of rock stardom became a way to reach the swelling audiences of arena rock. Terry Knight may have managed the rise of Grand Funk Railroad with the most careful attention to the desires of the crowd, but the enthusiasm displayed by that crowd at Shea Stadium, and at hundreds of other shows in arenas around the United States, suggested that far more than marketing acumen was afoot. The 1960s were over, and a new young audience had found a reason to raise its collective voice.

Notes

1. Sarah Thornton, *Club Cultures: Music, Media and Subcultural Capital* (Hanover, N.H.: Wesleyan University Press, 1996), 41.
2. Ibid., 29.
3. Ibid., 78.
4. Ellen Willis, "Crowds and Freedom," in *Stars Don't Stand Still in the Sky: Music and Myth*, ed. Karen Kelly and Evelyn McDonnell (New York: New York University Press, 1999), 153.
5. Ibid., 154.
6. Ibid., 156.
7. Ibid., 157–58.
8. Aerosmith with Stephen Davis, *Walk This Way: The Autobiography of Aerosmith* (New York: Spike, 1999), 54–55.

9. Quoted in Metal Mike Saunders, "The Case for Grand Funk Railroad," *Fusion* (December 1972). *Rock's Back Pages,* http://www.rocksbackpages.com/article .html?ArticleID=1423 (accessed April 16, 2007).

10. Kenny Kerner, "An Interview with Grand Funk Railroad's Mentor-Manager-Producer Terry Knight," *Circus,* September 1971, 29.

11. Ibid., 30.

12. Greil Marcus, "Rock-A-Hula Clarified," *Creem,* June 1971, 38.

13. Ibid., 42.

14. Ibid., 43.

15. Kristofer Englehardt, *From Grand Funk to Grace: The Authorized Biography of Mark Farner* (Burlington, Ontario: Collector's Guide Publishing, 2001), 268.

16. This can be heard on the recent reissue of Grand Funk concert material, *Live: The 1971 Tour* (Capitol, 2002), which includes several tracks recorded during the concert at Shea.

17. Timothy Ferris, "World's Biggest Car Radio Performs in N.Y.," *Rolling Stone,* August 19, 1971, 6.

18. For further discussion of the MC5 and their importance to the Michigan rock scene of the late 1960s and early 1970s, see Steve Waksman, *Instruments of Desire: The Electric Guitar and the Shaping of Musical Experience* (Cambridge, Mass.: Harvard University Press, 1999), 207–36; and David Carson, *Grit, Noise and Revolution: The Birth of Detroit Rock 'n' Roll* (Ann Arbor: University of Michigan Press, 2005).

19. Ferris, "World's Biggest Car Radio," 6.

20. Ibid., 8.

21. Ibid.

22. Richard Goldstein, "Thus Sprach Grand Funk Railroad," *Harper's,* October 1971, 42.

23. Ibid.

24. Lenny Kaye, "To Live Outside the Law You Must Be Honest," *Creem,* November 1971, 73.

25. Ibid.

26. Ibid.

27. Ibid., 74.

28. Elias Canetti, *Crowds and Power* (New York: Noonday Press, 1984), 18.

29. Robert Duncan, *The Noise: Notes from a Rock 'n' Roll Era* (New York: Ticknor and Fields, 1984), 29.

30. Kaye, "To Live Outside the Law," 74–75.

31. Marcus, Mystery Train: Images of America in Rock 'n' Roll (New York: Dutton, 1975), 6.

Jason King

The Sound of Velvet Melting
The Power of "Vibe" in the Music of Roberta Flack

11 Where is Roberta Flack? Since a 1994 album of jazz-pop covers, the North Carolina–born singer-pianist has hardly released any new solo material. Yet she still performs extensively and her catalog remains in vogue, as evidenced by perennial covers of her classics. The Fugees retrofitted "Killing Me Softly with His Song," D'Angelo did the same for "Feel Like Making Love," Scarface's "On My Block" sampled the ostinato piano lick from her 1972 Donny Hathaway duet "Be Real Black for Me," and Luther Vandross, who began as a Flack protégé, reinterpreted 1980's "The Closer I Get to You" as a duet with Beyoncé for his final studio album, *Dance with My Father.* Though she helped create the blueprint for piano-playing song essayists from Oleta Adams to Alicia Keys, Flack rarely receives the auteur status granted to male R&B innovators like Stevie Wonder or female virtuosos like Joni Mitchell. Most of her greatest hits, like "The First Time Ever I Saw Your Face" and "Where Is the Love," were not her original compositions, and sentimental interpreters are afforded less critical respect than autobiographical singer-songwriters. Flack, who was once the highest-paid female vocalist in the world, remains an underestimated trailblazer.

If we consider the role of energy as a defining factor in

the production and reception of music, Flack emerges as an auteur precisely because of her ability to use her voice and complementary musical skills to traffic in "vibe." Colloquial shorthand for vibration, vibe is ambient energy that can either be embodied auratically (a person "gives off" a certain type of vibe) or exist as nonphysical matter ("there was a strange vibe in the air"). Felt rather than physically perceived, vibe is more effectively qualified than quantified. In musical performance, a "positive" or "soulful" vibe refers to collective intimacy, the pleasurable feeling of oneness and synchronicity within, say, a dance club or live concert. Such a vibe can be generated between people communing on a musical and spiritual level. Here, vibe is a real-time "presence" that musicians often deliberately strive to capture.

Given optimal conditions for sensory reception and appreciation, Flack's languorous music has a consistently "magical" ability to transfix audiences in concentrated, rapturous attention. Her classic period, covering the six albums released on Atlantic between *First Take* (1969) and *Feel Like Making Love* (1975), is characterized by spellbinding vibe. Reviewing a 1975 live concert performance by Flack of the Janis Ian ballad "Jesse," one critic noted: "she sang with such feeling you could almost feel the pain from your seat. The completely filled theatre gave their attention on each song as if they were holding their breath and following each word."[1] Dramatic suspense and the imminent promise of danger are augmented in Flack's case because of the extreme pianissimo, aching slowness, and understated instrumentation of her balladry. That minimalist aesthetic, which runs directly counter to the tendency toward pyrotechnical virtuosity in funk and soul as well as the orchestral grandeur of mainstream 1970s pop and rock, positions Flack as an undiscovered experimentalist in the history of popular music.

The suite of mechanisms that informs how Roberta Flack generates a rapturous vibe in performance is the subject of this essay. The energy that her sound produces is rooted in her choice of material, her musical arrangements, the feelingful communication between Flack and her musicians, and the production of her recordings. To claim Flack as an auteur, one also has to reclaim quiet storm, a commercially successful but critically maligned style of smooth "slow jams" that debuted in the mid 1970s via artists like Smokey Robinson and the Isley Brothers. The deliberate minimalism of Flack's classically informed music not only confirms her status as a quiet storm pioneer: it is the basic ingredient in her technical ability to create a spellbinding vibe. In unexpected ways, quiet storm challenges and augments the aesthetic ideals of ambient, a mid-1970s genre of avant-garde atmospheric music that has tended to exclude musicians of color and women.

The spellbinding vibe in Flack's work also cannot be extricated from politics. In retrospect, Flack has been a human rights advocate and an early gay rights sympathizer—not just in her publicity but more importantly in her music. Because she displaces the masculine aggression customarily associated with funk-era protest in favor of feminine vulnerability, Flack's complex history of advocacy has largely gone underrecognized. The issue of vibe as energy, as it informs the profound risks and stakes in Flack's musical output, finally provides another way to redress some critics' laments over the shallowness in today's soul music.

Vibeology

A rock concert is in fact a rite involving the evocation and transmutation of energy.
WILLIAM BURROUGHS[2]

In 1972, at the height of her success, Roberta Flack received the *Billboard* "Trend-Setters" Award for "moving jazz into the pop market with her soft delicate style."[3] This kudo remains an oversimplification of her complex take on crossover. Flack glided onto the charts by extending (and sometimes copying outright) Nina Simone's fusion of multiple genres— musical theater, soul, gospel, classical, blues, jazz, spirituals, rock, and folk—into an unclassifiable mélange. In a pop context, Flack held jazz credentials for several reasons: her small-combo arrangements featuring the jazz likes of Ron Carter and Bucky Pizzarelli; the purity of her tone and the way she played piano while singing in a manner reminiscent of cool stylists like Ella Fitzgerald and Shirley Horn; and because jazz radio stations were the first to regularly play her music.

Flack's 1969 debut *First Take*—an album that only found commercial success two years later, after the director Clint Eastwood prominently featured "The First Time Ever I Saw Your Face" on his *Play Misty for Me* soundtrack—exemplifies her eclectic, "queer" approach to pop. Set to austere, acoustic jazz instrumentation, the songs include "The First Time Ever I Saw Your Face," Ewan MacColl's bolero-tempo Scottish folk ballad; "Los Angelitos Negros," an Afrocentric self-esteem anthem sung in Spanish; "Hey That's No Way to Say Goodbye," a languid, windswept reading of the Leonard Cohen ode; "Compared to What," a sardonic Gene McDaniels protest tune; "I Told Jesus," the plaintive Negro spiritual popularized by Nina Simone; and "The Ballad of the Sad Young Men," a musical theater lament about the plight of homosexual barflies. As with her subsequent recordings, *First Take* foregrounds the smooth, transparent sensuality of Flack's alto. Idiosyncratic and instantly recognizable, Flack's contemplative timbre has been accounted for by critics in a variety of ways: "pure, crystalline," "restrained," "lilting," "airy," "supple," "soulfully ethereal," "seasoned, subtle, smoldering." No literal or technical description of Flack's vocal accurately captures the magic of her tone because it conveys meaning most profoundly at a vibrational level. For part of a long-forgotten children's book series called "Women behind the Bright Lights"—the other subjects are Olivia Newton-John, Valerie Harper, and Cher—Linda Jacobs wrote an installment on Roberta Flack in 1975. The provocative title, *The Sound of Velvet Melting*, is perhaps the most sophisticated description of Flack's singing to date. "Her voice was rich and warm, like thick purple velvet," Jacobs notes, recognizing the metaphysical texture of Flack's lustrous tone. "It slipped easily between soft and loud, high and low, always flowing. 'If velvet could melt, that's how it would sound,' someone once said."[4]

For Jacobs, the physical structure and technical dressing of a concert space has the power to threaten the cultivation of soulfulness. "Thousands of people packed the auditorium," Jacobs noted. "Roberta couldn't see from her lake of light into their darkness. She couldn't touch them or even hear their individual voices."[5] Still, Flack generated collective intimacy and communion. "There was one way for her to make contact with each one of those people. She sat down to the piano. Her dark, graceful fingers danced across the polished keys, making lacy sounds where they touched. Other musicians took up the refrain. The drums thumped, the bass throbbed. Roberta began to sing."[6] Soulful musicianship emerges as the transformative force that overcomes individuation, alienation, and isolation: the moment when an audience falls into rapt, hushed silence. "Roberta Flack had reached her audience. 'That's what it's all about . . . making contact,' she says."[7] In contrast to the traditional binary communication model, soulful performance resembles a feedback loop. At the same time, Jacobs demystifies Flack by rooting her prowess in craft. "But soul alone can't produce the delicate control of Roberta's piano play-ing," she admits.[8] Soulful feeling functions in tandem with a reper-toire of concert skills, in direct opposition to the knee-jerk misconception that soul is exclusively about freedom or escape from the "prison" of technique.

Except for genres like free jazz and dub, vibe is usually overlooked in critical discussions of popular music. This neglect is especially egregious when one considers the fundamental nature of vibration to music itself. Science has long confirmed that sound is produced through the mechani-cal, acoustic, or electrical vibration of physical matter. In singing, sound is produced through the vibration of vocal folds, forcing air from the lungs causing the folds to open and close. "Vibrato" refers to the alternating pitch or frequency of a musical note that produces an oscillating or waver-ing effect. Beyond science, however, vibrations "magically" transmit in-formation, or content, in a nonrepresentational, sublime manner. The avant-garde composer and philosopher Anthony Braxton says: "What we call the blues is not just notes, it's a vibrational understanding that's been transmitted and encoded, and it's manifested in various forms of music in various different ways."[9] Braxton describes improvisation as the "vibra-tional fabric or liquid" of his music.[10] Music steeped in repeated pat-terns or motives produces collective spiritual transcendence, or group highs, toward the concept of "one nation under a groove." Affirmation of feeling and spirit—going with the flow, as it were—counters the fetishiza-tion of technique, form, artifact, and self-mastery commonplace in West-ern classical music. Spurred on by the success of *Vibe* magazine since the 1990s, the term "vibe" has become associated with African American urban slang.

Mood refers to an interior emotional state, usually temporary and shifting, as in Billy Joel's nostalgic "New York State of Mind." On the other hand, a person who "gives off" a New York vibe is being overtly expressive with an outward style. Similarly, there are external signifiers that register a soulful vibe in the popular consciousness: instrumenta-tion, chord changes, style of dress, gestures, and so on. Some performers attempt to appear soulful simply by accessing these external signifiers. Consequently, as LeRoi Jones notes in *Blues People*, R&B can be one of the most easily "faked" genres. "One gets the idea that a man who falls down on his back screaming is doing so, even though he might be genuinely moved to do so, more from a sense of performance than from any unalterable emotional requirement."[11] Yet it would be highly cynical to assume that soulfulness is automatically inauthentic simply because it can be stylized, manifested physically, or even commodified in the commercial marketplace. Jones himself identifies spirit and feeling as essential aspects of black music throughout his body of work, most notably in a 1987 chapter (writing as Amiri Baraka with his wife Amina) called "The Phenomenon of Soul in African American Culture."[12]

In the liner notes to *First Take,* the singer-songwriter Les McCann describes the 1968 "happening" through which he became acquainted with Flack's music, though only her backup singers were present. "Everybody in the club was into it—a lot of clapping, stamping and getting-togetherness. Then from out of somewhere, rose beautiful chitlinized voices in full harmony, and we all kept swinging right on through to the end of the song."[13] For McCann, the vibrations in the room contributed to the condition of "getting-togetherness": the erotic fusion of Self into Other, the moment where the ensemble on stage formatted the ensemble in the audience. Jazz musicians are said to play best when they are "vibin'," a complex form of interactive, improvisatory communication. In describing how he chooses which tabla player to hire for a project, the U.K. fusion artist Nitin Sawhney illuminates the link between flow, groove, and vibrational energy: "if I want to use someone who's really going to make everything flow and groove, I'll always use Aref. Aref's just like energy, man. He's got so much energy, he's always vibing."[14] Soulful music is the continual possibility of getting togetherness against the backdrop of unredeemable suffering and cosmic alienation.

Vibing is also an essential part of the reach for spiritual communion that occurs on dance floors. The groovy possibility of transcendent freedom has long been well mythologized in disco songs. When asked in an interview to describe the Loft, his legendary 1970s club, David Mancuso claimed: "It's a vibe. You're having a peace of mind or you're not. Usually the more you shed your ego the more peace of mind you will have."[15] Simon Reynolds's suggestively titled *Energy Flash* argues that the Ecstasy experience in rave nightclubs ranges from "open-hearted tête-à-tête through collective euphoria to full-blown mystical rapture."[16] This sense of "mystical rapture" can always be informed by ritualistic use of drugs and other substances. However, the end goals, achieved artificially or naturally, often remain the same: communion, getting togetherness, and synchronicity.

Just as fully, vibe anchors record producing. In his study of the craft of recording music, *The Poetics of Rock*, Albin Zak defines vibe as "consistency of expression and atmosphere."[17] Zak claims that vibe can be "difficult to maintain in the studio, [thus] pre-production often serves as a vital preparatory stage."[18] The producer Daniel Lanois, for instance, is famous for searching out unusual, charismatic recording environments (castles, New Orleans mansions, and such) not only for the acoustics but to create a shared feeling among musicians that will then transfer to the record itself. At the same time, capturing a vibe can be purely the result of creative accident. Wil-Dog Abers, the bassist for the fusion hip-hop group Ozomatli, claims that "you might be in the nicest studio, but then you might record something in the bathroom while you're on the road. And that ends up on the record because of a certain quality—the tone or vibe of whatever you captured at that particular moment."[19] In an interview with Joel Dorn, who produced most of Flack's classic Atlantic recordings, a writer noted: "Dorn feels good about Roberta's *First Take*. Even on that album there were technical mistakes which took him months to fix, [but] he finds a kind of magic in it—a magic that would be hard to capture again."[20]

Vice-president of Atlantic Records in the late 1960s, Dorn signed Flack to a recording contract after witnessing her perform live at Mister Henry's Capitol Hill, a legendary DC nightclub frequented by gay men and women to this day, where the owner, Henry Jaffe, had built an upstairs performance space, replete with church pews and a Mason and Hamlin piano, specially for her. Dorn claimed that on the night he went to see Flack perform there were only about "nine people in the bar," including "four dykes sitting at a table together," arguing loudly through the performance.[21] When Flack sang "Do What You Gotta Do"—just her sitting at the piano—the four fell into rapt silence, and when she finished singing they gave her a standing ovation. Dorn found it "really weird to see a standing ovation in an empty club" and he knew he wanted to sign her. Given a very small budget (approximately $10,000, Dorn recalls), the challenge became how to capture Flack's ability to spellbind a live audience on a studio record. Tony Taylor, the owner of another DC nightclub, actually enlisted thirty to forty of her fans as an audience for her to work off in the studio. Still not satisfied, Dorn brought in more experienced musicians and strings as overdubs. The final result is a series of composite takes that ironizes the album's documentarian title. But it also serves to demonstrate for soul purists that calculation sometimes informs spontaneity.

Still, much of the vibe of *First Take*, like Flack's other classic albums, has to do with the tremendous feeling that went into the performances: a shared fondness for vibing. Reminiscing about a live gospel performance with Cissy Houston, Flack remembered that "people were on their feet, and they stayed there. We got to that point all performers strive for when you and your audience are on the same wavelength. You become the person who pulls people into the music."[22] Flack's attitude toward vibin' is echoed by the statements of her musicians, an extraordinary communion of talents including King Curtis, Donny Hathaway, Bucky Pizzarelli, Ron Carter, Hubert Laws, Eumir Deodato, Bernard "Pretty" Purdie, Eric Gale, and Richard Tee. Ralph McDonald, Flack's frequent collaborator, producer, and co-writer of the hit "Where Is the Love," perhaps sums it up best: "There was no electronic music back when I was coming up. It was acoustic, so you *had* to listen to each other. That's how we created. That's how we played, off each other. It was all about the vibe."[23]

Caught Up in the Rapture: Reconsidering Quiet Storm

The distinctive magic of Roberta Flack is inextricably related to the minimalist quietude of her classic ballads. Songs like 1975's slinky "Mr. Magic" and the dreamlike "Feel Like Makin' Love" are some of the most hushed, low-key R&B recordings ever released. Writing in *Rolling Stone*, Julius Lester identifies her gift: "More than any singer I know, she can take a quiet, slow song (and most of hers are) and infuse it with a brooding intensity that is, at times, almost unbearable."[24] Some of Flack's album titles, like *Quiet Fire* and *Blue Lights in the Basement* (named after slow jam—only parties), confirm her penchant for damped understatement.

Clues to Flack's musical sensibility can be found in her cover of Lori Lieberman's "Killing Me Softly with His Song," a perfect song choice for Flack, winning her a second consecutive Grammy for Record of the Year, as well as Song of the Year and Pop Vocal Female trophies. The killing, of course, is both ironic and metaphorical: the narrator feels as if she is being sensually turned "inside out" by a guitar-wielding "young boy" singer. It is as if her intimate thoughts have been exposed, even though he is a "stranger" and they've never met. The lulling, delirious reverb and echo effects turn Flack's stacking choral harmonies into a pillowy, floating soundscape. Eumir Deodato's clever arrangement gradually fills out, particularly on the famously scatted bridge. But the subdued delicacy of the instrumentation remains consistent throughout the track. What's ingenious about "Killing Me Softly" is that form is inseparable from content: it's a rapturous, delicately rendered performance of a song about the process of being enraptured by a delicately rendered performance of a song. The laid-back breeziness of the record helped mark the drift toward more mellow sounds in American popular music of the 1970s. Soft rock, forged by artists like Carole King and Fleetwood Mac, found its R&B analogue in quiet storm, the tenderized style that became home to artists like Flack, the Isley Brothers, and Frankie Beverly and Maze.

For the uninitiated, quiet storm began in 1976 as a programming niche spearheaded by Melvin Lindsey at Howard University's WHUR-FM. The title came from Smokey Robinson's "Quiet Storm," the first recording ever played on the format. The opening lines of Robinson's bossanova–flavored tune hint at the format's overall aesthetic: "soft and warm, a quiet storm / quiet as when flowers stalk at break of dawn." Sensuous and pensive, quiet storm is seductive R&B, marked by jazz flourishes, "smooth grooves," and tasteful lyrics about intimate subjects. As disco gave way to the "urban contemporary" format at the outset of the 1980s, quiet storm expanded beyond radio to emerge as a broad catchall supergenre. Quiet storm stalwarts include Anita Baker, Luther Vandross, Stephanie Mills, and Sade, but the format is now roomy enough to incorporate hip-hop–influenced soul aspirants like D'Angelo, Alicia Keys, and Anthony Hamilton. Roberta Flack's *First Take* prefigured the 1975 rise of quiet storm by nearly six years. It would not be a stretch to say that her early Atlantic recordings helped create the aesthetic. During quiet storm's zenith in the 1980s, Flack continued to produce staples like the satiny Donny Hathaway duet "The Closer I Get to You" and the saccharine wedding anthem "Tonight I Celebrate my Love," featuring Peabo Bryson. "Set the Night to Music," a 1992 duet with Maxi Priest, became her last chart topper.

Rolling Stone's Ben Fong-Torres once described quiet storm as a "blend of pop, jazz fusion, and R&B ballads—all elegant and easy-flowing, like a flute of Veuve Clicquot champagne."[25] Fong-Torres's clever metaphor brings us to a discussion of class and status. Like other quiet storm artists, Flack is regularly referred in articles as "classy," "polished," and "slick." Some critics view quiet storm's reach for upscale hauteur as symptomatic of black assimilationism and false consciousness in the aftermath of civil rights struggles. In 1988's *The Death of Rhythm and Blues,* Nelson George lambastes sell-out artists who appear to be deluded by "crossover consciousness" and water down their music to secure white audiences. Peabo Bryson, an artist who first rose to mainstream popularity while singing with Flack, is held up as an example of an artist whose hubris for crossover success is ultimately met with the indignity of dwindling concert bookings and low record sales. In 1998's *Just My Soul Responding,* Brian Ward avoids this sell-out approach although he sees classy quiet storm as symptomatic of deep fissures in the black community, insofar as it bypasses "lower class black adults who tended to go for darker funk tones, deep soul classics and later for the rap stylings which spoke more directly to their still functionally segregated and disadvantaged black lives."[26] In his three-part assessment of the roots of soullessness in contemporary black music, Mark Anthony Neal notes that 1980s R&B sought to attract "upscale 'urban' audiences—whether legitimate members of the black middle class or working class strivers."[27] Targeted to mature audiences in the age of hip-hop, quiet storm became "increasingly out of touch with a generation of black youth consumers."[28] Quiet storm, with its easy-listening bent, avoidance of profanity, and neglect for street concerns, seemed complacent at a time when Reagonomics was widening the gap between black rich and poor. Rap also ushered in a new squadron of hypermasculine hardbodies, from Kurtis Blow to Rakim to LL Cool J, who were worlds away from mannered, feminized quiet storm maestros like Freddie Jackson and Luther Vandross.

I have previously written about how the aesthetics of upward mobility in soul, such as polish, class, and refinement, generates fears of effeminization as depoliticization.[29] Critics decried Vandross's lack of masculine "funk," inexorably tied to his fondness for glitz, operatic grandeur, and domestic glamour. With Flack—who launched Vandross's career as a session singer in the mid-1970s before firing him in an effort to encourage him to pursue his solo career—those fears are more directly linked to the effect of her classical music training on her (in)ability to generate soul. Like Nina Simone before her, Flack straddled an interest in classical music and gospel. Flack spent her Arlington, Virginia, youth in the African Methodist Episcopal Zion Church where she "grew up playing piano for the choir—Handel, Bach, Verdi, Mozart, and all those great, wonderful, intricately written Negro spirituals."[30] She would then sneak into the Baptist church down the street to get her fix of "the raunchy, wide-open, free, spontaneous, full-of-life thing" performed by gospel luminaries like Sam Cooke, Mahalia Jackson, Clara Ward, the Five Blind Boys, and the Mighty Clouds of Joy. She won a statewide, segregated classical piano competition at thirteen; preternaturally gifted, she enrolled in Howard University on a full music scholarship at the unusually young age of fifteen. After earning a master's in music education, Flack began her career teaching math and English in a small high school in Farmville, North Carolina, before returning to DC to teach in public schools. She earned money on the side accompanying opera singers at the Tivoli Club, where she discovered her ability to draw audiences with her singing voice.

Like Miles Davis, whose cool minimalism was rooted in his European classical training to lyrically hold notes as well as his own recognition of his limited technical virtuosity, Flack's restrained, economical style stems from her fusion of classical and gospel techniques. Her distinctively spare arrangements, predilection for spaciousness, and cool reflective tone are the result of her fondness for composers like Liszt and Bach. For instance, her minimalist piano accompaniment to Donny Hathaway's devastating 1972 reading of "For All We Know," which appears on *Roberta Flack and Donny Hathaway*, alters the harmonic structure of the jazz standard and is clearly inspired by classical counterpoint.

Yet that minimalist approach also seems to be a personal sensibility as much as it is a result of formal training. In a 1977 radio interview, Flack is asked to explain what she learned from classical training. She responds that she likes to "stay involved in the structure of music" in a "scientific and soulful way."[31] When asked about the softness of her music, she claims that she likes to represent that kind of "atmosphere, down into the basement, turn on soft lights."[32] She goes on: "everybody has that thing in them, that little quiet space. And I think fortunately that is probably my forte when it comes to performing popular music and that it's a blessing because there's a need for people to be able to play music that addresses itself to that little space too . . . I am more in tune as an artist . . . the most artistic part of my soul lends itself to that kind of song and that kind of melody that is so haunting and so beautiful and so soft and so spiritual."[33] Indeed, Flack's personal orientation to softness and restraint underscores her artistic choices.

While her classically informed minimalism could, as *Rolling Stone* notes, be seen as an elaboration of soul rather than its foreclosure, that economical restraint and reach for controlled purity also make her music less than properly soulful for any number of music critics. "Boring," "depressing," "uninteresting," "detached," "bland," "cold," "unsentimental," "lifeless," "studied," and "calculated" are some of the adjectives regularly used to describe her work. Flack's brazen intellectualism and concentrationist, classical approach to music making—qualities to some degree shared by her classically trained soulmate Donny Hathaway—are imagined to run up against the pursuit of soul. *The Village Voice*'s Robert Christgau japed in 1971: "Flack is generally regarded as the most significant new black woman singer since Aretha Franklin, and at moments she sounds kind, intelligent, and very likable. But she often exhibits the gratuitous gentility you'd expect of someone who says 'between you and I.' "[34] He then encourages readers to skip out on Flack "until she crackles a bit" and listen instead to a grittier soul singer, Ann Peebles. In 1981, in reviewing Flack's greatest hits collection, Christgau still resists: "On the evidence of these hits (the early albums were marginally livelier), she has nothing whatsoever to do with rock and roll or rhythm and blues and almost nothing to do with soul. The analogy isn't Donny Hathaway (who lives on in duet after duet), much less Stevie Wonder (also represented)—it's Barry Manilow. She made 'The First Time Ever I Saw Your Face' and 'Killing Me Softly With His Song,' he made 'Mandy' and 'I Write the Songs,' and who is to say which achievement will prove more durable? Flack has better taste, I agree—that's the point. In the long run, pop lies are improved by vulgarity."[35]

Christgau is hesitant to include Flack under the banner of soul because of her MOR aesthetic. He compares her lack of vulgarity and inability to "crackle" to the milquetoast output of Manilow, whom he describes elsewhere as having an "uncompromisingly inoffensive voice—a voice that never hints at sex or history or even chops."[36] In other cases, Flack's interest in polish over grit is read as a deliberate reach for whiteness.

Wilfrid Mellers notes that Flack's "pure-toned wistfulness" on her performance of Janis Ian's "Jesse" makes her sound "nearly as White as Janis
herself."[37] There is of course a danger of reaffirming a stereotypical racial
binary in which black music is hot, energetic, body-driven, and gritty and
white music, or music that aspires to whiteness or moves away from blues
traditions, is cold, uninspired, intellectual, and rational. In response to
the threat of pigeonholing, Flack has stated: "I want to be a singer . . . not
just a black singer. I am black. I grew up in a lower middle-class black
home. I think black is beautiful but there is so much gorgeous music in
the world that has nothing to do with black."[38] She turns the critiques of
her lack of soulfulness into a dissertation on racial marginalization and a
rejection of soul as vulgarity or pure grit: "I am not a black person who
sounds anything like Aretha Franklin or anything like Chaka Khan. I
know what I am and I don't want to, and I shouldn't have to, change in
order to be who I am."[39] Lest her pooh-poohing of soulful grit be read as a
desire to escape her blackness in pursuit of white upscale refinement, she
has also said: "I'm not interested in developing a growl so I can join the
ranks of several rhythm and blues artists. Nor am I interested in developing a pure white tone so I can sell records to people who buy Olivia
Newton-John."[40] Recall that for Flack, soul is more than grit: it's about
making contact and producing getting togetherness.

One of the defining elements of Flack's rapturous vibe—and the key to
the slow-burn aesthetic that is quiet storm—may be the phenomenon
of silent frenzy. Frenzy is the palpable yet understated manifestation of
spirit or ambient energy in kinetic motion. Frenzy is a key phenomenon
of certain strains of Afro-Christian worship and is discussed by Du Bois
in *The Souls of Black Folk* in the following manner: "Finally the Frenzy of
'Shouting,' when the Spirit of the Lord passed by, and, seizing the devo-
tee, made him mad with supernatural joy, was the last essential of Negro
religion and the one more devoutly believed in than all the rest. It varied
in expression from the silent rapt countenance or the low murmur and
moan to the mad abandon of physical fervor,—the stamping, shrieking,
and shouting, the rushing to and fro and wild waving of arms, the weep-
ing and laughing, the vision and the trance."[41] The notion of frenzy as
"silent rapt countenance"—which is only one possible expression of the
aesthetic—is related to the hypnotic rapture I've previously described in
Flack's work. Stemming from her training both in gospel and in classical,

Flack has the ability to generate silent or quiet frenzy in her work. Though the music is subdued it is nonetheless marked by simmering fiery energy, like the simmering heat that is velvet melting or the heat of intimacy and getting togetherness, akin to James Baldwin's notion of performance as electrical current corroborating flesh and blood between audience and performer. It is not surprising, then, that Flack has claimed to be inspired by the gospel legend Marion Williams, who, she says, "sings with the spirit of God's gift, serenely and quietly, but with fire."[42]

And still, despite the ubiquitous use of quiet storm samples like De-Barge's "Stay with Me" and the Isley Brothers' "Between the Sheets" in untold hip-hop songs, quiet storm—insofar as it is imagined to be soft, bleached, and assimilationist—is usually positioned opposite to the ideals of rap. For some, the avant-garde, futuristic aesthetics of hip-hop music, such as breakbeat science, sampling, and scratching, seemed light years ahead of quiet storm's retro orchestrations, slick strings, treacly electric pianos, and gated drum sets. While rap confirmed its political authority through bombastic loudness and percussive muscle, quiet storm's sluggish tempos, monotonous grooves, and dulcet decibel levels suggested impotence and lounge complacency.

One way to rescue quiet storm is to consider how it actually functions as "good background music." Defined by soft sounds that blend in with rather than overpower the environment, quiet storm can enhance a romantic vibe in the bedroom "between the sheets," at a candlelight dinner, at a lounge or any other subdued setting where getting togetherness and intimacy is the aim. Though the genre has been plundered over the years by record labels to produce endless recombinant hackneyed make-out compilations, quiet storm might be best considered a racialized take on—or redefinition of—ambient music.

Ambient, in its original coinage by Brian Eno, was a defocused, minimalist music. In the liner notes to his 1978 *Music for Airports,* Eno writes, "An ambience is defined as an atmosphere, or a surrounding influence: a tint."[43] Elaborated on by artists like Terry Riley, Pauline Oliveros, and Harold Budd, ambient is the opposite of Muzak, that "conventional background music" inherently designed to strip away "doubt and uncertainty" and to blanket over the "acoustic and atmospheric idiosyncrasies" in a listening environment.[44] Instead, ambient induces "calm and a space to think" and it can accommodate "many levels of listening attention without enforcing one in particular; it must be as ignorable as it is interesting."[45] The French composer Erik Satie, whose music arguably prefigured ambient, philosophizes about "Musique d'ameublement" or furniture music: he was among the first to muse explicitly about the way that music could be deliberately played atmospherically as background music for a dinner or at a party rather than in the foreground. Satie's concept, echoed in the work of Eno, seems directly related to the background function of quiet storm. The new age movement quickly appropriated the gauzy meditational sounds of Eno's experimental albums like *Another Green World* and *Music for Films*. Since then ambient has expanded to accommodate a variety of dream-like or atmospheric musics across genres, from dub and reggae to pop, rock, and house music, straddling the work of groups like Orb, Aphex Twin, Air, and Röyskopp. Ambient has received a significant amount of critical attention: two of the genre's major tomes include David Toop's richly evocative *Ocean of Sound: Aether Talk, Ambient Sound and Imaginary Worlds,* and Mark Prendergast's lengthy (but not exhaustive) *The Ambient Century: From Mahler to Moby—The Evolution of Sound in the Electronic Age.*

At first glance, quiet storm would seem to have little to do with ambient. The former is humanist and modernist in its earnestness, while the latter is decidedly postmodernist and flirts with computer technologies, posthuman consciousness, and cyborgian possibilities. Driven by artists like Vandross, Anita Baker, and Lenny Williams, quiet storm has always been popular and tied to commercial radio and major label concerns. Ambient, wrapped up in Eno's cerebral, philosophical musings, began as—and remains for some—an esoteric, acquired taste. Stemming from the work of minimalists like Steve Reich and LaMonte Young, ambient music can be characterized by an arythmic or nonexistent pulse, raga-inspired modality and droning, space-sounding electronic instrumentation, and tape loops. Quiet storm tends to be more conventionally structure-oriented and privileges melody and often pyrotechnical vocal performance. As Eric Tamm notes: "Ambient music was decorative, rather than expressionist; if not completely free of individual taste, memory, and psychology, as in [John] Cage's ideal, it nevertheless lacked the bathos of self-importance and confessional displays of open psychic wounds."[46] For Tamm, ambient would likely sidestep the confessional aesthetic of blues-based musics like soul.

These justifications become the implicit reasons for excluding a great degree of black music from the history of ambient. In Mark Prendergast's *The Ambient Century*, for instance, only a few black figures, such as Miles Davis, Goldie, Tricky, and DJ Spooky, show up in the book's five-hundred pages. While Prendergast devotes copious space to white artists like U2 who perform lyric-driven, narrative-driven, openly sentimental blues-based, gospel-inspired music, there's no mention of African American pioneers like the texture-driven free jazz artist Joe Harriott, who as early as 1963 described his music as "best listened to as a series of different pictures—for it is after all by definition an attempt to paint, as it were, freely in sound."[47] Men dominate *The Ambient Century*: few women, of any color, are mentioned. The author also completely avoids quiet storm; in fact, Marvin Gaye and Donna Summer are the only soul music artists mentioned. Such studies of minimalism and ambience are routinely defined by double standards stemming from patriarchal, Eurocentric approaches.

Yet there are plenty of shared similarities between ambient and quiet storm. Tamm's descriptions of ambient as "quietness, gentleness, an emphasis on the vertical color of sound, establishment and maintenance of a single pervasive atmosphere" and music that "surrounded the listener with a sense of spaciousness and depth, encompassing one on all sides, instead of coming *at* the listener" are equally applicable to quiet storm.[48] Both unobtrusive musics emerged in the mid-1970s as soothing counter-aesthetics to pop music's sheer loudness and bombast. In 1975, Smokey Robinson, who coined quiet storm, notes: "In our concerts we try to create a quiet storm, that is our aim in performing. . . . When I left the Miracles, I went to a lot of concerts and night clubs, I saw everyone, black, white[,] oriental and they were all loud, usually you can't hear what they're singing. So I decided that our act would be different so you can come, hear and dig what's happening."[49] Quiet storm and ambient equally concern themselves with tone and texture, washes and colors of sounds, and the use of effects to create intimacy and warmth that functions in the background or foreground. Ambient could be discussed in terms of vibe: we have already seen how the expressive balladry of a quiet storm artist like Flack has the capacity to "tint" or color the atmosphere of a location. Both musics draw on repeating patterns, motifs, or ostinatos to create a hypnotic mood: ambient drones parallel the smooth grooves of quiet storm.

David Toop's expansive definitions of ambient begin to make room for quiet storm. Ambient can include "recordings on which sheer noise, minimalism or non-narrative drift is sold and used as a kind of pop music," and it can also include "music exploring the language of physical sensation; music in which a blankness prevails, ambient dread or bliss, calm and near-silence, extreme minimalism, or a spacious landscape, a tropic or frozen atmosphere in which the listener can insert her or himself, occupy the foreground, wander the imaginary space for hours at a time."[50] Toop is also an accomplished musician and record producer, and in 1996 he released a quiet storm compilation entitled *Sugar and Poison: Tru-Life Soul Ballads for Sentients, Cynics, Sex Machines & Sybarites*, featuring drift classics such as "Sensuality" by the Isley Brothers, "Just Like a Baby" by Sly and the Family Stone, as well as less-well-known singles like "Chasin' a Dream" by Tashan and Chic's "At Last I Am Free." In his hallucinogenic, impressionistic liner notes about the travails of Dr. Horse, chock full of references to "sound word-feeling-rhythms" and music that is "far inside the vibration of a silent scream," Toop hints at the intertwined nature of ambient and sentimental soul music.[51]

However, Toop is a lone voice in the wilderness. The inclusion of Marvin Gaye in Prendergrast's *The Ambient Century* (in a section alongside Van Morrison) is a case in point. Given his experimental approach to multitracking and phase shifting, and his willingness to include psychedelic atmospherics on records like *Let's Get It On* and 1976's *I Want You*, Gaye was unquestionably an ambient innovator. Yet those same albums clearly define him as quiet storm royalty. There are numerous other figures in the history of R&B, and I would include Flack among them, who straddle both worlds or render such divisions untenable. Flack's classic recordings are experimentalist in their low-key approach to volume, texture, color, orchestration, and arrangement. But they are also avant-garde in more traditional ways. *Roberta Flack and Donny Hathaway* ends with a seven-minute classically inflected electric piano piece called "Mood" that is so self-effacingly pensive and driven by motif that one may even forget the record is still spinning. To my mind, it resembles one of the floating atmospheric tracks on an early Eno solo record. Though inconsistent and lightweight, Flack's 1975 *Feel like Makin' Love*, which she self-produced under the pseudonym Rubina Flake, is drenched in ambient, psychedelic effects. The last six minutes of the nearly twelve-minute Stevie Wonder–penned "I Can See the Sun in Late December" produce a druggy soundscape that sounds like nothing if not an early Rotary Connection avant-garde confection. The same goes for her self-produced 1977 *Blue Lights in the Basement,* where Eugene McDaniels's rapturous "25th of Last December" seems to float out of the speakers and linger in the air. Such hypnotic recordings are nearly self-conscious attempts at sustaining a quiet-fire vibe, decidedly experimental in the context of mainstream R&B. For any number of reasons, they deserve to be included in the history of ambient.

Softness and Gravitas

Reviewing 1971's Newport Jazz Festival, a writer claimed that Roberta Flack stood out on a bill involving such luminaries as Aretha Franklin, Thelonious Monk, Jimmy Smith, Charlie Mingus, Kenny Burrell, and Dizzy Gillespie. "An informal poll among the audience for unqualified heaviness," he concluded, "would have gone to Roberta Flack, though she brought the house down by being lyrical and so slinkily sensual."[52] The concept of "unqualified heaviness" is worth some consideration here insofar as it likely refers to the profound emotional depth and resonance that some hear in Flack's music. It also likely references the explicit political content in her repertoire. Besides her primary interest in songs about romance and interpersonal relationships, Flack has recorded any number of nakedly political tunes. Released in the midst of the infamous social strife of 1968–69, *First Take* contains "Trying Times," a topical commentary on social turbulence penned by Donny Hathaway and Leroy Hutson, and "Compared to What?," a spry tune about everyday hypocrisy and political apathy. Flack's 1971 follow-up, the sublime *Chapter Two,* contains the Kurt Weill-esque antiwar "Business Goes On as Usual." Flack also regularly included songs like Marvin Gaye's "What's Going On?," "Inner City Blues," "Mercy Mercy Me," and Ralph McDonald's soaring "Tradewinds" (later covered by Rod Stewart) in her live sets. Critics often cite Gaye's 1971 *What's Going On* or Curtis Mayfield's 1970 *Curtis* or any Stevie Wonder album of the era as classic soul protest albums, even as they usually overlook Flack's contributions. This omission is of particular significance because Flack's politically charged *First Take* was released two years before Gaye's album.

   I would argue that Flack's quiet-fire aesthetic—her tendency toward softness, quietude, tenderness, restraint, and understatement—categorizes her music in conventionally feminine terms that do not gel with the conventionally masculinist thrust of protest. Her reflective treatment of a song like "Compared to What?"—avant-garde both lyrically and musically —sidesteps the aggressive thrust of a song like the Temptations' 1970 "Ball of Confusion." Flack's heaviness works in tandem with her aesthetic penchant for softness to deconstruct the axiomatic link between soulful funk, hardness, and machismo. Her radical discourse on "ambient blackness" also challenges the racist conception of black music as automatically equivalent to masculine sweat, over-the-top loudness, and in-your-face bombast. As Anthony Braxton notes: "Jazz musicians are still viewed from the so-called 'cutting mentality' where whoever plays the longest and strongest will 'win.' This kind of criterion not only distorts the musicians' creativity—because some people will be tempted to play up to the image—it also reinforces 'the already over-accented position of the masculinity affinity slant of present-day black creativity'; that is, the music is reduced to empty displays of fake 'soulfness' and pyrotechnic machismo, or what is called 'power'—even though in actual fact, this phenomenon retards the real power of the music."[53]

The soulful heaviness of Flack's quiet-fire music also has to do with its sacred content. Like her Atlantic labelmate Aretha Franklin, and her musical peer Bill Withers, Flack made Christian-inflected music that spoke to African American uplift and pride in the immediate aftermath of civil rights struggles. *First Take* contains "Los Angelitos Negros," and the liner notes claim that Flack introduces the song in concert by asking: "Painters, why do you always paint white virgins? Paint beautiful black angels." *Quiet Fire*, from 1972, offers the scorching "Sunday and Sister Jones," a Eugene McDaniels–penned social commentary about life and death rituals in the black community, as well as an experimental tribal funk uptempo called "Go Up Moses." *Roberta Flack and Donny Hathaway* features the black love ballad "Be Real Black for Me": "Our time is short and precious / Your lips, warm and luscious . . . Your hair, soft and crinkly . . . be real black for me." In 1971 Flack appeared in the documentary *Soul to Soul*, in which African American artists like Mavis Staples and Tina Turner traveled to Accra, Ghana, to stage a concert commemorating the fourteenth anniversary of Ghanian independence from British rule. In 1973 Flack was in the documentary *Save the Children*, recorded during Jesse Jackson's Operation Push exposition in Chicago. In 1975 she performed with Bob Dylan at a benefit for a fighter unjustly convicted of murder, Rubin "Hurricane" Carter. Even as critics lambasted her for her proximity to whiteness and gentility, Flack had made mention of her desire to work toward her doctorate in language and logistics at the University of Massachusetts and to produce a textbook called "He Be Done Did," "an aid for ghetto-area teachers in understanding the language spoken by inner-city children."[54]

Flack's engagement with black pride and beauty was also cross-lateralized in her visual image. The singer emerged as a potent black fashion icon in the early 1970s, sporting a large Afro (captured in full glory on the cover of *Quiet Fire*) along with dashikis and Afrocentric baubles, bangles, and beads. In 1975 Flack was one of the winners of the "best dressed award" given by the National Society of Fashion, an organization "committed to the development and instillation of self-pride by bringing honor and recognition to outstanding sartorial members of the Black race."[55] Flack's Afrocentric glamour was part of the way she expanded the aesthetic terms of blackness toward the redefinition of soul. Perhaps no other mainstream musical artist of the 1970s more complexly brought black nationalism into discourse with European classical aesthetics and a proximity to whiteness. Early in her career, Flack received some publicity for her short-lived marriage to the white bass player Steve Novoselic. As with other singers like Diana Ross and Nina Simone who married outside the race, this information was presented matter-of-factly and was not positioned to challenge her relation to the black aesthetic. If anything, the frequent references to Flack's family life at the outset of her career seemed designed to promote an image of Flack that assured her heteronormativity: "she doesn't plan to entertain for long, but wants to have and adopt children and raise a family, including plenty of animals. A family and happiness and contentment are very important to her."[56]

Perhaps her publicity promoted her heterosexuality so vigorously because much of the rest of her career was implicitly devoted to destabilizing gender and sexuality. Throughout her career Flack has served as a champion of black male voices that represent alternative masculinity. Besides her work with Vandross and Peabo Bryson, Flack's ten-year creative association with her high school friend Donny Hathaway, before his untimely death in 1979, amounts to what was possibly the greatest male and female duo in R&B history. Hathaway and Vandross rose through the ranks to become two of the greatest balladeers of all time, not simply

Fig. 1. An Afrocentric fashion icon, redefining the parameters of soul: Roberta Flack in the early 1970s, publicity photo. COURTESY OF ATLANTIC RECORDS.

because of technical ability but more importantly because of the depth of feeling, vulnerability, and tenderness in their music. No other female singer in the history of soul music actively promoted and gave opportunities to help distinguish male balladeers in this particular way.

I have already noted that Flack was signed to Atlantic by Joel Dorn because of her ability to enrapture audiences that happened to have a strong gay core at a nightclub in DC. It is equally noteworthy that she included "The Ballad of the Sad Young Men" on her *First Take* debut. Written for the forgotten 1959 jazz musical *The Nervous Set*, the tune was penned by Fran Landesman and was recorded by Gil Evans and Anita O'Day. (Reportedly, Johnny Mathis recorded an aborted version.) Though the lyric never openly refers to the term "gay" in the context of the homosexual concept, its references are unmistakable: "All the sad young men, seek a certain smile / Someone they can hold, for just a little while, Tired little girl, does the best she can / Trying to be gay, for sad young men /

While a grimy moon, watches from above / All the sad young men, who play at making love." The song's last line confirms its empathetic tone: "Misbegotten moon shine for sad young men / Let your gentle light guide them home again." "Ballad of the Sad Young Men" was a staple in Flack's live concerts. As early as 1971, she openly discussed its meaning in her stage act, lest its impressionistic lyrics be misunderstood. Flack sang songs of substance that had meaning for gay audiences throughout her career. "Jesse," an ambiguously titled love song by then-closeted Janis Ian, likely had resonance for Flack's audiences. In 1982 Flack sang the theme song to *Making Love,* Arthur Penn's groundbreaking and highly controversial film depicting homosexual love between two men. There is no way to fully emphasize the political risks Roberta Flack may have faced as an R&B singer in the late 1960s, 1970s, and early 1980s performing—and discussing—songs advocating human rights for gay men and women. That risk is impacted by her instantiation within Afrocentric Christianity, rarely a safe space for progressive discourses on gay rights, as well as by the risks around quietude and softness in her politically inspired and mainstream work.

Flack's heaviness appears to be related to Paul Gilroy's 1998 discussion of the "ultraserious, sepulchral" quality of classic soul music. "When I went to see Curtis Mayfield that night or any night of five hundred nights, similar nights, that have passed since then," Gilroy reminisces, "the atmosphere retains that kind of sepulchral mood. That holy burden of expectation bound to those profane delights."[57] For Gilroy, soul music derived its essential power through the application of sacred feeling of Christian worship into secular or worldly contexts. "Soul for me, now," he notes, "is about marking those intensities of feeling that were readily assimilated into a religious language and experience, a spiritual exploration, but it allows us to value them as a secular and sometimes profane phenomenon."[58] Rooted in the history of slavery and that institution's legacy of unredeemable suffering in black communities, soul music is marked by a sepulchral mood—the sort of auratic, ambient energy one might expect at a funeral—even as it bespeaks utopian optimism. That heaviness, or what I would call gravitas, is part and parcel of soul music's moral authority, the music's ability to generate intense possibilities for human interconnectedness and collective intimacy, what Gilroy refers to as "a scale of sociality, which is denied everywhere."[59] Gilroy finds this degree of sociality missing from hip-hop era black music for a number of reasons: the rise of digital instrumentation forecloses real-time, face-to-face vibing; the prominence of rhythm over voice in electronic music forecloses the cultivation of soul; and the desire for instantaneous "carnal vitality" over spiritual transcendence instantiates shrinking "orbits of freedom" in the individualist post–civil rights era. Contemporary black popular culture is marked by collective nostalgia for the old school, a fetishized yearning for classic soul music's power to produce getting togetherness.

The Fugees' wildly popular 1996 remake of Roberta Flack's "Killing Me Softly with His Song," produced by Wyclef Jean and Lauryn Hill, is a case in point. Their stylized hip-hop cover closely follows the original, save for the inclusion of a synth sitar sound, Wyclef's blurted chants, Hill's vocal melisma on the scatted bridge, and a bombastic drum-loop track that replaces Ralph McDonald's kick drum. When asked for her opinion, Flack notes: "They were smart enough to keep my version right where it was, without taking it too far left or right. And it was wonderful in the video how Lauryn decided she wanted me to sit at the piano, as if I was teaching her the song."[60] The Fugees' desire to produce, or reproduce, soulful vibe was the inspiration for the track. Group member Pras notes: "All three of us grew up surrounded by music, music that was soulful and real. There's a powerful feeling to that kind of music, and that's the feeling we wanted to bring to hip-hop."[61] Wyclef confirms this: "The idea in covering these songs is they have filled us with inspiration all our lives. . . . And we want them to inspire others, too. It's about us and the music connecting with the audience. When that happens, we reach a real unity with everyone in the room, a real solidarity that's uplifting."[62] Particularly given Flack's ringing endorsement, it would be difficult to argue resolutely that because the mode in which it functions is nostalgic, the Fugees' cover has any less relevance or is any less soulful than the old-school original.

However, if we pay closer attention to the differences in the production of the recordings and how those differences inform energetic content, the Fugees' rousing cover clearly bypasses the rapturous spellbinding vibe of the original. Instead, producer-performers Wyclef and Hill privilege the percussive rhythm, which is what gives the track its explicit hip-hop sensibility, at the expense of Flack's quiet-fire delicacy. In the absence of the original's intense attention to dynamics, arrangement, rapturous effects, instrumentation, and feelingful interaction between vibe-driven instrumentalists, the Fugees' cover cannot—or doesn't attempt to—access the melancholic "heaviness" of Flack's original. Instead, as confirmed by Wyclef's and Pras's comments, the Fugees aim to produce getting togetherness by conjuring up a nostalgic vibe that is worshipful of "old-school" modes of getting togetherness. This somewhat ironic strategy is largely unique to a post-instrumental, sample-driven generation of music producers.

The nostalgic reach for soulfulness in the Fugees' cover is partly a consequence of the political energy of hip-hop itself. Hip-hop's privileging of bombastic masculine aggression, in terms of thematic and sonic content, forecloses the sort of subtle "danger" engendered in the soft-heavy work of Roberta Flack. Though Flack is routinely cited as the antecedent to neo-soul singers like Erykah Badu and Lauryn Hill, it has become virtually impossible in today's risk-averse marketplace and conservative political climate to imagine a black R&B or hip-hop artist contracted to a major label rising to commercial prominence through the support of gay audiences or openly demonstrating Flack's degree of empathy for gay rights. These aspects of Flack's career, though swept under the rug or misunderstood, are not at all incidental to her ability to create a spellbinding vibe in her work. The lack of danger in contemporary soul music—which is another way to contemplate its perceived shallowness or growing irrelevance—has everything to do with the retrograde affirmation of patriarchy and the concomitant accretions of identity in corporate-driven, commodity culture. No surprise that Flack's Gene McDaniels–penned anti-war "Compared to What" received a politically inert cover in 2003 by the singer Mya and the "conscious" rapper Common that served as the soundtrack for one of Coke's "Coca Cola . . . Real" commercial series. Mark Anthony Neal notes the unfortunate obliviousness of contemporary audiences to these sort of submerged histories: "While it is in some ways welcome to hear McDaniels' 'Compared to What' drift through the air courtesy of Common, Mya, and Coke, the fact remains that the song's appropriation is yet another example of how the marketing of 'classic cool' often obscures the political contexts in which some pop art was initially created, whether it be witnessed in Che Guevara tee-shirts (on Taco Bell commercials with a 'militant' Chihuahua) or celebrity recordings of Marvin Gaye's 'What's Going On' like those witnessed directly after the 9/11 attacks."[63]

By investigating the phenomenon of vibe, this essay has attempted to illuminate some of the contexts in which Flack's "sentimental," "soft" work emerges as politically efficacious. A soulful vibe is ultimately inseparable from the depth and sophistication—and sincerity—of one's desire for communion and oneness. Today, even when empathy is present in mainstream circuits—such as Kanye West's bold 2005 critique of hip-hop homophobia during an MTV interview—that empathy rarely spills over into the music itself nor does it shape the overall trajectory of the artist's career. Flack's ability to integrate her political choices with the sound and energy of her music is inseparable from her self-assessment as an artist whose chief power is to bring people together. She leaves us with a message that's relevant for anyone interested in the future of soulful music: "As strong as I believe in the black struggle . . . or anyone's struggle for equality and just basic human rights, I know that my best bet is to express this through music. . . . You see, that's the thing today. This communication—oneness—has to come out in music."[64]

Notes

1. Beresford D. Weekes, "An Evening with Roberta Flack," *Oakland Post,* July 13, 1975, 4.
2. Mickey Hart, ed., *Spirit into Sound: The Magic of Music* (Petaluma, California: Grateful Dead Books, 1999), 148.
3. Anonymous, "Roberta Flack's Special!" *Oakland Post,* May 16, 1973, 20.
4. Linda Jacobs, *Roberta Flack, Sound of Velvet Melting* (St. Paul: EMC Corp., 1975), 7.
5. Ibid.
6. Ibid.
7. Ibid.
8. Ibid.
9. Graham Lock, *Forces in Motion: The Music and Thoughts of Anthony Braxton* (New York: Da Capo Press, 1988), 166.
10. Ibid., 174.
11. LeRoi Jones, *Blues People: Negro Music in White America* (New York: Morrow Quill, 1963), 173.
12. Amiri Baraka and Amina Baraka, *The Music: Reflections on Blues and Jazz* (New York: Morrow, 1987), 269.
13. Les McCann, liner notes, *First Take,* Atlantic Records, 1969.

14. Nitin Sawhney, "Exclusive Interview with Nitin Sawhney," *Ethnotechno.com*, November 4, 2003, http://www.ethnotechno.com/ints/int_nitin_11.04.03 .php (accessed April 16, 2007).

15. David Mancuso, "David Mancuso of the Loft—Interview," *Discomusic.com*, March 14, 2003, http://www.discomusic.com/people-more/49_0_11_0_ M77 (accessed April 16, 2007).

16. Simon Reynolds, *Energy Flash: A Journey through Rave Music and Dance Culture* (London: Picador, 1998), xxii.

17. Albin Zak, *The Poetics of Rock: Cutting Tracks, Making Records* (Berkeley: University of California Press, 2001), 136.

18. Ibid.

19. Chris J. Walker, "Ozomatli: Eclectic, Multi-Ethnic and Bustling with Energy," *Mix*, August 2004, 127.

20. Charles Morse, Ann Morse, and Dick Brude, *Roberta Flack* (Mankato, Minn.: Creative Education, 1975), 17.

21. Joel Dorn, interview with author, July 2003.

22. Patricia Smith, "Roberta Flack: Still True to Herself," *Boston Globe*, November 8, 1991, 43.

23. Billy Amendola, "Percussion Legend Ralph MacDonald: Living the Island Life," *Modern Drummer*, July 2004, 74.

24. Julius Lester, "*First Take* review," *Rolling Stone*, October 29, 1970.

25. Ben Fong-Torres, "KBLX: The Station Goes Quietly Upscale," *San Francisco Chronicle*, April 26, 1987, 59.

26. Brian Ward, *Just My Soul Responding: Rhythm and Blues, Black Consciousness, and Race Relations* (Berkeley: University of California Press, 1998), 427.

27. Mark Anthony Neal, "Rhythm and Bullshit? The Decline of R&B, Part One; Rhythm & Business, Cultural Imperialism and the Harvard Report," June 3, 2005, http://www.popmatters.com/music/features/050603-randb.shtml (accessed April 16, 2007).

28. Ibid.

29. Jason King, "Any Love: Silence, Theft and Rumor in the Work of Luther Vandross," *Callaloo* (Winter 2000): 422–47.

30. Smith, "Robert Flack."

31. Interview with Linda Snow, archived at the Museum of Radio, Film and Television in New York, 1977.

32. Ibid.

33. Ibid.

34. Robert Christgau, "Consumer Guide Reviews: Roberta Flack," *Village Voice*, 1971, http://www.robertchristgau.com/get_artist.php?id=1157&name=Roberta +Flack (accessed April 16, 2007).

35. Robert Christgau, "Consumer Guide Reviews: Roberta Flack," *Village Voice,* 1981, http://www.robertchristgau.com/get_artist.php?id=1157&name=Roberta +Flack (accessed April 16, 2007).

36. Robert Christgau, "Consumer Guide Reviews: Barry Manilow," *Village Voice,* 1994, http://www.robertchristgau.com/get_artist.php?id=3275&name=Barry +Manilow (accessed April 16, 2007).

37. Wilfrid Mellers, *Angels of the Night: Popular Female Singers of Our Time* (New York: Blackwell, 1987), 86.

38. Anonymous, " 'In Person: Roberta Flack' On KPIX Tues.," *Sun Reporter* (San Francisco), July 15, 1972, 38.

39. Richard Harrington, "Comeback with 'Oasis,' " *Washington Post,* January 29, 1989, 1.

40. Jim Sullivan, "Roberta Flack, the Romantic," *Boston Globe,* March 6, 1981, 1.

41. W. E. B. Du Bois, *The Souls of Black Folk* (New York: Penguin Books, 1989), 192.

42. Octavio Roca, "For Marion Williams Gospel Is a Song of her Soul," *Washington Times,* December 5, 1993, D3.

43. Brian Eno, liner notes, *Music for Airports.* Editions EG, 1978.

44. Ibid.

45. Ibid.

46. Eric Tamm, *Brian Eno: His Music and the Vertical Color of Sound* (Winchester, Mass.: Faber and Faber, 1989), 132.

47. Lock, *Forces in Motion,* 24.

48. Tamm, *Brian Eno,* 132.

49. Smitty, "Entertainment Scene," *Oakland Post,* July 20, 1975, 5.

50. David Toop, *The Ambient Century: Aether Talk, Ambient Sound and Imaginary Worlds* (London: Serpent's Tail, 1995), 11.

51. David Toop, liner notes, *Sugar and Poison: Tru-Life Soul Ballads for Sentients, Cynics, Sex Machines & Sybarites,* Virgin, 1996.

52. Stephen Curwood, "Newport's Spirit Came on Strong at Garden," *Bay State Banner,* December 16, 1971, 16.

53. Lock, *Forces in Motion,* 115.

54. Anonymous, "An Evening with Roberta Flack," *Oakland Post,* June 15, 1975, 4.

55. Anonymous, "National Best Dressed List for 1975," *Sun Reporter,* December 28, 1974, 12.

56. Jack Miller, "Flack's Magic Is Indirect," *Bay State Banner,* September 10, 1970, 14.

57. Paul Gilroy, "Questions of a Soulful Style: An Interview with Paul Gilroy," in *Soul: Black Power, Politics, Pleasure,* ed. Monique Guillory and Richard C. Green (New York: New York University Press, 1998), 262.

58. Ibid., 252.

59. Ibid., 256.

60. Steve Morse, "Carrying On, Softly, with her Songs and Spirit," *Boston Globe*, October 26, 2003, N7.

61. Deborah Evans Price, " 'They're Playing My Song,' " *Billboard*, May 11, 1996, 37.

62. Ibid.

63. Mark Anthony Neal, "Real: Compared to What? Anti-War Soul," *Pop Matters*, March 28, 2003, http://www.popmatters.com/features/030328-iraq-neal .shtml (accessed April 16, 2007).

64. Morse, Morse, and Brude, *Roberta Flack*, 31.

Michaelangelo Matos

All Roads Lead to "Apache"

12 Jerry Lordan was not an American Indian. He was a Londoner who had served in the Royal Air Force, dabbled in stand-up comedy, and worked in advertising before he began writing song hits for Mike Preston, Anthony Newley, John Barry, and especially the Shadows, the backing band of Cliff Richard, Britain's premier rock and roll teen idol until the Beatles came along. In 1959, Lordan saw a Burt Lancaster movie called *Apache*, which had come out in 1954. In much the way Charlton Heston played a Mexican in *Touch of Evil*, Lancaster was Massai, the last Apache left after Geronimo's surrender to the U.S. Cavalry in Arizona, and a man out for vengeance. The story was based on fact—the real-life Massai did in fact escape the prison train after Geronimo's tribe was captured—but the movie was primarily a frame for non-stop action. This gave Lordan an idea for a song, also titled "Apache," and Lordan sold it to Bert Weedon, then the top-selling solo guitar instrumentalist in England.

Thirty-four years after Weedon cut the song, Lordan was still complaining: "He hasn't even played the music that I wrote," the songwriter told an interviewer in 1993, two years before he died. "I wanted something noble and dramatic, reflecting the courage and savagery of the Indian."[1] Soon after, Lordan, who also had some minor hits as a vocalist, went on the road with Cliff Richard and the Shadows. He introduced the song to them (stories vary about how), and after the band returned to London, they recorded "Apache" in less than forty-five minutes, expecting it to be a B-side. Instead, it became a hit.

Sonically, the Shadows' "Apache" functions as the missing link between the zany country guitarist Speedy West, the looming rock pioneer Link Wray, and the zany, looming Italian soundtrack king Ennio Morricone. The steady galloping rhythm is a cross between a military march and, thanks to the ride cymbal, a jaunty, Latin-esque dance beat, similar to Ray Charles's contemporaneous hit, "What'd I Say." The straightforward melody—especially its clear, ringing lead notes—is robust and instantly memorable, with Hank Marvin's guitar nicely laconic and laden with echo. As the British critic Tom Ewing put it, "It conjures a shimmer of desert heat," an effect helped along by the Chinese tam-tam drum Cliff Richard kept time on while the drummer Tony Meehan played his kit—the most "Indian" portion of the arrangement. But the Shadows' use of echo on "Apache" stayed out the realm of kitsch futurism. Instead, you could call it kitsch nostalgia, giving the Old West a kind of day-glo sheen.

The song went to Number One in England on August 27, 1960, staying there five weeks and selling a million copies; it did just as well all over Europe. It also became something else—a modern standard, in part because of its tough, cool melody line, in part because of its eminently variable tempo ("Apache" sounds equally good fast or slow), and in part because it was adaptable to any style of music you could imagine, though during the sixties most of the covers seemed to be by surf guitar bands from California.

A major exception was the version that hit Number One in America the year after the Shadows,' the one by Jorgen Ingmann, a Danish guitarist who would later win the 1963 Eurovision Song Contest along with his wife, Grethe, with a song called "Dansevise (I Loved You)." Credited to Jorgen Ingmann and His Guitar, the beat of this third version of "Apache" is played entirely on a tom-tom, losing the Shadows' drive but emphasizing the song's would-be Native American war-drum associations; though the acoustic that the lead line was played on had some slapback echo on it, it didn't answer itself the way Marvin's did. Instead, Ingmann overdubbed curlicuing slide playing on the higher-pitched electric that evoked Hawaiian and Pacific Island music, then enjoying a vogue in American pop, in part via artists like Les Baxter and Martin Denny, who mined those sounds for their own hi-fi head-trips.

In short, what Ingmann did was take something that was already sourced in the ersatz—it gets no less realistic than Burt Lancaster playing a Native American—and added a sonic patina of "exotica," turning a simulacrum of a simulacrum into a Möbius loop of third-hand representation. This was added to by the photo on the cover of Ingmann's album, which featured the musician in war paint and headdress—Comanche war paint and headdress, to be precise. Factor in Lordan's comments about nobility and savagery, and the cumulative implied condescension becomes thicker than Hank Marvin's guitar tone.

Yet "Apache" was evocative, conjuring dusty plains via echoing guitars, the Old West arrived at through modern methods. It loomed and sunk, cast long shadows and bided its time until the cavalry arrived. For a record that sounded like the soundtrack to the most somber Bugs Bunny vs. Yosemite Sam cartoon ever made, "Apache" didn't seem silly. It meant business. Until its legacy took a turn in the mid-seventies, the artist who deviated from its melody the most was the person who first recorded it, Bert Weedon. Yet pliability was built into the song's structure—you could do just about anything with it and have it remain recognizable. "Apache" is a song that both invites and resists interpretation—despite the many changes it would undergo, as a melody and as a piece of rhythm that first underpinned the melody and later everything under the sun, it usually retains the ferocity Lordan set out to evoke, albeit in a different manner with each stylistic overhaul, from the melody's cowboys-and-Injuns doominess to the urban-jungle grit of the classic breakbeat it would evolve into.

In the years following the Shadows and Ingmann/Guitar versions, "Apache" became something of a rebel-rock standard, usually via being taken out to the beach or out for a ride. Surf-identified artists like Seattle's Ventures honored it as a forerunner of their hollow, wave-riding guitars, while the wild-assed Davie Allan and the Arrows, from LA, revved it up and dragged it through black-tar roads, fuzzing it up. "Apache" it remained, which meant it stayed earthy. Guitar rock, however, did not—it got cosmic. Psychedelia began in earnest in the mid-sixties, and while a few of the surf vanguard were down—Davie Allan's best song was a seven-minute ditty titled "Cycle-Delic"—the old guard suddenly became the corniest thing going, a fate sealed in June 1967 by Monterey Pop, where the Beach Boys no-showed, the San Francisco sound began its long descent into classic-rock radio-programming tedium, and Jimi Hendrix introducing himself to America by lighting his guitar on fire and intoning, "You'll never hear surf music again." He was wrong, but the damage was done: Like girl groups and the Twist, the forms that "Apache" had nurtured would seem like relics, even—especially—when revived by future generations.

That might have been the fate of "Apache" itself if it hadn't been for Michael Viner. In the swirl of culture and politics that was the 1960s, Viner, who had worked on Robert Kennedy's 1968 presidential campaign, became an MGM talent scout and A&R man in LA, where his boss was Mike Curb, the Richard M. Nixon crony and future lieutenant governor of California, which is how an RFK man wound up overseeing the music at Nixon's second inaugural.[2] Viner was also a bongo player who did occasional film work. In 1972, the year of Nixon's reelection, Viner put a pair of songs on the *Psychotronic* magazine drive-in classic, *The Thing with Two Heads*, which starred fallen forties star Ray Milland and the football player Rosey Grier together as the title character. Milland was white, Grier was black, the joke got old fast, and Viner's cheesy "Bongo Rock" was a minor hit for MGM's Pride subsidiary. Viner recorded it under the name the Incredible Bongo Band with a revolving cast of studio musicians anchored by the drummer Jim Gordon, formerly of Derek and the Dominos, who later went on to kill his mother.

"Bongo Rock" was a remake of Preston Epps's 1959 instrumental hit; Viner reconstructed it as a goofy funk number. Like the original, it entered the charts alongside several other instrumental hits: Deodato's "Also Sprach Zarathustra (Theme from 2001)," Eric Weissberg and Steve Mandell's "Dueling Banjos," the Edgar Winter Group's "Frankenstein," Focus's "Hocus Pocus," and Love Unlimited Orchestra's "Love's Theme" were all top-ten in 1973. For the *Bongo Rock* album, Viner tried a few others in the same vein. The best of them was "Apache."

On the album, the Incredible Bongo Band reworked "Apache" into grandiose, kitschy funk. But something about that stentorian melody escaped camp, even when turned into a pitched battle between colliding horns, jetliner guitar, boiling-over organ, and massed percussion. Viner and his crew had concocted the most crazed piece of orchestral funk ever recorded, and what made it all the more ridiculous was that the song never lost its shape, never stopped being "Apache." It was, as Jerry Lordan had wished, noble and dramatic, and maybe a bit savage, though probably not all that courageous—apart from the biggest liberty it took, which was to extend the song via a minute-long percussion break, the trap drummer (probably Gordon) and the congaist (the legendary Nassau-born session player King Errisson) dueling to a draw, the congas winnowing into the beat, the drummer never losing pace. The song was never released as a single; after a second album in 1974, the Incredible Bongo Band—never really a band to begin with—was no more. It was around that time that a young man named Clive Campbell began playing the record at parties in the Bronx. "I'm not a DJ, I'm a disc jockey. I play the discs that make you jockey," Campbell, professionally known as DJ Kool Herc, told Terry Gross in March 2005 on *Fresh Air*.

> The breaks came out of an experiment. I'm watching the people dancing, a lot of people used to wait for some particular part of the record. I'm studying the floor . . . I was noticing people used to wait for the particular parts of the record, to dance to, just to do their special little moves. So I said, Listen, I'm going to do a thing, I'm-a call it the Merry-Go-Round. . . . At the time I had a record called "Apache," and it was off an album called *The Incredible Bongo Rock* [sic]. And when I did that, that experiment went out the window. Everybody would come and really wait for that particular part of my format for me to get into it. And that's when everybody started searching for the perfect beat, try[ing] to beat that record. They still can't beat that record until this day. . . . Everybody's still using *Bongo Rock*'s "Apache."

In other words, a record written by a white Englishman imitating Native Americans as portrayed by white Americans and made famous by a Dane with a vaguely Hawaiian sound, newly arranged by a Canadian, and rhythmically defined by a Bahaman, became the biggest record in black New York. Juggling multiple copies of the track's percussion break until they became a hypnotic rhythmic mantra, over which his accompanying MCs would rhyme, Kool Herc and the pioneering hip-hop DJs who followed him—the most storied being Afrika Bambaataa and Grandmaster Flash—turned the Incredible Bongo Band's "Apache" into an underground hit in the manner of other early-seventies records like Manu Dibango's "Soul Makossa" or TSOP's "Love Is the Message"—a

DJ specialty, played and treasured by those in the know. And like those songs, "Apache" eventually become a mass-cult hit. It just wouldn't do it as itself.

"Apache" became—it's a cliché by now—the b-boy national anthem. For one thing, Viner and company's nervy groove was perfect for battle-dancing—as Joseph Schloss demonstrated at the EMP Pop Conference in 2005, the song's conga-led breakdown lent itself to uprock moves, described by the website of the longstanding Brooklyn crew the Dynasty Rockers (who formed in 1973, the year of Viner's remake) as

> a soulful and competitive street dance . . . developed in the Bushwick area of Brooklyn between 1967 and 1968 by two men; Rubberband Man and Apache. Uprock is danced in synchronization to the rhythms of Soul and Funk music; and certain Rock songs. The dance consists of foot shuffles, spins, turns, "Freestyle" movements, along with sudden body movements called "Jerks" and hand gestures called "Burns." The ["Uprock"] dance involves two or more dancers who perform single or as a team, dancing alternatively or simultaneously. This performance is is called a "Battle." Uprockers or "Rockers" battle throughout the duration of a complete song—from the beginning to the end while in a line formation called the "Apache Line." The Apache Line allows two opposing dancers or Crews (dance groups) to face each other and execute their Burn gestures towards one another. Although Uprockers sometimes emulate violent or vulgar moves with their Burns, physical contact is never allowed. Physical contact is usually a sign of inexperience. . . . Experienced Uprockers are also familiar with the songs . . . they dance to. They use the lyrics and every element of the music to out-do their opponent.[3]

On the Dynasty Rockers' website, there is a list of essential uprocking songs, among them Viner's "Apache" and "Bongo Rock." It's possible that the Apache Line wasn't named after the song, but it seems too much of a coincidence for it not to have been.

Just as Viner's "Apache" proved irresistible to the dancers and DJS, so it would provide record producers with the impetus to recreate its feel. In early recorded hip-hop, live studio bands would replay and extend or rearrange the most popular breaks—Chic's "Good Times" was used on the Sugarhill Gang's debut, "Rapper's Delight," and reinterpreted by numerous others, and Cheryl Lynn's "Got to Be Real" underpinned several early records, such as Brother D & Collective Effort's "How We Gonna Make the Black Nation Rise?" "Apache" received the treatment in 1981 when the Sugarhill Gang issued a 12-inch of the same name, with the interpolated break replayed by the Sugarhill Records house band and the Chops horn section. The Gang took not only the groove but the implication of the original song, with faux–Native American party chants ("Tonto, jump on it . . . Geronimo, jump on it"). Considering the amount of western-movie imagery in early hip-hop (Disco Four's "Country Rock and Rap," Trickeration's "Western Gangster Town," Furious 5 rapper Cowboy), this should perhaps not be too surprising.

Two years after the Sugarhill Gang recreated it, the Bongo Band's "Apache" first made its way onto wax as a sample source, getting cut up on West Street Mob's "Break Dance—Electric Boogie." Here, "Apache" was brought into the space age—appropriate given that electro was the latest in a long line of primarily instrumental pop styles anchored by what were generally considered novelty sounds. Like the echoing guitars of surf music and psychedelic rock's wah-wah pedals, the Vocodered vocals and tinny drum machine beats of electro mark their time with an acuity that seemed old hat after five years and utterly classic after twenty.

The same year as "Break Dance—Electric Boogie," Double Dee and Steinski codified "Apache" as hip-hop's ultimate beat. Douglas DiFranco (Double Dee) and Steve Stein (Steinski) were a pair of New York ad men (Stein was a copywriter, DiFranco a sound engineer) who were also serious record collectors, and in the early eighties they became hip-hop fans. In 1983, to bolster sales of G.L.O.B.E. and Whiz Kid's single, "Play That Beat Mr. DJ," Tommy Boy Records, which had struck gold pioneering the electro sound thanks to hits by Afrika Bambaataa and the Soul Sonic Force (G.L.O.B.E. and Whiz Kid were Soul Sonic members), sponsored a remix contest for the record. DiFranco and Stein entered and proceeded to take "Play That Beat" at its word, cutting-and-pasting dozens of snippets over, under, around, and through the original track. "The Payoff Mix," as the ad men called it, won the contest handily, and its starkest moment belonged to a familiar bongo pattern that stood out on an otherwise jam-packed record. Everything else on "The Payoff Mix"—Humphrey Bogart snarling, "*Play it*," Culture Club repeating "I'll tumble, I'll tumble, I'll tumble, I'll tumble," a snatch of synth from Herbie Hancock's "Rockit"—attested to hip-hop's density, diversity, and wide-open range. But the steely implacability of the "Apache" snippet seemed to say something else—that this was the core, the root of the entire enterprise.

The first major rapper to utilize "Apache" was LL Cool J, with "You Can't Dance" from his 1985 debut, *Radio,* though it's hard to hear in the song—the producer, Rick Rubin, cut it into fragments. The Viner "Apache" received a boost, however, when it was included on the first volume of Streetbeat's *Ultimate Breaks and Beats* compilation series of popular hip-hop crate-diggers' treats, inspiring partial or wholesale swipes until the early nineties. According to The-Breaks.com, a website that tracks the use of samples in hip-hop, Viner's "Apache" was utilized in forty-five songs, thirty-nine of them hip-hop and the majority of those occurring between the mid-eighties and early nineties. The website's listing is far from complete, but it's a good starting point for determining the number of "Apache"-laden tracks out there, as well as their sheer variety—everything from the mall-ready pop-rap of C + C Music Factory's "Things That Make You Go Hmmm . . ." and MC Paul Barman's joke-laden novelty track "Burping and Farting" to the far more serious KRS-One's "Who Are the Pimps?" and original gangsta rapper Schoolly D's "Housing the Joint."

After the combined effects of sampling litigation (most famously, lawsuits were brought against De La Soul and Biz Markie by the Turtles and Gilbert O'Sullivan, respectively, for unauthorized use of their compositions as new backing tracks), and the played-live production on Dr. Dre's path-breaking album *The Chronic* ended the sample era, the "Apache" break didn't die—it migrated into the post-hip-hop dance music that falls under the broad umbrella "rave." Instead of reinforcing rappers' boasts with its sonic swagger, though, "Apache" became a kind of reality principle within the often ethereal, vocal-less soundscapes of the cavalcade of post-techno mini-genres. Drum and bass, for example, was created by speeding up hip-hop breakbeats, and its sonic menace became a natural home for the break. London's Metalheadz label, for a while the purveyor of the toughest versions of the sound around, utilized "Apache" multiple times on its 12-inch singles: The-Breaks.com lists Goldie's "Inner City Life," Digital's "Metro," and J. Majik's "Your Sound," and there are probably others. All three songs feature the break chopped to pieces, one element among many, but Viner's congas patter away within the tracks' precise rhythmic tics and skyscraper-like synth eddies, scurrying like a moth caught in stainless-steel girders. Something similar applies to "Apache"'s use in straighter techno songs as well—in this case, Future Sound of London's "We Have Explosives" and Moby's "Machete."

But as drum and bass and techno receded in popularity, "Apache" seemed fairly used up as source material. That changed in late 2002, when two big hip-hop names resurrected it for completely different reasons. On the Roots' "Thought @ Work," from *Phrenology*, the group looped a hefty chunk of "Apache" underneath Black Thought's rapid-fire flow, emphasizing the mc's playfulness—and, by extension, the group's and hip-hop's as well. Nas went the other direction: On "Made You Look," from *God's Son*, while Nas taunted, "You're a slave to a page of my rhyme book," the producer, Salaam Remi, isolated a guitar echo and slowed it down until the menace that had always been at the heart of the song's appeal oozed out of the grooves as if Remi and Nas had just discovered it for the first time. Hank Marvin would have been proud.

Notes

1. George Geddes, "Jerry Lordan," http://www.mcr26.freeserve.co.uk/shadows/Lordan/Default.htm (accessed April 16, 2007).
2. In 1970, Curb was awarded a special commendation by Richard M. Nixon for having cut eighteen artists the previous year from MGM's roster for supporting drug use, including Frank Zappa and the Mothers of Invention, the Velvet Underground, and . . . Connie Francis! The real reason he dropped the artists, of course, was that none of them were making MGM money—the Animals, who did, were kept on despite veiled drug references.
3. The Dynasty Rockers Web site, http://www.dynastyrockers.com/brooklynuprock.html (accessed April 16, 2007). This site also provides much more of the history of the Dynasty Rockers.

Discography

Davie Allen and the Arrows. "Apache '65." *Apache '65*. Tower, 1965.
Double Dee and Steinski. "Lesson One: The Payoff Mix." Tommy Boy, 1983.
Future Sound of London. "We Have Explosives." *Dead Cities*. Astralwerks, 1995.
Goldie. "Inner City Life." *Timeless*. Metalheadz, 1995.
Incredible Bongo Band. "Apache." *Bongo Rock*. MGM, 1973.
Jorgen Ingmann and His Guitar. "Apache." *Apache/The Many Guitars of Jorgen Ingmann*. Collectables, 2004.
LL Cool J. "You Can't Dance." *Radio*. Def Jam, 1985.
Moby. "Machete." *Play*. V2, 1999.

Nas. "Made You Look." *God's Son.* Columbia, 2003.

Cliff Richard and the Shadows. "Apache" (1960). *The Greatest Hits.* EMI UK, 2004.

The Roots. "Thought @ Work." *Phrenology.* MCA, 2002.

The Sugarhill Gang. "Apache" (Sugar Hill, 1981). *Sugar Hill Hip-Hop Box Set.* Castle, 2002.

The Ventures. "Apache." *The Ventures Play Telstar.* Capitol, 1963.

Weedon, Bert. "Apache." JAR, 1960. *Very Best of Bert Weedon.* EMI UK, 2003.

West Street Mob. "Break Dance—Electric Boogie" (Sugar Hill, 1983). *Sugar Hill Hip Hop Box Set.* Castle, 2002.

Lavinia Greenlaw

On Punk Rock and Not Being a Girl

13 When punk first came to town it didn't take any notice of me and I failed to go out and meet it, but it left behind a sense of disturbance that was tectonic, atmospheric, and microscopic. It only affected certain people, as if it hit their natural resonant frequency and set something off, the way a car starts to shake when it reaches a particular speed. It shook me up and in doing so, prompted me to shake off the girl I was trying to be.

I had moved from London to an Essex village when I was eleven. The girls at my new school laughed at my voice, my name, my fraying jeans and long hair, and called me "gypsy." I took this as a compliment, but I was lonely. At thirteen, the hormones kicked in and all of a sudden I wanted to belong—not among the serious girls with their knee-socks and violins; I wanted to be desirable and bad, which in that place at that time meant a disco girl.

And not just any disco girl. I wanted to be like Tina, whose every aspect conformed to some golden section of girldom: her height, her shape; her prettiness relative to her smartness, and her niceness relative to her toughness. Tina offered certainties. She issued instructions on how to dance, whom to like, what to wear. Clothes had to be pressed, shoes polished, bodies scrubbed, shaved, creamed, and deodorized. Just as her mother kept the house fanatically clean, so Tina attended to herself. Each morning, her face would be re-tuned—the brightness turned down, the color turned up—and she would stride into school, her hips and breasts armored, her hair a winged, blonde helmet. I wanted this tough bright shell, which she could use to attract or deflect at will. To me, Tina was wise and ruthless, a goddess of war.

In Essex, disco was for girls, and I was becoming a girl as instructed by girls but I knew I wasn't a real girl, at least not of this kind. My feet wobbled on platform-wedge shoes, and a pencil skirt curtailed my stride. How these clothes made us walk was how they made us dance—we minced, jerked, and shuffled, shoulders hunched, elbows tucked in. We danced in a circle or in line, and performed routines with the zeal of synchronized swimmers.

For all her control, the atmosphere around Tina was hysterical. If your makeup ran, your brastrap showed, or you had dogshit on your shoe, the others would mock you savagely. Nothing escaped notice and everything was judged, and I never matched up. The only release was in the music, which was everything Tina would not permit us to be—flamboyant, or-nate, deadly serious, light-hearted: KC and the Sunshine Band, Brass Con-struction, Disco Tex and the Sex-O-Lettes, Earth, Wind & Fire. Safely in place in our circles and lines, under cover of maximum volume, within the bounds of our pencil skirts, we could be fierce. Imagine ten girls in four-inch wedge heels stomping in time to War's "Me and Baby Brother" —hop, skip, jump, crash . . . I still love that music. For me it was a new chemistry, geometry, architecture, and physics. The village and its land-scape were locked in place, as I was within them until the bass beat opened up the earth, the brass section raised the roof and you had to move, everything had to start moving and, to quote Brass Construction, "Keep on Movin.'"

Although we talked about boys, we danced for ourselves and each other. Boys loomed out of the shadows during the opening bars of the first slow dance, which was usually the Chi-Lites' "Have You Seen Her?" with its repeated ponderous intro acting as subtitles to what passed between us and the boys who were crossing the floor: "Aaaaaah!" "Hhhhmmmm. . . ." We simpered and wilted—there would be no stamping or clapping now.

And then one day I had no more interest in love bites or dance rou-tines. The disco girls—with whom I had shared mirrors, loitered at bus stops, and danced in line—were all of a sudden strangers. Our separation was subtle, mutual, and absolute: one day we met and simply did not recognize each other. What happened? There was no revelation, no decision. I had stopped dancing, and would not do so again on a disco floor with a group of girls, all trying to look and move alike. There would be no more giggling and shrieking, and things would cease to be either mortifying or hilarious. It was as if some electrified self had been unplugged along with the disco lights.

I have no memory of throwing out my high heels and hairspray but I do remember the thoroughness with which I went about getting rid of my disco and soul records. There were a few I couldn't bear to throw out so I hid them at the back of a cupboard, with real fear of their being found. I had an extreme but abstract terror of exposure, as if the truth of me lay not in what I looked like but what I listened to. If someone found Marvin Gaye or the Chi-Lites in my room, they would discover something *terrible* about me. But what?

By the summer of 1976, I had heard of punk rock only I hadn't really heard it. The village I lived in was just thirty-five miles outside London but at that time music, like most things, traveled slowly. And then, that September, punk bounced through town like a stage fight bounces through a set. Eddie and the Hot Rods, along with Chelsea and the Damned, played at a so-called rock festival nearby. I didn't know anyone who actually went, but there was said to have been a riot and I remember the excitement at school that this thing was out there, close by and possibly dangerous.

My first small step was to buy a pair of straight-legged jeans which were so new to Essex that I was mocked. Just a few months earlier I would have died of shame but now being different felt like a strength, or at least it felt like me. I was abrasive, discordant, and impatient and had found music to match, and clothes that were, like the music, thrown together, ill-fitting, falling apart. I burned photographs of myself in high heels, lip gloss, wide trousers, smocked dresses, peardrop collars, and puffed sleeves. It was like putting a pin in a blow-up doll. I was now a skinny kid who cut her own hair, and who wore big boots and a torn army jacket covered in scribbled quotations. Tina would have thought me scruffy and pretentious, and she'd have been right.

The next year, 1977, I was watching television one afternoon and there was Marc Bolan interviewing the Jam: a man with ringlets, in a floppy shirt, talking in a floppy voice to three boys who buttoned down their collars and measured the turn-ups on their trousers. They approached one another as if from different planets. The Jam played "All Around the World" and here was a speeded-up, pared-down sound that would take me further and faster than any boy in his car: "All around the world I've been looking for new." I could never connect the list that followed to that phrase and so it remained for me an all-round imperative. I was looking for new and it lay in these collisions and detonations and two-minute songs; in this acceleration out of a time in which I felt the passing of every minute.

That winter, our English teacher took us to see *Othello* at a theater marooned in a shopping precinct in Basildon New Town. It was just another long afternoon to be got through and then, as we were ushered off the bus, I caught sight in a shop window of the cover of the Sex Pistols' *Never Mind the Bollocks*. The offending word had been covered in tape, but that didn't thrill me as much as the bubblegum pink and acid yellow of the cover. It was strident, lurid, and magnificently out of place in that damp concrete mall. It buzzed. So the colors of punk, like its rumor, set off a vibration and the drab crust of provincial England cracked. Flashes of color were everywhere—orange socks, blue hair, lime-green nails, pink trousers. 1970s Essex was a world of painted pub signs rather than of neon; of black-and-white television, early closing time, and the corner shop. In my house, we ate whole food—brown food—and craved the processed stuff which in those days was manufactured in unregulated technicolor. The fishfingers, peas, and pudding on our school lunch trays glowed. We were so color deprived that we were impressed by a set of six winking red, yellow, and green lights lined up in front of a DJ's deck.

At this point, I took a backwards step. When I stopped dancing, I sat down and began to listen. I felt serious about music and also serious about boys, only they had to be older, and the only ones I met were my elder brother's friends. He lived in a bus, wore a coat he'd fashioned out of a goatskin rug, and went barefoot in winter, which gives you some idea of his friends. The girls he knew, with their long hair and earthbound clothes, were gentle, serious, and annoyingly calm. They seemed to me like grownups and so now that it was time to try out womanhood, I dug out my mother's afghan coat (from sixties London), grew my hair, and acquired a quilted Indian jacket and an embroidered skirt. I listened to Santana and John Martyn; I even went to see Uriah Heep, but it didn't stick.

I was listening to punk but looked like a hippy, or at least like a confusion between the two. For a while this was tolerated. Punk did not emerge into an empty world and those making their way toward it were given time to catch up. Crowds were a mix of the shaven, spiked, pierced hardcore and those who had just got round to ripping a few holes in their school blazer. I went to see the Vibrators at the Marquee Club with a friend. We were wearing jeans while the rest of the girls were in bin liners. My friend sat in the corridor and read Herman Hesse's *Siddhartha* until someone staggered past and threw up on her book. At Knebworth Festival, I watched Devo being pelted with beer cans and then slept through Genesis. I was on Devo's side, or wanted to be. Their surgical outfits made it seem as if they were setting up a sterile field on stage so as not to be infected by these filthy English hippies.

Essex was a tribal place and soon allegiances had to be clear. Punks hated hippies and skinheads hated everyone. I decided it was time to draw the line and began by finishing with my boyfriend, who had just begun his own metamorphosis by shaving off one side of his hair. I then went to get my own hair cut off. My two best friends and I skipped class, bought a bottle of wine, and went to the hairdressing salon upstairs in the clothes shop, Miss Selfridge. This was a girly shop—its logo was a lipstick kiss— but the hairdresser was young and kind and excited at the idea of doing her first punk cut. She turned up the music and let us pass the bottle of wine back and forth. I walked back through town feeling lighter, and not just because I had got rid of a grown-out shaggy perm. A boy called out "Punk!" and I was thrilled. The pleasure was more than that of being different. The boy had meant to be insulting and another time might have shouted "Slag" or "Cow." But "Punk" had nothing to do with being a girl. It neutralized, rejected, and released me.

I made myself strange because I felt strange and now I had something to belong to for which my isolation and oddness were credentials. Suddenly the skinny pale boy with spots and bad teeth was sought after; the fat girl in braces was a goddess in chains. For years I had hated being so pale; now I made myself paler. In that little Essex world, there were so many taboos that it took little effort to break them: buy clothes from a jumble sale in plain sight, men's clothes, and then wear them: pin-stripes, cricketing whites, vests, ties, belts, and braces. I was reversing out of being a girl, perhaps in the hope of regaining the freedom of my tomboy childhood. I stole my father's fifties coats and suits; a school blazer from my younger brother, and my ex-boyfriend's leather jacket. It was as if I were borrowing a little bit of masculinity from each.

In the spirit of appropriation, adaptation, and do-it-yourself, I was constantly on the lookout for something that could be cut up, ripped apart, dyed, bleached, and pinned back together. I didn't want to add up. I didn't want to be a story, form an argument, or make a point. I had a weakness for the then-fashionable term "eclectic," but the outfits I put together were just plain odd—too big, too heavy, too much: thirties men's flannels with a brick-red cropped and tailored Chanel jacket and a Victorian silk shirt with a lace collar and cuffs that was so fine that I shivered putting it on; skin-tight plastic trousers bought from Chelsea Market, and my great-uncle's World War I leather flying coat—so enveloping and soft and brown that it was like walking around inside a cow. Then there would be chains, scarves, badges, gloves, and lurid, shapeless garments knitted out of synthetic mohair on the biggest knitting needles I could find. We traveled down to London to buy cheap, synthetic, metallic, graphic tat on the King's Road, and to peer through the windows of Vivienne Westwood and Malcolm MacLaren's shop, Sex.

As I became more guarded, the colors I wore became more subdued until most of the time I just wore black. I had already dyed my hair black, which did not suit me, and then bleached out streaks which I tinted aubergine or peacock blue with Krazy Kolor. I went for a university interview on a rainy day and sat talking about Russian folktales to a kind professor as my hair dripped pink on his books. I dyed most of my clothes black, which in those days was done by piercing tins of acrid powder, which was then tipped into a cauldron of boiling water on the stove. It was my mother's enamelled preserving pan but it looked like a cauldron to me, and as I added salt and stirred in the clothes, a bitter cloud of steam filled the room and it did seem as if I were performing a spell that would dissolve me and my world into shadow.

Perhaps I wanted to be shadow. Certainly, I did not want to be known but then again, I barely knew myself. Perhaps I did not want to know myself. I was still a child, in that I operated instinctively and while I could be horribly talkative, on certain matters I was mute. I was discovering the pleasure of belonging to a different kind of gang—in which name, appearance, sexuality, and personality were so confusingly and overtly constructed that we were all strangers. Identity was worn rather than embodied, and it was a collection of parts. We were keeping ourselves apart and it was a respite from becoming, and having to be, clear. Crammed together in the punk club under the stands of the football ground where Eddie and the Hot Rods had played, we drank and kissed and fought and collided, but never got to know one another. We never knew who the band was either as nobody famous played there—why would they? Whoever it was would play for a while then fall off stage into the fixotropic swirl of that dark room. The village-hall disco looked like an eighteenth-century ball in comparison.

Maybe we girls didn't bond so much because we didn't dance. That was left to the boys, lurching around in their bondage trousers, and bouncing off one another. It was as if someone had choreographed the ways in which they usually communicated—football and fighting. If girls went off to the Ladies to giggle and conspire, they would find some boy snorting speed, throwing up, or doing his makeup. Punk had its girls, though. I admired those who were aggressively sexual, but I could not be like them.

The queen of the local scene was called Rat and she was a *girl*. She was so sweet; the spikes of her sugar-blonde hair were tipped in candy pink. I remember seeing her emerge from the club, walking daintily among puddles of vomit and urine, wearing a white muslin top without a mark on it. She was confident and nice enough; she could have been Tina. What I envied most was that she looked as if nothing could touch her. I wanted to look untouchable.

Punk made its way smoothly out of the backstreet clubs and into the town halls and dance halls and cinemas: the Electric Ballroom, the Lyceum, the Hammersmith Palais. We saw the Buzzcocks or Adam and the Ants in the Chelmsford Odeon, where we were serried in rows of red plush seats and told not to dance in the aisles by the old ladies who usually sold ice cream.

I don't think punk was perceived as dangerous so much as an excuse for a good fight. The local police, who were bored and liked a chance to dress up, routinely turned out in riot gear. They pushed us up against walls, prodding us with batons until someone reacted. They would be taken aside; some were beaten unconscious. The most terrifying experience of my life was being caught up in a battle after a punk band played in a small town on the coast where local men decided to surround the hall and beat everyone up, starting with the girl on the door. The police arrived but stayed in their cars and watched as these men, some of whom had bottles and knives, set about a bunch of kids who dressed differently and dyed their hair, as if ridding the town of its demons.

We were stopped routinely but I felt immune—because I was young but also because I was a girl, which was ironic given that I felt protected by the fact that I didn't look like one. I would walk through town late at night and if men called after me it was in mockery rather than pursuit. To most of them, a girl with blue hair was not a girl at all.

Punk evolved into new wave, which suited my seriousness and pretentions. I smoked Gauloises and carried Russian novels in my raincoat pockets. The colors of punk refined into graphic blocks of red, white, and black, and the brute homemade noise refined into the colder simulations of electronica. Music was more ambitious, more serious, but also suddenly lyrical again. I remember listening with amazement to the sleigh bells cascading through Joy Division's *Atmosphere* and the moment when Phil Oakey and Martyn Ware (the original Human League) stepped out from behind their synthesizers to give an austere, passionate rendition of "You've Lost That Loving Feeling." It was alright to know the words, to look back, to remember and feel.

Clothes were also growing up as gym-slips, blazers, kilts, and nappies gave way to suits and dresses. Girls started growing their hair again, and sugar and water were replaced by hairspray and gel. The shop Sex was renamed Seditionaries. In the summer of 1979, I went to Paris for my seventeenth birthday with a group of friends. I was armed with my grandparents' pre-war map of a city that no longer existed. Every bar played the one Belgian new wave hit, Plastic Bertrand's "Ça Plane Pour Moi," a year old and already Muzak. I was standing outside the Pompidou Centre wearing a Westwood mohair top when a boy shouted at me, "Punk est mort!" He turned out to be from Yorkshire, which placed him hundreds of miles further away than I from the epicenter of London. If punk was dead in Yorkshire, it ought to have been long buried everywhere else. I felt like a map of a place that no longer existed.

Punk lyrics were the same old love thing after all—the Buzzcocks' "Love You More," the Vibrators' "Baby, baby, baby, won't you be my girl?" I was a girl and here were boys, and while I aspired to the fuck-off looks of Siouxsie Sioux, I fell in love. I am of that confused generation who were told that the gender war was over, that all was nurture and not nature, by parents who were enacting traditional roles. I thought I had escaped being a girl, but what else could I be? I talked to boys about music and they tried to take off my clothes, which were after all tactile and sensual—leather, mohair, muslin, silk, net, and lace. I saw myself in a shop window wearing a black raincoat and beret, a white collared shirt and spotted chiffon scarf. Even with my dyed and spiked hair of course I looked like a girl, and a good one at that.

We stood around in our buttoned-up raincoats wondering what to do next. Then out of the west came the Pop Group, A Certain Ratio, Rip Rig and Panic, the New Age Steppers, and we took our coats off, let down our hair, and started dancing to music that threw jazz, funk, and reggae at one another and was, well, *musical*.

I changed my appearance once more, and went on changing. The punk masquerade was a game of disguises and while it did not reveal a true self, it revealed truth about the self as a construction of parts, as fluctuating, incoherent, susceptible, and resistant. Music was instrument, language, and atmosphere; it changed the shape of the world and my shape within it, how I saw, what I liked, and what I wanted to look like. It made my noise for me. It did what it could.

Eric Weisbard

The Buddy Holocaust Story
A Necromusicology

14 There is a bleed in the recording, audible on both the often duplicated cassette that I first heard twenty years ago and on the remixed CD sent me, with the note "At long last," in the winter of 2005. It's 1981. A college student billing himself as "Buddy Holocaust" introduces the set he is about to play with pseudo-sociopathic wit: "This is a dinner hour concert. If any of you want to eat dinner, feel free, but if you throw up it's your fault and not mine." And: "This is not going to be too mellow. In fact, if you leave during a song you'll be shot." Meanwhile, bleeding in, is the sound of him singing "we have our reasons for dropping bombs on you," from five songs ahead in time. There won't be any fixing the problem, since it's the only recording of the only performance he ever gave. Like so much about Buddy Holocaust, it's creepy, funny-tragic, and sort of perfect.

Buddy Holocaust was a protest singer who protested the protest movement. His first song on the tape is called "Another Kent State." As in, he wants another one: the first might have been misperceived as an unfortunate accident. Yes, the Vietnam War is over, but then again, as will be heard two manifestos along, he still thinks "We Will Retake Saigon." And anyhow, it's the No Nukes concert that has set him off most: Bruce Springsteen, Jackson Browne, and the rest of the rock elite in 1979 at Madison Square Garden, so self-inflated with celebrity and sanctimony that they mistook the grounds of their country estates for the world they thought they were saving. "They'd replace our cooling towers / With a field of smelly flowers / They'd kill our fine reactors / Bury them for good with tractors." The singer knows that he's being irrational. He enjoys it, strumming away in his best imitation of a Phil Ochs politically positioned somewhere to the right of Dr. Strangelove: "They made us lose in Vietnam / Don't they know that war is peace / They always exaggerate the harm / When we shouldn't care in the least / Each fair sized tank should have a nuke / America is great / These worthless hippies make me puke / We need another Kent State."

So he's kidding, right? Well, sure. He's satirizing everyone: dummies on the right and dummies on the left alike. A born smartass—with girl troubles, of course. The second ditty, "Give Me Your Love or I'll Destroy the World," has a music hall lilt, a passage about Adolph wreaking genocide when Eva acted coy, and the couplet "Yes you can say no / But earth will have to go." But as the singer's invective finds new targets with every song, the sense of alienation becomes all-encompassing. Jonathan Richman had twitted hippies too as a horny young man, singing "The modern world is not so bad / Not like the students say / In fact I would be very glad / If you'd share the modern world with me." Recorded in the early 1970s and left unreleased for several years, the *Modern Lovers* album would be a crucial influence on punk: the Sex Pistols covered "Roadrunner" in one of their rare moments of affirmation. Buddy Holocaust strummed like a folkie but talked like a punk. Introducing "Concrete and Steel," he says: "Some people don't like the modern world. They don't like cities, they don't like skyscrapers. Highways scare 'em. I love technology. I think there's as much beauty in a speeding automobile as in all the paintings in the Metropolitan Museum of Art." There is no reason to think he doesn't mean it, like ten thousand Futurist art students before him posing in exactly this same brutalist manner.

I was first given a copy of the Buddy Holocaust tape in the mid-1980s at Princeton, where a couple of songs of his lived in permanent rotation at our campus radio station, WPRB. Buddy Holocaust, it was said, had been a Dartmouth College student. And he had gone on to kill himself, not long after his concert was recorded, by driving into a freeway embankment. If

"Concrete and Steel" was a pose, he had died fulfilling it. Maybe that gave the songs an extra note of credibility. Maybe we were also drawn to Buddy Holocaust's utter obscurity, as committed indie rockers come to punk rock late in the game, at a time when the scene's momentum had switched from take no prisoners art statements to revival (the Velvet Underground and all their heirs) and the grassroots construction of an archipelago of record labels, "left of the dial" radio stations, self-distributed fanzines, barebones clubs, and boho shops all across America.

In Ronald Reagan's America this felt like political resistance but it was also identity politics, as much an act of privileged self-separation in its way as white suburbanization. Fundamentally, much of indie America was collegiate—in love with serial killer novels as literature, deconstructionist aporia as revelation. Buddy Holocaust, a student at the most famously right-wing university in the United States, had gotten there early: his rants were inherently undergraduate. "Coathanger Blues," which defies the otherwise conservative line to support abortion, since naturally Buddy Holocaust favored euthanizing the weak, has the rhyme "I say Malthus, he won't defeat us / Evidence this bloody dead foetus." The songs took crazy ideas to absurd extremes, with no regard for consequences. It resonated with who we were. I remember, back then, turning over the phrase "it's academic" with utter glee. That was true. It was!

Nonchalant, we broadcast Buddy Holocaust as if he were Buddy Holly, from central New Jersey to the suburbs of Philadelphia. "Laura," which he introduces on the tape as the first song he ever wrote, trills out: "It was springtime / The birds were singing / Your neck, I thought of wringing." "Declared War on Love" finds him murdering his girl and her family too, concluding: "Since I finally broke your heart / I'll have to blow my brains apart / I guess this means that we are through / But I proved my love was true." It's a competitive category, but Holocaust's most incendiary number, or as he would have put it, "rudest," was likely "Drugs Did This to Me," aka "Forced to Kill on PCP." He introduced it with a wink ahead in time to Nancy Reagan's Just Say No campaign. "This next song is about another one of my girlfriends. [General laughter.] I'm sorry about what happened, but it did happen. And it was because of drugs. I just want to tell you all that drugs are really evil. And you really shouldn't take any because something like this might happen. I mean, if you take the right drugs." Then he cut loose:

I shot into her golden hair
I sighed and laid her body bare
I took my knife and stuck it in
It ripped apart her fair white skin
I sliced her belly open wide
And then [giggling] I shoved my hand inside
It's true, drugs did this to me

Forced to kill on PCP
Yes, I escaped reality
Now she seems dead
Guess I lost my head

I pulled her entrails out at once
I stopped and rested, had her lunch
Then to enhance her quiet charm
Carved my initials in her arm
I pulled her limbs out one by one
I took a bite, but just for fun

What needs to be retained here is how Buddy Holocaust, even then, could have seemed only one step beyond the indie norm. We relived the zombie flick *Night of the Living Dead* and that Ramones favorite *The Texas Chainsaw Massacre* at the film society, lynchpins in an evolving "psychotronic encyclopedia." Cheered on the Butthole Surfers and Big Black as their industrial carnivals showcased genital surgery and a state official blowing his head off at a news conference. Simon Reynolds's recent account of 1978–84 postpunk, *Rip It Up*, documents the stylized extremity that dominated the scene. A new wave group as seemingly innocuous as Human League formed as Musical Vomit, playing a space called Meatwhistle, with songs about masturbation and necrophilia. "Slug Bait," by Throbbing Gristle, was about a psycho cutting open a pregnant woman and biting off her foetus's head. Scraping Foetus off the Wheel was considered a pretty cool name for a band. Back at Princeton, this all registered as pop of a kind. Local high school kids called our station wanting to hear the Violent Femmes, Suicidal Tendencies, Sid Vicious, and the Misfits: potentially gigantic suburban cult hits that no one had had the guts or stomach to promote. Eventually, and I do mean eventually, *Violent Femmes* would go platinum, Kurt Cobain would rise and fall, *South Park* would air episodes like "Cartman Gets an Anal Probe," and Johnny Cash, resurrected for his dark streak, would turn a song by that "pretty hate machine," Nine Inch Nails, into his last anthem. Postpunk's "pigfuck" underbelly had somehow become Americana.

All those years later, a friend of mine from college, Ken Katkin, mentioned that he had put the old Buddy Holocaust tape on CD and did I want a copy? Quickly saying yes, I then wondered if anyone had ever discovered the story behind the music. Within seconds, it seemed, Ken had tracked down a Dartmouth alum who had known Bill Tate, aka Buddy H. The legends were true: Bill Tate had killed himself a few months after the concert, which had been given at the Collis student center. Tate's fellow student Rob Graff summarized the details in an e-mail that struck what would turn out to be the characteristic note of all accounts of Buddy Holocaust: confusion and awe. "He performed dress[ed] in a military uniform to an audience that was not certain if he was serious or not (I'm not sure whether he knew himself for sure). . . . Stark music. It's been over 20 years, but some of his lines still haunt me."

My own subsequent inquiries proved that Bill Tate's friends had worked to preserve his legacy. There was the story of a tape deck disassembled, and permanently broken, out of fear that it might have eaten the only extant copy of the recording. There was a documentary film that had not come to fruition. One social circle had had a mass discussion of Buddy Holocaust, with the e-mails compiled into liner notes for an edited CD version of the concert. Bill Tate's best friend, David Goldstein, e-mailed me a copy of the amazing flyer for the show, which he had held onto: a headshot of Tate, wearing military gear, over a nuclear explosion, with the words: "In the midst of decay, in the midst of decadence, in the midst of destruction, one man stands fast with truth: the explosive Buddy Holocaust." I now knew the exact date of the concert. July 29, 1981, exactly as Prince Charles celebrated his wedding to Lady Diana.

Bill Tate was almost as fascinating to those who knew him as Buddy Holocaust. His friends remembered the freshman who vowed that he would either become a rock star, dictator of the world, or kill himself. Who was obsessed with Nietzsche and went nine straight terms without a vacation break. Which surprised no one, as with the same energy he

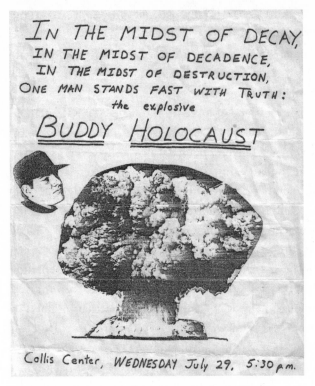

Fig. 1. The Explosive Buddy Holocaust: concert flier, Bill Tate performing as Buddy Holocaust, July 29, 1981, at Collis Center, Dartmouth College. COURTESY OF DAVID GOLDSTEIN.

would send thirty-page letters to a girl he was interested in, freaking her completely. He called the songs he blitzed out (there were twenty-four on the tape) "punk folk." Nobody was quite sure how much of their content he believed.

He had worn his dad's air force uniform at the concert, Goldstein remembered. There were about thirty to fifty people in the audience, maybe fifteen of them friends who had heard some of the songs before while just hanging out, which explains why the crowd on the tape sounds more pleasured than stunned. Not long after, the two of them drove west, where Tate's family had moved from the Midwest: his dad, formerly of Merrill Lynch, was now vice-president of sales for Monex, a vendor of precious metals in Newport Beach. In California, Tate fruitlessly gave a copy of the tape to a friend of Goldstein's father, who was an executive at Arista. The last time they saw each other Bill was working at a Carl's Jr. to earn some income. A week later he had killed himself. He had looked hard and found the only freeway underpass in LA that you could drive into at high speed. "Biographical note," one friend late wrote. "Bill Tate was from Chagrin Falls, Ohio. The irony of that never escaped me."

It still seemed mythical, and after all Chagrin Falls is just a suburb of Cleveland. But a hit on the right ProQuest Historical Newspapers database yielded a photo and caption from the *Los Angeles Times*, November 4, 1981: "Grim task—County firemen use 'Jaws of Life' to cut open wreckage to recover body of William F. Tate, 21, of Newport Beach. He was killed when his car went out of control, crossed into divider and slammed into concrete post on north-bound Corona del Mar Freeway at Red Hill Avenue." The car, bunched like crumpled wrapping paper, demands to be viewed with "Concrete and Steel" playing underneath, part of a toxically pastoral industrial landscape.

You may recall an overused quote, taken from Nietzsche: "Whoever fights monsters should see to it that in the process he does not become a monster. And if you gaze long enough into an abyss, the abyss will gaze back into you." Bill Tate kept on his dorm-room door photos of Nietzsche and the pope, looking at each other, with a mushroom cloud in-between them. Inside, the only decoration was a Sid Vicious poster. Tate called his personal philosophy "pragmatic nihilism." One friend described it as "something along the lines of 'none of this means anything—deal with it.'" Another elaborated: "He described Pragmatic Nihilism as a result of his ongoing 'War with God.' God did not know what s/he was doing and was responsible for the foolishness and triviality of human endeavor. . . . It was useless to try anything worthwhile, so we might as well do nothing . . . i.e., pragmatic. In my opinion back then, I had categorized him (hah) as being one of the ones who are too smart for their own good." A third friend, balancing tragedy and farce, called pragmatic nihilism "a response to the cold war and his inability to find a sexual partner."

Yes, we know the Bill Tate type: brilliant but lost, and above all young. Still, there is nothing like Buddy Holocaust. Those who hear him remember it and demand more. The tape spread through the Ivy League: you can Google footage on the Internet of Columbia students in 1990, at the second installment of an annual "Weirdo Party," performing a choral version plus tuba of "That'll Teach Ya, Hiroshima," with the 1981 concert introduction repeated verbatim. A later Dartmouth student studied the

Holocaust repertoire: "I even performed some of the tamer ones at the very same campus house where Buddy was recorded. But unlike Buddy, we cared too much about what people thought about us to wear fatigues and sing about mutilation and eugenics." More recently, Buddy Holocaust songs have been getting regular airplay on New York's hippest radio station, WFMU. A record label issue may not be out of the cards.

I think that Bill Tate's single performance as Buddy Holocaust deserves to be heard, puzzled over, celebrated for what a college student achieved in one manic flash of self-invention, and mourned for the human being sacrificed on the altar of Nietzsche, punk rock, and prolonged adolescence. After twenty years of listening to every garden variety of underground shock rock, or what Martha Bayles once spent a book denouncing as "perverse modernism," I still find that Buddy Holocaust claims a spot in my personal pantheon. But I can understand those who find such attention incomprehensible. "What makes you think that I'm not serious?" Buddy Holocaust asks in one of his songs. The question lingers, as does its mate: and why should we care? One of Bill Tate's friends remembered playing his tape for his or her parents, who were horrified, "perhaps realizing at age 60 what I did not at age 19." Another, the only one hostile to my inquiries, which he called "necromusicology," e-mailed me a demurral: "This really isn't so painful as it is forgotten and very sad. Bill was a very lost soul who had a talent for writing nihilistic poems and setting them to catchy pop melodies. I don't really know what there is to tell."

In time, my questioning led me to Bill Tate's parents: they had a right to know about their son's strange legacy. One morning, I spoke with his mother, Ann Tate. Jack and Ann Tate were from Iowa; when they met and married, however, the family name was the Germanic Toedt, changed legally when Jack began working for Merrill Lynch and wanted something that didn't sound so foreign. (Bill Tate had told Dartmouth friends, fancifully, that there was a family connection to Hitler's lieutenant Fritz Todt.) Before that, Jack Toedt had just about been one of those people who could destroy the world: he served overseas in the air force, flying B-47 bomber planes in the late 1950s on missions up to the border of the Soviet Union. There were three siblings, born in short succession: Janice in 1956, Karl in 1959, and Bill, the youngest, in September, 1960. The family moved around a fair amount: Indiana for nine years; then Manhattan for the summit of the sixties, 1968; Iowa again; Montlake, New Jersey; and finally Chagrin Falls in 1974, just as Bill began high school. The year that everything broke down for Bill Tate, 1981, Jack and Ann moved one last time, to Orange County, where they still live today.

Jack Tate's people were farmers, but Ann Tate's father, Joseph Ellis Baker, was an English professor at the University of Iowa, and the author of several books, including a study of the Oxford Movement, a period of Catholicized ferment within the Church of England. The Tates were Catholic, but Bill Tate as he grew up came to hate the church, or any kind of authority. He was a quiet kid, able to make friends but closest to his older brother Karl. They made elaborate home movies together, enacting military battles. They argued about politics, siding with their Democrat mom against their Republican dad, particularly hating Richard Nixon. And they were arty, quoting Kipling, sometimes reading *The Village Voice,* listening to music: Bill Tate taught himself to play rock on guitar and Bach on piano. They were weird for a buttoned up village like Chagrin Falls, though perhaps the isolation was inspiring for troubled young satirists— one of their classmates, and a friend, was Bill Watterson, later the recluse who drew the anarchically philosophical *Calvin and Hobbes* cartoons; a few years before, Doug Kenney, the founding editor of *National Lampoon,* co-writer of *Animal House* and *Caddyshack* (and suicide in 1980), had come out of Chagrin Falls too. As punk crested—Ann Tate remembers the boys following the story of Sid Vicious stabbing Nancy Spungen and then killing himself—Karl Tate began studying in the New York University film program. The next year, Bill left for Dartmouth. He had still never had a girlfriend.

But at college he finally met someone, a student at the University of New Hampshire named Wendy, and it may have been his undoing. Ann Tate doesn't deny that Bill was already brittle before that: he wrote songs like "We Will Retake Saigon" and declared his intent to be a rock star and duel with God ("It was almost like he could be God, would replace God," she says) long before he met Wendy. Still, the laughter on the tape when Bill Tate mentions "another one of my girlfriends," Ann says, is because his friends knew there were no other ones. And when Wendy dumped him he crashed: as the final Buddy Holocaust songs were being written, in the summer of 1981, he was prescribed drugs at the campus clinic and had to suspend his studies. In September, when he and David Goldstein drove west, they stopped in Iowa City to be with Ann and her parents on his twenty-first birthday. Bill played them the Buddy Holocaust songs: Ann was proud of the political ones, her English professor dad horrified by the misogynist ones. Still, all could see how depressed Bill was. In California, he took the fast-food job but he also began talking about suicide and was placed in a seventy-two-hour hold in a psychiatric facility, leaving against the doctor's advice. There was talk of lithium, for potential bipolarity, but it wasn't prescribed in time. On November 3, a sheriff came to Ann's door, to deliver the awful news and ask if her son might have been suicidal; there were no skid marks where his car had smashed into the bridge abutment.

"If you are depressed, the negative becomes the positive," Ann Tate told me. She has seen a lot of this: Karl has battled depression much of his life and, at forty-six, has lived with his parents for the past thirteen years; Janice, their eldest, had alcoholism dissolve her marriage. Ann is open about these matters and counsels other couples dealing with family grief: she is not quite sure what even Buddy Holly's music was like (though she reminds me that his plane crashed in Iowa), let alone punk attitudes, but she knows more about the limits of human behavior than aesthetes could hope to. And she is able to listen with appreciation to "Coathanger Blues," a song as revolted by humanity as the Sex Pistols' "Bodies." Can those of us with punkish pasts and parental presents, weary survivors of edginess, remain equally appreciative?

I still believe that being sophomoric, partially educated but sure that you know it all, irrationally committed to impossible positions, so full of yourself that you burst, is as much a vital part of the rock masquerade as blackface or drag. But I know that this is exactly why the particular expressiveness of rock strikes some as so miraculous and others as an unbearable travesty of privilege impersonating oppression. Like other forms of art school shenanigans, it's a way of impersonating modernity, taming it, murdering it. But rock goes further down this path. Even at the level of an unreleased cassette like Bill Tate's it's a pop, mass, commodified medium of art, youth, and transgressive impulses, whose status as an aesthetic form is constantly in question.

Buddy Holocaust, from this perspective, represents the limit point of an attitude we haven't yet fully named—perhaps because it's so common in its various, less toxic strands as to be virtually a given. Bill Tate was a privileged Ivy League punk in one guise, impossibly far from his show biz dreams and headed for suicide at Carl's Jr. in another, and the crafter of a performance whose misogyny, diseased wit, and bravura would horrify most and improbably entice a few. Tate called his philosophy pragmatic nihilism, a phrase combining inherently European and American schools of thought every bit as much as punk did schools of style. So too, I think, for his sophomoricism, a particularly American, pop culture–infused brand of European dissidence. It's a bohemianism of the provinces and suburbs, where the issue isn't so much parody vs. pastiche, or art vs. commerce, but centers and margins, originators and inheritors. Those who are small and dream of becoming big. Late in the concert, the singer sounds exhausted, as if it has just occurred to him how strange it is to have thrown his life into these routines, into becoming a prophet of stylized inhumanity. For an encore, Tate partially steps out of character and does "And I Haven't Decided," where he is watching himself: the medicated inmate he would briefly later become, staring in the song at shadows on padded walls, not sure in successive choruses if he's Napoleon, Admiral Byrd, or Genghis Khan after all.

So yes, the "sick humor" of the baby boomers was a kind of holiday in other people's misery, as Johnny Rotten might have put it. Alongside Chagrin Falls native Kenney, the other principal *Animal House* co-writer was a Dartmouth alumnus (strange coincidences: this is a film, mind you, that also featured John Belushi smashing a sensitive folksinger's guitar into last year), Chris Miller. In Tony Hendra's well-titled history of sick humor, *Going Too Far,* Miller recalled:

> There was an upside down sense of values. . . . There was a fraternity motto, a variation of the 1984 one: "Sickness is health, blackness is truth, drinking is strength."
>
> Blackness, in this case, didn't mean being [like] black people as much as it meant black as in black humor. To behave "black" was a compliment in my fraternity and it meant that you behaved in a perverse way. Because we were sitting there in one of the straightest colleges in the world; this is a place that turns out Republican politicians and guys who head up big companies like American Express. There was a sense that "We got four short years here, guys to raise bloody hell because after that every one of us is going to be working in a corporation, or sitting in a boardroom, or an officer in the Navy, and we're not going to be able to do this *ever again* . . ."

National Lampooners tended to be as Ivy League collegiate as Buddy Holocaust, and as committed to sophomoric humor. *Radio Dinner,* the magazine's first LP, featured a Joan Baez impersonator singing "Pull the Triggers, Niggers," while its 1973 stage musical, *Lemmings,* featuring Belushi and Chevy Chase with the future *Spinal Tap* auteur Christoper Guest as musical director, spent its whole second act satirizing the "Woodshuck Festival of Love, Peace, and Death."

The sophomoric bohemian, the pragmatic nihilist, formed out of a moment when mass culture still largely worked in a top-down fashion and yet certain kinds of rebels had become widely known figures. Rock stars, Beats, existentialist and nihilist philosophers, poets like Sylvia Plath were a relatively new kind of celebrity anti-hero, viewed by a nation of affluent kids now more likely to go to college than not with an envy that could approach (to pose as a Nietzschean) *ressentiment.* The still startling anger of punk on the one hand and sick humor on the other came in large part from people denied access to this privileged realm of dissent—however privileged, in other ways, they may have been themselves. Arguably, punk, zines, the dramatic rise in small publishing across every genre, the Web, and numerous other technological shifts have democratized, or at least suburbanized, the means of cultural reproduction. As a result, perhaps, and paradoxically, the varieties of rock rebellion to be found are far more numerous and individually far less consequential.

Should we take Buddy Holocaust seriously? Only, I guess, to the extent we take rock seriously, and the inflated identities that it insists upon at just the place in a young adult's life when it feels like everything is about to dissolve. When it's possible to get up on stage in your dad's military gear and sing, "Give me your love or I'll destroy the world. Give me your love, it's useless to resist me girl."

Robert Fink

ORCH5, or the Classical Ghost in the Hip-Hop Machine

15

Germany has a very long classical music tradition.
RALF HÜTTER OF KRAFTWERK

I The DJ plays your favorite blasts,
Takes you back to the past—
Music's magic! (poof)
AFRIKA BAMBAATAA, "PLANET ROCK"

"Tomorrow's Music Today"
ADVERTISING SLOGAN FOR THE FAIRLIGHT COMPUTER
MUSIC INSTRUMENT, CA. 1983

Prelude: The Great Liberation, or, Is There Life after Death?

The "death of (European) classical music" may seem a somewhat tired, even irrelevant trope with which to start an essay in the present volume—which is, after all, devoted to the study of the magical moments within (clearly quite healthy) popular music. Certainly there is no consensus among critics and scholars as to the survival of the literate, "cultivated" tradition of Western music as the twenty-first century advances, and even if there were, why should anyone doing popular music studies care, other than to register a small but real sense of satisfaction at avoiding what looks like a losing horse in the music history championship stakes? It oughtn't matter much to the study of popular music whether, as partisans within the classical world indignantly retort, audiences for the symphony and opera are actually holding steady; whether, as classical record label executives report, the latest crossover hit has temporarily stabilized their bottom line; whether, as contemporary classical composers now hasten to assure us, they really *do* care if you listen.[1]

And indeed, these material-cultural issues are of little import for the discussion that follows. What cannot be ignored is the fundamental epistemological crisis that besets Western music as it heads into what more than one commentator has labeled its "post-classical" era.[2] I have argued elsewhere that the incipient collapse of our paradigmatic cultural hierarchy of music, along with its canon of "classical" masterworks, was easily discernable as European musical culture careened toward the millennium, ushering in a fundamental (and salutary) "de-centering" of its musical worldview. As I pointed out then, under the somewhat whimsical rubric "Why You Need a Musicologist to Listen to Beck," one of the most disorienting consequences, ripe for scholarly study, was the collapse of the classical canon's segregating function, its ability not only to keep the "low" music out but to keep the high-art classical music of the European past safely walled in, where mass culture could mostly ignore it, occasionally gesturing at it from afar, whether to resist ("Roll Over, Beethoven"), parody ("Bohemian Rhapsody"), or appropriate ("A Whiter Shade of Pale") its snob value, along with (at times) its sounds and structures.[3]

The story of ORCH5 is, accordingly, set within the de-centered world of Western music during the slow twilight of its classical canon. It will lead us from Düsseldorf to Detroit, and from avant-garde German modernism to Afrocentric hip-hop. It is a story of technology, of machines fetishized, appropriated, mistrusted, misused. It also turns out to be a ghost story, the story of what happens to a particular fragment of classical music after it stops being classical, when it is not quite dead, but, as Buddhists might put it, in the *bardo* realm halfway between death and new life. The classic description of the bardo appears in what is popularly known as *The Tibetan Book of the Dead*: the actual title, though, is (roughly) the *Book of the Great Liberation, through Hearing, in the Bardo Realm*. This is, accordingly, a story of death—but there will also be an attempt at post-canonic hearing, and at least some intimation of the great liberation(s) to come. Reincarnation, what Pythagoras called "the transmigration of souls," is not an exotic, foreign concept; it has always been deeply woven into the European musical consciousness, brought to us by the same mind to which we mythically attribute the foundational observations of Western music theory. The story I have to tell is of musical reincarnation, of the transmigration of *tones*. It is a tale of the afterlife of "classical music," transmigrated through digital technology, the commodity form, and myriad fortunate cultural misreadings of a single famous chord.

It is the story of the classical ghost in the hip-hop machine.

Kastchei the (Digitized) Immortal

ORCH5 is low-resolution, eight-bit digital sample, a very early one, perhaps the first one to become famous. It was digitized around 1979 by David Vorhaus, a computer programmer and classically trained electronic musician. The file appeared on disk 17 of the twenty-five-or-so eight-inch floppy disks that made up the sampled sound library shipped with each *very* expensive Fairlight Computer Musical Instrument. (In the United States, the going rate for a Fairlight Model IIx in the early 1980s was over $25,000.)[4] The Fairlight CMI, originally cobbled together in 1979 by two Australian inventors out of the ruins of the Quasar, a failed analog modeling synthesizer, was the first commercially available electronic musical instrument that, in addition to generating musical sounds through analog/digital synthesis, gave its owner the ability to sample pre-existing sounds into digital memory, process them, and play them back through a keyboard. It is thus the single evolutionary starting point for an entire phylum of ubiquitous (and much cheaper) digital samplers, including the Akai S-series (1984) and the Ensoniq Mirage (1985), so crucial to the rise of sample-based hip-hop.

Kim Ryrie and Peter Vogel, the inventors of the Fairlight, considered its digital sampling capability a technical hack, a clever shortcut on the way to their ultimate audio workstation. Digital conversion allowed them to implement complex tools for sound synthesis while bypassing processor-intensive tasks too difficult for its parallel pair of primitive Motorola 8800-series microprocessors. Nobody really took sampling per se seriously at first: company apocrypha identifies the first sound sampled for melodic playback as the barking of an employee's dog. But early Fairlight users singled out the CMI's sampling power as a key differentiator, and soon company brochures touted the system's ability "to incorporate literally ANY type of sound—not only classical and modern instruments but sounds of the world; sounds reflecting the full spectrum of life, from the subtlety and force of nature to the sounds of civilization and synthesis."[5] This is why Fairlights began shipping with floppy disks full of sampled sounds. Many of these soon-to-be famous samples had been somewhat casually appropriated by an adventurous first generation of users. Vorhaus, an orchestral double-bass player as well as founder, with members of the BBC Radiophonic workshop, of the British electronic "pop" group White Noise, was a typical early adopter of the Fairlight; he brought his classical training very much to bear as he contributed to what would become the standard set of samples included with every new CMI.

ORCH5 was just one of a series of ORCH samples that Vorhaus and others culled from (one assumes) a quick troll through their classical record collections. The orchestral samples provided with the Fairlight feature short snippets of full-orchestra chords from the symphonic literature, usually just a single attack, often pitched (TRIAD), but also percussion-dominated (ORCHFZ1), occasionally looped to provide a pulsating pattern capable of sustained use (ORCH2). ORCH5, the most famous of these, is almost certainly sampled from Igor Stravinsky's ballet *The Firebird;* as I have verified myself using digital sound processing, the loud chord that opens the "Infernal Dance of All the Subjects of Kastchei," pitched down a minor sixth (and also slowed down, since digital technology did not in 1979 yet allow independent manipulation of frequency and sampling rate), can be made to match with tolerable precision an iteration of ORCH5 on the pitch C4 easily obtainable from several Internet websites devoted to the mysteries of the Fairlight CMI.[6] It's not hard to fathom why Vorhaus picked this spot: the piece is famous, the sound is impressive, and, crucially, in every one of Stravinsky's three suites from the ballet, this forceful blast is neatly isolated at the beginning of a movement, framed by complete silence on one side and only a low *pianissimo* rumble on the other (see examples 1a and b).

Here, as classical music steps into the bardo realm, is where a musicological ear is of use; the Russian provenance of ORCH5 gives rise to some quite strikingly ironic overtones, mostly pitched at frequencies that require at least some music-historical training to perceive. The sampled chord in question was notated in 1909, quite close, as Horowitz argues, to the absolute apogee of classical music culture in the West.[7] It is the

Example 1a. Stravinsky, *The Firebird Suite* (1919 version), Khorovod.

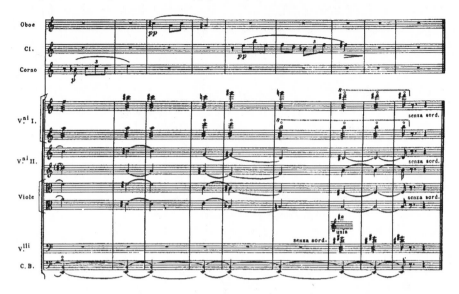

creation of the Western composer most famously and consistently fascinated with the use of recording technology to fix and transmit his music to
future generations; and yet, Stravinsky would undoubtedly have been
horrified that the first digital sample to enshrine, as pure information for
all time, a fragment of "classical music" happened to preserve this particular chord from this particular work. Long before his own death in 1971,
Stravinsky had become hag-ridden by *The Firebird;* he often wished in
print and conversation that the piece, an inveterate request every time
he proposed to conduct or record, would just go away. For most of Stravinsky's life, *The Firebird* was, to him, already dead; audience fetishiza-
tion of his first concert success simply got in the way of an ongoing
creative life. As the musicologist Joni Steshko argues, Stravinsky's two re-
orchestrations of the ballet suite are not just practical (the first, in 1919, to
reduce the orchestra to generic proportions; the second, in 1945, to re-
establish copyright): they impose a programmatic "dehydration" (the word
was the critic Olin Downes's, in an exchange following on a concert review
to which the composer had bitterly objected) on Stravinsky's lush original
that shows the composer so increasingly out of sympathy with his old
creation that he seems to be attempting to exorcise—or at least tame—an
unwelcome ghost from his past.[8]

Example 1b. Stravinsky, *The Firebird Suite* (1919 version), Infernal Dance.

Vorhaus appears to have sampled either the soggy 1910 suite or its 1919 reduction, *not* the 1945 "dried-up" version of the ballet; but the limitations of his eight-bit digital-to-digital conversion process produced a brittle, grainy sample whose frequency spectrum is shifted noticeably toward the upper registers of the orchestra.[9] This has the paradoxical effect of making the sample sound both "old" (because its low fidelity cannot capture the full range of the orchestra, as in the pre-LP era), and "new" (because the sound itself is noticeably devoid of romantic lushness). As it happens, Stravinsky's successive re-orchestrations of the ORCH5 chord had a similar bass-filtering (and thus modernizing) effect: by 1919, in search of a drier, lighter sound, he had replaced two of the harps with the ringing sound of the piano's top octaves, asked for the bass drum to be struck with a leather mallet, and instructed the timpanist to use his hardest wooden stick. In the final 1945 version, his remixing went even further, with a xylophone glissando and a new snare drum roll producing a distinctively dry, crackling spray of dissonant upper partials. In effect, Stravinsky had been down-sampling his younger self long before Vorhaus captured the dried-up digital remains of Kastchei the Immortal on an eight-inch floppy disk.

How much of the original juice could possibly be left?

Stravinsky Joins the Zulu Nation

ORCH5 led a quiet life for about two years. Only wealthy or well-connected pop musicians had access to a Fairlight CMI, and the complexities of programming its intricate waveform editor and its quirky music sequencing module (the famous "Page R") made harnessing Fairlight samples the province of methodical experimenters with big budgets, lots of time, and notably progressive tastes. When ORCH5 showed up in their work, the temporal and acoustic distance it encoded, the grainy, slowed-down, "half-dead" sound of a classical orchestra taken out of context, often worked toward a kind of Orientalist exoticism. This is how Kate Bush used the sample in the title track of her 1982 album *The Dreaming:* blasts of ORCH5 under heavy reverb lance through the chanting, didgeridoos, and pounding drums of the song's fadeout, the whole a spooky musical depiction of Australia's aboriginal "dreamtime" under attack by industrial modernity ("'Bang!' goes another kanga / On the bonnet of the van . . ."). Other early Fairlight owners, especially in Europe, used its sampling capability to reactivate the subversive agenda of the "historical avant-garde" within popular dance music.[10] Presumably this is why Anne Dudley released her essays in Fairlight-enabled sound collage—where ORCH5, jostling for space with the sound of chainsaws, breaking glass, and motorcycle engines, functions as pure alienation-effect—under the retro-Futurist moniker "The Art of Noise." (Dudley and Trevor Horn, her main collaborator, may well have known firsthand from Vorhaus whence the sample came; in any case, the final moments of their 1984 hit single "Close (to the Edit)" wittily close the loop, mixing ORCH5 back into a congeries of sampled orchestral blasts from Stravinsky's *Rite of Spring*.)

But in late 1982, Stravinsky and Vorhaus started hanging with a blacker, funkier crew; ORCH5 joined the Zulu Nation. "Planet Rock," an interracial collaboration between the pioneering hip-hop DJ Afrika Bambaataa and the dance producer Arthur Baker, was a massive R&B hit; it remapped the sound and practice of hip-hop, defined several new musical genres, and spawned hundreds of imitations. Bambaataa himself immodestly claims at least *six* genres of dance music were born when "Planet Rock" launched the style that he himself called "Electro-Funk," and which would ultimately be known simply as "electro"; as he enumerated them, they included "the Miami Bass to the Latin freestyle, Latin hip-hop, to the house music, hip-house, techno."[11] Baker agrees: "I knew [it was a historic track] before we even mixed it. I knew before there was even a rap on it. I went home the night we cut the track and brought the tape home and I said to my wife at the time, 'We've just made musical history.'"[12]

Bambaataa and Baker didn't just make hip-hop history; they also made world-famous a particular orchestration of ORCH5. African American musicians have been asking other musicians to "hit them" for decades; but "Planet Rock" is the first time that the hit came down in the form of a digital sample. Baker claims technical priority, since Bambaataa knew the beats and breaks he wanted, but "didn't know about the studio,"[13] and since it was through Baker's industry connections that the "Planet Rock" sessions took place in a fully equipped New York recording space—the kind that had an expensive Fairlight CMI just sitting around ready to transform the sound of African American popular music.

On one level, "Planet Rock" was pure serendipity. Bambaataa and Baker had no idea how to use the machine, no one to show them, nor any time to learn: "It was pretty quick to make because we didn't have much money. We'd get downtime—night time—sessions. The guy who owned the studio gave us a deal. Maybe it was three all night sessions. We did all the music in one session and a bit of the rap. Then we did the rap. Then we mixed it."[14]

John Robie, the keyboard player, hacked around until he figured out how to trigger eight versions of ORCH5 simultaneously, using both hands, on the pitches of a root-position minor triad. The Fairlight IIx, with its eight independently operating audio cards—and which in all other respects seemed to Baker and Bambaataa an unprogrammable "$100,000 of useless space thing"—responded beautifully.[15] A hip-hop cliché was born.

But one might ask why the first sampled hit should be so dark, portentous, and *classical*-sounding. Why did Robie filter Stravinsky-by-way-of-Vorhaus through that brooding minor triad? Could it have something to do with the dark synthesizer tune, full of Germanic *Weltschmerz*, that he knew he would be asked to play a few moments later?

Eleganz und Dekadenz, or, Kraftwerk Throws Classical Music from the Train

That tune is, as most everyone knows, a quotation from Kraftwerk's 1977 non-hit, "Trans Europe Express." Using Kraftwerk (not to mention "The Mexican," a transcription by the British progressive rock band Babe Ruth of Ennio Morricone's tune from *For a Few Dollars More*) was an attempt to capture in the studio the unpredictable range of Bambaataa's live DJ-ing. Bambaataa enjoyed throwing things like Kiss, the Monkees, calypso tunes, bongo breaks, movie soundtracks, even the Pink Panther theme into a funky set; though the group's appearance reminded him of "some Nazi type of thing,"[16] he particularly liked the electronic sound of Kraftwerk, an esoteric taste he shared with Baker, and which was partly responsible for getting the white disco producer and the black hip-hop DJ working together.[17] Standard histories of hip-hop credit Kraftwerk's robotic drum machines with kick-starting electro, and it is clear that the beat of "Planet Rock" is copied verbatim out of the track "Numbers" from their futuristic 1981 *Computer World* album. (Copied, *not* sampled: Baker found, for twenty dollars, someone who owned one of the newly released Roland TR-808 "drum machines" and who was able to program the Kraftwerk beat into it.) But the minor-key ORCH5 and dark synthesizer tune of "Planet Rock" also transmigrate the resonances of an earlier Kraftwerk

Fig. 1. United States front cover, Kraftwerk, *Trans Europe Express*.
COLLECTION OF,ROBERT FINK.

project, a darker record whose concerns were more political, more historical, and more narrowly European. Bambaataa reports that, given the early
1980s absence of listening booths in used record stores, he tended to pick
up vinyl whose cover art and lettering "looked funky";[18] it's hard to imagine what would have made him pick up *Trans Europe Express*. Figure 1
reproduces the U.S. front cover of the Kraftwerk LP; its nostalgic glamour
seems worlds away from beat-boxes and the Bronx. In fact, the German
front cover was a stiff shot of the four members of Kraftwerk in black and
white, taking what they called their "string quartet" poses. The album's
packaging features carefully staged and colorized pictures that evoke not
technological modernity but ambiguously pastoral images of the 1930s,
as when the four members of the group, dressed in darkly conservative
wool suits, arrange themselves stiffly and formally around a café table
draped with a red-and-white checked tablecloth, all in front of a painted
photographer's backdrop of quaint Bavarian landscape. They might indeed be waiting for a local train—or perhaps something a little less *volk-
stümlich*, like a meeting of the local NSDAP (see figure 2).[19]

Fig. 2. "Like extras from the film *Cabaret*": 1930s imagery recaptured for
Trans Europe Express. COLLECTION OF ROBERT FINK.

The nostalgia really cranks up, though, with the album's idiosyncratic table of contents, which takes up the entire inside sleeve (see figure 3). Drawn on a background of music staves, using musical notation, even introducing a hand-drawn caricature of Franz Schubert, the Austro-German composer we can most easily imagine picnicking with the boys around a Bavarian checkered tablecloth, this guide to the album sets us up to hear it as an extended meditation on classical music, on German identity, and—given the psycho-symbolic import of trains and traintrips—on *loss.* Thus it is hardly surprising that the entire record is unified both tonally and motivically—not implausible for a pair of conservatory-trained German musicians who worked for a time under Karlheinz Stockhausen, but also, here, an expressive strategy: to use the structural apparatus of European classical music to comment on its decline and death.

To be fair, this reading of *Trans Europe Express* is conspicuously unsupported by definitive statements from Kraftwerk's creative team, the composers Ralf Hütter and Florian Schneider. Artistic pronouncements emanating from their Kling Klang studio, of which there have been many over

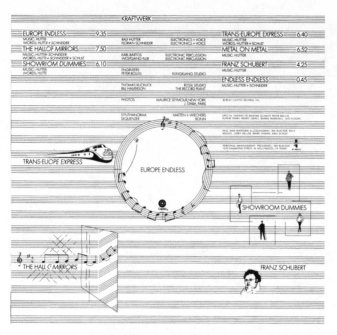

Fig. 3. Musical "table of contents" on staff paper background, *Trans Europe Express*. COLLECTION OF ROBERT FINK.

the years, are in general useless for hermeneutic purposes, since a large part of the group's conceptual aesthetic is based in deadpan irony and Dada-esque media jamming. Some of the interpretive frames placed by Hütter and Schneider around *Trans Europe Express* are patently silly, even offensive, like the notion that since Kraftwerk made "electronic blues," and classic Negro blues often involve trains, they ought to record a song about the European train network.[20] Foolishness aside, Kraftwerk and their fans have seen the group's paean to high-speed train travel as congruent with their positive embrace of modernity and technology, a fitting sequel to albums themed around the *Autobahn* (1974) and *Radio-Activity* (1975): "movement fascinates us . . . all the dynamism of industrial life, of modern life."[21] Yet a fundamental incongruity remains. How to reconcile a briskly unsentimental view of industrial modernity with faded images of pre-war *gemütlichkeit*? What do old-fashioned musical notation and a wan little cartoon of Schubert have to do with the futuristic embrace of "musical machines" that eliminate the very possibility of spontaneity or virtuosity? One possibility, not to be followed up here, is the critique of routinized classical music performance that would become explicit as soon as Kraftwerk began using robotic dummies in "live" performance:

"The interpreters of classical music, Horowitz for example, they are like robots, making a reproduction of the music which is always the same. It's automatic, and they do it as if it were natural, which is not true."[22]

Internal music evidence seems to suggest, however, that it is not just classical music's star interpreters who are "dead"; *Trans Europe Express* manipulates its musical material so as to let us hear, if we wish, the death of classical music itself. Consider example 2d, which transcribes the mournful synthesizer melody Baker, Bambaataa, and Robie lifted and made famous in "Planet Rock." Its minor-key chromaticism and, as we'll see, its signifying function within the album's motivic web will justify the slightly portentous label of "*Weltschmerz*" theme. (Within an interpretive community based in European tonal music, the theme's specific habit of repeated leaps up to the lowered sixth degree of the minor scale will overwhelmingly be read as expressive of pain and sorrow.) With its syncopated chuffing, track-rattling ostinato, and sampled screeches of metal on metal, the song "Trans Europe Express" is an onomatopoetic train ride, certainly; but its real expressive significance does not become clear until we hear it as the dark night-time echo, the negation, of an earlier trip taken in broad daylight. "Europe Endless," the first song on the album, is in many structural ways the expressive double of "Trans Europe Express": the latter begins in the gloom of dissonant stacked fourths resolving to E-flat minor (see example 2c, left), and then modulates, via Doppler effect, down a third to C minor; while the earlier track, opening with radiant G-major arpeggios, modulates *up* a third to an even more sunny B major. A motivic transformation clinches the connection: the same rhythm and contour that outline soggy C-minor *Weltschmerz* in "Trans Europe Express" first appear at the climactic moment of "Europe Endless," at the peak of an endless, rhapsodic prolongation of the dominant and its energy. (The "painful" appoggiatura progression from flat sixth scale degree to the fifth accordingly starts off as the more sanguine use of the natural fourth scale degree to decorate the major third; see examples 2a and b.)

Just before that ascent, Schneider murmurs a verdict on European culture: "*Eleganz und Dekadenz*." The synthesizer theme that Baker and Bambaataa will later borrow is made, over the course of Kraftwerk's album, to act out that decay; at the end of "Metal on Metal," the track that follows and extends "Trans Europe Express," it is buried beneath dissonant fourths and finally crushed under the wheels of technological modernity. (Bambaataa would have been quite familiar with this process;

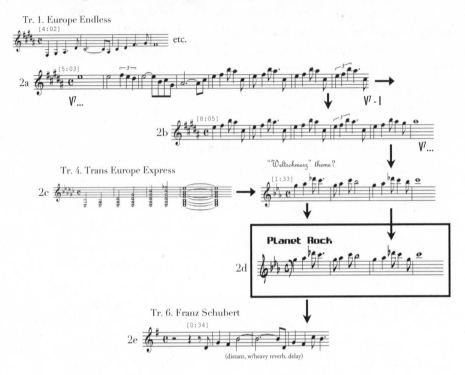

Example 2. Motivic relationships in Kraftwerk, *Trans Europe Express* (1977).

we know that one of his early-1980s Zulu Nation tricks was layering the fiery rhythms of speeches delivered by Malcolm X over the unbroken thirteen minutes of "Trans Europe Express" plus "Metal on Metal" as they followed one another on the B-side of *Trans Europe Express*.)[23] And, if the album cover's musical notation and nostalgic imagery are not enough, consider the penultimate track, "Franz Schubert," in which the decay of the *Europa-Weltschmerz* theme is explicitly linked to the most *gemütlich* of German classical composers. Back in the G major of the album's opening, the basic theme itself decays, contour and pitch dissolving under massive reverb and delay effects (see example 2e). It sounds like a dream . . . or a ghost.

Welcome to the bardo realm.

Lost in Space: ORCH5 and the Retro-Futuristic Sound of Electro Funk

Thus my fundamental hermeneutic leap: if Kraftwerk's *Trans Europe Express* album is about the collapse of European culture as embodied in the decay of its classical music; and if the appropriation of the *Weltschmerz* theme by Baker and Bambaataa transferred some of that anxiety and gloom into African American music; then John Robie's ORCH5 blasts capture, perhaps by accident, the sad revenant of European classical music in a single digital sound. This is how the classical ghost (Stravinsky, standing in here for Schubert, who is standing in for the entire Germanic concert music tradition) gets trapped in the hip-hop machine.

Or, should we rather say, is *liberated* by the hip-hop machine? There is an argument to be made that ORCH5, through a complex transmigration of tones, was soon able to stand expressively by itself without the entire structure of feeling I have just outlined, since nobody in the Bronx actually linked it consciously to the death of European art music, about which, presumably, they couldn't have cared less. Baker's original idea for "Planet Rock" was to avoid, for copyright reasons, any direct use of Kraftwerk's tunes;[24] you can hear the first version of the track, which he actually thought was better than the version the label ultimately decided it was perfectly safe to release,[25] underneath the smooth vocals of his next production, Planet Patrol's "Play at Your Own Risk." That track uses a different synthesizer tune, while a new and funky clavinet riff gives the groove a more soulful feel; but ORCH5, the signature sound of "Kraftwerk in NYC, ca. 1982," remains, now doing all the signifying work by itself. As sonic synecdoche, minor-key ORCH5 began to take on an (after)life of its own: what carried the weight of the decaying European tradition in Düsseldorf or Berlin was understood quite differently by African American musicians in Brooklyn and the Bronx.

The transmigration seems to have proceeded in two phases. In the first, electro producers troped directly off the science-fiction imagery of Baker and Bambaataa's "Planet Rock"; ORCH5 was heard within the matrix of the later, more overtly cybernetic Kraftwerk, the orchestral blasts and doom-laden synthesizer lines resonating, after the fact, more with *The Empire Strikes Back* than with Schubert and Weimar fascism. This played perfectly into an Afro-futurist cultural project that Bambaataa consciously took over from Sun Ra and George Clinton, and, as we'll see below, provides a key imaginative linkage to the house and techno music that the Zulu Nation pioneer claimed as the logical consequence of his "electrifying" hip-hop.

Science fiction, presumably, is the intended referent of the *alla breve* minor-key synthesizer tune that begins its methodical climb, punctuated

Example 3. Afrika Bambaataa, "Planet Rock," 1982

by brassy orchestral "explosions," at about 2:50 into "Planet Rock" (see example 3). Although it sounds dark and serious enough to be from *Trans Europe Express,* this skeletal scalar ascent was invented expressly for "Planet Rock." The grainy string-like timbre and plodding tension evoke Kraftwerk's mordant, robotic version of classical music pretty well—but they also sound a lot like the bombastic pastiches of late Romanticism that lent excitement to battle scenes in Reagan-era space and adventure epics like *Star Trek* and *Raiders of the Lost Ark.*

This Kraftwerk-meets-John-Williams-on-the-synthesizer trope was easy to imitate, but it demanded appropriate content. The desire to copy that distinctively stiff keyboard sound forced electro producers to emphasize exotic, futuristic topics—the ones that would, paradoxically, justify the retrograde sound of dead European music in their grooves—and they rose to the challenge with rap songs based on science fiction, computers, video games, and nuclear annihilation. A constellation of sonic cues assembled itself into the style called "electro": vocoders applied to the MC for a cold robotic sound; the rigid bounce of electronic percussion, with static-laden snares and the distinctive chiming "cowbell" of the Roland TR-808 well to the fore; long unison synthesizer tunes in regular, unsyncopated rhythms; and, slicing through it all, minor-key blasts of ORCH5 providing a dark cinematic edge.

The spread of minor-key ORCH5 was thus not just a consequence of digital sampling getting cheaper—it was a precise, deliberate imitation of Bambaataa imitating Kraftwerk. The original Stravinsky chord sampled by Vorhaus was an orchestration of the open fifth A-E, and thus had no modality; only the multiple-voiced version in "Planet Rock" is minor. As example 4 demonstrates, imitation was often the maximally sincere form of flattery: Larry Johnson and Maurice Starr of the Jonzun Crew changed just enough notes in their version of the "Planet Rock" riff to keep their

Example 4. Jonzun Crew, "Pack Jam (Look Out for the ovc)," 1982–83.

Example 5. Twilight 22, "Siberian Nights," 1984.

"Pack Jam," a catchy paean to the popular video game Pac Man, from actually infringing copyright. (Baker himself had set the precedent by releasing "Play at Your Own Risk" under the group name Planet Patrol, the title of a popular Atari video game.) "Siberian Nights," programmed by a young Fairlight whiz named Gordon Bahary (who had worked on one of the first Fairlights in America while helping Stevie Wonder get ready for his *Secret Life of Plants* tour), used a lowered second scale degree to give its riff a Soviet Russian accent (see example 5); but the combination of high-tech electronic percussion, classical-sounding minor-key organ solos, and meditations on technologically enabled cultural extinction ("You got nuclear war, atomic rain / And nuclear winter gonna freeze your brain!") seems, like "Planet Rock," nicely balanced between the futurist dystopianism of Kraftwerk and the retro-futurism of George Lucas.

Or should we rather name-check another George, George Clinton? The Jonzun Crew's 1983 album was, appropriately enough, entitled *Lost in Space*. On it, their project to continue the psychedelic Afro-futurism of Sun Ra and Parliament-Funkadelic as reinvigorated by Afrika Bambaataa is made explicit: "Pack Jam" rubs shoulders with freaky tracks like "Space Cowboy" and "Space is the Place." Mark Dery argues that "if there is an Afro-futurism, it must be sought in unlikely places, constellated from far-flung points."[26] His example is the opening of Ralph Ellison's *Invisible Man*, in which the "proto-cyberpunk" narrator's desire to hear Louis Armstrong on five simultaneously spinning turntables prefigures the cut-and-splice adventures of Grandmaster Flash and his "Wheels of Steel." But what more unlikely constellation than the one just outlined, where sonic ghosts of Stravinsky and Schubert battle each other inside a funky evocation of a video arcade, where Kastchei, the medieval Russian sorcerer, break-dances through the endless Siberian night of nuclear winter?

A key aspect of the Afro-futurist imagination lies in a complex identification with the science-fiction Other, with *alien*-ness, on the part of a Afro-diasporic culture still dominated by the dark legacy of subjugation to a more technologically advanced colonial power. From this technological domination springs a powerful desire for the Mothership Connection, a desire to appropriate and unleash the power of alien technology—usually imagined simultaneously as ancient technology—on behalf of the oppressed.[27] It only remains for the post-canonic musicologist to point out that, in the sound-world of electro-funk, it is European art music that is cast, deliberately or not, in the role of ancient, alien power source. Kastchei is riding the Mothership, and ORCH5 is his talisman, the classical jewel hidden beneath the hip-hop Pyramids. "Music's magic!" cry the members of the Soulsonic Force, and we know what they mean. It has the power to fill the tank of Stravinsky's *Firebird* with rocket fuel.

Techno Scratch: ORCH5 as a Break

In the second phase of ORCH5's transmigration, the sample loses even the vestigial association with orchestral art music afforded by Bambaataa's "sci-fi soundtrack" trope and is absorbed completely into the generic musical practice of early-1980s hip-hop. Other NYC DJs and producers heard Bambaataa's polyphonic orchestral "blast from the past," those eight sets of grace notes sliding up to the tonic, and imagined not the laser cannons from *Star Wars* but a new and funky kind of digitized turntable scratch.

The precedent had been set by the first generation of hip-hop DJs. Most of the cutting and scratching of early performers like Grand Wizard Theodore, Kool DJ Herc, and Grandmaster Flash has been lost to posterity, and if one is familiar only with recorded output from the period, the connection between hip-hop beat-juggling and ORCH5 might seem obscure. But a trace here and there allows provisional reconstruction of how sampling Stravinsky could function like scratching vinyl in the Bronx, ca. 1982. Consider the track "Flash Tears the Roof Off," a 2002 recreation of a classic turntable mix from the early 1980s. In it, Grandmaster Flash (Joseph Sadler) cues up two copies of a famous break from Funk, Inc.'s 1972 soul-jazz record, "Kool is Back." (This drum break—sampled and played back, probably, on a Fairlight CMI—was made famous among white folk in 1983 when Trevor Horn used it to spice up his production of Yes's

"Owner of a Lonely Heart.") Flash proceeds to execute *the* classic maneuver of Bronx sound system DJ-ing, which he more or less invented, alternately rewinding and releasing the records, looping, stretching, and chopping up the short drum fill into an extended dance break. So far, standard hip-hop practice, and hardly worth mentioning, except for a strangely familiar sonic intruder, lurking in the grooves of the record. Unlike the everywhere-sampled breaks in tracks by James Brown ("Funky Drummer") and the Winstons ("Amen, My Brother"), which start "clean," the first beat of this drum fill is punctuated by a loud splat from the entire quintet, cutting loose on a jazzy added-sixth chord. As voiced and swung in "Kool is Back," this "G-added-sixth" chord sounds enough like ORCH5 that unwary listeners often mistake one for the other: in both cases, members of the ensemble attack early and slide up to meet a sharp, staccato downbeat with heavy emphasis on an open fifth, which then reverberates into recorded space.

I wouldn't insist on the resonance, were it not for what Grandmaster Flash does with the sound. As he juggles this break, he picks up the "kool" chord attached to its first beat and—intentionally or not—juggles it, too. The sharp ensemble attack is now the direct result of a turntable scratch, and it marks the syncopated downbeats of chopped and sampled breaks. When hip-hop DJs and producers heard ORCH5 in "Planet Rock," some of them quickly realized that it could be used in precisely the same way, and they began dropping it into tracks filled with sampled breakbeats and digitized techno-scratches to create an up-to-the-minute, "electro-funky" style of hip-hop. ORCH5, no longer just the sound of science fiction but also "the-hit-before-the-breakbeat-starts," could then be rhythmically activated through (often faux) scratching and beat juggling.[28] Used this way, as in Mantronix's 1985 classic, "Needle to the Groove," the *Firebird* chord becomes a purely percussive accent, stripped not just of dark, minor-key glamour but of any tonal function at all. This must be the reason Kurtis Khaleel of Mantronix simply couldn't be bothered to adjust the pitch level of his ORCH5 sample to that of the surrounding track, triggering it instead at a consistent and grating half-step below the tonic. The effect is, to musicological ears, genuinely avant-garde (if probably serendipitous). "Needle to the Groove" recycles most of the aural signs of electro: vocoded chanting; mechanical-sounding TR-808 drum beats; and, of course the ubiquitous ORCH5 sample, but now on the off-beats, syncopated, within an expressive context that betrays no hint of futurism, Afro- or other-wise. The song's infectious refrain, spinning out of its self-referential title phrase ("We got the needle to the groove / We got the beats that'll make you move"), makes it clear that classical music, or at least the fragment of it trapped within ORCH5, had achieved, through systematic musical trans-migration, a great liberation.

This is how it happens: by the mid-1980s, ORCH5 is thoroughly natu-ralized within hip-hop, to the point that one need neither invoke the death of European culture nor the incipient descent of the Mothership to use it. It doesn't have to sound melodramatic and minor, and you don't even have to put it on the downbeat. It's just one of the many funky things that can happen when you put the needle to the groove.

Postlude: Strings of Life

At this point it would be possible to follow dozens of tracks toward the present day; but let us follow the most direct route, the high-speed techno train that runs between Düsseldorf and Detroit.

Few people in the pop music world of 1982 even knew what a Fairlight was. After the huge success of "Planet Rock" and Baker's follow-ups, many urban musicians casting around for an ORCH5-like sound settled on what one might call the "techno minor" triad. A staccato minor chord played through a grainy analog string patch, with its envelope tweaked to provide both a sharp percussive "chuff" at the attack and a pronounced reverb at the release, sounded pretty much like ORCH5, if you weren't too particular. Techno minor plus beats from a machine was all you needed to get the sound.

This is the sound of very early Detroit techno, for instance the group Cybotron, a group of suburban black teenagers who everybody took for "some white guys from Germany." "Clear," Cybotron's first (and only) hit, features rhythmically syncopated repetitions of the techno minor triad over a lopsided *Computer World*–style mechanical beat. When a pyramid of synthesizer tones dissolves into a melancholy tune right out of "Trans Europe Express," it is clear that Juan Atkins, the brains behind Cybotron, really *wanted* to be heard as white and from Germany, and that "Clear" is meant as overt homage to the paradigmatically white German guys who made up Kraftwerk. Its relation to "Planet Rock," Afrika Bambaataa, and the Zulu Nation was much more equivocal; "Clear," and the Detroit techno music that sprung from it, programmatically eliminated all traces of hip-hop from the sound (no rapping, no inner-city accents)—which looks, in retrospect, like an attempt to synthesize a futurist electronic music by filtering out the "Afro" (that is, the Bronx) in Afro-futurist hip-hop. As the Detroit style matured, the techno minor triad was featured in front of minimalist spiraling keyboard riffs and the rat-a-tatting of the Roland TR-808, as in the classic track "Off to Battle," a more sophisticated effort by Atkins, now working under the *nom-de-microprocessor* Model 500. (He took the name from the Roland MC-500 Micro Composer, one of the first affordable digital sequencers.)

In 1997, Derrick May, another crucial innovator of the Detroit sound, released a CD of his early tracks. It was the tenth anniversary of his first major hit, a track often cited as the single inspiration for the global techno scene. In a short new track called "A Relic Mix," he reached back and collected some of the sounds of his early career, most notably the techno minor triad. For the project, he took out of mothballs his 1985-model Ensoniq Mirage, the first eight-bit digital sampler to be priced under $2000: the sounds are relics twice over, because May, famously, took the Mirage to Detroit's Orchestra Hall and did some surreptitious sampling during rehearsals, thus making some cold and grainy versions of ORCH5 for himself.

Relics of relics; we appear to have looped back to the beginning, an endlessly decaying Europe of dead sounds and music. But May's ghostly relics, his blasts from the past, whisper of liberation, at least for classical music, in the bardo realm. Ten years before, May, producing under the no-nonsense moniker Rhythim Is Rhythim, had used these orchestral samples to make one of the seminal leaps forward in the Detroit techno explosion, an unsentimental masterpiece of irrepressible energy that is on every dance music historian's list of the most influential tracks of all time. In it, stabbing tones derived from the sound of an orchestral violin section (the attacks are grotesquely exaggerated, so that each keystroke sounds a little like ORCH5) pile up in irregular, accelerating drifts over a stuttering, vaguely Latin piano riff. It inhabits some of the sound-world of Kraftwerk, but none of its aesthetic: both sampled piano and sampled violins have a nervous, un-quantized intensity—a *swing*, one wants to call it—that is continents away from the ponderous, lacquered decay of Kling Klang Studios. The Roland TR-808 and 909 that drive the track forward no longer sound like machine guns, laser cannons, or dot-matrix printers gone mad; instead we hear congas, djembes, shakers . . .

If Kraftwerk trapped the classical ghost in their machines; and Afrika Bambaataa let it out of his, to break-dance for a little while; then May offers up his machines to be ridden, hard, by an electronic Orisha. Rhythim *is* Rhythim, after all.

There is nothing decadent about this music.

It manifests a fierce joy, the joy of *starting over.*

May called it—how unexpected, how *perfect*—"Strings of Life."

Notes

The sources of the epigraphs to this chapter are as follows: Hütter interviewed by Sergey Chernov, *St. Petersburg Times,* May 28, 2004, 972; "Planet Rock" lyrics as transcribed by the author; Fairlight slogan as quoted in G. Holmes, *The Holmes Page: Fairlight CMI,* http://ghservices.com/gregh/fairlight (accessed April 16, 2007).

1. The reference here is to Milton Babbitt's infamous article in *High Fidelity,* often anthologized under his preferred title, "The Composer as Specialist," but which appeared in 1958 with the more journalistically apropos editorial title "Who Cares if You Listen?" For the revisionist soul-searching to which I refer above, see Evan Ziporyn, "Who Listens if You Care?" in *Strunk's Source Readings in Music History,* ed. Leo Treitler (New York: Norton, 1998), 1311–18.

2. Joseph Horowitz, *The Post-Classical Predicament: Essays on Music and Society* (Boston: Northeastern University Press, 1995). Kyle Gann, who in 1997 published a wicked and witty parody of the perennial "death of classical music" article (as a hard-boiled detective story) in his *Village Voice* column, has titled his Web log (and associated radio station) simply "PostClassic." The Web log is hosted by www.artsjournal.com, and the (highly recommended!) radio station, winner of a Deems Taylor award, is streamed on www.live365.com.

3. Robert Fink, "Elvis Everywhere: Musicology and Popular Music Studies at the Twilight of the Canon," *American Music* 16, no. 2 (1998): 142–56.

4. See Holmes, *The Holmes Page.*

5. Brochure for Fairlight Computer Music Instrument (Fairlight Instruments Pty. Ltd., 1983), online at http://www.hollowsun.com/vintage/fairlight/brochure.zip (accessed April 16, 2007).

6. Audio samples of the Fairlight's sound library, including ORCH5 can (as of early 2007) be accessed at Holmes, *The Holmes Page.* See also the larger downloads of sound banks from the Hollow Sun website, http://www.hollowsun.com/vintage/fairlight (accessed April 16, 2007).

7. Joseph Horowitz, *Classical Music in America: A History of Its Rise and Fall* (New York: Norton, 2005).

8. Joni Steshko, "Stravinsky's *Firebird*: Genesis, Sources, and the Centrality of the 1919 Suite," Ph.D. dissertation, UCLA, 2000, 230–49.

9. It is not possible for me to tell exactly which *recording* of Stravinsky's *Firebird* was sampled by Vorhaus. One could, of course, ask him, but I refrain as a matter of principle: to ask Vorhaus to identify the recording would be to open huge swaths of the hip-hop world to the possibility of copyright infringement lawsuits. In the hip-hop world, this is called "snitching." Joseph Schloss, in his recent study of hip-hop producers, refuses for this reason to transcribe into musical notation any of the chopped and looped samples he discusses. Joseph Schloss, *Making Beats: The Art of Sample-Based Hip-Hop* (Middleton, Conn.: Wesleyan University Press, 2004), 12–15; 120–30.

10. Andreas Huyssen, *After the Great Divide: Modernism, Mass Culture, Postmodernism* (Bloomington: Indiana University Press, 1986).

11. Jim Fricke and Charlie Ahearn, *Yes Yes Y'all: The Experience Music Project Oral History of Hip-Hop's First Decade* (New York: Da Capo, 2002), 315.

12. Bill Brewster and Frank Broughton, *Last Night a DJ Saved My Life: The History of the Disc Jockey* (New York: Grove Press, 2000), 242–43.

13. Arthur Baker, interview with Bill Brewster and Frank Broughton, January 25, 1999, reproduced in full at http://www.djhistory.com/books/archiveInterviewDisplay.php?interview_id=8 (accessed April 16, 2007).

14. Ibid.

15. A technical note: this eight-voice polyphonic mode, in which the same sound is assigned to each one of the machine's eight audio registers, is the default setting on the Fairlight's Register and Keyboard Control Page (Page 3). Thus a high level of computer literacy would be required to get the CMI to do *anything else but* simply play eight iterations of the sample in Register A when eight keys were pressed down. The only other "programming" skill one would need to produce "Planet Rock" was the ability to use a light pen on Page 2, Disk Control, to select a file like ORCH5 from the contents of the floppy disk and load it into the default memory location, which is, of course, Register A. The recording engineer could have shown Robie or Baker how to accomplish this in less than thirty seconds. As so often in the history of electronic dance music (analogous stories could be told about the Roland TB-303 bassline generator and the birth of acid house), using the machine correctly, to make conventional music—the Fairlight, for instance, could be laboriously programmed, using register control and keyboard mapping, to play in real time all the sounds of a jazz or rock combo—was extremely difficult. Using the

machine incorrectly, "hacking" it, on the other hand, was easy, and the sounds resulting were often, as in this case, more interesting than the sonic output intended by the machine's creators. For details on programming the Fairlight CMI, as well as screen shots of its control pages, see Holmes, *The Holmes Page*.

16. Fricke and Ahearn, *Yes Yes Y'all*, 310–11.

17. Baker, interview.

18. Fricke and Ahearn, *Yes Yes Y'all*, 46.

19. This may seem a far-fetched reading—but it appears to be exactly what Pascal Bussy meant when he imagined Kraftwerk in this picture "almost as if posing as cardboard cut-out extras for a scene in the film *Cabaret*." Pascal Bussy, *Kraftwerk: Man, Machine, and Music* (London: SAF Publishing, Ltd., 1990), 85. The reference can only be to the mise-en-scène of the movie's one daytime exterior number, "Tomorrow Belongs to Me," with its chorus of apple-cheeked Brown-shirts giving an impromptu, menacing concert in the sunshine of a suburban *Biergarten*.

20. Bussy, *Kraftwerk*, 86.

21. Hütter as quoted in Bussy, *Kraftwerk*, 88.

22. Hütter as quoted in Bussy, *Kraftwerk*, 161.

23. Brewster and Broughton, *Last Night a DJ Saved My Life*, 243.

24. Baker interview, 1999.

25. They were wrong, and he was right to worry. Kraftwerk, once they became aware of this appropriation, responded in a distinctly un-postmodern way: they immediately sued Baker and Bambaataa for plagiarism, furious that they had not been correctly footnoted: "If you read a book and you copy something out of it, you do it like a scientist, you have to quote where you took it from, what is the source of it" (Kraftwerk percussionist Karl Bartos as quoted in Bussy, *Kraftwerk*, 125).

26. Mark Dery, "Black to the Future," in *Flame Wars: The Discourse of Cyberculture*, ed. Mark Dery (Durham, N.C.: Duke University Press, 1994), 124.

27. Robin D. G. Kelley, *Freedom Dreams: The Black Radical Imagination* (Boston: Beacon Press, 2002).

28. There may have been iterations of ORCH5 or ORCH5-like sounds on DJ records, but I have never seen one. One could, of course, have attempted to scratch with "Planet Rock" itself, but that would have been unutterably lame (Schloss, *Making Beats*, 114–19).

Discography

Art of Noise. "Close (to the Edit)." *(Who's Afraid of) The Art of Noise* (1984). Universal, 1998.

Bambaataa, Afrika, and the Soulsonic Force. "Planet Rock" (1982). *Don't Stop . . . Planet Rock*. Tommy Boy, 1992.

Bambaataa, Afrika. *United DJs of America Presents Afrika Bambaataa: Electro Funk Breakdown* (mix CD, 1999). DMC, 1999.

Bush, Kate. "The Dreaming." *The Dreaming* (1982). Capitol, 1990.

Carl, Aaron. "Down (Electro Mix)" (ca. 1986?). *Timeless: The Essential Metroplex Classics Mixed by Juan Atkins*. Metroplex, 2003.

Cybotron. "Clear" (1983). *Clear*. Fantasy Records, 1990.

Funk, Inc. "Kool is Back" (1972). *Funk, Inc.* Prestige, 1995.

Grandmaster Flash. "Flash Tears the Roof Off" (turntable mix). *The Official Adventures of Grandmaster Flash*. Strut, 2002.

The Jonzun Crew. "Pack Jam (Look Out for the OVC)." Originally released on *Lost in Space* (Tommy Boy, 1983). Reissued on *Street Jams: Electric Funk, Vol. 2*. Rhino, 1992.

Knights of the Turntables. "Techno Scratch" (1984). *The Wild Bunch: Story of a Sound System*. Strut, 2002.

Kraftwerk. "Numbers." *Computer World*. Elektra/Asylum, 1981.

——. *Trans Europe Express*. Capitol, 1977.

Mantronix. "Needle to the Groove." *Mantronix: The Album*. Warlock, 1985.

May, Derrick. "A Relic Mix." *Derrick May: Innovator*. Transmat, 1997.

Model 500. "Off to Battle" (1987). *Timeless: The Essential Metroplex Classics Mixed by Juan Atkins*. Metroplex, 2003.

Planet Patrol. "Play at Your Own Risk" (1983). *Electro Science Mixed by the Freestylers*. Urban Theory, 2000.

Rhythim Is Rhythim. "Strings of Life" (original mix, Transmat MS 4, 1987). *Derrick May: Innovator*. Transmat TMT CD 4. 1997.

Twilight 22. "Siberian Nights." Originally released on *Twilight 22* (Vanguard, 1984). Reissued on *Street Jams: Electric Funk, Vol. 2*. Rhino, 1992.

Vorhaus, David, et. al. "Fairlight IIx Sample Library, Disc 17." *Pro-Rec Audio Sampling CD*, 2003.

Yes. "Owner of a Lonely Heart." *90125*. Atlantic, 1983.

Mark Anthony Neal

White Chocolate Soul
Teena Marie and Lewis Taylor

16 Tears in my bedroom when they chased me home from school
Nigger lover this and nigger lover that
Oh yes, I've been called it all
TEENA MARIE

There has been no greater tension within black pop, tra-
ditionally, than that associated with the performance of
"black" styles by white musicians. This dates back to the
early nineteenth century, when white performers began
to get their "charcoal" on, donning blackface and tattered
clothes and acting out what they perceived as authentic
black style. One of the very first images of a "black" male
in film—a Thomas Edison short made at the beginning
of the twentieth century—was a white male in blackface,
and black men have been chasing, affirming, challenging, and running away from this cartooned caricature for
the last one hundred years.[1] In jazz, Mezz Mezzrow
could live an "authentic" life (meaning black) while Paul
Whiteman could arrogantly claim that he was sanitizing
the music via his "symphonic" arrangements. But no
one has elicited more concern on this front than Elvis
Presley, given his status as the "King" of rock and roll
(anybody wanna query Little Richard or Chuck Berry on
this point?). Feelings about Presley among black au-

diences were perfectly captured a few years ago when the late Ray Charles responded to a Bob Costas query about Elvis with the quip, "What the hell was so special about Elvis . . . all Elvis did was shake his ass and black folks been shaking their ass for hundreds of years."

Paul C. Taylor calls the unease behind comments like Charles's the "Elvis Effect," adding that it could easily be called "the Benny Goodman, the Dave Brubeck or the Vanilla Ice effect."[2] There is a clear legacy of artists like Presley, Eric Clapton, Pat Boone, and most recently Eminem who have had huge commercial success essentially because they were white artists performing so-called black music. It is not simply a question about cultural interlopers—and I'm not accusing any of these men of being cultural interlopers—but the impact that their dexterity at performing "black" music has within the political economy of popular music. Amiri Baraka, for example, asserts that the music industry must "either cover [black music] or the music must be wrestled away from its originators and its creation ascribed to others. Elvis Presley is at once a cover and a fake originator."[3] Carl Hancock Rux notes that "race inclusivity diminishes the organic intention of race music until it simplifies into yet another popular entertainment form in the marketplace, where its inventor will compete for the right to exist."[4]

I am less interested here in defending or challenging black attitudes toward white cultural interlopers, or citing the continued problematics of the "Elvis Effect," than in dealing with the aesthetic issues surrounding white appropriation of black musical styles, particularly in the context of "soul music." Taylor notes that "knowing of the historically racist trajectory of white American appetites for cultural commodities can change the way one hears Eric Clapton—or the Canadian dancehall dj Snow . . . can erect affective obstacles to the reception and enjoyment of otherwise impeccable arrangements of sounds."[5] It is in the context of Taylor's observations that I'd like to forward an alternative view—one that suggests that there are artists who transcend, to varying degrees, the kinds of "affective obstacles" that make it difficult for some audiences to derive pleasures from so-called white performances of black musical idioms. More specifically, in opposition to a notion of "blue-eyed soul," I'd like to argue for a separate category known as "white chocolate"—that which "looks" different (and for all intents is different since white chocolate isn't really made of chocolate) but contains all the "flava" and the texture of the original.

By "white chocolate" I mean artists—ostensibly R&B and soul performers—who challenge essentialist arguments about who is *allowed* to sing black music (and this essentialism travels in all directions including in the direction of those black artists who are not deemed "black enough") and who also provides examples of white performances of black pop that transcend simple appropriations (and in the worst case theft) and legitimately add to the tradition. Thus clear distinctions could be made between Michael Bolton (still a hack after all these years) and George Michael or Vanilla Ice and Eminem or the Righteous Brothers and Laura Nyro. Of course "white chocolate soul" could easily be interpreted as a simple confection, contrived by major recording labels to mainstream white performances of black pop. As such I use the term "white chocolate" not so much as a descriptive term as a theoretical idea that can be employed to discern white performances of so-called black style from caricatures of "blackness" performed by whites (or blacks for that matter), be it the examples of the professional basketball player Jayson Williams—his nickname "White Chocolate" was the inspiration for the title of this essay—the spoken-word and dramatic performances of Danny Hoch, or the prose of Adam Mansbach. As such I am less concerned about whether or not such performances are "black enough" or authentic, but rather, to borrow a theoretical framework argued by the cultural anthropologist John L. Jackson, Jr., concerned by whether or not such performances can be read as "sincere." In his book *Real Black: Adventures in Racial Sincerity,* Jackson argues that "sincerity presumes a liaison between subjects . . . Questions of sincerity imply social interlocutors who presume one another's humanity, interiority, and subjectivity. It is a subject-subject interaction, not the subject-object model that authenticity presumes—and to which critiques of authenticity implicitly reduce every racial exchange."[6] For very different reasons, figures like Teena Marie and Lewis Taylor complicate our thinking about the cross-racial performance of musical blackness.

Born in the multiracial town of Venice, California, in 1956, Teena Marie was introduced to a wide range of musical styles via her parents. She recalls hearing Mozart and Schubert as often as she heard Sarah Vaughn and Aretha Franklin during her childhood but says that Al Green's "Tired of Being Alone" was the song that began her affection for soul and R&B: "I just leaned against a locker and went Wowww! I had never heard a sound like that before."[7] To her credit, Marie was cognizant of what it meant to be a "white" soul singer but made no excuses for her musical taste, admitting that she "never thought that you had to be any particular color to sing whatever is in your heart . . . I was born to sing rhythm 'n' blues. I just know that."[8] In another interview she juxtaposed her status as white soul singer to that of black women in opera, noting that " some of the great opera singers in the world are black women."[9] One of the things that has made Marie so appealing to many of her fans is her ability to own up to the contradictions of her talents. In a *New York Times* profile Carol Cooper wrote, "From the start [Marie] was a walking contra-diction—a tiny woman with a huge voice; a formally trained musician able to improvise like a storefront gospel soloist; a white singer whose au-dience is overwhelmingly black."[10]

When Marie signed with Motown in 1976, the label wasn't sure it knew what to do with all those contradictions—her first project languished in development, as she recorded uninspired retreads of songs like "Every Little Bit Hurts." Motown clearly realized that a "white soul singer" could be a valuable commodity, particularly at a time when the label was very much struggling to maintain its footing in the commercial marketplace. The Jackson Five, the most important act that Motown had developed since their relocation from Detroit to Los Angeles, ended their relation-ship with the label the year before Marie signed with the label. With the burgeoning Philly Soul empire of Gamble and Huff reigning dominant in the field of black pop and many of the "white"-owned labels aggres-sively pursuing and promoting black artists, Motown was forced to rely on the star power of some of its aging solo acts like Smokey Robinson, Diana Ross, Marvin Gaye, and Stevie Wonder and a new group of acts that included Lionel Richie and the Commodores, Switch, and Rick James.

Though Richie would become the most popular of these next-generation Motowners, it was clear in the late 1970s that James was the label's most charismatic artist and creative force. James is generally credited with "discovering" Marie and was behind the boards (along with longtime Marvin Gaye engineer Art Stewart) for Marie's debut *Wild and Peaceful*, released in March 1979. According to James, he first heard Marie sing at Motown's Los Angeles offices: "I expected to see a writer-producer. And instead I found this short tiny white body sitting at the piano sing-ing like the gods had come into her spirit."[11] Motown brass and Marie's manager Winnie Martin encouraged James to take a more active role in Marie's initial project. The collaboration was the beginning of what would be an intensely personal and often volatile relationship between the two.

Marie was not Motown's first white act—Charlene had moderate success in 1977 with the single "I've Never Been to Me" and Rare Earth released several albums for the label in the early 1970s, including a rollicking "Rock" cover of the Temptation's "Get Ready." There has been speculation that Rare Earth was really a front band for Motown's famed studio musicians the Funk Brothers (an interesting subversion of the classic cover scam, if true). The difference between Marie and the aforementioned white acts is that Marie's sound was decidedly "black," and Motown—by then a clarion example of cultural nationalist sentiments within some black communities in the United States—was in a quandary as to how to market her. Accordingly, the cover art for *Wild and Peaceful* lacks any photographic reference to Marie—clearly an effort by Motown to obscure Marie's white identity. In this regard the "story" of James's discovery of Marie (like Diana Ross's fictional discovery of the Jackson Five) and his presence on her initial recording was thought to be a crucial component of black audience acceptance of her music.

At the time James was riding a wave of popularity courtesy of his post-Parliament-Funkadelic "Punk Funk" sound and signature tracks like "You and I," "Mary Jane," and "Bustin' Out." James's role in the promotion of Marie would anticipate Dr. Dre's nearly two decades later in the career of Eminem. One of the tracks on *Wild and Peaceful* critical to understanding Marie's artistry and her racial politics is "Déjà Vu (I've Been Here Before)." The song's lyrics, written by James, highlight the malleability of identity through the concept of reincarnation—a metaphor for the cultural hybridity that Marie embodied with her voice.

Marie followed up her debut with *Lady T* (1980), which was produced by Richard Rudolph, a founding member of Rotary Connection, a multiracial soul-rock band, and dedicated to Rudolph's late wife Minnie Riperton (also a one-time member of Rotary Connection). Given Riperton's own ability to challenge essentialist notions of soul music, it's not surprising that Marie found inspiration in Riperton's music and career. According to Marie, "people thought Minnie Riperton was white because she didn't have that same soul sound as Aretha. . . . I think people have embraced me because they really can feel that I'm real, and that I'm who I am and I play the music that I love."[12] Among the standouts on *Lady T* were the dance hit "Behind the Groove" and the sensual "Aladdin's Lamp." Six months later, Motown released Marie's *Irons in the Fire* (1980). The disc was the first that was wholly produced by Marie and included her first foray onto the American pop charts with "I Need Your Lovin.'"

It Must Be Magic, Marie's fourth recording, was released by Motown in May 1981 and marks Marie's most extensive use of her songwriting, vocal skills, and production talents—it is the project most emblematic of her "white chocolate" aesthetic. The recording was propelled by the assertive lead single "Square Biz," which provided Marie with the opportunity to "speak out" about her identity and influences. The song's title is taken from a then-popular colloquialism within some black communities in the United States, which affirmed something as the "truth" (a few years later "word" or "word-up" would function the same way within hip-hop vernacular). Though Deborah Harry is frequently cited as the fly white girl who first did the rap thing on Blondie's "Rapture," the significance of Marie's own rap on "Square Biz" is too often ignored. And it is with her rap that Marie lays claim to her intimate connection to black culture. Addressing the name calling she faced as a child, Marie states, "I've been called Casper, Shorty, Lil' Bit / And some they call me Vanilla child / But you know that don't mean my world to me / Cause baby names can cramp my style." Showing audiences "what's really good in the hood," Marie proclaims her love of " 'chickiken' and Buff's [Buffalo, New York] collard greens." But ultimately the power of Marie's rap is evidenced in the wide range of influences that she cites—"You know I like spirituals and rock / Sarah Vaughn, Johann Sebastian Bach / Shakespeare, Maya Angelou and Nikki Giovanni just to name a few"—many of whom might have been obscure to the black teenagers who formed her core audience at the time. In this instance, it is Marie's whiteness that emboldens her transracial/ multiethnic project. While I hesitate to accuse Marie of the kind of racial tourism that marks so much transracial desire in the age of the Internet, I do want to suggest that Marie's "whiteness" makes her testimony credible in a way that might likely be read as suspect or "acting white" if uttered by an African American performer.

Throughout *It Must Be Magic* Marie pays tribute to John Lennon, who was murdered in front of the Dakota Hotel in New York in December

1980. On the heartbreaking "Where's California," Marie alludes to Lennon's death in the opening line "Manchester, England looks a lot like me today / ain't no sunshine in the feeling," and later: "I couldn't find the fog, the Beatles or myself." The introspection of "Where's California" is juxtaposed to the strident political tome "Revolution," which symbolically responds to Lennon's own critique of that name. Though the song captures the urgency of the Black Power and student protest movements of the late 1960s, its intent is closer in spirit to the nonviolent movements of Gandhi and Martin Luther King, Jr. Marie's rejection of violence is then read onto the legacy of John Lennon, as she links his murder to lax gun laws: "Brother Soul has gotten killed and he's just standing there / reading captions from *The Catcher in the Rye* / It didn't take too many dollars to get his hand on a revolver." The reality of violence is again echoed in the song's closing breakdown as Marie openly asks "why must they kill off all our leaders?" As a white performer, Marie does not have access to the "black rage" narrative that black artists could more easily traffic in, thus her embrace of a nonviolent politics is logical on both a personal and a musical level.

The centerpiece ballad on *It Must Be Magic,* if not the most significant solo ballad in Marie's body of work, is "Portuguese Lover." Nearly eight minutes in length, the song features a three-minute closing breakdown that highlights call-and-response exchanges between Marie and the saxophonist Danny Lemelle (reminiscent of those between Phillip Bailey and Larry Myricks on the live version of Earth, Wind & Fire's "Reasons"). The call-and-response performance is a prominent feature of the black gospel tradition, though it is not surprising to find such exchanges on soul and R&B performances, particularly during live performance. In the case of Marie's "Portuguese Lover," the performance conveys yet more evidence of Marie's authenticity as a soul performer. The song's title alludes to an exoticism that helps to mask the more obvious interracial sexual tension between Marie and James, who sings background throughout in what seem like postcoital exchanges. Similarly, the vocal pairing "Fire and Desire," featured on James's crossover breakthrough *Street Songs* (1980), remains a remarkable tribute to the power of desire. Never before had a white woman and black man sung so passionately to each other and for each other. "Fire and Desire" reversed years of unrequited sexual desire across the "color line," though of course Marie's "black" voice obscured this fact to those who were not aware of her actual racial identity, thus muting some of the transgressive potential of the song.

It Must Be Magic was Marie's last studio recording for Motown; she next signed with Epic Records, then home to Michael Jackson and Luther Vandross, and released Robbery in 1983. But it was with the breakout success of the lead single of her follow-up Starchild (1984) that Marie finally crossed over to the mainstream. "Lover Girl" catapulted Marie to the top-ten pop charts in an era that was dominated by pop acts like Michael Jackson, Lionel Richie, Van Halen, Culture Club, and Cyndi Lauper. "Lover Girl" is easily the least "black" song that Marie had recorded to date (at least in the context of 1980s-era American pop music) and thus was the irony of her career up to that point—the "munchkin white girl" was perhaps too "black" for some white audiences and pop radio in particular. The musical strategy of the song was not unlike that employed by Michael Jackson and his producers on the track "Beat It," which relied on fairly standard rock guitar riffs and thus cemented Jackson's transition from an R&B artist to full-fledged pop star. In this regard, "Lover Girl" found Marie ironically performing "whiteness," and given the success of that recording it's not surprising that subsequent recordings by Marie, notably Emerald City (1986), suffered from attempts to please audiences beyond her base.

Marie's last major success as an R&B artist occurred with the release of Naked to the Word (1987) which featured the single "Ooh La La La." Nine years later the chorus from the song was prominently reconstituted as part of the Fugee's "Fu-Gee-La" from their critically acclaimed The Score (1996). The Score featured several revisions of classic R&B recordings including "Ready or Not," a remake of the Delfonics' classic "Ready or Not Here I Come (Can't Hide from Love)" and a nuanced version of Roberta Flack's "Killing Me Softly." Their use of Marie's song suggests the extent to which she was perceived by the group as a legitimate purveyor of the soul tradition among the hip-hop generation. Such a notion was later articulated by Mary J. Blige, who suggested that Marie was "the queen of every black person's home" when she was "a little girl growing up in the projects."[13] In other words Marie possessed a "ghetto pass," one that Cash Money clearly recognized when they signed Marie to their subsidiary Cash Money Classics in early 2004. The subsequent release La Dona (2004) was Marie's first top-ten album release since Starchild (1984).

Rick James once told *People* magazine that Marie was the "most important white female singer since Barbara Streisand; and her own race forgot her."[14] As one journalist once described Marie's career, "the more Top 40 radio ignores [Marie], the more valid becomes her place in the world of rhythm and blues."[15] Marie's success as a "white chocolate" soul singer was ultimately rooted in her comfort with and convincing performance of black vernacular traditions of the late 1970s and 1980s. Marie was also always honest about her musical influences and her intent to be "just" an R&B artist. Though there are many white women artists who were as adept as Marie in the performance of black vernacular musical styles, Laura Nyro, Dusty Springfield, and Janis Joplin being the most prominent examples, the popularity of these women wasn't solely premised on their use of black musical idioms—they were perceived by audiences and critics as having broader musical interests, whether that was the reality or not. In this regard it was Marie's lack of musical ambition that likely endeared her to black audiences—this was not an artist who was trying to push the boundaries of the form.

If Teena Marie has rarely distanced herself from her soul roots, Lewis Taylor's music represents a more complicated view, which at once affirms the possibilities of expanding the available language associated with soul music and contemporary R&B while actively obscuring the obvious influences of black artists on his music. I would argue that Taylor's proclivity to record music that, as he describes it, is "born of a disintegrated mind" is an attempt to undermine the socially constructed image of the "blue-eyed" soul singer.[16] Whereas Teena Marie hails the productive value of embracing her soulful influences, Taylor attempts to obliterate the blue-eyed soul figure (and its gendered investments) in an act inspired as much by the need to further the soul tradition as to distance himself from "blue-eyed" commercial hacks. But ironically, at least in a critical sense, it is Taylor's whiteness (his real-time racial privilege) that allows him the space to experiment—experimentation that the critical establishment, especially in the United States, was ambivalent about in the case of some black artists. I'm thinking specifically of the second full-length studio recordings from D'Angelo (*Voodoo*) and Maxwell (*Embrya*).

Born in North London, in the town of Barnet, Lewis Taylor got his start playing guitar in the Edgar Broughton Band in the 1980s. In the late 1980s, Taylor changed his name to Sheriff Jack and recorded two psychedelic discs under that name. By the time he came to the attention of the Island Record A&R executive David Gilmour, Lewis Taylor was positioning himself as an R&B singer. Taylor admits that it was "generic" R&B: "nothing with any identity, there wasn't anything particularly unique about it."[17] Taylor's feelings changed when he wrote and recorded "Lucky," the song that became the foundation for his debut recording *Lewis Taylor* (1996). According to the singer, he was listening to artists like Tangerine Dream and Tim Buckley and Miles Davis's *Bitches Brew* (1969)—music that trafficked in "atmospherics"—while recording later segments of *Lewis Taylor*. This particular production style is apparent on songs like "Track" and "Betterlove," where one can hear echoes of Brian Wilson's production on the Beach Boys' *Pet Sounds*, specifically "Caroline No," "I Just Wasn't Made for These Times," and "Don't Talk (Put Your Head on My Shoulder)." On a track like "Betterlove," though, one can also hear vocal phrasing and cadences that are clearly borrowed from a figure like Bobby Womack. Initially Taylor was very open in acknowledging the influences of black soul artists on his music, telling *Blues and Soul*, "As a kid the kind of music I was exposed to at home was black music . . . it would range from Louis Armstrong and Count Basie to Sam & Dave and Marvin Gaye, and with that always being around the whole black music thing quickly got instilled and became important to me."[18]

Taylor's vocal debt to Marvin Gaye is particularly pronounced throughout *Lewis Taylor*—rumor has it that Leon Ware, who wrote and produced Gaye's *I Want You* suite (1976), broke down in tears after first hearing Taylor's music—and Taylor admits that he was also listening to Gaye's *Trouble Man* (1972) and *Here, My Dear* (1978) during the recording process. Taylor confesses as well to listening to acoustic blues recordings from Robert Johnson, Son House, and Charley Patton.[19] Even as Taylor tried to obscure these influences via his production style, it was clear that many critics and fans were more interested in portraying him as the cutting edge of a new generation of neo-blue-eyed soul singers. As one reviewer described Taylor's debut, "You will hear much that is familiar: echoes from the sweeter end of the Philadelphia period, that almost ethereal wah-wah guitar sound that was at the heart Curtis Mayfield's finest work. . . . And there's the voice, like a born-again Marvin Gaye."[20] As critics began to weigh in on *Lewis Taylor*, the artist lamented, "They pushed me into a place that's not representative enough of what I'm interested in."[21]

Taylor bristled at the British press's anointing of him as the "new British blue-eyed soulster." At the time Taylor candidly told *Blues and Soul*, "Well, I suppose the most unintelligent answer I could give to that is '*Fuck off!*' . . . Because any person making popular music these days who isn't black is automatically a blue-eyed soul boy!" Continuing his indictment of music critics, Taylor stated, "It doesn't matter if you're Led Zeppelin, Jamiroquai or whoever. I don't care what anybody says, at the end of the day we're all blue-eyed soul boys! And the only way it gets measured today really depends on the degree of how close to Black music you are!"[22] Taylor's annoyance at the blue-eyed soul construct and critics that aligned him to the neo-soul style of Maxwell and D'Angelo was palpable. He asserted, "I'm interested in a much wider span of music than that. I think if you scratch below the surface you can hear that it isn't just about soul"— "It all depends on how you display your references and there are so many other influences in what I do that there's no way this is black, soul music."[23] Left unspoken in Taylor's comments is the fact that his "whiteness" is a key ingredient to the expansive musical project that he desires. In other words, Taylor will never have to defend or explain his extensive musical tastes, because such fluidity is emboldened by his whiteness. In comparison, black artists, particularly in popular forms like R&B, soul, and hip-hop, who also exhibit a wider musical palate will often be viewed as "exceptional" in large part because of the presumption that black artists —and black people for that matter—were the products of singular and limited cultural and social experiences.

For his follow-up recording Taylor consciously sought to distance himself from the blue-eyed soul construct, by submitting to his label Island Records an album that has been described as an "unholy marriage" of Radiohead and the Beach Boys. While it is unclear whether it was the label's or Taylor's decision to scrap the project, Taylor's eventual second release, *Lewis II* (2000), was closer in style to his debut. When asked about the shelved project Taylor told a writer, "[I] lost [my] nerve. It was a knee-jerk reaction to everything that had been going on, an attempt to eschew all my black influence," adding that he was "trying to fuck things up in a way . . . to get back some control."[24] Taylor eventually released the aborted recording on his own label (Slow Reality) as *The Lost Album* (2004). In a telling review of *Lewis II,* the critic Ray Douglas writes of Taylor "Here's a bloke with an abundance of talent and he's damn sure he's going to be the only one to display it. And therein lies the reason why [Taylor's] not a household name—Taylor is so intent on making sure we know just how smart he is, dazzling us with his cerebral, convoluted chord structures."[25] There's little doubt that Taylor wants to show audiences and critics how smart he is, and while it is easy to suggest that Taylor's reactionary comments about the blue-eyed soul tradition and his music's affinity for African American styles is somehow born out of racist notions of black expressive culture, I would argue that Taylor's comments are inspired by his desire to achieve a far more complex cultural project.

Taylor's desire to resist being packaged as a "blue-eyed soul man" was largely about not being inscribed by recording industry politics as a "product." "It was very difficult at the time," Taylor recalls; Island "really struggled to understand it."[26] It's not that Island didn't recognize the value of a "skinny little [white] lad who can sing like a soul singer" but that they didn't know how to market Taylor's music. Taylor recalls one exec at Island who kept asking, "When's he gonna come out with his 'Money Is Too Tight to Mention?'" in reference to the 1985 recording that introduced the so-called blue-eyed soul of Mick Hucknall and Simply Red to American audiences with the album *Picture Book.*[27] Simply Red's chart-topping crossover "cover" of Harold Melvin and the Bluenotes' "If You Don't Know Me by Now" (1988) was indeed the blueprint that Island hoped to follow with Taylor, had the singer been willing. But I would suggest that Taylor was also driven by the reality that artists such as himself are often interpreted as borrowers and even outright thieves of a tradition that they are not deemed as legitimately contributing to. By highlighting the influences of acts like Tangerine Dream, Captain Beefheart, and Radiohead within a decidedly African American soul idiom, what Taylor is actually doing is expanding the available musical language that exists within that tradition. In other words, Taylor is not just an appropriator of the soul tradition but is actually contributing to its development; and it is the failure of critics and fans to pick up on this that likely grates on Taylor more than anything. Though in many ways *Lewis II* is more accessible than *Lewis Taylor,* particularly in terms of melodic structure, it is also a project that Taylor likely intended to be interpreted within the context of the burgeoning neo-soul movement in the United States. The project's title, which supposes both an intimate self-exploration and the conceit that audiences were on a first-name basis with Taylor, can also be understood as an attempt to position his music alongside first-name artists such as Maxwell and D'Angelo. Comparisons to Maxwell and D'Angelo were inevitable, given how each artist represented a clear alternative to the standard R&B fare of the mid-late 1990s (R. Kelly notwithstanding), but the two artists were also given high praise for embarking on aesthetic projects that Taylor had arguably advanced further.

The journalist Larry Katz's assertion that *Voodoo*'s "originality is impressive. . . . its disdain of convention is admirable" was indicative of how most critics in the United States thought about the music of D'Angelo and Maxwell, particularly their respective sophomore releases *Voodoo* (2000) and *Embrya* (1998).[28] This was often the case, even when critics were not necessarily enamored with those projects, though some were much less kind to Maxwell in this regard. For example, Dream Hampton, writing in the *Village Voice*, described *Embrya* as "listless and unfocused," also chiding him for projects self-centeredness.[29] But I am less interested in critical interpretations of *Embrya* and *Voodoo* than I am the commentary from the artists themselves about their projects. In the case of *Embrya*, Maxwell admitted to Jim Farber that the recording "wasn't about song form in a traditional way . . . I was creating an atmosphere and giving myself time to move on. I knew it was going to be hated. But I've got to do what I've got to do."[30] D'Angelo projected a much different sensibility, instead taking aim at the genre of contemporary R&B, which he described as a "joke," adding that the "people making this shit are dead serious about the stuff they're making . . . they've turned black music into a club thing."[31]

The comments from Maxwell and D'Angelo can easily be read as self-indulgent and pretentious—attributes emboldened, no doubt, by critical reaction to their work. But my point here is that Maxwell's and D'Angelo's stance is commercially viable in a way that Lewis Taylor's can never be. In the case of Maxwell and D'Angelo their self-indulgence and pretentiousness helps sell them (not necessarily their music) as musical spectacle—singular, worldly savants who stand out among the denizens of corporate R&B music. Of course this was also part of the strategy of marketing so-called neo-soul artists—the idea that they were somewhat removed from the tastemakers of mainstream urban culture—though much of their complexity was owed to classic soul artists of the late 1960s and 1970s. Taylor's whiteness and to a lesser extent his "Britishness" (which surely further reifies his whiteness) normalizes his experimentation among non-urban audiences, but among mainstream American urban audiences (and I'm reading neo-soul fans as outside the "urban") Taylor is forced to apologize, as he does above, for attempting to push the boundaries of R&B as a white performer. This is an example of the complexity associated with what Taylor outlines with the "Elvis Effect" and what I'm trying to articulate with the concept of "white chocolate": whiteness may be of value in the marketplace of soul and R&B when it sells records—Justin Timberlake rings true here—but it is clearly a detriment for those artists who have a legitimate investment in the aesthetic development in those genres. The irony of course is that if Taylor had "dumbed-down" his music and played up his black musical influences (even to the point of caricature), he would have likely experienced the kind of relative commercial success afforded a white R&B act like Jon B, who had unremarkable but consistent sales throughout the mid-to-late 1990s.

Taylor was dropped from Island Records shortly after the release of *Lewis II*. Island simply did not know how to promote Taylor, as was the case with some of the labels Taylor talked with after leaving Island. According to Taylor, "everyone was looking to devise a complicated marketing plan to justify what they do. The reality is that [the music] doesn't need that much. The people that hear it like it—It's as simple as that."[32] Taylor has subsequently released four recordings—*Stoned, Part 1* (2003), *Stoned, Part 2* (2004), *The Lost Album* (2004), and *Limited Edition 2004*—on his own label. *Stoned, Part 1* was released in the United States is 2005 by Hacktone Reords to critical claim, though sales of Taylor's music here have been sluggish. These recordings, with the exception of *The Lost Album*, are the most accessible and commercially viable of his career. The openness with which he expresses his black influences on these recordings suggests that the convoluted nature of his earlier recordings was directly affected by his attempt to resist the efforts of his former label and the British critical establishment to cast him as the traditional "blue-eyed soul" singer. Telling are the several tracks on *Stoned, Part 2* and *Limited Edition 2004* that are essentially remixes of earlier recordings, suggesting the multiple ways that Taylor envisions his music. Taylor's whiteness may not help him sell records in this regard, but ironically it allows him the freedom to explore the broader contours of rhythm and blues and soul in ways, I would argue, that the mainstream of R&B is rarely permitted.

Notes

1. Clyde Taylor, "The Game," in *Black Male: Representations of Masculinity in Contemporary American Art,* ed. Thelma Golden (New York: Whitney Museum of American Art, 1994).

2. Paul C. Taylor, "Funky White Boys and Honorary Soul Sisters," *Michigan Quarterly Review* (Spring 1997): 320–36.

3. Amiri Baraka and Amina Baraka, *The Music: Reflections of Jazz and Blues* (New York: William Morrow, 1987), 264.

4. Cark Hancock Rux, "Eminem: The New White Negro," in *Everything But the Burden: What White People Are Taking from Black Culture,* ed. Greg Tate (New York: Broadway Books, 2002), 24.

5. Taylor, "Funky White Boys and Honorary Soul Sisters."

6. John L. Jackson, Jr., *Real Black: Adventures in Racial Sincerity* (Chicago: University of Chicago Press, 2005), 15.

7. Lisa Russell, "Teena Marie Brings a Whiter Shade of Pale to Soul Music," *People Weekly,* May 6, 1985, 98.

8. Steve Holsey, "Teena Marie: 'I Was Born to Sing Rhythm 'n' Blues,'" *Michigan Chronicle,* April 6, 2004, C1.

9. Dan DeLuca, "Teena Marie Still Surprises: Soul Diva Returns on Rap Label," *Philadelphia Inquirer,* May 28, 2004.

10. Carol Cooper, "Teena Marie's Heart Belongs to Rhythm and Blues," *New York Times,* May 8, 1988, H23.

11. Russell, "Teena Marie Brings a Whiter Shade of Pale to Soul Music," 99.

12. DeLuca, "Teena Marie Still Surprises."

13. Raymond Fiore, "Take It from Mary J.: Teena Marie, R&B's Secret Weapon?" *Entertainment Weekly,* May 28, 2004, 122.

14. Russell, "Teena Marie Brings a Whiter Shade of Pale to Soul Music," 98.

15. Cooper, "Teena Marie's Heart Belongs to Rhythm and Blues."

16. Paul Lester, "Boiling Bunnies," *Guardian,* August 25, 2000, 14.

17. "About Lewis Taylor—Part One," http://www.geocities.com/SunsetStrip/Arena/7463/aboutone.htm (accessed April 16, 2007).

18. Peter Lewis, "Deliverance," *Blues and Soul* (Summer 1997).

19. Jim Irvin, "Young Soul Rebel Who Knows his Onions," *Mojo* (September 1997).

20. Mengel N, "Slo-Mo to Soothe the Soul," *Courier Mail,* November 16, 1996, 12.

21. Irvin, "Young Soul Rebel Who Knows His Onions."

22. Lewis, "Deliverance."

23. "About Lewis Taylor—Part Two," http://www.geocities.com/SunsetStrip/Arena/7463/abouttwo.htm (accessed April 16, 2007).

24. Lester, "Boiling Bunnies."

25. Ray Douglas, "The Big Album," *Times* (London), September 9, 2000.

26. Interview with author, September 2005.

27. Ibid.

28. Larry Katz, "D'Angelo's Voodoo Needs More Magic," *Boston Herald*, February 4, 2000, S21.

29. Dream Hampton, "He Wants You to Want Him," *Village Voice*, July 14, 1998, 63.

30. Jim Farber, "Maxwell Stands Alone," *New York Daily News*, August 12, 2001, 2.

31. Errol Nazareth, "Some Voodoo Magic," *Toronto Sun*, January 21, 2000, 64.

32. Lewis Taylor, "Off the Record: If a Label Won't Put Your Record Out, Put It Out Yourself," *Music Week*, December 7, 2002, 23.

Daphne Carr

Dancing, Democracy, and Kitsch
Poland's Disco Polo

17

For some, Polish disco is the ultimate sonic oxymoron.

First, there's the Polish. Polka-dancing, pierogie-eating, and Pope-loving Poles in the United States have for over a hundred years been the besotted and bumbling protagonists to all manner of blonde, light bulb-turning, boat-sinking jokes and other abuses not so funny. To be Polish in the United States today is to be part of a history of arguably incomplete assimilation from the marked ethnicity of the dumb Polack to a less conspicuous shade of white. Then there's disco. Thanks to a great crop of relatively new books, disco has been well documented as preternaturally cosmopolitan as well as big, gay, black, and proud of it. So disco polo, a 1990s post-disco musical hybrid by new Poles, seems not only a sonic smash-up but potentially an intercultural carnal sin.

Liking disco polo can be a sin for Poles. They know they shouldn't do it, but many do. They enjoy it and enjoy it in public but will not admit to enjoying it when asked. For them, it is *that* bad. In 1998, the *Warsaw Voice* characterized disco polo as "music that has thumped the legacy of Chopin well and truly into the gutter. In fact, disco polo . . . has less to do with music, it seems, and more to do with repetitive rhythms, nursery rhyme lyrics and wooing dyed blondes with promises of paradise."[1] This is one of the most explicit and often-stated reasons that Poles hate disco polo—it is perceived as frontal attack on high culture. Played on digital synthesizers by amateur musicians, it is often simple in concept and execution and has lyrics that appeal to multiple generations of listeners, including the least cool cultural consumers—children and the elderly. In short, it displays the bottled blonde of the wildest ethnic stereotype to the world, the world the Poles perceive as waiting to make them into a punch line.

The polka, the mazurka, the polonaise. *These* are the dances of Poland. In the spring of 2005 I was invited to a folk costume show in Greenpoint, Brooklyn, home to the second-largest Polish immigrant population in the United States. A group of local Polish children, pre-teens, and adults danced the polonaise while wearing traditional peasant costumes. The MC talked of how each costume reflected the struggles of its particular time and place, but the composite group of brightly colored, neatly pressed, and hand-stitched garb was only fancy dress from pre-industrial Polish villages. If one went searching in these same villages in the 1990s, one would be less likely to see peasant skirts and more likely to hear, and dance to, disco polo. Still, in the romantic vision of the folk as the vehicle of expression for the nation, the idea of disco polo as the next step in the aural tradition is tantamount to suggesting that contemporary Poland is a nationalistic, illiterate, or even nihilist dystopia. Disco polo became the dominant sonic expression of village life in the 1990s and remains so in the lives of Polish ex-pats in the United States. Christenings, weddings, name days, and other holidays—moments of sacrament and celebration shared with family—are all remembered with a disco polo soundtrack. Although disco polo is folk in origin and folk in use, upper-class, urban Poles recoil at the thought of it as an expression of national identity, perhaps because it tells of a Polishness they wish to leave unarticulated.

The sonic genealogy of disco polo begins with Giorgio Moroder, the Italian dance music producer. Moroder's signature production style swapped the strings and organic funk of disco for synthesized melodies, drum machines in basic four, and English-language lyrics (often more like utterances) simple enough to transcend national boundaries. This became the formula for Italo disco, the first truly popular European electronic dance music. As a form of new wave, Italo disco's formula was simple and adaptable enough to inspire a generation of Europeans to pick up synths.

The phenomenon, Eurodisco, took shape in countries across Europe, the U.S.S.R., and North America, mutating into Hi-NRG, Eurodance, and Euro-pop. In Europe, Eurodisco's popularity gave way to house and hip-hop, but its producers moved on to shape mid- and late-1980s synth-based dance pop mega-hitmakers like Boney M and Modern Talking. One-hit-wonder obscurities in the United States, these artists dominated the pop landscape of Europe.

Many successful Italo disco records were made by DJs-turned-producers who had no formal music training. The raw, unpredictable, and simple sounds of early synths and their recorded spatial dryness came from technological necessity but became an aesthetically desirable trait of the genre. On a website dedicated to European dance music, Alex Nikitin wrote, "[Italo dance singles] always sound like they're dead cheap. I think that's their appeal. They're a bit like punk records—they go in and get very excited by the most banal sounds. The banality of them often makes them strangely moving, somehow. The thing is, of course, that *this music is terribly unhip* in Europe."[2]

In *Rock around the Bloc,* Timothy Ryback wrote, "By 1979, rock and roll in Poland was virtually non-existent." A disco craze had swept the country. Musicians were being fired and replaced with DJs and young people danced to an international selection of disco records instead of domestic rock, a situation lamented by Ryback, who praised the December 1981 start of martial law as jolting "the Polish rock scene from a decade of lethargy."[3] An urban-led political punk explosion occurred in Poland in the 1980s. Eurodisco flourished simultaneously, but nearly all English-language writing on the Polish popular music of this time focuses on socially significant musical moments like the youth protests at Jarocin, the first punk festival in the Soviet Bloc. Perhaps that is because these movements fueled the romantic ideology of rock as power for the power-less, an obvious mapping of how pop can serve as cultural resistance. Western scholars and historians of Slavic popular music during commu-nism have relatively ignored musical genres that did not correspond to this ideology, and the consequence is a void in which other forms of pop—like Eurodisco and disco polo—have gone relatively undocumented.

U.S. and European dance music—disco, early techno, Italo- and Euro-disco—had a profound impact on Polish culture in the 1980s. Major Eurodisco artists like Modern Talking, a German group that has sold

120 million records worldwide but remains relatively unknown in the United States, and Italo disco artists such as Kano and Lectric Workers were played by DJs in village fire-hall dances and other social gatherings in rural Poland. Today, the repackaging of Eurodisco and Italo disco hits has even become a nostalgia industry, sold in compilations with flat, bright graphics similar to those used in early U.S. new wave packaging. It's a totally different awesome eighties than the one enjoying a retro boom in the United States but functions similarly as new wave nostalgia for pop-loving Poles.

Disco polo's cultural roots trace back to a genre called *piosenka chodni-kowa,* or sidewalk music. During World War II, Polish musicians had few opportunities for public performance and would travel door to door playing and singing songs to raise money. As part of the resistance movement, young children committed the "little sabotage" of writing graffiti or singing anti-occupation songs in the streets. These melancholic, patriotic sidewalk songs continued to be sung through the 1950s and 1960s and were recorded by small, private record labels. The Polish scholar Leszek Koczanowicz likened the sound of these recordings to that of Bobby Vinton.[4] Later, as the genre was adapted into disco polo, the "sidewalk" shifted from performance space to retail outlet, as Polish record stores would not stock the albums. Sidewalk music became the ubiquitous rural wedding band music of the late 1980s, and the most popular songs became standard repertoire for local bands playing at receptions and country fairs. As these bands became more popular through the distribution of cassettes, they began to add their original songs to the repertoire but still played from the tradition. While disco polo artists produce albums, it is label and genre compilations of these hits that drive the industry, suggesting that disco polo is largely song-, not artist-, driven. In this, among other ways, it resembles both folk and country music.

The patron saint of pavement music was Sławomir Skręta, an entrepreneur sensing that this homegrown form had an audience but no industry. He coined the term "disco polo" and began the label Blue Star in 1992, first distributing tapes and then CDs to the villages through a variety of grassroots efforts. At the time, music piracy was at an estimated 95 percent in Poland, and disco polo cassettes routinely cost one-fifth as much as international and major-label–based artists.[5] Foreign-owned labels like EMI wouldn't sign disco polo artists. But the genre's three main labels—

Blue Star, Green Star, and Omega Music—ultimately sold huge volumes, regularly around 400,000 units. This was done without the benefit of traditional print, radio, and television advertising, which is remarkable considering that Top One, whose "Ciao Italia" from 1989 is said to be the first far-reaching disco polo hit, sold 2.5 million copies of their album *White Teddy Bear* in 1995. Likewise, Polish MTV and other major television stations in Poland ignored the genre, but Poland's first private, low-budget terrestrial commercial station, Polsat, presented a video show featuring disco polo artists, *Disco Relax*, which immediately gained a wide following in Polish villages.

In the 1996 disco polo documentary *Bara Bara*,[6] Skrêta, who founded Blue Star, defended the criticism of his artists as primitive, saying, "We don't want bands to create music too professionally, because this professionalism can kill the authenticity of the songs and would for sure reduce the public." That Skrêta feels the genre's authenticity (here meaning amateur-style songwriting, populist lyrics, and unmannered musical performance style) actually ensures a continued audience is a populist music business articulation of the folk model. Another reading, that of the Frankfurt School, would be that the genre ensures its widest reach by the production of work of a lowest common dominator of complexity, depth of emotion, or sophisticated expression. To urban Poles in the 1990s, now completely free to engage in the soft cosmopolitanism of distinctive consumption of not only Polish music but that of the international marketplace, this latter reading expressed their deepest anxieties over the spread of disco polo. The music was *really bad* and really popular. It threatened to overtake Poland's serious cultural expressions, so championed by the international literary, music, and theater communities during communism, as the primary postcommunist cultural export. By the mid-1990s, disco polo was so popular that the blackout it received in mainstream media coverage became an obvious calculation. Intellectuals did not want the genre's influence to spread, its existence to be known, or its implications to be recognized outside Poland. Critics who would acknowledge disco polo characterized it in extremely negative terms. It was made by artists "old enough to travel free on buses, while the rest still believe in the Santa Claus that gave them their first cheap Casio synthesizer."[7] It was "very loud, cheap pop music played in clubs which are very brightly colored, and sung by women with long dark hair and short skirts."[8] Nearly every critic pointed to the class-based markers of its vapid-ness (cheapness, naiveté, sexual candor) and few would acknowledge any familiarity with its actual sonic formulation. Disco polo is a genre where people even refuse to call what they hear *music*. Some people, like the journalist Tadeusz Sobolewski, went as far as to hear it only as absence, "Disco polo occupies the place abandoned by art."[9]

What does the place abandoned by art sound like? In its earliest form sidewalk music was made by groups of young to middle-aged men, with an occasional female singer, who lived in villages in the historically agri-cultural eastern part of Poland, formerly of the Russian partition. While in the late 1980s it had been a mix of acoustic and electric instruments, sidewalk music became disco polo in part by the introduction of and reliance on electronic keyboards that became widely available immedi-ately following the collapse of communism. Their use in disco polo is ubiquitous and uncomplicated: a bouncing electronic bass carries the root, with synth upbeats blocking out either 2/4 or 4/4 rhythms. If there are drums, they are pre-set. Vocals carry the melody, moving stepwise in short phrases without embellishment but often heavy processing to fit within the layered synth pads. Early 1990s artists like Bayer Full stay with the heavily Italo disco model of sparse arrangements mostly mirroring acoustic instruments, while later 1990s artists like Shazza or Boys move into a slicker production style and rhythms that often drop the keyboard upbeats, holdovers from folk dance forms, to fit into European electronic dance or pop models.

The lyrics, always in Polish, celebrate freedom, domestic bliss and childhood in the abstract, and specific traits of Slavicness—hospitality, bravery, or ability to hold stiff vodka—in particular. With their overt na-tionalism and celebration of rural Polish values, disco polo lyrics are most often compared by Poles to American country music. Take the popular disco polo group Boys, who formed in 1991 and whose first and most popular hit, "Wolność I Swoboda," was reportedly recorded on borrowed equipment in a garage shortly thereafter. A synth horn fanfare, bells, and chorus pad play the melody for "And crown thy good with brotherhood / From sea to shining sea," the final couplet from "America the Beautiful." The intro ends in an ominous timpani roll. A surging synth bass line carries the root of the melody, and when the vocals and synth pads come in on the verse, a keyboard catches the upbeat of each bass note.

The verses tell a story sung by a boy whose voice is bathed in reverb and pushed high in the mix. Here is the story. "A mother had an only son / She wanted to raise him well (to be a gentleman)" but, "When she raised him and cared for him / She had to see him sentenced to prison," then, "When they were taking him, the music was still playing / The people laughed and the young girl cried" which caused the mother to cry, "Oh people, people what is it you're doing / You're taking my boy away for life." In the chorus, the keys double, the rhythm is more complex, and drum blasts, a synth reed run or a horn fanfare punctuates each statement. "Long live liberty, liberty and freedom (*wolność i swoboda*) / Long live playfulness (partying/letting go) and a young girl (youth)." Each chorus is more fiercely orchestrated, then returning to relative calm after the closing repetition of the first verse, "A mother had an only son." The plain tone of the singer's voice, lacking vibrato, emphasizes the everydayness of his story, which is in one way the tale of a young, rural boy whose mother dreamed of his upward mobility but whose fate is sealed when he commits an unnamed crime. Given the framework of "America the Beautiful," however, the song can also be read as the metaphorical lament of a mother who did raise her son to success. Unfortunately, this means he must leave the village to take part in a new economy overseas or in the Westernized Polish cities. The final line of the chorus, then, is a nostalgic statement, calling for the long life of playfulness and youthful innocence of the village troubled in the transformation to modernity.

Villagers, the primary consumers and creators of disco polo, were the "losers" of the transition to capitalism in the 1990s. While collective farms were dissolved as early as 1956, eastern agriculturalists had been farming collectively until the end of communism, and with its end came a void of governance and the ensuing chaos of rapid market transition. Not only was the East's supposedly secure position as Poland's breadbasket undermined by the opening of the market but the increasing prestige and importance placed on the cosmopolitanism of the new Pole—multilingualism, emphasis on higher education, willingness to travel, toleration—furthered the gap between the rural and the urban. This space has come to be filled by alcoholism, depression, crime, and increasingly active hate groups. Anger and frustration about the lack of opportunities for advancement and the decreased standard of living in rural areas created a vast societal schism in Poland. In the 1990s, disco polo became the sound of this frustrated body.

Similar music movements occurred among many rural and recently urbanized populations in Central European postcommunist and post-socialist countries in the 1990s, but none so vividly as in Serbia. There, traditions of rock as resistance were worn away by a distinct brand of homebrew—turbo folk. Eric Gordy wrote in *The Culture of Power in Serbia,* "The urbanites and peasant urbanites were publicly differentiated by taste, particularly musical taste. Whereas the urban residents of Belgrade . . . looked to the European and American West, developing a strong domestic jazz and rock culture, the peasant urbanites developed a taste for neofolk, a hybrid form that married the conventions of traditional folk songs with contemporary themes and also increasingly with contemporary instrumentation."[10] Complicit in Milosevic's nationalist agenda, turbo folk was best symbolized by its leading romance—Ceca, a folk-dance pop star since the age of fourteen, and Arkan, who one journalist described kindly as "a charming and baby-faced war criminal, mafia leader and psychopath."[11] The marriage of music and warmongering gave critics a tangible reason for turbo folk's badness—it espoused, or at least condoned, bad politics.

Disco polo artists initially maintained that their music was celebratory not political, but in 1995 two of disco polo's original bands wrote campaign songs for the presidential election. Top One's "Ole Olek" toasted the postcommunist party SLD's Aleksander Kwaniewski and Bayer Full's "The President" celebrated his opponent Valdemar Pavlak of the Polish Peasants Party, also a postcommunist party. Seen in public dancing to their campaign songs and celebrating the domestic cultural production of disco polo, both candidates were heavily criticized for pandering to a populist audience. In media coverage since this time, the term "disco polo" has occasionally been applied to politicians who attempt quick, unsophisticated, or gratuitously populist fixes to domestic politics, a thinly veiled expression of liberal anxiety about the growing power of the radical left wing. As disco polo aesthetics mixed with disco polo politics, it amplified the voice of the rural village. In doing so, it highlighted an embarrassingly unfulfilled promise of higher living standards and better education for small Polish towns passed by in the rush to catch up with the West. Disco polo's unapologetic nationalist sentiments, and the nostalgia and betrayal they implied, were now a plainly heard critique of the present Polish political system.

Philip Bohlman writes of nationalism, "[it exaggerates] all that we find most repulsive and ugly. Music that might otherwise represent individual, local or regional traditions must undergo a process of aesthetic leveling, in which it speaks in a language shared by the broadest cross-section of a nation's populations. Once leveled, tradition communicates itself as kitsch."[12] Kitsch in Poland has a close relationship with propaganda, and one can say the opposite—the pursuit of art has historically had a close relationship with freedom, or at least, the desire for it. The Polish philosopher and disco polo scholar Leszek Koczanowicz told me, "Because of losing independence in the eighteenth century, Poles always are considered a locus of resistance against foreign power and the supporter of national identity. So it is very difficult for Polish intellectuals to accept any kind of art which is a pure entertainment."[13] Art has needed, then, to be both a form of resistance and distinctly Polish, infused with some quality that will serve as domestic and international signifier of high Polishness: the poet Czeslaw Milos, the filmmaker Andrzej Wajda, or Chopin.

Polish rock and punk music enjoyed a place in this hall of fame—interviewees called it "deep," "artistic," "philosophical," and "complicated," all words describing lyrics, while the blues-sound form taken was not mentioned, being naturalized as part of the Polish gaze on the West. Artful Polish popular music finds particularity within hybridity while resisting stereotyping as Slavic, nationalist, simple, or backward. Disco polo, as a form of romantic pastoral longing, revels in such things. Milan Kundera wrote that what was wrong about kitsch is the static, simplistic way it fixes complex emotions, such as feelings for the homeland. "Kitsch causes two tears to flow in quick succession. The first tear says: How nice to see children running on the grass! The second tear says: How nice to be moved, together with all mankind, by children running on the grass. It is the second tear that makes kitsch kitsch."[14] Disco polo's lyrics are nostalgic kitsch, creating false worlds of escape through space, time, and happiness in an era marked by schizophrenic disconnect to history—songs for the end of history's history. But the dreamland is ironic, both sonically and lyrically, as it presents not a utopian vision of futuristic techno-pop but a 1980s synth-led romp into capitalism's spoils re-imagined.

Given postcommunism's freedom of the marketplace, these visions remain unfulfilled for many lower-income, uneducated Poles. For them, disco polo serves as sonically and lyrically hopeful but is driven by and is responding to intense skepticism about the integrity of rural Polish life.

Disco polo artists' power comes from dedication to the celebration of their perceived shortcomings, as in country music or Eminem's Rabbit character in the *8 Mile* battle scene. By making weakness obvious, by preemptively exposing all the redneck tendencies, disco polo flattens its critics by not only understanding its own badness but also basing its whole shtick on this brand of bad. *Here's* your punch line. Let's dance.

In 2000 the disco polo artist Shazza performed at Poland's number one pop music festival. It was the end of an era—the era of disco polo as pavement music, of its threat to Polish intelligentsia and media. It was not because of a great cultural shift, however; the genre disappeared. Some of its artists had evolved into true pop stars whose eyes were set on horizons beyond Poland—they became Euro-pop and Euro-house stars with sounds and images less Polish and more global. Others faded back into local wedding band status.

In America, the disco polo phenomenon continued unabated. Polonia, as Polish Americans call their culture, is big in Greenpoint, Brooklyn. There are 600,000 Poles in the metropolitan area. Wanderers on Greenpoint's Manhattan Avenue encounter a little Warsaw displaying marquees, overhangs, vinyl and handwritten signs in Polish offering all the goods and services of the homeland plus daily needs for new Brooklynites. Poles from all three waves of immigration—the early twentieth century, the years following World War II, and the 1980s—mingle, although gentrification is forcing middle-class Poles to buy homes in neighboring Slavic communities like Ridgewood, Queens.

In the Polish record stores of Greenpoint—Music Planet and MegaPol—ample shelf space is reserved for CDs of disco polo artists and popular compilations released in even intervals, the *Now That's What I Call Music* of disco polo. Music Planet still sells racks of disco polo cassettes although the owner, Jancesz, said that sales of disco polo have dropped to about 10 percent of his total, down 15 percent from opening in 1998. At both stores, disco polo is stocked with Polish folk music, patriotic tunes, and Romani music. Both stores sell more Polish hip-hop than anything else. Hip-hop, it seems, is what happened next after the Polish underclass's bubble burst on hopes for a place in the new economy.

Ania, a striking blonde twenty-year-old Polish American born in Greenpoint, studies Polish folk dancing but said that she loves disco polo. "When we used to go on family trips and my siblings and I would misbehave, they would put on the disco polo music as our punishment. That's sort of how we were introduced. We knew all the songs because that's what they play at weddings and family parties. When I was at my cousin's wedding in October, she had disco polo nonstop. Nobody was sitting." In addition to the church and Catholic school halls and Polish-owned banquet facilities, two Polish nightclubs, Exit and Europa, serve the community, playing disco polo between hip-hop and dance sets and when they expect an older crowd.

Ania's boyfriend is a member of the Polish rock band Present Perfect, a name in tribute to the eighties Polish new wave band Perfect. He is from Poland but lives in the States and teases Ania about liking disco polo. "But when he goes to weddings with me, I make him dance. He is always smiling so it can't be that bad. People from the city look down on disco polo because they think it's sort of simplistic and that music should have some deeper meaning. They say, 'Oh that's *weiska* music'—country-side music, which is sort of seen as backward, compared to the city. They listen to rock, rap, and techno," she said.

Ania's mother is from the town Białystok in Eastern Poland. She came to the States in the eighties because, as a farmer, she had few opportunities. She brought with her a love of disco polo, and Ania calls Białystok "the homeland of disco polo." She is not ashamed of her heritage, she said. "My parents are proud of their Polishness, but I know a lot of people whose parents never taught their kids Polish and they never learned English fully, so they have a hard time communicating. It depends on how you feel about your ethnicity. Most people in Greenpoint hold on to their Polishness in some way."

Ania runs the Polish Club at her university. Many of her members are Poles studying in the States, and they look down on cultural consumption of Polonia. "When we have the Polish parade, the girls in my club were embarrassed that I was wearing a folk costume and doing folk dancing. They think things like that are kind of backward and they'd like us to be playing Chopin while we're walking down the avenue instead of a disco polo band keeping up the tempo, making people smile."

Another Polish Club member named Monika, daughter of a Polish doctor, moved to the States two years ago. Her family lives in Tenafly,

New Jersey, because her mother "isn't very attached to the Polish community. She prefers to live in a more expensive neighborhood with better schools."

"I try to be open" about the Polish American community, she said. But what does that mean? "Polish people living in Poland are not very tolerant of Polish Americans living here. It's true that most of the people who've come here are people who are not educated, who came *z chlebem*—for the bread. They're not cultured and don't know about Poland. When Ania asks me to go to folk dances I say, 'No, that's too much.'" As for disco polo, she said, "I was ashamed that something like that could be produced. You have two people, one with a keyboard and the other with guitars, and these infantile lyrics about the same crap. It was just bad. It didn't make me angry; it was more just a way for people from the city to make jokes about people from the village."

Krzysztof, a young Polish-born pianist practicing for the Chopin Piano Competition, spends his time between his family's home in Greenpoint and Madrid, where he studies. He sometimes works at Music Planet and laughed when I asked why no one admits to listening to disco polo. "It's a shame for me to listen to it. The arrangements are poor, low. . . . Why is it popular here? Greenpoint is people mostly from the village and they like disco polo. I don't dislike them for it, it's just that they don't have as much education in music."

Ania suggested that while she knew the music was "bad," she still enjoyed it because it accentuated her Polishness and allowed her to have fun and dance. Her position on disco polo—a not-guilty pleasure—allowed her to both anticipate critique and to disarm it through the same irony that disco polo artists themselves used against the intelligentsia in Poland. The scholar Leszec Koczanowicz understood this as part of a larger phenomenon of material and cultural nostalgia in Greenpoint, where he told me he felt like he was "walking through a Polish village twenty years ago." The feeling of the street, the way shops and restaurants were decorated, was, to him, like nostalgia for the communist era. Greenpoint, to Koczanowicz, was disco polo.

What part does disco polo play in this essentializing quality of Polishness in Greenpoint? Bohlman writes, "More skillfully and subtly than other forms of artistic expression, music finds its way into the temporal boundaries where the myth and history of the nation overlap to create complex myths about what we want a nation to be and what it is. . . . The musical representation of the nation, however, constantly reminds us that there is a difference between national myth and history."[15] In Greenpoint, the spatial distance from the homeland creates a temporal lapse—there are trends in Polish music listening in Polonia, but not trendiness. For those choosing to hold onto their Polish identity, the distinction between cultural signifiers of Polishness—the taste hierarchies and value judgments that mark folk, popular, and art music consumption—collapse under the need for a spatial and temporal bridge back to the motherland. In the Poland of Greenpoint, these class-based value distinctions do not matter—only Polishness matters. Nostalgia divorces choice from taste in just this way, rendering value judgments meaningless and class distinctions based on these judgments moot. Perhaps *this* is what bugs "real" Poles about Polonia. In Greenpoint, they can have their Chopin and their disco, too.

Notes

Thanks to my New York City interviewees, to Leszek for general disco polo culture chats, to Marcin (www.80s.pl), Alex (www.Euro-Flash.net), and Rich for insight on the history of Euro-, Italo-, and polo discos, and to Monika for the lyric translation. Thanks too to the Polish popular culture scholars and writers I consulted along the way for this project.

1. Tom Galvin, "Backwater Blues: Disco Polo—The Music with the Hole," *Warsaw Voice*, October 25, 1998.
2. Alex Nikitina, "Italo Disco—History 101," *Euroflash: For the Love of Music*, http://www.ld-sign.com/italo/italo.php (accessed January 2005).
3. Timothy Rybeck, *Rock around the Bloc* (New York: Oxford University Press, 1990), 181.
4. Bobby Vinton is something of a hero among Polish Americans. The rock-era ballad singer had a 1974 bilingual Polish-English hit with "My Melody of Love." The song became a standard in the Polish American community and earned him the accolade "The Polish Prince."
5. "Majors Enter Polish Soundcarrier Market as Piracy falls," *Music and Copyright*, May 22, 1996, via LexisNexis.
6. Maria Zmarz-Koczanowicz, *Bara Bara*, VHS recording, 1996.
7. Galvin, "Backwater Blues."
8. Ben Partridge, "Central Europe: Culture Reflects Shift to Market Economy," *Radio Free Europe*, July 3, 1998.

9. Tadeusz Sobolewski, quoted in Agnieszka Zembrzuska and Leszek Koczano-wicz, "Post-Communism and Pop-Music: Annihilation or Restoration of Memory in Disco Polo," *Focaal, Tijdschrift voor antropologie*, no. 33, 1999.

10. Eric D. Gordy, *The Culture of Power in Serbia* (University Park: Pennsylvania State University Press, 1999), 107.

11. Dominic Hipkins, "Music for Militias," Greatreporter.com, September 13, 2003, http://greatreporter.com/mambo/content/view/151/2 (accessed April 16, 2007).

12. Phillip Bohlman, *The Music of European Nationalism* (Santa Barbara, Calif.: ABC Clio, 2004), 20.

13. Leszek Koczanowicz, interview with the author, December 2005.

14. Milan Kundera, *The Unbearable Lightness of Being* (London: Faber and Faber, 1999) 248.

15. Bohlman, *Music of European Nationalism*, 24.

Drew Daniel

How to Act Like Darby Crash

18 In March 2004, the Los Angeles punk rock band the Germs played a reunion concert in conjunction with an attempt to sustain momentum on a beleaguered film project about them, called *What We Do Is Secret*. The concert had a perverse and telling sequence of events: first the actors playing the Germs in the film performed, and then the surviving members of the original lineup, Pat Smear, Don Bolles, and Lorna Doom, walked onstage and replaced them, with the actor Shane West remaining onstage and playing the role of Darby Crash as the reunited Germs played around and against him. I hope to read this concert as a symptom of the representational crisis engendered by Darby's suicide and the necessity/impossibility of mourning that it enforces, and as a particularly flagrant site of conflict between punk rock, Hollywood, and history.

The actors walked onstage to *Gong Show* go-get-'em hoots. They dogpaddled into the Germs song "Sex Boy," clearly struggling. Their hesitancy, their odd little Shaggsy lurches and stapled-together quasi-competence started to make the proceedings vaguely cute, and then, perversely, perfectly Germs-like. If you think this is unfair, consider the recorded evidence of early Germs shows (before they had Don on drums, before they had made

"Lexicon Devil," before they had Joan Jett passed out on the couch "producing," and in all senses premature): when they started, the Germs used to sound like this too, all slipshod stops and starts, absentee drumming, tentative guitar stabs, awkward as a newborn baby giraffe. Their performance, immortalized on the *Germicide* recording made in June 1977, reeks of "we don't care" delivered not as a strident, aggressive stance (they weren't Fear) but "we don't care" at a molecular level, saturating the air with a misshapen, ugly din. Yet it twitched all the same. So, the actors weren't all that far off really. Playing "My Tunnel" to titters from Steven McDonald and others in the crowd whose crows-feet and bemused expressions implied that they clearly Were There the first time around, a kind of stomach-churning historical vertigo ensued.

So why were we here? Were we here to rock out, as if this was just the same as seeing any other presently active punk rock or hardcore band with some but not all of the original members present and accounted for, in the same Bush era space-time continuum as Warped tours, *O.C.* tie-ins, and stadium emo? Were we here to ironically snicker at the actors' offensive presumption and applaud the original Germs for being the Real Thing? And if so, doesn't that reek of precisely the historically ossified politesse and established canonical deadweight which punk rock was supposed to have violated? Didn't the original members' participation in the event imply an at least tacit support of the film project? If the show itself was being filmed for potential fund raising and promotional purposes in support of the movie, didn't that mean that we in the audience were now extras, assistants, collective props whose presence assisted in the production of the film, thus vitiating any attempt at critical distance from it? Merleau-Ponty has a handy slogan for this: "The act by which I lend myself to the spectacle must be recognized as irreducible to anything else."[1] We were all on loan to the spectacle that night. But where does the spectacle start? Or, once you notice its presence at the heart of things, where does it ever stop?

Darby's suicide proposes a simple, elegant answer: death. Death's "undiscover'd country," an absolute zero outside the reach of representation, would seem to afford a shelter from participation in the spectacle. It's a way out of the painful process of staying punk while getting old, an absolute means of tethering your fidelity to aesthetics. It's a refusal to stick around to watch punk enter history as another youth movement which must yield its adolescent expressive rationale before the onrush of middle age, compromise, and reunion tours. Yet, of course, in this case it is precisely Darby's suicide which maintains the persistence of the spectacle as it rushes in in response to the seductive vacuum which that suicide all too conveniently opens out and sustains. In true punk rock fashion, Kim Fowley put it very bluntly: "Now we can all jack off to the futility of his life *as* the art form."[2] Was that what this concert was about? Pious necrophiles accessorized with prophylactic irony? Is that what my own remarks amount to? A discursive smoothie of formaldehyde and lube?

Multigendered and multiracial, but reassuringly commanded by a slim, good-looking white male frontman, the Germs seem all too castable when cynically imagined from the perspective of youth-obsessed, demographics savvy. But the screenplay for *What We Do Is Secret*, co-written by Rodger Grossman and Michelle Baer Ghaffari, is in fact an insider's view (that's Michelle cooking eggs with Darby in Penelope Spheeris's *The Decline of Western Civilization*, the two blithely camping at heteronormative domestic bliss). It's also a labor of love, whose ten years of increasingly tentative circlings through development hell outstrips the longevity of the band it chronicles by a factor of three. (Rather like the *M*A*S*H*-episodes-to-Korean-War ratio) Looking at the gung ho kids onstage doing their best to act like a punk band, one felt tossed between knee-jerk hipster scorn for these pretenders and a brazenly parental fawning at their pep. Behind the scenes, lawsuits were pending as the film's funding was yanked, and nobody at Rhino Films was answering the phone this week. Aware of the apparently imminent financial collapse of the film project for which they had rehearsed, learned their lines, learned to play the instruments and the songs, not to mention passing up more lucrative offers of employment elsewhere, their showbiz trooper sticktoitiveness took on the narrative momentum of an Andy Rooney film. "Hey gang! Let's put on a show!" Once they were onstage, you had to feel for them. People in the crowd flexed their punk rock history cred by shouting out classic Germs show heckles. But then, in kicking off with an "I'm bored. Gimme a beer," Shane was really asking for it. I'm ashamed now to admit it, but I took part in the trivia hounding, crying out, "Get your teeth fixed!" and hoping to hear Darby's sour, Bette Davis-esque response: "Why don't you get your braaaaain fixed?"

A strapping, presentable Hollywood citizen, Shane West played Tom Sawyer in *The League of Extraordinary Gentlemen* (2003), his last film role before taking on the task of playing an acid-gobbling punk rock cult figure. TV fans know him as Dr. Ray Barnett on the popular medical drama *ER*. My boyfriend's first thought on seeing Shane West in his Darby outfit ordering a drink at the bar was that he was far too conventionally handsome to play at being Darby Crash. But this is not exactly right. Revisiting the photos from the late seventies, what leaps out at once is that Darby was in his tattered way as iconic as Doris Day, his Aryan beefcake status tricked out with tight pants and Iron Crosses like the biker camera assistant in Fassbinder's *Beware of a Holy Whore*. The camera liked him: painted in his own blood, eyes leaping out of his skull, splayed flat on the floor, halfway between Mantegna's *Dead Christ* and a porn shoot. But, thanks to a rock thrown at him by a sister who took him for someone else, Darby had fucked up teeth and Shane West didn't. Shane West had the high pro glow of a Labrador retriever and flawless skin. (I have been told since the show that Shane West has now had himself permanently tattooed with Darby's tattoos in preparation for the role.) But beneath the skin, Shane West clearly didn't hate himself, and why should he? So, not Darby, but for all that, eerily correct: the shirt, the bracelet, the haircut, the too-tight everything, and the vague affectless "off"-ness.

Still, once he was onstage, something very basic was wrong. Shane sang into the mic. He just couldn't help it. Singing into the mic doesn't make you a singer, but it's a very good start—unless you're trying to act like Darby Crash, in which case you should groan unintelligible, awkward smears at a forty-five-degree angle tilted away from any sound-carrying devices, then swerve past it so that single words come through:

eeeeaaghghhcammmeintothisWURRLLLD

You have to stop singing entirely, wander off the stage to pursue ghostly, puzzling errands, then stagger back in time to miss your cue. Ask for more beer. Tell people, "Do damage. Hit the person next to you." Don't enunciate. Slur whenever possible. It helps to be high, preferably on something randomly handed to you by a Germette fan who is buying your groceries this week.

Yet the very looseness of these Hollywood kids, their dumpy cardboard drumrolls and seat of pants power chord jerkings and geewhiz facial expressions as they went through their moves (better not fuck this up well on second thought who cares this movie is never getting made)—it all began to seem increasingly Germs-like. Cracked actors in a school play about punk rock, their stammers and clams and flubs became a kind of second-order version of the original Germs manic ad hoc scribbling. They weren't performing *as if* they were a barely together punk rock band that had only learned to play a few weeks ago. They really were a barely together punk rock band that had only learned to play a few weeks ago.

Then the Real Germs came on, and the mosh pit exploded—with the flashes of seemingly hundreds of handheld digital cameras. The audience was enraptured with the band and with itself for being at such a cool, once-in-a-lifetime event, yet sagged internally with a creepy sense of the tenuous status of what it was that we were participating in and affirming. The poet Thom Gunn once quipped that there's no such thing as an insincere hard-on—but what would he have said to an ironic mosh pit? Weirdly, this one came complete with an internal split that itself reconstructed the original historical moment of the Germs, poised as they were between their roots in the artier, faggier Hollywood scene and their speedy appeal to the testosterone-poisoned brutes of the emergent Huntington Beach hardcore contingent. This pit was split: half of the people, with fists flailing, were trying to skank in a circle . . . and half of the people were jumping up and down in a spirited re-enactment of pogo-ing, looking as historically quaint as Morris Dancers at an English country fair. I actually got lectured to by some prissy dork because I was moshing and this wasn't a hardcore show, it was a punk show, man.

Then something odd and perfect happened at the end of the show. It wouldn't stop ending. The song "We Must Bleed" was played as a finale. It ruled. Pat would wait two beats, then start it again. Then he'd wait two beats, then start it again. They played it five times. Or was it four? I lost count, precisely because every "I want out now" shouted by Shane-as-Darby seemed to index a new deictic now, a now of the immediate present without any possibility of return to the past. Pat Smear kept time with this absolute now. Restarting "We Must Bleed" over and over, reveling in this song's punishing capacity to renew and amplify impossible, endless demands. I want out now. Beneath the jocularity of a coach blowing his whistle and making the track star run extra laps, there was something desperately aggressive, human, and embarrassing, about Pat Smear and

Shane West's playing with and against each other that slipped out. It was a very uncomfortable tipping point in the evening's uneasy truce—not just the truce between the actors and the musicians but the truce between the present and the indomitable deadness of the past.

Each time these quasi-Germs played "We Must Bleed" Darby's words seemed to redouble and mutate. Especially the line "I'm not one, I'm two." Who is this I that speaks? Punk rock names answer this question by proffering a fake name; they disavow identity and claim it at the same time (which is why John Doe is the ultimate punk name). Spitting out the paternal property logic and phallic transcendental signified of the Name of the Father, they assert, in quite uncertain terms: I am (a fake) somebody. Darby: a new spelling of my name. "I'm not one, I'm two": birth name Jan Paul Beahm and punk name Bobby Pin. "I'm not one, I'm two": stage name Bobby Pin and stage name Darby Crash. "I'm not one, I'm two": the role of Jan Paul Beahm as played by Shane West. Onstage in Hollywood in 2004, the Germs are not one, they are two: Real Germs and the Actor Germs who masquerade as them. But then the Real Germs are not one, they are two: the Real Germs of history and mourning, memorialized in youthful album sleeve photos and decaying copies of *Slash* and *Flipside,* and the Real Germs onstage participating in their own reunion spectacle. But then the Real Germs of that very reunion spectacle are not one, they are two: the Real Germs playing bass and guitar and drums, looking alternately sheepish and jubilant, and the supplementary actor whose presence wedges the constitutive split into view and keeps the melancholic wound of Darby's stubborn, absolute absence open for inspection. And on closer examination that actor isn't one but two: Shane West is itself a stage name, taken up to ease the passage into fame of someone who was born Shannon Bruce Snaith.

This return of the Germs which somehow compromises the original legacy by introducing falsehood, self-citation, an ironic, knowing attitude toward one's own schtick, hell, which inserts play-acting into the playing of music: is this not itself the hallmark of the Germs themselves, precisely because the Germs did reunite, with Darby playing himself by way of embarrassingly London-derived Adam-Ant-esque feathers and Mohican finery, shortly before his death? Travesty: according to the OED, the word enters English through Juan Florio's 1592 translation of Montaigne, who uses it simply: "to disguise [one's self], or take on another man's habit."

Before his death, Darby did precisely this, disguising himself in the habit of Adam Ant, returning from a trip to London as Darby Crash by way of the leather body armor and faux–Native American kitsch of Adam Ant's own faux-colonial exoticism. In a secondary definition of travesty as an action, to make a travesty of something is to debase what was originally serious, to harrow it and render it ridiculous. But can you travesty something that started out ridiculous? What wormholes of self-cancellation or unexpectedly serious dead ends arise when you try to travesty travesty? Of course, travesty also connotes the performative switching of gender. Before the Germs were Sex Boys and Manimals, they were Queens, referencing makeup and artificial meat in their first moniker, Sophistifuck and the Revlon Spam Queens, who were a notional band, a band that consisted entirely of t-shirts and flyers and bragging.

This evening shook me up and made we wonder about how to grow old with punk rock, wonder about the means and ends of sustaining fidelity to it, and the costs of that. What does it mean to try to remain faithful to something as it passes before your eyes into history? Darby had clearly spent time thinking this over, and his first strategy for securing a certain longevity was the Germs burn, a cigarette burn to the inner left wrist administered by members of the band to their closest friends. In a kind of parody of venereal infection this burn can then be passed on by those who have it to others; as the circle expands, it leaves in its wake a permanent, ghostly white mark, a circular hole, a zero in the skin. As Pat Smear put it: "It was his idea of something permanent, so that in ten years you'd be at the supermarket and some lady would give you change, and you'd see the burn and make a connection."[3] But as I can personally attest, Germs burns fade. Skin isn't quite permanent enough.

Proleptically imagining the suburban dead end that awaited punk rock's survivors, Darby branded his faithful with a logo whose circular logic and graphic zero said it all. Darby opted out, and shut down. Does Darby's suicide, overdetermined by its multiple and cruelly compatible explanations (heroin addiction, alcoholism, the closet, burned bridges, changes of fashion, ambitions both impossible and prematurely satisfied, enough fame to be banned from performing but not enough fame to make the rent), represent an attempt to violently wrench himself out of time or to disappear into it? Is it a refusal to enter history, or the shortest path toward ensuring a place within it? In "Mourning and Melancholia"

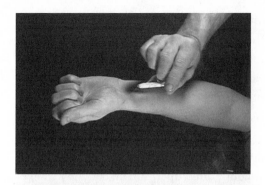

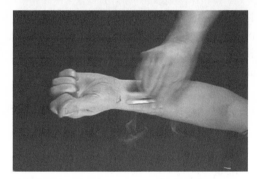

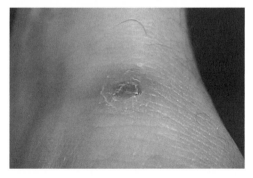

Figs 1a, b, c, and d.
The Germs burn.

Freud famously describes melancholia as a parasitic form of mourning: what has been lost may or may not have died—it has simply been lost as an object of love. Normal mourning celebrates the memory of the lost object in order to allow it to fade, or in Freud's parlance, in order to subtract libidinal investment from it in a process of decathexis. But melancholiacs do something unique: their ego splits in half, and on one side of this cleavage they encrypt a kind of relic of the lost object which they refuse to allow to fade, while with the other side of their ego they sadistically attack this object and pour hatred upon it. The corny psychobiographical move would go like this: In the wake of his failed attempt to survive the Germs with the Darby Crash Band, an ill-starred entity that limped along for a few shows after the Germs broke up, and in his own reunion of the Germs, Jan Paul Beahm seems to have both encrypted and grown to hate his own identity as "Darby Crash," and his suicide confirms the failure of his attempts to preserve that icon from the ravages of self-criticism. At a different level of description: our own contemporary enjoyment of Shane West's performance as Darby represents a certain refusal to mourn Darby Crash; it is itself the ultimate melancholiac strategy, a rejection of decathexis, a desperate clinging to a virtual/theatrical simulation in the face of an absolute loss. Postmodern celebrations of punk rock as just one more gloriously inauthentic surface to be played with remain, for all that, haunted by the void opened out by those who can't show up to smirk at the reunion tour.

Yet "travesty" is not, quite, a violation of the real object which has here been lost. Resisting both the ethical turn toward a "morally serious" tsk tsk from a bystander outside the punk rock scene and the pious survivor-guilt–inflected variant of the same voiced from within by its older and wiser alumni, I must insist on purely aesthetic grounds that, in addition to being an act of murder, suicide is already an act of theater, complete with a script, a costume carefully attended to, its own rehearsals, its stagings, and its props. I say this not to slight some mother's son as a poseur even unto his final breath but to attempt to look steadily into the circular logic, overdetermined circumstances, and representational degree zero achieved by Darby's untimely/all-too-timely death. It was a piece of showmanship in perfect synch with the "showy" display of archived suffering constituted by the ad hoc community of Germs burn victims, and in resonant sympathy with the struggles of a Hollywood kid to play out his part onstage—Jan Paul Beahm playing the part of Darby Crash, Shane West playing the part of Darby Crash, hell, even Shannon Bruce Snaith playing the part of Shane West.

Epilogue: Righting itself financially and soldiering on, the Rhino Films project *What We Do Is Secret* completed shooting in the summer of 2005. More Germs reunion concerts featuring the Shane West-as-Darby lineup are scheduled to coincide with the release of the film. It seems that the Germs reunion spectacle is more durable than any of us would have suspected while watching things teeter to a close at the Chameleon. Reeling with acute historical whiplash, my boyfriend and I left the show that night with Don, got into his rattling behemoth of a primer-black van (which he starts, pirate style, by jerking a butcher knife he keeps permanently wedged into its ignition), and headed over to pick up the members of Pretty Girls Make Graves and drive on to a warehouse party where Mahjonng were playing and underage teenagers were smoking outside and drinking beer to ironic DJ sets chock-a-block with New Order songs so long gone they might as well be doo-wop. In short, we returned to the present, where Darby Crash is still dead, and my Germs burn is still healing.

Notes

1. Maurice Merleau-Ponty, *Phenomenology of Perception,* translated by Colin Smith (New York: Humanities Press, 1962), 184.
2. Brendan Mullen et al., *Lexicon Devil: The Fast Times and Short Life of Darby Crash* (Los Angeles: Feral House Press, 2002), 265.
3. Ibid., 106.

Greil Marcus

Death Letters

19 "Somebody has to black hisself up / For somebody else to stay white." That's a line from the 1930s Harlem poet Melvin B. Tolson's "Sootie Joe." I've been trying to figure it out.[1]

I've been trying to figure it out by listening to the way modern primitives—another way of saying "folkie," maybe, maybe not—have taken up certain touchstones of old American music. It's odd how, again and again over the last few years, people have been drawn to two pieces in particular: the Mississippi blues singer Son House's 1930 "My Black Mama"—as, after House's rediscovery by 1960s blues cultists, the song was rewritten as "Death Letter Blues"—and, summing up the morbid mountain music the Virginia banjo player Dock Boggs made in the late 1920s, his queer "Sugar Baby." Whatever it is that's going on here, with the White Stripes, the Kills, John Mellencamp, the Eagles of Death Metal, David Johansen, and more diving after this music, it isn't the blackface—or whiteface—of the 1960s. Usually the original lyrics are intact and the songs are unrecognizable as covers of anything, yet there's a certain legitimacy, or the thrill of the illegitimacy of cultural appropriation, that gives these new recordings their shared spark. It's the sense of venturing into forbidden or foreign territory, in disguise—

and then the thrill of ripping off the disguise, not to show others who you really are, but to find out.

I'm interested in the way old music seems to be heard, today, as punk. It's heard as music of values: the values of harshness, cruelty, even sadism if that's what it takes to get rid of euphemism in ordinary speech, at funerals, in religion or politics. The values of say your piece and get off the stage: get it over with, tell the truth as you see it and then shut up. There's a sense of affinity, not the smell of a raid on someone else's culture. What's going on could hardly be more different from the slavish folk-revival attempts at self-erasure of Jo-Ann Kelly ("You might remember her from those British Blues Anthologies, where she sounded exactly like Memphis Minnie," wrote Charles Burton in *Rolling Stone* in 1969, be-fore he turned into rockabilly singer Charlie Burton, "but like it says in the liner notes, she's been woodshedding for a long time, and now she sounds exactly like Robert Johnson"),[2] Geoff Muldaur, the New Lost City Ramblers, or even Bob Dylan in the early sixties—as opposed to the Bob Dylan of *"Love and Theft,"* of his "High Water (For Charley Patton)," spinning lines from old folk songs as if he were throwing dice.

It's a lack of sanctimony, caught perfectly in *Ghost World,* a modern punk movie made by Terry Zwigoff, a one-time sixties country blues cultist who, in his liner notes to the soundtrack album, makes it clear he has abandoned none of his original values of soil and blood and reality and who still has a collection of more than fifteen hundred 78s. "My own likes and dislikes musically speaking are so out of touch with the rest of the world, that it was problematic choosing tunes to use in *Ghost World* that would connote the same message to the audience as to myself," Zwigoff writes. No kidding: he fails completely, and so the movie sings its own tune. Thora Birch's Enid finds the truth: she picks up an old country blues LP at a garage sale, puts it on the turntable she probably got for her fifth birthday, and hears Skip James's 1931 "Devil Got My Woman." Her life doesn't change, it deepens—and then it returns to where it was, leav-ing her stranded. She goes back to the guy who sold her the album, Steve Buscemi's geek collector, and asks for "more records like that." "There aren't any more like that," he says. ("A big fantasy for Terry," the comix artist R. Crumb, subject of Zwigoff's film *Crumb,* says. "The eighteen-year-old thinks the cranky, alienated old record-collector nerd is a cool guy and they end up having sex!")[3] He takes her to a club to see an ancient black singer, and she fixes him up with a blonde at the bar. "Wow!" says the blonde, trying hard after Buscemi has baffled her by carefully explaining that the singer isn't really blues, but perhaps closer to ragtime, depending on how you define . . . "If you're into blues, you've got to hear Blueshammer!"—which turns out to be the white trio the old man is opening for. They come storming onto the stage, the apotheosis of fake, of cultural theft and blues rape, smashing out their own "Pickin' Cotton Blues." Buscemi sinks even further into the depression that hangs over him like a cloud. "For the world at large in the film," Zwigoff says in his liner notes, "I wanted horribly contrived commercial slop . . . I wanted this music to heighten the alienation and fit into the general feeling of paranoia and cynicism I was attempting to create"—so Zwigoff wrote "Pickin' Cotton Blues" himself. "You want the audience to get the fact that the music is supposed to be bad," he writes, even if "that can make the scene hard to sit through." But the Blueshammer song doesn't work. The song isn't terrible. The performance is obnoxious, and it's alive. It's not nearly as awful as it's supposed to be!

The punk reinvention of old American music begins in the mid- to late sixties, with people taking the ancient sound as a foreign language in which you could say absolutely anything, mean every word, and pretend you were only kidding. There were the Holy Modal Ramblers in Greenwich Village in 1963, incapable of taking anything seriously, but nevertheless getting to the bottom of folk songs other people sang as if they were obvious—but their soulmates were in Los Angeles, where everything was corrupted the minute it hit the sun: Kaleidoscope making "Greenwood Sidee" and "Cuckoo" into satanic rituals the Manson Family wouldn't have recognized. Taj Mahal cakewalking through "The Celebrated Walking Blues" in 1967. Captain Beefheart's scratchy, fierce live versions of Howlin' Wolf's 1954 "Evil" and Blind Willie Johnson's 1930 "You're Gonna Need Somebody on Your Bond" in 1966 and 1968, the singer's voice filled with resentment for the songs, for what he could never be, and so making them cheap, mean, hateful, and strange. Canned Heat's 1968 version of Tommy Johnson's 1928 "Big Road Blues," their starts-on-earth "On the Road Again"—which ends in the afterlife, if not the underworld.

From London, but onstage in San Francisco for music that would appear in 1968 on *Wheels of Fire*, Cream found its way into Robert Johnson's 1936 "Crossroads" and then out of it, as the onetime country blues fanatic Eric Clapton was, for a night, unafraid of the music he knew he could never really get his arms around, the best description of the music merely the name of the album that carried it. And then Jeffrey Lee Pierce and the Gun Club, again in Los Angeles, punk Los Angeles in 1981, with all knowledge lost and all books burned, the old songs discovered as if they were scribbles no one had even tried to decipher. So the Gun Club makes *Fire of Love* in 1981, with voodoo art on the front cover and shelves of the sort of hoodoo elixirs you can still buy on Beale Street on the back sleeve—including a bottle where the label shows Elvis being whipped by Ann-Margret—and on the album itself Pierce is flattening Son House's 1930 "Preaching the Blues" and Tommy Johnson's 1928 "Cool Drink of Water Blues" as if he's a truck and the songs are just road. Pierce may be mired in sixties authenticity-mongering only in that he doesn't really find his own voice—but it's his flailing for it that brings the tunes to life.

In 1930 Son House was twenty-eight; his deep, thick voice made it sound as if he'd already lived more than one life. The first three minutes of his nearly six-and-a-half-minute "My Black Mama"—two sides of a 78—were a pastiche of floating verses about trouble with women. When the second side began a letter arrived and a story came into focus: "The gal you love is dead." He rushes off to see her, finds her "on the coolin' board." He looks "down in her face." Just like that, you're somewhere else—somewhere between this world and another world.

When in 1965, in a Columbia studio in New York City, House recast those last three minutes as "Death Letter Blues," he had twenty-three years left to live. He sounded little older than he had thirty-five years before, but the song is completely different in tone and lyrics and structure. The folk-lyric verses from what in 1930 was Part 1 are smeared into what had been Part 2, which now covers its own six minutes. Compared to "My Black Mama," this is much more self-consciously masterful, with House pressing hard vocally, from the chest, and it's no longer a story. Wisdom is being passed on; the sense of inevitability, of fate as a black hole, is gone.

In 1976, at the 100 Club in London, Malcolm McLaren put on the first punk festival, with Sex Pistols, the Clash, Siouxsie and the Banshees, the Damned, the Buzzcocks. But six years earlier Son House was sitting in a chair on the same stage. "Well, I tell y'all the truth, children, I been drinkin' this kinda medicine now, ever since—'27, I think it was. I started—" "1827," someone whispers. House breaks up cackling. "Something slipped my remembrance, there." This is blackface: a studied parody of the drunken old blues wreck. House goes on, straightening up: "Fact of the business, habits and habits. Sometimes you think you just can't do without a thing. The way you look at it, you just can't—that old word, caint. Just can't. Well—any thing that you get it in your mind, and your mind tell you, that you can't do it—don't try." Laughter from the crowd. "'Cause you're bound to fail." He sounds very drunk again. "When you think you can—you can pretty well, well, when you thinkin' you can, if you think you can't, because some people, I used to hear 'em say, tell others that something happened, just say, man, you know, my mother told me not to do that thing, but if I'd just followed my first mind, my mind told me! I oughta done something. Say what? Yay-ehhhh." He whispers: "If I had just done followed my first mind," and then he raises his voice: "Well, that's the bad one. You oughten'da followed it. Don't ever follow your first mind—'cause that's the one that's wrong. 'Cause the devil beats God every time." There's laughter. House laughs: "Think twice —and speak once." He goes into the song.

There's hot, hard guitar. The voice is free, rangy, full, in the air. The story unfolds: the woman in the song is dead and you are in her presence. House is a bird, looking down on the man looking down on the dead woman—this is the second mind, playing the song. "See you on Judgment Day" is not a tag line. "I didn't have a soul, to throw my arms around / I said, I didn't have a SOUL—to throw my arms around." "I wouldn't mistreat you, for my weight in gold"—and you hear how he has mistreated her. The voice is escaping from his body.

When the Detroit one-man one-woman guitar-and-drums punk combo the White Stripes take up the song thirty years later, in 2000, they take it straight, stridently, like everything else on *De Stijl;* they rise to the occasion as if they're getting out of bed. "Got up this morning / The break of day / Just hugging the pillows / Where my baby used to lay"—the language is classical, from another country, and it fits seamlessly into the songs around it. This song is merely more shapely, more striking. The fact that it opens into a larger world seems almost an illusion: the ten thousand people at the burying ground aren't present anywhere else on the album, and you wonder why not.

Two years later it's one-time New York Dolls singer David Johansen, aka lounge lizard Buster Poindexter, now working as a tramp folklorist on his album *Shaker,* with his band the Harry Smiths, named for a real tramp folklorist. The guitarist comes up with a wonderful bottleneck; Johansen offers a smeared, embarrassing blackface vocal, but you get the funny sense that his respect for the song is so great that the only way he can sing it is to make a fool of himself. But the guitarist is playing tiny figures, undercutting Johansen's overstatements, or pushing him into himself, or out of himself. You don't hear Johansen understanding the words he's singing, but you hear him catch the rhythm and ride it. "Just huggin' the pillow where the good gal used to lay"—that's the line that seems to get them. Now the rhythm is harder, hammering down at the end of phrases, and Johansen steps forward as himself, going from loud to soft, reaching for melodrama. "Hush!—I thought I heard her call my name—you know it wasn't loud—it was kind of nice and plain." He is in the song; no one is telling him to leave.

And then it's the Indiana rocker John Mellencamp, a year later, on *Trouble No More,* a shining album where he dared to take up not only "Death Letter" but Howlin' Wolf's 1961 "Down in the Bottom," Hoagy Carmichael's 1942 "Baltimore Oriole," and Dicky Doo and the Don'ts fabulous doo-wop "Teardrops Will Fall," and closed the album by changing Charlie Poole and the North Carolina Ramblers' 1926 "White House Blues" from a sardonic number about the assassination of William Mc-Kinley in 1901 into a meaninglessly clumsy, heartbreakingly bitter tale about an election ninety-nine years later. Mellencamp looks Son House in the face as he sings, and it's this, his acknowledgment that the song does not belong to him, that allows him to claim it as Jack White of the White Stripes and David Johansen do not quite dare to do. Mellencamp is singing the song in his own voice, in his own style—and yet he brings less that is new to the song, perhaps because there is no distance.

In each case, the song is demanding more from the musicians than they have to give. They could pretend to be something they aren't; they could dress up, they could attack the song with parody and satire, take revenge on the way the song resists them. The singer is thrown back on himself, and so he leaves the song as an ordinary person, and with a sly, secret grin. The singers sing to each other: the song has become a new kind of pop lingua franca. As a death letter it's a chain letter.

It's 1997, and Jeff Tweedy and Jay Bennett of the Chicago old-timey punk band Wilco, along with Roger McGuinn, are taking up Dock Boggs's "Sugar Baby" at a Harry Smith tribute concert. "Why don't you start it off,

Jeff," McGuinn says, as if the old folk-rocker knows Tweedy has no idea what a vortex he's about to be sucked into. Boggs's 1927 recording is one of the most fierce and unyielding performances in American music, the killer quietly teasing his victim, a child howling in the next room—and from the first instant, in Tweedy's fingers, the song is a dream, a swirl. The three musicians are at once at the center of the circle and above it, looking down only for an instant, then disappearing into the clouds. "That kid! How did he get that song?" said a woman in her fifties, astonished, as the song seemed less to end than to go back where it came from, wherever that was. How could this kid take the song so completely, she meant, make it altogether his own, as if it had never been played before?

From the Eagles of Death Metal you learn that Boggs's songs don't hold still, that they demand from you what you and nobody else can give. It's 2004, with the hilarious, very folkie, very aluminum *Peace Love Death Metal*, and leader Jesse "The Devil" Huge, aka J Devil Huge, is having the time of his life. "Who'll love the devil? Who'll kiss his tongue? Who'll kiss the devil on his tongue?" he roars, and he answers himself: "I'll love the devil! I'll kiss his tongue! I will kiss the devil on his tongue!" But it turns out that "Kiss the Devil" is just the lightest rewrite of Boggs's "Sugar Baby."

"Sunday morning gonna wake up crazy," the great blind country guitarist Riley Puckett sang happily in 1940 in his version of "Nobody's Business," as if he were about to go out for a cup of coffee. "Kill my wife and slay my baby / Nobody's business if I do." This isn't Boggs's tone. His song is more demonic than these Eagles, not to mention the other Eagles, would every dare to be. "Who'll rock the cradle, who'll sing the song? Who'll rock the cradle when you gone?" Boggs's singer asks his wife. He answers for her: "I'll rock the cradle, I'll sing the song / I will rock the cradle when you gone." Huge steps back from this with parody, with absurdity—"Peace Love Death Metal," right—and his step back is why his rewrite works. He heard Boggs; he understood him. He also understood that the only way he could ever sing Boggs's song, the only way he could drape Boggs's skin over his, was to turn the song into a joke.

In 2003, the one-woman one-man punk chamber band the Fiery Furnaces, from Oak Park, Illinois, by way of Brooklyn, took up Boggs's "Old

Rub Alcohol Blues" on their odd, word-drunk debut, *Gallowsbird Bark.* I know Boggs's music, and I played the Fiery Furnaces album for months without realizing they were covering him; one day, I just happened to notice something in the album credits. Otherwise I still wouldn't know. Matthew Friedberger plays a rolling, gonging, Dylan-style piano—the way Dylan plays on "Dear Landlord" or "I'll Keep It with Mine." There is no referent to the past present anywhere, not in the music, especially not in Eleanor Friedberger's singing.

The song was written by W. T. Meyer, who owned a variety store in Richland, Virginia. He'd shuffle lines from blues and country songs, practicing folk-lyric song-making, and send them to performers he liked —Mississippi John Hurt was a favorite. The idea was that they'd fit his words to melodies and record the results, for his own record company: Lonesome Ace, with a picture of the *Spirit of St. Louis* and the motto "Without a Yodel" on the label, because Meyers loved Charles Lindbergh and hated yodeling. Boggs recorded the little blues pastiche in 1929, at his last session before the Depression all but wiped out blues and country recording: the last recordings Boggs would make until the folklorist Mike Seeger located him in 1963, within miles of where Boggs had lived his whole life. As the punk duo the Kills—V. V., from the United States, Hotel, from the United Kingdom—do with their 2003 version of "Sugar Baby," Boggs sings it as a scratchy drone, suppressing the tune. He is going through the motions. Boggs himself made folk-lyric songs—but *he* made them, and he could have heard Meyer's "Old Rub Alcohol Blues" as a parody of what he'd already done, or who he was. He wasn't going to say no; it was a chance to make another record.

There's no hint of this in the Fiery Furnaces' version. Of Meyer's ten verses, they use five—just enough for Eleanor Friedberger to sing as if she's worked out every idea in the lyric for herself, fingering her own scars. At the same time there is a second dimension in her singing, a second mind, where every word travels on a stream of consciousness, as if the idea in any given line has just occurred to her. Nevertheless, by the time she reaches the second-to-last verse she'll use she is testifying, with her hand over her heart, as when Boggs sang the lines he all but turned his back: "No, I've never worked for pleasure / Peace on earth I cannot find." But by her last verse she is drifting again, floating through the song, as if it has already long outlived her. By now what might be a clavinet is keening be-hind the piano, which seems to play itself, seems like a player piano, the high, disembodied sound like something the song is generating for itself, not something anyone is playing. "I'll soak up all the old rub al-co-hol," Eleanor Friedberger sings carefully, distinctly, pressing on each syllable, as if to nail what each one means into her tongue like a stud, as if she's looking herself in the face. "Ease all trouble off my mind," she sings. "I'll ease all trouble off my mind / My mind / My mind"—and Dock Boggs is gone. The song is hers, absolutely. She wrote it. No one else can sing it now.

"Somebody has to black hisself up / For somebody else to stay white"— is that true? Sometimes you can hear that; other times you can't.

Notes

1. Melvin Tolson, "Sootie Joe," in *Blues Poems*, ed. Kevin Young (New York: Everyman's Library, 2003), 37.
2. *Rolling Stone*, December 27, 1969, 58.
3. Personal communication, September 16, 2002.

Discography

Captain Beefheart and His Magic Band. "Evil Is Going On" (1966) and "Yer Gonna Need Somebody on Yer Bond" (1968). *Grow Fins—Rarities [1965–1982]*. Revenant, 1999.

Boggs, Dock. "Sugar Baby" (1927) and "Old Rub Alcohol Blues" (1929). *Country Blues*. Revenant, 1997.

Canned Heat. "On the Road Again" (1968). *Uncanned! The Best of Canned Heat*. ERG/Liberty, 1994.

Cream. "Crossroads." *Wheels of Fire*. Atco, 1968.

Eagles of Death Metal. "Kiss the Devil." *Peace Love Death Metal*. AntAcidAudio, 2004.

Fiery Furnaces. "Rub Alcohol Blues." *Gallowsbird Bark*. Rough Trade, 2003.

Ghost World: Original Motion Picture Soundtrack. Shanachie, 2001. Includes Skip James, "Devil Got My Woman" (1931), and Blueshammer, "Pickin' Cotton Blues."

Gun Club. *Fire of Love*. Slash, 1981, reissued Rhino, 2001.

Holy Modal Rounders. *The Holy Modal Rounders*. Fantasy, 1999. Reissue of *The Holy Modal Rounders* (Prestige, 1963) and *The Holy Modal Rounders II*. Prestige, 1964.

House, Son. "My Black Mama Part I and Part II" and "Preachin' the Blues Part I and Part II" (1930). *Son House and the Great Delta Blues Singers: 1928–1930*. Document, 1990.

——. "Death Letter" and previously unissued alternate take. *Father of the Blues: The Complete 1965 Sessions*. Columbia, 1992.

——. "Death Letter Blues." *John the Revelator: The 1970 London Sessions*. Sequel, 1992.

Johansen, David, and the Harry Smiths. "Death Letter." *Shaker*. Chesky, 2002.

Johnson, Blind Willie. "You're Gonna Need Somebody on Your Bond" (1930). *The Complete Blind Willie Johnson*. Columbia, 1993.

Johnson, Tommy. "Big Road Blues" and "Cool Drink of Water Blues" (1928). *Tommy Johnson (1928–1929): Complete Recorded Works in Chronological Order*. Document, 1990.

Kaleidescope. "Greenwood Sidee" (1967) and "Cuckoo" (1969). *Pulsating Dream: The Epic Recordings*. Acadia, 2004.

Kills. "Sugar Baby." "Fried My Little Brains" EP. Rough Trade, 2003.

Taj Mahal. "The Celebrated Walking Blues." *Taj Mahal*. Columbia, 1967/2000.

Mellencamp, John. "Death Letter." *Trouble No More*. Columbia, 2003.

Tweedy, Jeff, with Jay Bennett and Roger McGuinn. "Sugar Baby." *The Harry Smith Connection*. Smithsonian Folkways, 1998.

White Stripes. "Death Letter." *De Stijl*. Sympathy for the Record Industry, 2000.

ACKNOWLEDGMENTS

Listen Again compiles work presented at the second, third, and fourth years of the Pop Conference at Experience Music Project. I write these thank yous having just concluded a fifth installment. It has been one of the great experiences of my lifetime to see the conference taken to heart by so many people. I'll be happy if this book conveys even a little of the feeling of being at EMP during these April weekends. Three sets of rock 'em sock 'em panels happening simultaneously, ratio of killer to filler so high that participants come away energized, with a new sense of appreciation for the breadth and possibilities of this field. My immense gratitude to all who have presented over the years. For more conference related writing, check out *This Is Pop: In Search of the Elusive at Experience Music Project* (Cambridge, Mass.: Harvard University Press, 2004), as well as a special October 2005 issue of the journal *Popular Music,* "These Magic Moments," from which a couple of these chapters have been adapted.

Funding for the conference and for this book was provided by a generous gift from the Allen Foundation for Music, administered through a collaborative partnership between EMP, radio station KEXP, and the University of Washington School of Music. Thanks to the leaders at all three institutions who recognized the value of securing and preserving this unusual event, and to coordinator Rob Carroll for making sure that the partnership never blew up. At Experience Music Project (whether now or formerly), Bob Santelli, Shannon O'Hara, Janine Logsdon, Gwen Wilson, Chris Clevish, Anthony Angelora, Danny Bland, Brian Epps, and Liam Barksdale are among the many staffers who went far beyond the call of duty. Thanks, too, to the various program committee members—too many to name singly—who vetted proposals and recruited participants.

Each of the contributors to this book revised and expanded their initial presentation, often undertaking multiple drafts. They are, as a rule, very busy people. I thank them all for valuing this project enough to deliver such ambitious material and I count myself fortunate to have gotten to know them a bit better through our work here. It is worth noting that this collection has an entirely new set of contributors when compared to the last one. And it still only scratches the surface: the ranks of journalists, academics, and musicians (or some combination, as is usually the case) capable of producing magnificent, insightful prose on the subject of pop appears to be virtually limitless. Ken Wissoker of Duke University Press is as enthusiastic about good music writing as I am. He has attended every single Pop Conference, and I am thrilled that his patience has finally yielded a manuscript.

Finally, Ann Powers has been my co-host at the conference each year, my co-worker at EMP for much of this time, a constant member of the program committee, and one of the gathering's star attractions. She can't be in this book as a writer, because she was in the last one, but trust me, she's in this book. All this and we're married (and raising Rebecca, who wasn't alive for years one and two, but has bobbed gleefully through the past three). If *Listen Again* didn't give you enough of a hit of people arguing about pop music, just come over to our house.

CONTRIBUTORS

David Brackett is an associate professor of musicology and chair of the department of theory (Academic Affairs) at the Schulich School of Music of McGill University. His publications include *Interpreting Popular Music* (1995) and *The Pop, Rock, and Soul Reader: Histories and Debates* (2005). His current research focuses on the relationship between genre and identity in twentieth-century popular music.

Franklin Bruno is the author of *Armed Forces* (2005), in Continuum Press's "33 1/3" series. His criticism has appeared in *Best Music Writing 2003*, *The Believer*, *Slate*, and *Village Voice*. Since 1990, he has released over two hundred songs, solo and with Nothing Painted Blue, as well as collaborating with Jenny Toomey and the Mountain Goats. He holds a Ph.D. in philosophy from the University of California, Los Angeles, and has taught at Pomona College, Northwestern University, and Bard College.

Daphne Carr is a Brooklyn-based freelance music writer and a graduate student of ethnomusicology at Columbia University. She is the series editor for Da Capo's *Best Music Writing*. Her dissertation focuses on popular music after the fall of communism in Central Europe.

Henry Chalfant is the co-producer of *Style Wars* and the co-author of the groundbreaking graffiti books *Subway Art* and *Spraycan Art*. He collaborated with Rita Fecher on *Flyin' Cut Sleeves*, a documentary of the Bronx gangs. His film *From Mambo to Hip-Hop* tracks the development of Latin music in the streets of the South and West Bronx from the post–World War II mambo era to the rise of hip-hop.

Jeff Chang is the author of *Can't Stop Won't Stop: A History of the Hip-Hop Generation* (2005) and the editor of *Total Chaos: The Art and Aesthetics of Hip-Hop* (2006). He co-founded the hip-hop indie label SoleSides, now Quannum Projects.

Drew Daniel teaches at the San Francisco Art Institute. He is currently writing a book about Throbbing Gristle and revising his dissertation on melancholy in sixteenth-century literature and painting. He has published music criticism in *The Wire* and *Sound Collector* and is a recent contributor to the music websites Pitchfork and eMusic. He is also one half of the band Matmos, and all of the band The Soft Pink Truth.

Robert Fink is an associate professor of musicology at the University of California, Los Angeles. He is the author of *Repeating Ourselves* (2005), a study of American minimal music as a cultural practice, and his work has appeared in the *Journal of the American Musicological Society, Cambridge Opera Journal, Popular Music, American Music,* and *Nineteenth-Century Music,* as well as the *Cambridge History of Twentieth-Century Music* and the collections *Beyond Structural Listening* (2004) and *Rethinking Music* (1999).

Holly George-Warren is the author of *Public Cowboy No. 1: The Life and Times of Gene Autry* (2007). A contributor to more than forty books on popular music, she has written for the *New York Times, Rolling Stone, MOJO,* the *Village Voice,* and other publications. She is an adjunct professor of journalism at the State University of New York, New Paltz.

Lavinia Greenlaw has published three books of poems, most recently *Minsk* (2003), and a memoir, *The Importance of Music to Girls* (2007). Her first novel, *Mary George of Allnorthover* (2001), is a study of adolescence and music in 1970s provincial England. Her second, *An Irresponsible Age,* was published in 2006. She has also published a collaboration with the photographic artist Garry Fabian Miller, *Thoughts of a Night Sea* (2003). She wrote the libretti for Ian Wilson's chamber operas *Hamelin* and *Minsk.*

Marybeth Hamilton is the author of *In Search of the Blues* (2007) and *When I'm Bad, I'm Better: Mae West, Sex, and American Entertainment* (1995). She is the writer and presenter of documentary features for BBC radio on women's film melodrama, blues record collectors, and Little Richard. She teaches American history at Birkbeck College, University of London.

Jason King is the artistic director of the Clive Davis Department of Recorded Music at New York University. He has written for *Vibe, The Village Voice,* and the journal *Callaloo,* among other publications. His book *Blue Magic: Spirit and Energy* *in Black Popular Music* is forthcoming from Duke University Press, and he is working on an alternative history of hip hop.

Josh Kun is an associate professor in the Annenberg School of Communications at the University of Southern California, where he also directs the Popular Music Project at the Norman Lear Center. He is the author of *Audiotopia: Music, Race, and America* (2005) and a contributor to the *New York Times*, the *Los Angeles Times*, *Los Angeles* magazine, and *Tu Ciudad Los Angeles*.

W. T. Lhamon, Jr., is the author of *Deliberate Speed: The Origins of a Cultural Style in the American 1950s* (1990 and 2002); *Raising Cain: Blackface Performance from Jim Crow to Hip Hop* (1998); and *Jump Jim Crow: Lost Plays, Lyrics, and Street Prose of the First Atlantic Popular Culture* (2003). For some years in the 1970s and 1980s he reviewed fiction and wrote a regular column on jazz and pop music for *The New Republic*. He is an emeritus professor of English and American studies at Florida State University and now lives in southern Vermont.

Greil Marcus is the author of *The Shape of Things to Come: Prophecy and the American Voice* (2006), *Lipstick Traces* (1989), *Mystery Train* (1975), *The Dustbin of History* (1995), and other books. He teaches at the University of California, Berkeley, and at Princeton University. He lives in Berkeley.

Michaelangelo Matos is a freelance writer in Seattle and the author of *Sign 'O' the Times* (2004), part of the "33 1/3" series. He contributes to eMusic.com, MSN Music, *Baltimore City Paper*, and the *Seattle Times*.

Benjamin Melendez formed the Ghetto Brothers gang while still in his teens and later became its president, then played a central role in brokering the Bronx gang peace treaty. He also sang lead vocals for the Ghetto Brothers band, and along with his late brother, Victor, was the primary songwriter. He still lives in the South Bronx, where he teaches martial arts and works with at-risk youth.

Mark Anthony Neal is the author of *What the Music Said: Black Popular Music and Black Public Culture* (1998), *Soul Babies: Black Popular Culture and the Post-Soul Aesthetic* (2002), *Songs in the Keys of Black Life: A Rhythm and Blues Nation* (2003), and *New Black Man: Rethinking Black Masculinity* (2005). Neal is also the co-editor (with Murray Forman) of *That's the Joint! The Hip-Hop Studies Reader* (2004). Neal is an associate professor of African and African American studies and director of the Institute for Critical U.S. Studies at Duke University.

Ned Sublette is the author of *Cuba and Its Music: From the First Drums to the Mambo* (2004) and the forthcoming *The World That Made New Orleans*. His most recent CD release is *Cowboy Rumba* (Palm Pictures), and his song "Cowboys Are

Frequently Secretly" has been recorded by Willie Nelson. His contribution to this volume was written while he was a John Simon Guggenheim fellow.

David Thomas, founder of and singer for the legendary avant-rock band Pere Ubu, has been rewriting the rules of popular music for more than twenty-nine years. Formed in Cleveland in 1975, Pere Ubu integrated found sound, analog synthesizers, and musique concrète into a hybrid of overdriven Midwestern garage rock tempered by abstract sensibilities.

Steve Waksman is an assistant professor of music and American studies at Smith College. A guitarist since age nine, he is the author of *Instruments of Desire: The Electric Guitar and the Shaping of Musical Experience* (1999) and is currently working on a cultural history of heavy metal and punk titled *This Ain't the Summer of Love: Rock Music and the Metal/Punk Continuum*.

Eric Weisbard organizes the annual Pop Conference at Experience Music Project, where he also co-curated the exhibit *Disco: A Decade of Saturday Nights* and edited the book *This Is Pop: In Search of the Elusive at Experience Music Project* (2004). Before that, he was music editor at *The Village Voice* and a senior editor at *Spin*, where he edited the *Spin Alternative Record Guide* (1995). He is the author of *Use Your Illusion I and II* (2007) about the Guns N' Roses albums of those titles.

INDEX

Rakim, 181

Ramone, Joey (Jeffrey Hyman), 56

Ramones, 222

Ramsey, Frederic, 36, 41

Rascals, 89

Ray, Johnnie, 64

Record Changer, 38

Record collectors, 26–49

Reed, Jimmy, 127

Reed, Lou (Lou Rabinowitz), 56

Reich, Steve, 186

Residents, 95

Reynolds, Simon, 177, 222

Rhumba, 77–78, 82, 84

Rhythim is Rhythim, 251–52; "Strings
   of Life," 251–52

Rhythm and blues (R&B), 172–99,
   256–71

Rhythmic key, 80

Rice, T. D., 21, 23

Richard, Cliff, 200

Richards, Keith, 90

Richie, Lionel, 259, 263

Richman, Jonathan, 220

Righteous Brothers, 258

Rik, Rik L., 147

Riley, Terry, 185

Rilo Kiley, 126

Riperton, Minnie, 260–61

Rip Rig and Panic, 218

Rizo, Marco, 69

Robie, John, 239, 245

Robinson, Smokey, 173, 180, 187, 259

Rock, 157–71, 296–305

Rocket from the Tombs, 101

Rodgers, Jimmie, 65

Rodriguez, Arsenio, 88

Rodriguez, Pete, 90

Rogin, Michael, 57–58

Rolling Stone, 164–65, 179–80, 183

Rolling Stones, 21, 89–90, 114

Ronk, Dave Van, 12, 65

Roots, The, 208

Ros, Edmundo, 81

Ross, Diana, 191, 259–60

Rotary Connection, 189, 260

Roth, David Lee, 63

Roth, Philip, 50

Rubin, Barry, 55, 64

Rubin, Rick, 207

Ruiz, Rosendo, Jr., 71

Rush, Otis, 86

Russell, Leon, 131

Russell, William, 36, 38

Rux, Carl Hancock, 257

Ryback, Timothy, 274

Sade, 180

Sam and Dave, 126, 265

Santana, 88–89, 155, 213

Satie, Erik, 186

Sawhney, Nitin, 177

Scarborough, Dorothy, 32

Scarface, 172

Schacher, Mel, 161, 167

Schloss, Joseph, 205

Schneider, Florian, 241–43

Schoolly D, 207

Schubert, Franz, 241, 244–45, 247, 258

Scorsese, Martin, 64

Scraping Foetus off the Wheel, 222

Sedgwick, Eve, 54

Seeger, Pete, 38

Sex Pistols, 213, 220, 228

Shadows, The, 200–202

Shazza, 281

Shuman, Mort, 59, 84

Sidewalk music, 275

Eric Weisbard organizes the annual Pop Conference
at Experience Music Project in Seattle.

Library of Congress Cataloging-in-Publication Data
Listen again: a momentary history of pop music / edited by Eric Weisbard.
p. cm.
Includes bibliographical references and index.
ISBN 978-0-8223-4022-5 (cloth: alk. paper)
ISBN 978-0-8223-4041-6 (pbk.: alk. paper)
1. Popular music—History and criticism. I. Weisbard, Eric.
ML3470.I59 2007
781.64—dc22   2007018000